Advances in Human Factors/Ergonomics, 1

Human–Computer Interaction

Advances in Human Factors/Ergonomics

Series Editor: Gavriel Salvendy, Purdue University, West Lafayette, IN 47907, U.S.A.

Vol. 1. Human—Computer Interaction (G. Salvendy, Editor)

Advances in Human Factors/Ergonomics, 1

Human–Computer Interaction

Proceedings of the First U.S.A.–Japan Conference on Human–Computer Interaction, Honolulu, Hawaii, August 18–20, 1984

Edited by

Gavriel Salvendy
Purdue University, West Lafayette, IN 47907, U.S.A.

ELSEVIER

Amsterdam — Oxford — New York — Tokyo   1984

ELSEVIER SCIENCE PUBLISHERS B.V.
Molenwerf 1
P.O. Box 211, 1000 AE Amsterdam, The Netherlands

Distributors for the United States and Canada:

ELSEVIER SCIENCE PUBLISHING COMPANY INC.
52, Vanderbilt Avenue
New York, NY 10017, U.S.A.

ISBN 0-444-42395-8 (Vol. 1)
ISBN 0-444-42396-6 (Series)

© Elsevier Science Publishers B.V., 1984

Printed in The Netherlands

PREFACE

This book consists of 72 of the 78 papers presented at the First U.S.A. - Japan Conference on Human-Computer Interaction held at the Sheraton Waikiki Hotel in Honolulu, Hawaii 18-20 August 1984. The following organizations cooperated in this conference:

- Human Factors Society
- Japan Ergonomics Research Society
- National Institute of Occupational Safety and Health (NIOSH)
- Japan Management Association
- Software Psychology Society
- Japan Information Processing Development Center
- Japan Electronic Industry Development Association
- Purdue University

The conference organization consisted of:

Gavriel Salvendy, General Conference Chairman, Purdue University

Masamitsu Oshima, Conference Co-Chairman and Chairman of
    Japanese Delegation, Medical Information Systems Development Center

Richard Morgan, Director of Local Arrangements, U.S. Marines

Loretta Bowman, Conference Secretary

Advisory Board

Kasuo Aoki, University of Tokyo

H. E. Dunsmore, Purdue University

Ray E. Eberts, Purdue University

Richard S. Hirsch, IBM Corporation

Kageyu Noro, University of Occupational and Environmental Health

Bernhard Zimolong, Purdue University

Michael J. Smith, NIOSH

Ben Shneiderman, University of Maryland

Akira Watanabe, University of Tokyo

The rationale for this bi-national conference stems from the fact that in 1983 over 50 million people interacted with computers in Japan and the U.S.A. When computer systems are well designed and used then they can significantly enhance industrial productivity, job satisfaction, health and safety and leisure time activities. Hence, the objective of this conference was to bring together research workers and practitioners to share and exchange information, ideas, theory, and experience in applying human factors and computer science concepts and methodologies to the design, planning, control and operation of human-computer interactive systems. By so doing, computer systems may be better designed and used.

The many contributing authors came through magnificently. I thank them all most sincerely for agreeing so willingly to create this book with me. This would not have been possible without the diligent work of the Advisory Board, the Conference Secretary, the Director of Local Arrangements and Masamitsu Oshima, the Co-chairman of the Conference.

Gavriel Salvendy
Conference Chairman
West Lafayette, Indiana
May 1984

CONTENTS

VI. STRESS, HEALTH AND PSYCHOLOGICAL ISSUES IN COMPUTERIZED WORK

VII. APPLICATIONS OF HUMAN-COMPUTER INTERACTIONS

VIII. SPEECH

XII

ADDENDUM

Human—Computer Interaction, edited by G. Salvendy
Elsevier Science Publishers B.V., Amsterdam, 1984 — Printed in The Netherlands

MAN-MACHINE INTERACTION IN "C&C" AGE

K. KOBAYASHI

NEC Corporation, 33-1, Shiba 5-chome, Minato-ku, Tokyo (Japan)

ABSTRACT

Kobayashi, K., 1984. Man-machine interaction in "C&C" age.

Interaction functions between human and machines are categorized in three hierarchies and corresponding technological means are discussed. Current status and problems in regard to hardware and software for man-machine interaction are presented. The concept of "C&C", the integration of computers and communications, is described. In order to make "C&C" system as friendly as possible, improvement in man-machine interaction is emphasized. Hence, the concept of "C&C" is extended to "Man and C & C", which is "C&C" with human as the axis. A perspective of man-machine interaction is also discussed.

I. INTRODUCTION

Rapid advances in science and technology have improved the productivity of modern industry and have enriched our social life. However, as society advances richer and more complex, we are facing ever more difficult problems. These problems are more human oriented and demand much more interdisciplinary approaches than what demanded in the past. Nevertheless, I am sure human wisdom will overcome these problems by advancing new forms of technology.

For the past several decades, among many technological innovations, computer and communication technologies have made remarkable progress. These technologies are rapidly merging together. The integration of computers and communications, as what I call "C&C", (Kobayashi, 1977, 78, 79), will provide an important infrastructure for the information society. The worth of information is increasingly valued as we advance into the information society. Hence, the general public demands the popularization of information services that can be accessed by anyone, anywhere and anytime for their individual purposes. This demand creates many difficult problems technologically and socially.

To meet this demand, we have to challenge to overcome various technological barriers that exist mostly at the interface between human and machine. In other words, all machines, especially computers, have to be made more friendly to human so that anyone can communicate intelligently with machines, similar to persons communicating with each other. Hence, this conference on human-computer interaction is a very important and timely event.

I have long recognized and advocated the importance of human-machine interaction. Next, I shall present my concept and perspective of man-machine interaction in the coming "C&C" age.

II. HUMAN INTERACTION WITH "C&C"

I joined NEC Corporation as an electrical engineer in 1929, just after graduating from Tokyo Imperial University, and have worked for over 55 years since then, especially in the latter half of the period, to develop communications, computers and semiconductor technologies and put them into commercial use. I have done so in the hope of contributng to world peace by helping create an international communications network by which anyone anywhere in the world can talk to anyone else at any time.

During this period, worldwide telecommunications has advanced through various technological innovations, such as automatic switching system, digital microwave communications system, satellite communications system, fiber-optic communications system and others. A definite trend is the digitalization of traditionally analog oriented communications. Communication technology is rapidly becoming congruent with digital-based computer technology. Meanwhile, computers have progressed from the early stand-alone, single function types, via multi-function types to large centralized units, and on to decentralized and distributed processing types. Now, office computers and personal computers are widely used in offices and even homes. Multi-dimensional distributed processing naturally means the formation of a total system linking individual computers and subsystems via the communication network. This is where we can see the technological interaction and integration of computers and communications through rapid progress in semiconductor technology. My use of the term "C&C" is an attempt to express the trend toward mutual contact and integration that we now see emerging in these three leading areas of electronics.

How exciting it has been to participate in such great technological advancement; however, I have always questioned in my mind the lack of consideration for human factors in machines and computers. Technological innovations in the past have created great impacts on our society and life. However, such impacts have not always been for the satisfaction of the public. Because of technological immaturity and lack of understanding of human factors, advanced machines have demanded much advanced knowledge and painful training for users. Automatic service machines have often irked customers to the end of their endurance, due to lack of humane service considerations and of proper interaction. Personal computers have helped to popularize computers, but from a human friendly point of view, they are still far from satisfactory.

One thing that I feel we must keep in mind along with the technological factors, is the human factors. This point is especially important in the "C&C" age, since human beings are the main actors who will be using and commanding data and information through the "C&C" media. At the same time, they are, in every sense of the word, the principal

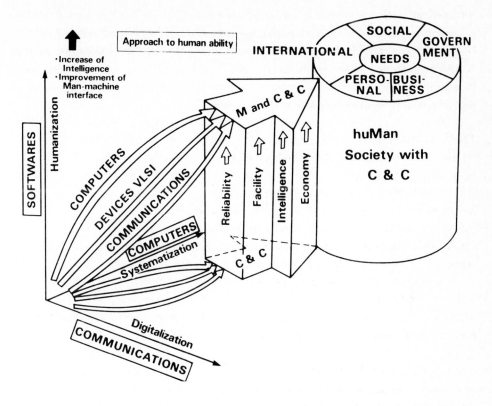

Fig. I. "Man and C&C" concept and perspective

developers of "C&C". For this reason, as shown in Fig. I, I extended my concept of "C&C" to "(hu)Man and C&C" to represent the integration of computers and communications along a human axis. (Kobayashi, 1980, 81, 82)

In the use of computers and communications, it has conventionally been necessary for peopole to strive to draw closer to the machine system in order to use it more effectively. While we can say the amount of labor required has now been greatly reduced, it is still necessary to put considerable effort into approaching and using sophisticated systems. Our ideal is to arrive at a stage of fulfilling social and cultural life through the use of information systems that anyone, not only specialists, can use quickly and easily without any special burden. For this goal, better human interaction with the "C&C" system, that is "Man and C&C", has to be aimed at, and computers with increased intelligence and improved man-machien interface have to be developed.

III. MAN-MACHINE INTERACTION

If we aim at "Man and C&C", we must progress in machine functions by incorporating human intelligence into the machine so that it ever more closely approaches human functions. In this context, the most important aspect of "Man and C&C" becomes the

4

hardware and software related to man-machine interactions. If the functions of "C&C" system are compared with those of human, they can be related as shown in Table 1.

Interaction functions between human and machines may be categorized in the following three hierarchies, as shown in Table 2. Man-Machine interactions have been improved by the development of various technologies and comprehension of such technologies in corresponding hierarchies, as shown in Table 3.

TABLE 1
Relation between "C&C" system and human factors

Computers	⟶	Artificial brain
Communications system	⟶	Artificial nerve system
Input terminals	⟶	Artificial five senses
Output terminals	⟶	Artificial vocal codes, hands and legs
Semiconductor devices	⟶	Artificial cells
Software	⟶	Intellignce

TABLE 2
Hierarchies of man-machine interactive functions

1. Sensory level (Physical phenomenal level)
   Interaction by acoustic, visual and motional means

2. Media level (Information presentation level)
   Communications by letter, language, video and image

3. Concept level (Semantics level)
   Communications through knowledge, idea and intention

TABLE 3
Technological approaches in each hierarchical levels

1. Sensory level
   I/O hardware, receiver and speaker, keyboard and tablet, display ..... Ergonomics
2. Media level
   Voice recognition and synthesis, character recognition, natural language understanding and composition, video recognition and understanding, computer graphics
3. Concept level
   Knowledge expression, conceptual construction, knowledge processing

As the hierarchy proceeds from the sensory level to the media level and further to the concept level, man-machine interactions depend heavily on the progress of software technology. New technologies in the concept level are still limited within the frame work of academic interest. Next, I would like to discuss various technological problems, beginning from input-output hardware problems.

Hardware

The telephone set has been the major input-output hardware item used in communications. As the switching technology advances from manual exchange switching via automatic switching to electronic switching, the telephone set added new functions, such as dialing and simple keyboard function by pushbuttons, on top of the basic functions in sending and receiving voice signals. The telephone set has not essentially changed for the past one hundred years. However, supported by rapid progress in microelectronics technology, modern telephone sets are acquiring intelligence by incorporating repertory dialing, message recording, display of receiving telephone number and other functions.

The teletypewriter that has long been used as an input terminal of record communications, and modern keyboards, as computer input terminals, are the machines that have deeply rooted into Western culture. Therefore, they are not necessarily friendly machines in a society such as Japan, where the culture is based on ideographs. An alphanumeric typwriter has only about fifty keys. However, a Japanese language typewriter has to have more than one thousand keys for two types of phonetic symbols, 44 characters for Katakana and the same number for Hiragana, and a minimum of one thousand Kanji or Chinese ideographs in common daily use. Therefore, a Japanese typewriter is a tool for use by specialists with a high degree of training, and it is highly ineffective compared with English typewriter. In order to increase the manipulative ability of Japanese typewriter or keyboard, a pen-touch system was developed, but the improvement in input speed has been insignificant.

As the computer usage has been moved from numerical data processing to information processing, the input of Japanese characters into computer has become indispensable. To attain a desirable input efficiency, Katakana, a Japanese phonetic symbol, has been used to input Japanese information. However, printing or displaying information using only Katakana is a very unfriendly method to achieve machine to human interaction. Japanese efficiency in understanding information is greatly reduced, when only Katakana symbols are used. The trend toward increased use of Japanese word processors and the development of ultra high level computer language definitly demand the use of Kanji as input characters. This requirement has imposed upon Japanese engineers the requirement to develop a very difficult technology compared with inputing alphanumeric characters. In order to limit the number of keys to within a practical limit, transfer technology from Katakanas to Kanji or Chinese ideographs has been developed. To let computer choose the right Kanji among many homonyms, very sophisticated software, similar to automatic translation of language, has to be developed. Currently, the choice of very difficult Kanji is done throguh man-computer interaction; however, input efficiency has greatly been improved.

The number of key positions on a Japanese language keyboard is about twice the number on an English keyboard, since it has both alphanumerics and Katakana. Therefore, using a Japanese keyboard requires much training for the users and it is yet poor in operation. In order to solve these problems, Dr. Morita of NEC has developed a new keyboard. A photo of the Morita keyboard is shown in Fig. 2. The Morita keyboard has only 30 character keys and provides exactly the same functions as the current standard

Fig. 2. Photograph of Morita Keyboard

keybord that has 48 character keys. The arrangement and angles of keys are well designed ergonomically for improving operability. Training time is reduced to about one third and input speed is increased 2.5 times, in comparison with the performance of a standard keyboard.

CRT display is most commonly used for machine to man interaction. Its information display function and operability have been greatly improved by acquiring higher definition, color display capability, character and video process functions and others. However, its performance is still insufficient to display documents, especially Japanese documents. Due to rapid penetration of OA (Office Automation) systems, the number of workers, who are using CRT display extensibly for long working hours, has increased. As a result, VDT (Video Display Terminal) disease such as deterioration in eyesight and headache has become a social problem, and further technological and ergomomic attention has been demanded.

As the use of various terminals increases to interact with the "C&C" system, desk and office spaces may be fully occupied by terminals, creating enviromental pollution.

Therefore, most devices and equipment have to be made as small and light as possible within the limit of ergonomic consideation. Further, the functions of several terminals should be combined and composite terminals should be developed.

SOFTWARE

In order to improve man-machine interaction by adding intelligence to a computer, many extensive advances in hardware and software technologies are necessary.

Machines that read characters started out from printed letters and now can decipher handwritten scripts. Some machines can recognize 3,000-odd Japanese or Chinese ideographs, a recognition rate that makes them more or less commercially practical. On the other hand, machines that can distinguish human speeches are already on the market. These devices are able to recognize single syllables or individual vocabulary, and we will soon see devices that can recognize continuous speech spoken by anyone, not just the voiceprints for a given individual.

NEC is now developing a machine for use by the blind, which turns over pages automatically, recognizes words and sentences, processes them to add proper accent and intonation, and speaks with a synthesized voice. Our finger print recognition machine has greatly improved the productivity of finger print database and the speed of identifying criminal suspects. The final identification is carried out by a finger print expert, interacting with the machine. The machines have helped to arrest many criminals of long unsettled cases.

The advancement of these man-machine interaction technologies in the media hierarchy level has depended upon the progress of hardware and software, relying heavily on the latter. In order to make machine more friendly so that anyone can handle daily works in harmony with machines, much advancement in high level language and software is necessary.

As Chairman and Chief Executive Officer of NEC, which is known as the "C&C" company, I am often questioned by the press whether I am freely using a personal computer at home. Then, I reply that I am still not using one since it is not friendly enough to me. I am asking to engineers at NEC to advance technology so that old man like me can utilize computers willingly. I wish I could communicate with computers as easily as I instruct and question my family and company members. I sincerely hope such days will arrive while I am still alive.

NEC engineers have advanced technology a step closer to my desire. They have developed an OA system that they nicknamed the Aladdin system. This system is in operation at our new Abiko works, which develops "C&C" office systems and equipment, and connects the terminals at major offices and engineering rooms, several computers and data banks via a fiber-optics local area network. As soon as the terminal is switched on, Aladdin appears on the VDT screen and says "May I help you". Soon after, a procesable work menu appears on the screen. When a desired menu number is pushed, for example a visual display of desk environment, as shown in Fig. 3, appears on the screen. If I point at

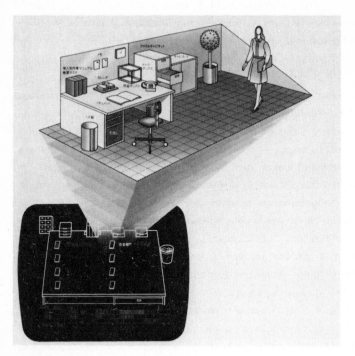

Fig. 3. A CRT display of office work menu

a desired item or key in a proper number, I can access to a desired document or information. Even I can use this system after receiving a short instruction.

Man-machine interaction for the new OA systems has moved a step closer to my desire; however, there are still many unsatisfactory points. Necessary hot informations are not always available just on time. The input efficiency and speed must be greatly improved. If the process deviates slightly from a routine, costly and time consuming program maintenance are required. Automatic software manufacturing tools, which can accept a programing diagram or a programing instruction written in Japanese as input information, are desired. SDMS (Software Devlopment and Maintenance System) developed by NEC engineers is advancing toward this goal. How can computer troubles caused by incorrect operations be avoided? How can computer crimes be completely eliminated? The technology for computer security has to be studied much further.

As computer applications expand broadly into every social sector through OA and FA (Factory Automation) stage to HA (Home Automation) stage, a great variety of software must be manufactured and maintained rapidly and economically to meet the variety of demands for "C&C" systems. Hence, without a great advancement in software production automation technology, it may be difficult to provide a man-machine interaction friendly to the public.

IV. PERSPECTIVE OF MAN-MACHINE INTERACTION

Man-machine interactions have been improving rapidly, owing to the great advancement in microelectronics and software technology; however, if machines are made to serve mankind, much improvements in man-machine interaction are necessary as discussed previously. I think the ideal man-machine interaction is that machines can be integrated naturally and in harmony with our culture and way of living, which have been created for thousands of years. I recognize that there are various criticisms against the development of automatic machines that do not require high skill and training. But, I think that without relieving humans from the burden of heavy and extensive training, popularization of technology is difficult to realize.

It is desirable to interact with machines using natural languages, even if some restriction is imposed upon usage of language to make it easier for the machines to understand. As new media technology is aiming at, if we could file and access any information in data banks as easily as we write memos and read books and documents, the utility of "C&C" system could be greatly popularized. In order to bring man-machine interaction closer to our natural way of living, there are mountainous technological problems to be challenged.

We Japanese are living in the culture that is based on ideographs and is vaque compared with Western logic. In order to develop "Man and C&C" for people with such cultural backgrounds, we have to challenge research and development of video, voice and knowledge processings in media and concept hierarchy levels. This is why we are working on the development of the 5th generation computer.

Within my professional carrier of 55 years, the world communications has advanced greatly. However, I feel the world today still lacks the mutual understanding that is necessary among the people of different nations. We in Japan feel particularly keenly that linguistic differences are a major barrier. In this regard, I believe that, in parallel with improving man-machine interaction, the development of automatic interpreting

JAPANESE **ENGLISH**

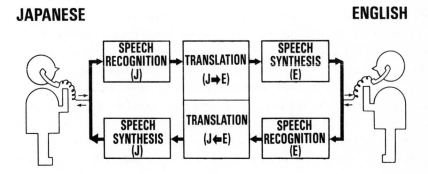

Fig. 4. Concept of automatic interpretation telephone

systems will be one of the indicators for the realization of "Man and C&C". Fortunately, we at NEC have at our disposal sophisticated voice recognition and synthesis technologies that have been cultivated for over 20 years. We hope that, by merging these technologies with machine translation technology, we will be able to achieve the dream of automatic interpretation. As shown in Fig. 4, if we could simultaneously hear what is said by the speaker at the other end of an international telephone call and have it interpreted by machine translation into our own mother tongue, more people could speak readily to foreigners, thus immensely increasing the opportunities for greater mutual understanding. At Telecom 83 in Geneva, Switzerland, NEC demonstrated a simple model of such a system and received high evaluations from participants.

To make the such systems practical, I realize very difficult problems in both hardware and software should be overcome, and that international cooperation is inevitable. I have personally witnessed how ideas for a new technology were brought into practical use through nearly 20 years of human efforts. For this reason, I am confident that automatic interpretation systems will be realized before the close of this century. I have made it my life goal to be able to confirm for myself, with my own eyes and ears, the coming of that day. I sincerely wish all of you will apply your endeavors and cooperations to advancing man-machine interaction and to further man to man communications.

REFERENCES

Kobayashi, K., 1977. Shaping a communications industry to meet the ever-changing needs of society. INTERCOM 77, Atlanta.

Kobayashi, K., 1978. The Japanese computer industry: Its roots and development. 3RD USA Japan Computer Conference, Sanfrancisco.

Kobayashi, K., 1979. A perspective on the new situation: "C&C". INTELCOM 79, Dallas.

Kobayashi, K., 1980. Computers, communications and man. 7th International Conference on the Use of Computers in Radio Therapy. Tokyo.

Kobayashi, K., 1981. Computers, Communications and man. 23rd IEEE Computer Society International Conference, Washington, DC.

Kobayashi, K., 1982. Man and "C&C": Concept and perspectives. IIC Annual Conference, Helsinki.

Human—Computer Interaction, edited by G. Salvendy
Elsevier Science Publishers B.V., Amsterdam, 1984 — Printed in The Netherlands

COGNITIVE ENGINEERING PRINCIPLES IN THE DESIGN OF HUMAN-COMPUTER INTERFACES

D. A. NORMAN

Institute for Cognitive Science, C-015, University of California, San Diego, La Jolla, California 92093 (USA)

ABSTRACT

Norman, D.A. Cognitive Engineering Principles in the Design of Human-Computer Interfaces. *Proc. of the First USA-Japan Conf. on Human-Computer Interaction.*

This paper provides a quick review of major issues facing the designer of the human-computer interface. The major points are these:

- There really is a problem: As we expand the base of user population, we must attend more and more to the needs and abilities of a variety of users.

- Special skills are needed: Skills in programming, psychology, and in the tasks to be accomplished.

- Software engineering: The interface should be separated from the rest of the system—modularized so as to be functionally independent. With an interactive system, the interaction is the system. Therefore, specification of the interface should be among the first tasks during the design of a computer system— not the last, as is now often the case.

- Formal design tools for the human-computer interface need to be developed. Until we have better design tools, design must be iterative, with cycles of design and experimental tests frequently repeated. Rapid prototyping tools are essential.

The details of the arguments discussed in this short paper have been made in other publications. Therefore, I take the opportunity to summarize, to provide a higher level overview of the points and issues. The most important points are listed in the abstract and they form the main sections of this paper. The points are easily summarized: There really are problems with the human-computer interface; users are not well served by existing practices; and solution of the problems requires concentrated and dedicated efforts, with new techniques of software engineering, new evaluation procedures, and a specialized breed of interface designers.

This research was supported by Contract N00014-79-C-0323, NR 667-437 with the Personnel and Training Research Programs of the Office of Naval Research and by a grant from the System Development Foundation.

THERE REALLY IS A PROBLEM

It should be unnecessary to dwell upon this point, yet somehow it always seems necessary. Conventional computer systems simply do not take real user needs into account, sometimes not even the needs of the programmers who designed them (Norman, 1981a). Others at this conference will also speak to this issue. But I wish to emphasize several issues, some which are the *slogans* that have guided our research, others which are fundamental design considerations.

The user space

There is a wide class of users for any given computer system, perhaps best characterized along three dimensions: Knowledge of computer systems in general; experience with the particular computer system; knowledge of the topic domain of the system. These dimensions map out a large space of user capabilities and concerns that must be met by an interface. No single, fixed interface can satisfy all users.

Tradeoffs

There are no correct answers, only tradeoffs. Each technique has its virtues and deficits. The designer should know the space of design issues described by these tradeoffs and choose the design accordingly, tailoring the system for the particular set of users that are of most importance. In another paper (Norman, 1983a), I present both the case for tradeoffs and also a quantitative design technique that allows one to assess the relative psychological importance of the *User Satisfaction* for one variable against the *User Satisfaction* for another.

Stages of interaction

Just as there are different users with different needs there are different stages of interaction even for a single user at a single task. When a person interacts with a computer it is possible to identify four distinct stages in that interaction: *Intention, Selection, Execution,* and *Evaluation.* Each stage has different goals, different methods, and different needs. An interface design that is appropriate for one stage may not be for another (Norman, 1984a, b). This is an important and subtle point, one made more thoroughly in the original paper. This point interacts strongly with the philosophy that there are no correct answers, only tradeoffs. Not only are there tradeoffs in the attempt to help one class of users over another, but there are also tradeoffs even with a single user doing a single task, for assistance toward one stage of interaction can detract from what is desired for another.

Mental models, conceptual image, system image

The user develops a *mental model* of the computer system that helps in learning and trouble-shooting, and in interpreting the current state and output of the system and, thereby, in determining what to do next. This mental model is derived from the *system image* provided by the computer system, which means by the outputs, the input requirements, the messages and help provided by the system, and by the manuals and training sessions. The designer usually starts with a *conceptual image* of the system and assumes the user's mental model matches that image. But the user develops the model through the system image. Therefore, the designer must aim at creating a system image that allows the user to get the proper mental model. The point is that the designer and user communicate via the system image (Norman, 1983b).

Humans err, so recovery must be built-in

Human error is fundamental to our operations. We can use the analysis of error to help design systems (Norman, 1983c). Because all of us err, the responsible system allows us to recover gracefully. Irreversible actions should not exist. The *undo* command should be considered essential to all systems. As with all such guidelines, there are exceptions to these strong statements, but it is useful to keep the strong forms as the goals.

Activity structures

We are not single purpose creatures. We do many things simultaneously. Most single tasks are complex, requiring multiple subtasks and taking so much time that we must interrupt to do other things, or even pause for long durations. A system that can support the real activity structures of people, that can support interruptions and later resumptions, and that can minimize the overhead required to switch tasks will be a better match for real human activities than systems that do not (Bannon, Cypher, Greenspan, and Monty, 1983; Norman, 1981b).

Interaction as conversation

HCI should be thought of as a conversation, with the participants iterating toward their goals. The conversational style should mirror the needs of the conversants. Just as we have no need for an "error message" in conversation there should be no such thing as an "error message" in computer interaction. Rather, each utterance should be thought of as another iteration toward the goal, and if it is incompletely formed, ambiguous, or uninterpretable, nonetheless it represents an honest attempt toward the goal. Feedback, comments, and offers of assistance, yes: error messages, no. Recognition of this point of view changes the nature of the dialogue considerably.

FORMAL DESIGN TOOLS FOR HCI NEED TO BE DEVELOPED

We need a number of tools for HCI. Qualitative rules are essential for ensuring the proper flavor of the interaction; quantitative tools are essential for making the design choices and for getting the details right. Debugging tools are essential for ferreting out the interface problems and fixing them. At the moment, none of these tools are well developed. Card, Moran, and Newell (1983) provide a start at developing a set of quantitative design rules. I have suggested a quantitative scheme for evaluating the tradeoffs in design (Norman, 1983a).

SOFTWARE ENGINEERING

The interface should be considered a specialized piece of software, one in which the user is a fundamental part of the system. Earlier, Draper and I suggested that the user and the interface be thought of as co-routines, each communicating with the other, but with users running their "code" on machines of unknown design, with unknown characteristics (Draper & Norman, 1984).

Debugging the interface requires special skills and special tools. An interface "bug" should be defined as any failure of the total system—including human and program—to meet specifications, borrowing Shneiderman's (1982) suggestion of establishing formal usability specifications at the start of the design phase. If a user fails to perform the task properly in a specified time, or fails to recover from an error, then there is a bug in the system, even if the information needed has been presented to the user. What matters is how real users actually perform, not what designers believe the ideal user is capable of doing. (And real users are overworked, fatigued, continually interrupted. Moreover, they tend not to read documentation or messages. These statements apply for system programmers as well as for first time computer-users.)

One important software engineering design tool is that of modularization. If the interface is properly modularized, only it communicates with the user. Then, changes in communcation protocols are easily made without disruption to the rest of the system. Similarly, system changes can be made without changing the interface (again, see Draper & Norman, 1984).

ITERATIVE TESTING IS IMPORTANT

Because we lack good design tools, the interface has to be developed through iterative experimentation with the user. Indeed, the user probably does not know the real interface requirements until the designs have been tried out. Think of interface design, therefore, as an iterative process. To make this work properly, several tools must exist. First, there must be good evaluation techniques so that the strengths and weaknesses of the design can be determined. Second, there must be rapid prototyping tools that make it easy to try out new ideas.

Rapid prototyping

Rapid prototyping has the advantages that ideas can be tested immediately while they are still fresh in mind, and that users and designers get immediate feedback, thus rewarding their sense of participation in the design. By making interface design simpler, one avoids the heavy emotional commitment that is naturally formed with computer code that has taken a lot of time and effort to design—commitment that can cause great resistance to modification, even if the modification is agreed to be an improvement. Rapid prototype tools do not always lead to efficient code, so that these tools do not eliminate the need for extensive programming efforts. Still, they are essential for iterative experimentation. One has to be careful in this work not to restrict the format or class of interfaces. It is easy to make a rapid prototyping system for menu-driven interfaces: difficult to do a system that moves beyond this one, limited class of interaction. A number of promising starts toward the development of rapid prototyping systems for interfaces have been made, including the work by Buxton (1983), Jacobs (1984), Perlman (1983), Roach, Hartson, Ehrich, Yunter, and Johnson (1982), and Wasserman and Shewmake (1982).

WE NEED INTERFACE DESIGNERS

Design of an interface requires special skills: knowledge of programming, knowledge of the task domain, and expertise in human psychology. It is unlikely that a single person, be it programmer or psychologist, has these skills. But without this combination of skills, the interface is apt to be deficient. I strongly recommend that interfaces be designed by teams consisting of programmers, psychologists, and task specialists, all working together. As programmers learn modern experimental (cognitive) psychology, and as psychologists learn modern programming techniques, we may develop people with special expertise in interface design, people who can do the whole task. Today only a few such individuals exist, so the team approach seems necessary.

There is a danger that programmers might fool themselves into thinking they understand psychology simply because they have thought about how they themselves do things, or that they might think they have evaluated a system when they have asked a user or two how they felt about it. There is less danger that psychologists will think themselves programmers simply because they have taken an introductory course in BASIC or PASCAL, but that danger should be guarded against as well. Both areas are complex: both require good training and experience. And a successful interface design is going to require expertise at both.

HARDWARE IMPROVEMENTS

Hardware advances do not suffice to improve the interface. The mouse (or other pointing device) offers benefits as well as deficits. High resolution screens and windows can help some problems, but not all. Menu selection and pop-up menu design help in one of the stages of interaction (*selection*), but can get in the way of other stages (e.g., *execution*). [1] Color is pretty and sometimes useful, but not a universal solution to problems. And speech input and output adds its own bevy of virtues and problems, including whole new classes of errors and misunderstandings for designers to contemplate.

On the whole it would be best to have design principles that are independent of hardware. In the absence of these, we need principles that can guide us in the best use of particular hardware advances. We already have some of these. New hardware makes no substantive changes to the difficulties of proper design of the interface.

----

1. This is one place where the analysis of the interaction into stages provides a more precise description of the conflict between menu driven "pointing" systems and command-language systems, one thought to be superior for novices, the other for experts. In fact, the conflict is not between novice and expert nor between menus and command languages, but rather between demands at the stage of selection and at the stage of execution.

CONCLUSION

Because I have spelled out the problems of interface design in many places, this paper serves primarily to alert those new to the field to the fact that the problem of interface design is real, difficult, and challenging. It requires special skills and expertise. System designers should attend to what is already known and discussed in the literature (see references in this and other papers for the conference). The most important starting point is to take the design of the interface seriously, to recognize that both programmers and psychologists must cooperate to do the task.

REFERENCES

Bannon, L., Cypher, A., Greenspan, S. and Monty, M.L., 1983. Evaluation and analysis of user's activity organization. *Proceedings of the CHI '83 Conference on Human Factors in Computing Systems*. Boston.

Buxton, W., Lamb, M.R., Sherman, D. and Smith, K.C., 1983. Towards a comprehensive user interface management system. *Computer Graphics*: 35-41.

Card, S., Moran, T. and Newell, A., 1983. *The Psychology of Human-Computer Interaction*. Erlbaum, Hillsdale, NJ.

Draper, S.W. and Norman, D.A., 1984. Software engineering for user interfaces. *Proceedings of the 7th International Conference on Software Engineering*. Orlando, FL.

Jacobs, R.J.K., 1984. An executable specification technique for describing human-computer interaction. In: H.R. Hartson (Editor), *Advances in Human-Computer Interaction*. Ablex, New York.

Norman, D.A., 1981a. The trouble with UNIX: The user interface is horrid. *Datamation*, 27, No. 12: 139-150.

Norman, D.A., 1981b. A psychologist views human processing: Human errors and other phenomena suggest processing mechanisms. *Proceedings of the International Joint Conference on Artificial Intelligence*. Vancouver.
(Also translated into Japanese and printed in *Psychology*, 1983, *38*, No. 5: 60-65.)

Norman, D.A., 1983a. Design principles for human-computer interfaces. *Proceedings of the CHI '83 Conference on Human Factors in Computing Systems*. Boston.

Norman, D.A., 1983b. Some observations on mental models. In: D. Gentner and A. Stevens (Editors), *Mental Models*. Erlbaum, Hillsdale, NJ.

Norman, D.A., 1983c. Design rules based on analyses of human error. *Communications of the ACM, 4*: 254-258.
(Also translated into Japanese and printed in *Psychology* 1983, *4*, No. 8: 62-69.)

Norman, D.A., 1984a. Four stages of user activities. In: B. Shackel (Editor), *INTERACT '84, First Conference on Human-Computer Interaction*. North-Holland, Amsterdam.

Norman, D.A., 1984b, in press. Stages and levels in human-machine interaction. *International Journal of Man-Machine Studies*.

Perlman, G., 1983. *Software tools for user-interface development*. Presentation at the 1983 Summer USENIX Conference, Toronto, Canada.

Roach, J., Harston, H.R., Ehrich, R.W., Yunter, T. and Johnson, D.H. 1982. A Comprehensive System for managing human-computer dialogue. *Proceedings of the CHI '82 Conference*. Gaithersburg, MD.

Shneiderman, B., 1982. The future of interactive systems and the emergence of direct manipulation. *Behavior and Information Technology, 1*: 237-256.

Wasserman, A.I. and Shewmake, D.T., 1982. Rapid prototyping of interactive information systems. *Proceedings of the 2nd SIGSOFT Symposium — Workshop on Rapid Prototyping*. Columbia, MD.

Human—Computer Interaction, edited by G. Salvendy
Elsevier Science Publishers B.V., Amsterdam, 1984 — Printed in The Netherlands

SYMBIOTIC MAN-COMPUTER INTERFACES AND THE USER ASSISTENT CONCEPT

H.-J. BULLINGER[1] and K.-P. FAEHNRICH[1]

[1] Fraunhofer-Institut für Arbeitswirtschaft und Organisation (IAO), Stuttgart,
W. Germany

ABSTRACT

The paper discusses Human Factors issues of different modes of communication between man and computer. "Generic" classes of communication modes are suggested and their respective pros and cons are considered in a framework of evaluation criteria. A "symbiotic" use of different communication modes in an integrated interface and the concept of a user assistant capable of managing these different communication modes is discussed.

INTRODUCTION

Human Factors in the area of man-computer interface design are looking for a focus. Taking into account several areas of theoretical and empirical work necessary, one could try to formulate some overall areas of research:

o Models for man-computer interfaces (including the allocation of relevant influencing factors) and languages to model them.
o The isolation of certain "generic" classes of communication modes and their respective Human Factors profiles. And as an outcome of that: the definition of integrated multimodal dialogue modes.
o The definition of advanced "intelligent" interfaces that serve as a "user assistant" or "user assistant" - as an adaptation mechanism on the computer´s side simulating some of the human´s methods of cognitive adaptation.

Some of the ideas presented in the following sections are to a high degree speculative. Nevertheless, considering the development in computer science (especially in the area of artificial intelligence, computer linguistics or cognitive science) and ongoing big research programmes (Fifth Generation Computers programme, ESPRIT programme) Human Factors research should stay in contact with computer science and guide the development where possible and desirable.

GENERIC COMMUNICATION MODES

As a hypothesis for future work, it is proposed to span the space of man-computer communication by the following generic modes:

o Natural language,
o Programming languages,
o Direct manipulation.

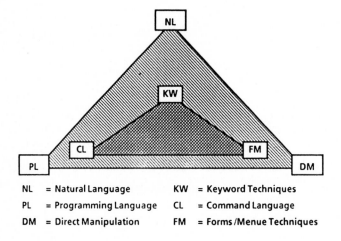

NL = Natural Language   KW = Keyword Techniques
PL = Programming Language   CL = Command Language
DM = Direct Manipulation   FM = Forms/Menue Techniques

Figure 1:   Proposed generic communication modes in man-computer interaction

For a definition or characterization of direct manipulation compare /1/, /2/, /3/. A good overview over natural language dialogue systems is given in /4/.

Other communication modes, like keyword techniques, command languages or forms/menu techniques /5/, can be allocated in this space. A more thorough discussion of this paradigm can be found in /3/. As a starting point for a more theoretical foundation, appropriate models for man-computer communication can serve. The following preliminary model (cf. /6/, /7/, /3/) is suggested:

Based on models like this, there exist some approaches describing man-computer communication in a more formal way /6/, /8/. On the other hand complementary to this approach sets of Human Factors oriented evaluation criteria for man-computer interfaces have been developed (cf. /9/, /10/). Bringing together these approaches the generic dialogue modes discussed above can be classified hypothetically in the following way (cf. /3/):

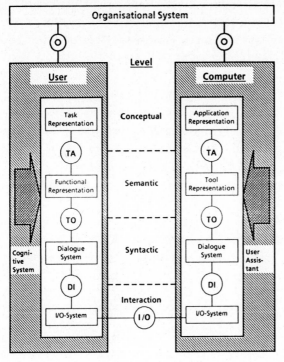

Figure 2: A model of the man-computer interface

O	: Organisational Interface
TA	: Task Interface
TO	: Tool Interface
DI	: Dialogue Interface
IO	: Input /Output Interface

Evaluation criterium	PL	DM	NL
Appropriateness for closed tasks	−	+	−
Appropriateness for open tasks	+	−	+
Self-explanatoriness, learnability, error tolerance	−	+	+
Expert user steady state performance	+	−	−
Controlability, reliability	+	+	−
Adaptivity of communication	−	−	+

PL = Programming Language
DM = Direct Manipulation
NL = Natural Language

Figure 3: Evaluation of generic interaction modes

It must be pointed out that at present these characterizations are mainly
speculative. A broad empirical and theoretical foundation is lacking. Nevertheless, they can serve to build hypotheses for later work. Some empirical work is
under way /3/.

Seeing the problem of man-computer communication from different angles, either more formal languages, natural languages or direct manipulation are regarded as being especially "user friendly". Disregarding problems of operationali-
zing this term, we don´t share this reductionist view. Concerning NL systems
e.g. conflicting views like "NL is the only natural means of man´s communication capabilities" to "The last thing a designer needs is a NL interface" are
reported.

To overcome this reductionist view, our work is based on two hypotheses
whose evidence is supported by the rough characterization of the generic dialogue techniques given above:

o There is no "best" overall dialogue technique - all techniques have their
   specific "pros" and "cons" when different user groups, tasks and application
   areas are taken into consideration.
o Although there are of course some "straight forward" cases (natural language
   dialogues in telephone based query systems) - generally the man-computer interface of the future will be a "symbiotic" mix of the generic communication
   modes[1].

To present more evidence for these theses, the term "user groups", often
operationalized by categories in pairs of opposites like "novice-expert" or
"trained-untrained" must be criticized. It seems to us that for a wide range of
applications those terms are misleading or areat least only a first approach to
the problem. It seems more appropriate to take a general view taking into account the time dependence (the usage history) of the problem. The following
picture tries to demonstrate this:

[1] We are not quite sure whether "symbiotic" in this context might not be a
   misleading term. It is not necessarily implied that there is a symbiotic interface between man and computer - although some research in artificial intelligence at least is pointing in that direction. Rather the problem of a
   multimodal, integrated adaptive system formed of the generic communication
   modes and supported by knowledge based techniques in the computer is
   addressed.

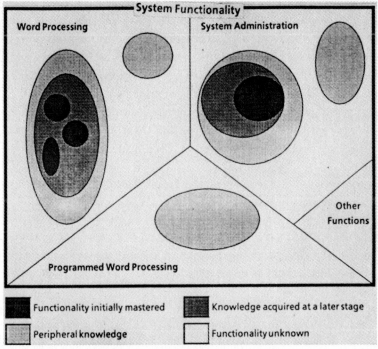

Figure 4: Acquisition of knowledge by the user

According to the interface model suggested in Figure 2, the following scheme
for the user´s knowledge is suggested:

o Pragmatic knowledge (conceptual knowledge) -
   the user model of the application.

                                                            know what

o Semantical knowledge - the knowledge of
   the detailed functionality.

o Syntactical knowledge - knowledge about
   valid input/output sequences.

                                                            know how

o Interaction knowledge - knowledge about
   formulating valid input/output sequences
   according to the underlying physical I/O
   devices.

It seems attractive to call the first two layers "know what"-knowledge and
the two later ones "know how"-knowledge. It is assumed that the mastering of
the higher levels is a prerequisite for meaningful communication on the lower

levels. As a result, a system has functionality areas where the user has a complete "know what" and sufficient "know how", others, where the "know what" is appropriate but the "know how" is not sufficiently developed and (often large) areas where even the "know what" is missing. Users can be classified according to the relative size of those areas, their exact location in the functional space and - this is of highest importance - their time-dependent development (respectively the developments which can be expected). Central in this approach is the expected learning behaviour of the user.

Accepting this view of the user-computer-interface, it would be a straight forward next step to generate dialogue technique profiles related to it, of course more detailed than the one given in Figure 5 - work on this topic is under way - and, as a result, to define time and context (task, user group) dependent "mixes" of generic communication modes which we have dubbed "symbiotic" dialogues. We see three advantages in this:

o Context dependent switching mechanisms could be built into the user interface (depending on the application: start with natural language or direct graphical manipulation - in appropriate areas switch to formal dialogue techniques for efficiency reasons).
o If the user interface supports all "generic" communication modes - redundancy could be built into the man-computer interface thus avoiding a lot of communication mismatches and resulting corrections or clarification dialogues. Weaknesses due to technical problems or our lacking ability to produce real convenient systems (natural language understanding!) could be compensated for.
o Beyond this compensation effect, real symbiotic communication could be defined. This seems for various applications the real natural language anyway.

As a side effect, we could get guidance to compensate e.g. some of the known disadvantages of direct manipulation (missing of programmable control structures, programmed macro building etc.) in certain situations by adding elements from other generic dialogue techniques (formal dialogue languages) in a way consistent with direct graphical manipulation. Incidentally, this approach is at present already in use (e.g. in spread sheet systems where direct manipulation is combined with formal techniques to specify formulas).

As Bijl /11/ states "drawings have a similar role to words in communications that pass between people, or people and computer information systems. Similar problems are represented by the use of both graphics and text as a natural means of expression "and" ... the meaning of natural expressions is anchored to reality by various means of deixis - pointing, showing, demonstrating etc.".

For many application areas, where graphical representations are involved in the man-computer interface anyway, the possibility to "anchor" natural language by means of pointing to objects, giving them names, manipulate them etc. would increase the expressive power of natural language as a means of man-machine communication and on the other side increase the scope of graphics systems: concepts like quantification, negation or "where" and "what" questions are hardly expressible by graphical means alone. Even in areas where graphics are not that much involved momentarily (e.g. big database systems - e.g. VIEWDATA systems) graphics could be used to guide the user in his "browsing" of the information space. Again natural language or more formal languages could be integrated "symbiotically".

For natural language and graphics systems first work in this area is reported in /12/ and /11/. "Symbiotic" interfaces in that sense will significantly improve the quality of the human computer interface. To give some evidence to that, Figure 5 shows a dialogue step in the domain of aircraft design for data base queries based on natural language and graphics.

With those integrated, multimodal interfaces a lot of natural language problems as reported in /16/ e.g. could be overcome. Systems like that will have to be knowledge based. They will need an adaptive coordination mechanism.

Figure 5: Example for a "symbiotic" dialogue

INTELLIGENT, ADAPTIVE USER INTERFACES AND THE CONCEPT OF A USER ASSISTENT

Existing man-computer interfaces normally represent application dependent interfaces. This concept has the following disadvantages:

o The implementation effort is high, due to the multiplication of implementations. Thus good solutions are cost intensive.
o The integration of different applications in the user interface is not straightforward. There is a high danger of non-uniform interfaces.
o The man-computer-interface software is distributed over the whole system and difficult to maintain.

Some efforts are directed at overcoming these disadvantages. The man-computer interface model mentioned above is a layered model for an application independent man-computer interface and its respective software structure. Its main benefit for Human Factors oriented work is that influencing factors can be better operationalized and located and that software structured according to this model can in principle overcome the afore mentioned problems. Without a component called "user assistant" its main disadvantage is that man-computer communication is reduced to mere input/output actions. Intentions and goals of the user, implicit communication in general or meta-communication with the system are either not represented or must be coped with by the user alone. In the artificial intelligence and cognitive science area complementary work such as the RITA-project /14/ or COUSIN-project /13/ is reported. At Stuttgart University, a work program was designed recently to study intelligent, adaptive and portable user interfaces /15/.

Before going into details, it must be remarked that at present such an interface is far removed from overall implementation. Nevertheless, for our work it represents a long distance goal. The main idea behind all this is to divide the man-computer-interface into two primary components:

o A "dump", but of course parameterized "virtual terminal" representing mainly the ideas of the man-computer interface model (cf. Figure 2) and
o an intelligent "user assistant" dealing with higher level communication problems. This "user assistant" is assumed to be knowledge-based.

Several sources of knowledge seem of importance for the user assistant:

o A user model:
User (group) characterization, learning state information (compare Figure

4), performance information, general session intentions, long and short term strategies, actual stress and strain situation etc. Two questions of course arise from this concept. How can we operationalize those factors and then get the relevant data and represent it in the system? Of course the user must be monitored to a high degree (another way would be to let him "meta-communicate" about those factors with the system: "I feel tired" ... or, "please suppress detailed output for a while"). On the other side, how will society (and of course the user) react to "monitoring" systems?

o A dialogue model:
   Tracing the dialogue history (updating the user model), keeping the dialogue technique profiles (cf. Figure 3), thus having basic knowledge about their context dependent advantages and disadvantages etc.

o A tool model:
   Represents information about objects the tool can manipulate, possible operations on them and their result. Keeps examples about the application of tools.

o An application model:
   Due to the tool set concept, tool/application mismatches can occur. So knowledge about pragmatically and semantically correct compilation of the application from tool sets with appropriate examples must be kept (think of the many examples of bad empirical work due to "automatic" unreflected usage of statistical packages!).

o An organizational model:
   Knowledge about possibilities to allocate or reschedule work, workload of certain components of the organizational system or simple things like technical component resource allocation support. The questions discussed in the context of the user model are valid here as well.

The user assistant now has the task to adapt the interface on the computer´s side to the actual communication context: Due to the degree of his sophistication he can be called in cases of communication mismatches to help to resolve them, he could "listen" to the explicit man-computer interaction all the time, he could be called by the user for meta-communication or could even play a by far more active role - allowing more implicit communication (highly efficient if it works - the old dream: do what I mean, not what I say) between man and computer.

For the moment being most of the suggested features of the "user assistant" concept are out of actual range of implementation. Nevertheless in a stepwise procedure the following goals could be achieved:

o Definition of man-computer interfaces with the capability to switch between different modes on the basis of long term usage history.

o Definition of man-computer interfaces that allow for user influence on the interface by meta-communication capabilities. This means that the interface can be switched into different modes by the user in an actual task context.

o Definition of interfaces that allow more implicit communication.

LITERATURE:

/1/ Shneiderman, B.:
The Future of Interactive Systems and the Emergence of Direct Manipulation. Behaviour and Information Technology, Vol. 1, No. 3, 1982, pp. 237 - 256.

/2/ Smith, D. C. et al.:
Designing the STAR User Interface. In: Degano, P.; Sandewall, E. (Eds.): Integrative Interactive Computing Systems. Amsterdam: North-Holland, 1983.

/3/ Fähnrich, K.-P.; Ziegler, J.:
Workstations Using Direct Manipulation as Interaction Mode. Proc. of the 1st Conf. on Human-Computer Interaction, INTERACT ´84, London, 1984.

/4/ Fauser, A.; Rathke, Ch.:
Studie zum Stand der Forschung über natürlichsprachliche Frage-Antwort-Systeme. Univ. Stuttgart, Inst. für Informatik, 1981.

/5/ Martin, J.:
Design of Man-Computer Dialogues. Englewood Cliffs: Prentice Hall, 1973.

/6/ Moran, Th. P.:
The Command Language Grammar: A Representation for the User Interface of Interactive Computer Systems. Int. J. Man-Machine Studies, 15, 1981, pp. 3 - 50.

/7/ Williamson, H.:
User Environment Model. Rep. of the 1st Meeting of the European User Environment Subgroup of IFIP, WG 6.5, 1981, pp. 6 - 7.

/8/ Shneiderman, B.:
Multiparty Grammars and Related Features for Defining Interactive Systems. IEEE Trans. Systems, Man, Cybernetics, Vol. SMC-12, No. 2, 1982.

/9/ DIN:
DIN 66 234, Part 8, "Dialoggestaltung", Draft, 1984.

/10/ Dzida, W. et al.:
Factors of User-Perceived Quality of Interactive Systems. Gesellschaft für Mathematik und Datenverarbeitung, Bonn. Institut für Software-Technologie (IST). Bericht Nr. 40 des IST der GMD, 1978.

/11/ Bijl, A.; Szalapaj, P.:
Saying What You Want With Words and Pictures. To be published in: Shackel, B. (Ed.): Proc. of the 1st Conf. on Human-Computer Interaction, INTERACT ´84, London, 1984.

/12/ Brown, D.; Chandrasekaran, B.:
Design Considerations for Picture Production in a Natural Language Graphics System. Dept. of Comp. & Inform. Science, Ohio State University, 1983.

/13/ Ball, B.; Hayes, P.:
Representation of Task Specific Knowledge in a Graceful Interacting User Interface. Report CMU - CS - 80 - 123, Dept. of Computer Science, Carnegie-Mellon-University, 1980.

/14/ Anderson, R. H.; Gillogly, J. J.:
Rand Intelligent Terminal Agent (RITA): Design Philosophy. Report R - 1809 - ARPA. Santa Monica, CA.: Rand Co., 1976.

/15/ Bullinger, H.-J.; Gunzenhäuser, R.; Lauber, R. et al.:
Rechnerunterstützte Arbeitsplätze. Antrag an die Deutsche Forschungsgesellschaft (DFG), Universität Stuttgart, 1983.

/16/ Winograd, T.:
Understanding Natural Language. New York: Academic Press, 1972.

Human—Computer Interaction, edited by G. Salvendy
Elsevier Science Publishers B.V., Amsterdam, 1984 — Printed in The Netherlands   27

DESIGNING TRANSITIONALITY INTO THE USER-COMPUTER INTERFACE

ALBERT N. BADRE

Information and Computer Science, Georgia Institute of Technology, Atlanta, Ga.

ABSTRACT

   In designing user/computer transaction languages, the designer needs to
consider that the user is not a static entity; that the same user can be a novice
at one time and become an expert sometime later. The design therefore should
allow for transitionality such that after a time the user finds him/herself in
an experienced mode of interaction simply by having practiced as a novice. This
paper describes some conditions a system should meet to provide transitionality,
and how the Infoscope* information management system was designed to meet these
conditions. Some preliminary results regarding the observed transitionality
paths taken by Infoscope users are discussed.

INTRODUCTION

   A computer neophyte browsing through the advertisements in a popular computer

magazine might come to the quick conclusion that software and computers are "easy

to use", "user-friendly", and "human-engineered". These and similar phrases are

encountered very frequently in advertised descriptions of end-user computer

products. In fact, usability has become such an important topic in software

design that one rarely ever reads a software review that does not include a

section on ease-of-use. At a closer inspection of the software that carries the

ease-of-use claim or is given a high usability rating by the reviewer, one may

conclude that "ease-of-use" means using menus to interact.

   There seems to be a perception among reviewers and designers that building

usability into the computer-human interface means specifying a menu-driven

interactive strategy. A menu is a list of items from which the user makes a

selection whereby he/she goes to a next screen. The next screen could either be

another menu screen or a transaction screen (such as data entry). Usually one

has to travel through several menus, sometimes interspersed with prompts, to get

to the intended transaction screen. The menu approach has the advantage of

guiding the novice user through a task, with the least effort spent on learning

how to perform the task. The effort is minimized because interacting successfully

does not depend on having learned and committed to memory the rules and

---

* Infoscope is a trademark of Userview Corp. It is published by Microstuf, Inc./
1845 The Exchange/Suite 140/Atlanta, Ga. 30339.

vocabulary of interaction as would be the case with a command or transaction code language. With a menu approach, interacting successfully requires recognizing and selecting familiar choices. Even if the selection items are not familiar, trial and error is an acceptable strategy. The "let me select and see what happens" approach of the novice problem solver works well in menu interaction.

The main disadvantage of the menu/prompting approach is that once one becomes familiar with performing a specific task, and no longer requires memory-by-recognition, then having to travel through a menu sequence becomes itself an obstacle to ease of task performance. The problem is that there is a continuum of user levels, from novice to expert. Software usability must deal with this continuum. Usability involves both ease of learning the software as well as ease of performance once one becomes proficient at a given task. We refer to a person who as a result of practice becomes familiar with a task domain and proficient at a given task within that domain as "experienced". An expert is at least an experienced user. The expert differs from the experienced user in that the expert can be said to understand the system, whereas the experienced user is performing tasks by rote. The expert needs to be able to molecularize, chunk, the atomic actions required for novice interaction (Schneider, 1982). This need to chunk, to summarize, and to abstract is instanced in varied circumstances such as representing chess positions (Chase and Simon, 1973), interacting with displayed information (Badre, 1982a, 1982b), or creating "shell" commands by experienced users as it is possible to do with the UNIX operating system.

Some software designs attempt to solve the problem of the two-level, perhaps multi-level, user by including both menus for the novice/occasional user as well as commands for the experienced one. Usually, however, each of these modes of interaction is independent of the other so that a user, experienced with the menus, remains a novice to the command interaction mode. The unstated assumption of such designs is that a user is static. He/she is either a novice or an expert. This is a false assumption of course because a user who is a novice at one time, with frequent use may become experienced or an expert sometime later. It is possible to be coterminously experienced and novice. One can be experienced with some of a system's functions and a novice relative to other functions. A more appropriate assumption for the designer is that the user may undergo transition from a novice to an experienced level. The design therefore should allow for transitionality such that after a time the user finds him/herself in an experienced mode of interaction simply by having practiced at being a novice. Using expert interactive strategies should derive from experience with the novice mode of interaction. The Infoscope information management system was designed to permit the novice-to-expert transition to occur.

DESIGNING FOR TRANSITIONALITY: THE INFOSCOPE INFORMATION MANAGEMENT SYSTEM

Design requirements

In planning a design for transitionality, one begins with the assumption that the novice user can gradually develop into an expert by practicing at being a novice. This assumption requires that several conditions be met in the design and its implementation.

(1) The system must allow the user to perform the same task in at least two different modes; let's call these the novice and expert modes.

(2) The novice mode should depend on recognition memory strategies to guide the user's actions; menus, prompts, and instructional screens are examples.

(3) The expert mode should depend on free recall of a language of interaction.

(4) It should be possible to learn the expert's vocabulary and syntax as a byproduct of having practiced at being a novice. Linguistic continuity should be maintained across modes.

(5) The expert's language of interaction should make it possible to: (a) bypass novice interactive strategies; and (b) introduce new vocabulary and generate new sentences for chunking and summarizing actions.

Design strategy

Before looking at transitionality designs in Infoscope, it is important to understand the Infoscope design basis and screen management environment. If usability of a software package is the most important design objective, then the designer should begin by describing the user interface environment, and make that a basis for all other specifications. In describing the user interface, transitionality specifications should be among the first to be considered. It is this approach to usability design that was adopted in developing the Infoscope information management system. The objective with Infoscope was to make the management of information on a screen similar to that on a desk. The desk analogy meant that the user should be able to maintain visual control over various information clusters. For example, it should be possible to check one's calendar of appointments while working on compiling a list of references for an article by manipulating screen information that is already visually present. One should be able to operate on either data cluster directly because the two occupy the same visual workspace, as in the case of a desk top, and not because it is necessary that they be related in substance.

The Infoscope interactive environment accordingly was designed to accommodate the information management practices of the desk top user. The Infoscope screen (see Fig. 1)* can hold up to eight files, called scopes, simultaneously. It is a

*All figures have been reproduced with permission of Userview Corp. and Microstuf, Inc.

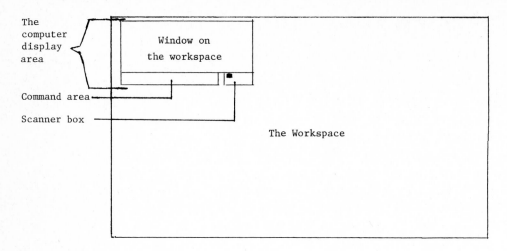

Fig. 1. The Infoscope screen.

virtual screen called the workspace. It is 253 characters wide and 62 lines
deep. The display area of the workspace contains a window onto the workspace,
an area in the lower portion for entering commands, and a scanner box in the
lower right-hand corner containing a smaller box. The scanner box represents
the workspace. The smaller box represents the location of the display area
relative to the workspace.

Modes of interaction

   After the user loads Infoscope and presses the ENTER key, the command line
reads:

        Press / for choices, ? for help, or type a command name. Ready.

This prompt immediately lets the user know that he/she can interact with
Infoscope in at least one of two modes, either by making a selection from a menu
or by typing a command name directly. In fact, it is possible to interact with
Infoscope in any of six modes:

        Menu prompting

        Command name prompting

        Command statement

        Command statement abbreviation

        Definitionals

        Command files.

Those six modes are inherently related. Having learned any one of them implies
ability to perform successfully with at least one other and most likely several

other modes. Becoming experienced with the menu prompting mode relative to a set of functions implies operational knowledge of the elementary vocabulary and syntax required for the other five modes. The linguistic continuity between an easy-to-learn mode for the novice and an easy-to-perform mode for the experienced user is an essential condition for transitionality, and one that formed the cornerstone for designing the Infoscope interactive environment.

A brief explanation of each of the interactive modes with examples of how to accomplish specific tasks in each mode will help demonstrate the linguistic continuity between modes.

Menu prompting. To enter into the menu mode, the user presses the / key. The result will look like Figure 2.

```
Tier 1     Add a new field or record to a file
SELECT:    Add  Change  Delete  Focus  Look  Quit  Sort  ?
           ↑
```

Fig. 2. The first tier of the menu mode.

The menus are stacked into seven tiers of commands. The user selects a command by typing the first character in the command name or by moving the arrow pointer to the desired word and pressing the ENTER key. The user moves the arrow in either direction by pressing the spacebar and the backspace keys. The definition of the command word to which the arrow points is always displayed on the line above the selection list. Tier-to-tier movement is accomplished by using the slash / and backslash \ keys.

Example: To list the Infoscope files of data in the menu mode, the user performs the following sequence:

    Press / to get the first menu tier as in Figure 2.
    Press / again to get the menu in Figure 3.

```
Tier 2     Compute an average
SELECT:    Average  Check  Font  List  Map  Print  Report  Total  ?
           ↑
```

Fig. 3. The second tier of the menu mode.

Type   L   to get the menu in Figure 4.

```
┌─────────────────────────────────────────────────────────────────┐
│                                                                   │
│   LIST:   Commands, Files, Keys, Switches, or Vocabulary ?        │
│          ↑                                                        │
│                                                                   │
└─────────────────────────────────────────────────────────────────┘
```

Fig. 4. A second level menu.

Type   F   to get the menu in Figure 5.

```
┌─────────────────────────────────────────────────────────────────┐
│                                                                   │
│   LIST:   Commands, Data, Format, Help, Key, Scope, or Other Files ? │
│          ↑                                                        │
│                                                                   │
└─────────────────────────────────────────────────────────────────┘
```

Fig. 5. A third level menu.

Type D to get the data files listed.
In summary, the user presses the keys //LFD to see a list of data files in the
menu prompting mode.

Command name prompting. This mode can be initiated directly from the command
line. After typing the command name, Infoscope will respond with either a menu
or a prompt. To list data files, the user types LIST; gets the menu in Figure
4; types F; gets the Figure 5 menu; then types D. The action sequence for this
mode uses the same elementary vocabulary as in the menu prompting mode, except
it permits actions to be initiated directly from command level.

Command statement. Here the user types, directly from the command line, the
command statement in English-like syntax. The important feature about this mode
is that the need to express new actions in terms of complete English words and
sentences is accommodated. This complete sentential structure is simply the
concatenation in the correct order of the elementary vocabulary present in the
menu sequence of the earlier modes, with "noise words" such as "of" being
allowable.

Example: The user types:
    LIST FILES OF DATA or LIST FILES DATA and presses the ENTER
    key to get the data files listed.

Command statement abbreviation. Infoscope recognizes abbreviations for the
frequently used command words, such as L for LOOK, A for ADD, and D for

DELETE. If words start with the same letter, then the ones judged to be more frequently used get a one character abbreviation; the others are abbreviated by the first two characters, for example, LI for LIST, MA for MAP, AL for ALIGN, and AV for AVERAGE. To take an action in the command abbreviation mode, the user enters at command level the abbreviations of the words that were used in the command statement. The abbreviations must be entered sequentially with spaces between them.

Example: To list the files of data, the user types LI F D .

The last two modes of interaction are designed to allow the expert user to summarize and chunk command statements and command sequences. The experienced user differs from the expert in that at the experienced user level, rote underlies achieving successful performance; at the expert level, successful performance requires divergence.

Definitionals. These allow the user to make a transition from the Infoscope learned command lexicon to a user defined one. The user can redefine command names, assign commands to function keys, and define new abbreviations for existing commands. New words and abbreviations that are not already in the Infoscope lexicon may be defined as synonyms to existing words by using the command MEANS. For example if one preferred the word VIEW to the word LIST, then he/she could add it to the Infoscope lexicon to perform the LIST function by typing "VIEW" MEANS LIST. (The quotes are necessary so that Infoscope will not try to execute VIEW as a command.) Words can be assigned to function keys in an equally simple way. To put LIST on key 1, the user enters at the command line: KEY 1 LIST.

Command files. The expert user may build on his/her knowledge of the language of interaction to tailor it to specific preferences, habits, and needs. If, for example, a sequence of commands is performed frequently, then it may be desirable to chunk the action sequence by writing a command file. This procedure may be done within Infoscope by first creating a one-field Infoscope file, whereby each record is a command in the sequence, then using the WRITE command to create a text file. To invoke the command file, the user types the file name used in the WRITE command.

TRANSITIONALITY PATHS: ONGOING RESEARCH

A question that may be important for the designer is whether there are transitionality patterns that are more appropriate than others relative to factors such as user levels and task complexity. Identifying transitionality patterns can allow the designer to build "transitionality prompts" into the system. Then at appropriate times, those prompts are automatically invoked to anticipate preferred practices and to define transitionality paths relative to user/task profiles.

Based on preliminary data from ongoing research, all users, whether they are neophytes (no previous experience with computers) or advanced (adept at using various software), begin by using the menu prompting mode, even though they were initially exposed to several of the modes. This tentative finding may suggest that under time limits, imposed purposely in the experiment, effort spent in recalling earlier learned information is minimized via a recognition memory format. We expected the beginning user to switch to some combination of command name prompting and statement abbreviations as he/she learned, since the menu prompting mode requires single keystrokes. The preliminary data however indicate that from menu prompting a majority of the users tend to migrate to the command statement mode where they type the complete statement instead of abbreviating it.

Some of the issues that we are still investigating in our current research are: Which of the six modes of interaction does a beginner select to perform assigned tasks? Is there a relationship between duration of experience on the system and migration to another mode? Does the level of expertise affect either the mode initially selected or the transitionality path? After a transition has been made from an initial mode to another, on one function, how long does it take to make the same transition on a new function? Is there a relationship between the complexity of a task and the choice of modes or transitions, where task complexity is defined in terms of: (a) the minimum number of functions required to complete a task; and (b) the type of control structure required to perform a task, e.g. concatenation, while structure, conditionals.

REFERENCES

Badre, A.N., 1982. Selecting and representing information structures for visual presentation. IEEE Transactions on Man, Systems and Cybernetics.
Badre, A.N., 1982. Designing chunks for sequentially displayed information. In: A.N. Badre and B. Shneiderman (Editors), Directions in Human/Computer Interaction. Ablex Publishing Corp., Norwood, N.J., pp. 179-193.
Chase, W.G. and Simon, H.A., 1973. The mind's eye in chess. In: W.G. Chase (Editor), Visual Information Processing, Academic Press, New York.
Schneider, M.L., 1982. Models for the design of static software user assistance. In: A.N. Badre and B. Shneiderman (Editors), Directions in Human/Computer Interaction. Ablex Publishing Corp., Norwood, N.J., pp. 137-148.

Human—Computer Interaction, edited by G. Salvendy
Elsevier Science Publishers B.V., Amsterdam, 1984 — Printed in The Netherlands

DESIGN OF HUMAN-COMPUTER DIALOGUES

R. C. Williges
Virginia Polytechnic Institute and State University,
Blacksburg, Virginia 24061 USA

ABSTRACT

Williges, R. C. Design of human-computer dialogues. Proc.
First USA-Japan Conf. on Human-Computer Interaction.
Honolulu, Hawaii, August 18-20, 1984.

This paper provides an overview of a multidisciplinary
research program on human-computer dialogues design which
involved the combined efforts of behavioral and computer scientists. The major components of the program included the dialogue
operating environment, the role the dialogue author, the role of
the applications programmer, and the end user interface.
Research findings are summarized in terms of dialogue models/-
concepts, dialogue design tools, and dialogue principles. The
implications of this program as discussed in terms of both the
overall research impact and the unresolved research issues.

OVERVIEW

For many years now, the computer boom has created an unparal-
leled demand for sophisticated software systems, and, since its
onset, the demand for functionality has been so large that much
of the design effort has been concentrated on the system code.
With the steady increase in software sophistication has come the
realization that the state of designs for human-computer interfaces is lagging behind, and computing system users are beginning
to demand better treatment. Management of human-computer dialogues is essential for the enhancement of the information processing and decision making capabilities of computer users working in real-time, demanding environments.

A solution to the interface problem requires a comprehensive
approach that considers the applications programmer, the dialogue
author, and the end user as well as the environments in which
they must function. This research dealt not only with specific
dialogue techniques, but also with the nature of software design
methodologies, the tools necessary to facilitate the development
of high-quality, flexible human-computer interfaces, and the
allocation of tasks between the human and the computer.

A sketch of the major aspects of the program is shown in
Figure 1. Essentially, there were four major thrust areas of
research which had the combined goal of understanding the
factors that might lead to improved human-computer communication
through the development of quality software interfaces. The
major components of the research program included the Dialogue
Management System (DMS) operating environment, the role of the
dialogue author, the role of the applications programmer, and
the end user interface.

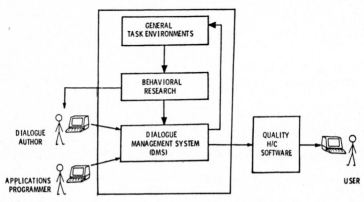

PROJECT OVERVIEW

Fig. 1. Program overview.

The core of the research is the software system, the DMS,
which is a complete system for defining, modifying simulating,
executing, and metering human-computer dialogues. Research emphasis in the DMS system involved the development of an execution environment that supports a Generic Environment for Interactive Experiments (GENIE) as a means of conducting behavioral
research; the construction of an overall human-computer system
development methodology which provides the developer with a
graphical programming language for producing an executable software requirements specification; and new methods for modeling,
designing, and development human-computer interfaces based on
syntactic and semantic specification. The DMS environment is
based upon the hypothesis that dialogue software should be designed separately from the code that implements the computational parts of an application. To achieve the goals of DMS two
distinct roles were defined for the production of a software application, the dialogue author and the applications programmer.

Dialogue author

The role of the dialogue author is an extremely important concept that has evolved during this research effort. If the dialogue, or communication, component of a software system can be kept independent of the computational component of the system, one can develop, modify, and monitor the communication interface in a straightforward and efficient manner. Much of the research conducted on the dialogue author was concerned with the development of tools to facilitate the authoring process which, in turn, is based on a transaction model. The toolkit developed for authoring dialogues involves a variety of components including a dynamic language executor, a behavioral demonstrator to exercise prototype interfaces at various stages of design or implementation, and a dialogue author interface called AIDE (Author's Interactive Design Environment). Dialogue authors, for example, may use these interface design tools to implement keypad, menu, textual, and graphic designs.

Applications programmer

Research dealing with the programmer's role dealt primarily with techniques and procedures that enabled the programmers and dialogue authors to work separately but cooperatively under the DMS environment, levels of interactive-ness in programming environments, and the application of software metrics to human-computer interfaces. In addition to these activities, a corollary effort was directed toward validation of the ADA programming support environments.

End user

A third role shown in Figure 1 is the end user. Research dealing with the end user was divided into three major areas. The first was in the area of sophisticated dialogue design for novice users, and here some of the problems investigated include command language design, adaptive information retrieval, interactive help information, and expert design systems. The second area concerned new technologies, specifically voice input and output. Here problems of interest included format of synthesized emergency messages and user feedback and error correction with voice recognition. The third area dealt with dynamic human-computer task allocation. Both dialogue-based communication and model-based communication for dynamic task allocation were studied.

RESEARCH FINDINGS

This research program resulted in a large variety of behavioral research studies and software implementations. The emphasis of these activities are summarized in terms of human-computer dialogue models/concepts, dialogue design tools, and dialogue principles.

Dialogue Models/Concepts

Many of the products resulting from this research program are direct outgrowths of fundamental conceptualization and model developments which were a focal point of the basic research. First, a series of dialogue concepts evolved. These included the concept of dialogue independence, dialogue author, human-human communication model, a transaction model, interface models, supervisory methodology, holistic design, meta-communication model, and cognitive structures. (Hartson and Johnson, 1983; Ehrich, 1982; and Roach and Nickson, 1983.) Second, techniques for building user models for commanding computer action (Folley and Williges, 1982 a & b) and for dynamic task allocation (Revesman and Greenstein, 1983) were developed for the end user interface.

Dialogue Design Tools

Three general categories of dialogue design tools evolved throughout the course of this project. These tools included system services, programming tools, and dialogue authoring tools. The system services include all the tools developed to facilitate the conduct of the behavioral research and the execution of the DMS environment. These include the dialogue database, metering, internal communications, process creation and deletion, device input/output timing, and debugging procedures (Ehrich, 1982; Cohill and Ehrich, 1983). Tools developed to aid the programmer include a programming environment (Ku and Lindquist, 1982), a graphical programming language (Yunten and Hartson, in press), and a behavioral demonstrator of software interfaces (Callan, 1983). Most of the effort in dialogue design tool building, however, centered around tools used by the dialogue author. These tools included a rapid prototyping tool, expert consultation tool, an expert profile generation tool, a general dialogue design environment, a dialogue author's tool-kit, and various tools for voice I/O. (See Johnson and Hartson, 1982; Elkerton and Williges, 1983; Spine, Williges, and Maynard, in press; and Lindquist, Fainter, Gray, Hakkinen, and Maynard, 1983.)

Dialogue Principles

The results of many of the behavioral studies not only were used to evaluate dialogue models and concepts, but they also provided a database to aid in the development of empirically derived dialogue design principles. This research focused on three general areas of dialogue design principles which were particularly lacking in research data. First, new dialogue technologies using voice input/output were considered. Principles for voice output included message cueing and syntax and the use of visual redundancy (Hakkinen and Williges, in press). Design principles for voice input were concerned with user feedback and error correction (Spine, Maynard, and Williges, 1983). The second area of concentration was concerned with sophisticated dialogue design for novice end users. Screen layout principles for interactive window size (Elkerton, Williges, Pittman, and Roach, 1982) as well as principles for providing novice user assistance in terms of interactive help (Cohill and Williges, 1982) and expert aiding (Elkerton and Williges, 1983) were investigated. And, third, dialogue principles for dynamic human-computer task allocation were developed. These included both dialogue-based task allocation principles for command types and input device types (Rieger and Greenstein, 1982) as well as model-based task allocation princples dealing with model implementation and computer feedback (Revesman and Greenstein, 1983).

PROGRAM IMPACT
Research Impact

A broad approach to human-computer dialogue design was followed throughout this research program rather than adopting a more focused investigation on one aspect of the dialogue design problem. Obviously such an approach results in less depth in investigating any of the four major areas depicted in Figure 1.

However, the broader approach taken in this research program had a tremendous impact on defining and organizing the problems associated with human-computer communication interfaces. The cross-fertilization of ideas from one aspect of the problem to the other major areas could only be realized through this broad approach. Indeed, there are probably no comparable laboratories with such broad perspective of the problem of producing software systems with human-computer interfaces. For example, the concept of role, training, and activities of the dialogue author could only have come from close interaction of computer and behavioral scientists. The tools and advanced techniques used in implementing studies could only have been achieved through the efforts of the computer science team members, and the recognition and resolution of the human factors issues in DMS could only have been achieved through daily work with the human factors team members. These relationships were manifest not only in the many joint seminars and workshops but also in daily contacts and activities.

The programmatic support is this program provided a mechanism to consider such a large-scale approach. The research team was also able to capitalize on the individual areas of expertise of all the researchers in a synergistic fashion which, in turn, resulted in multidisciplinary solutions to the various research problems. Rather than forcing researchers who have recognized expertise in certain research areas to become expert in every associated field, this multidisciplinary approach resulted in sophisticated, interdisciplinary strategies.

Research Implications

Although a great deal of research was completed during this three year program, the results of this work suggest additional areas of concentration. These future reseach issues include extensions of the dialogue management system, an author's interactive dialogue environment, multichannel concurrency, supervisory methodology, adaptive human-computer interfaces, bandwidth effects, multi-mode interfaces, verification and error processing, training novice users, multi-operator interfaces, dynamic interfaces, and implementation of human-computer guidelines.

ACKNOWLEDGEMENTS

This research program was supported by the Office of Naval Research under ONR Contract Number N00014-81-K-0143, Work Unit Number NR SRO-101. The effort was supported by the Engineering Psychology Programs under the technical direction of Dr. John J. O'Hare.

REFERENCES

Callan, J. The behavioral demonstrator: A requirements executor. Technical Report CSIE-83-14, May 1983.

Cohill, A.M. and Ehrich, R.W. Automated tools for the study of human/computer interaction. In Proceedings of the Human Factors Society 27th Annual Meeting (pp. 897-900). Santa Monica, CA: The Human Factors Society, 1983.

Cohill, A.M. and Williges, R.C. Computer-augmented retrieval of HELP information for novice users. In Proceedings of the Human Factors Society 26th Annual Meeting (pp. 79-82). Santa Monica, CA: The Human Factors Society, 1982.

Ehrich, R.W. DMS -An environment for building and testing human-computer interfaces. In Proceedings of the International Conference on Cybernetics and Society. (pp. 50-54). New York: IEEE Systems, Man and Cybernetics Society, 1982.

Elkerton, J. and Williges, R.C. Evaluation of expertise in a file search environment. In Proceedings of the Human Factors Society 27th Annual Meeting (pp. 521-525). Santa Monica, CA: The Human Factors Society, 1983.

Elkerton, J., Williges, R.C., Pittman, J.A. and Roach, J.W. Strategies of interactive file search. In Proceedings of the Human Factors Society 26th Annual Meeting, (pp. 83-86). Santa Monica, CA: The Human Factors Society, 1982.

Folley, L.J. and Williges, R.C. User models of text editing command languages. In Proceedings of Human Factors in Computer Systems (pp. 326-331). Washington, D.C.: Association for Computing Machinery, 1982.

Folley, L.J. and Williges, R.C. Validation of user models for interactive editing. In Proceedings of the Human Factors Society 26th Annual Meeting (pp. 616-620). Santa Monica, CA: The Human Factors Society, 1982.

Hakkinen, M.T. and Williges, B.H. Synthesized voice warning messages: Effects of alerting cues and message environment. In Proceedings of the Human Factors Society 26th Annual Meeting (p. 204). Santa Monica, CA: The Human Factors Society, 1982.

Hartson, H.R. and Johnson, D.H. Dialogue management: New concepts in human-computer interface development. Technical Report CSIE-83-13, November 1983.

Johnson, D.H. and Hartson, H.R. The role and tools of a dialogue author is creating human-computer interfaces. Technical Report CSIE-82-8, May 1982.

Ku, C. and Lindquist, T.E. PEEP: A Pascal environment for experiments on programming. Technical Report CSIE-82-9, September 1982.

Lindquist, T., Fainter, R., Guy, S., Hakkinen, M. and Maynard, J. GENIE -A computer-based task for experiments in human-computer interaction. Technical Report CSIE-83-10, October 1983.

Revesman, M.E. and Greenstein, J.S.   Application of a model of
    human decision making for human/computer communication.   In
    CHI '83 Conference Proceedings: Human Factors in Computing
    Systems (pp. 107-111).   New York: The Association for Com-
    puting Machinery, 1983.
Rieger, C.A. and Greenstein, J.S.   The allocation of tasks
    between the human and computer in automated systems.   In Pro-
    ceedings of the International Conference on Cybernetics and
    Society (pp. 204-208).   New York: IEEE Systems, Man and
    Cybernetics Society, 1982.
Roach, J.W. and Nickson, M.   Modeling and developing human/
    computer communications.   In CHI '83 Conference Proceedings:
    Human Factors in Computing Systems (pp. 35-39).   New York:
    The Association for Computer Machinery, 1983.
Spine, T.M., Maynard, J.F. and Williges, B.H.   Error correction
    strategies for voice recognition.   In Proceedings of the
    Voice Data Entry Systems Applications Conference. Palo Alto,
    CA: American Voice Input/Output Society, 1983.
Spine, T.M., Williges, B.H. and Maynard, J.F.   An economical
    approach to modeling speech recognition accuracy.   Interna-
    tional Journal of Man-Machine Studies, in press.
Yunten, T. and Hartson, H.R.   A SUPERvisory methodology and
    notation for develop-ment of human-computer systems.   In
    Advances in human-computer interaction. Norwood, New Jersey:
    Ablex Publishing Corp., in press.

Human—Computer Interaction, edited by G. Salvendy
Elsevier Science Publishers B.V., Amsterdam, 1984 — Printed in The Netherlands

NEW OPPORTUNITIES IN THE HUMAN FACTORS ENGINEERING OF COMPUTERIZED SYSTEMS

D. MEISTER[1]

[1]U.S. Navy Personnel Research and Development Center, San Diego, California, USA

ABSTRACT

Meister, D. New opportunities in the human factors engineering of computerized systems

This paper discusses the practical problems of how the human engineer makes behavioral inputs to the design of the computer-human interface (C-HI). Although such inputs should ideally depend solely on technical knowledge, non-technical factors such as conservative resistance by software managers and designers to Human Factors Engineering (HFE) may determine the success of those inputs. Factors leading to increased HFE opportunities are the relative novelty of software design which may help to counteract conservatism; the human engineer's background in computer use; and increased capability of securing C-HI performance data.

INTRODUCTION AND OVERVIEW

The theme of this discussion, from which its title has been derived, is that because of the distinctive characteristics of computerized systems and their software, the possibility exists for applying HFE to these systems more effectively than has been the case with non-computerized systems. To examine this possibility it is necessary to compare HFE as it has been traditionally performed with older systems with what is possible in applying HFE to computerized ones. What HFE has been and is, is fact; what it may be, may become fact if behavioral specialists working with computerized systems are intelligent enough--and perhaps, even more--lucky enough--to take advantage of their opportunities. The reality of system development is that the impact of HFE on the design of the C-HI depends in part on certain conditions that are not technical at all.

In examining the opportunities in the title of this paper the following questions must be answered: (1) What are the implications of the special features computerized systems possess? (2) Has the nature of what human engineers must do in system development changed with the advent of computerized systems? (3) Will human engineers entering the discipline in the future and working with computerized systems be the same type of practitioner as the older generation of human engineers? (4) Are HFE design guidelines presently being developed for computerized systems adequate to assist that human engineer?

DEFINITIONS AND DISTINCTIONS

Logically we begin by defining what we mean by a computerized system. A system is not truly computerized if its operator does not interact directly with the computer. Many large systems may contain small (micro) computers which function as components of a larger system, e.g., as in regulating the tuning of a television set, but the user is not even aware of them. The computerized system for purposes of our discussion is one in which there is communication between the operator and the computer. The system acts in a collaborative mode with the operator by performing such functions as: asking questions of the operators; presenting him with choices (e.g., a menu); providing feedback, error notices and correction opportunities; organizing and analyzing data; suggesting strategies; recommending decisions. All these functions will be possessed by only the most sophisticated system, although it seems reasonable to expect that as technology advances, systems will add to their repertoire of functions.

Since computer-human interaction is the essence of such systems, the human engineer will be most concerned about the C-HI. Smith (1982) defines the C-HI as all aspects of the system configuration that influence the user's participation in the interaction. While this is correct in a general sense, the factors of most immediate C-HI concern are the ways in which data are stored and manipulated, the way in which information is presented to the operator and the ways in which the operator must respond to that information. This difference is critical for HFE because the C-HI is oriented around cognitive rather than the psychomotor behaviors characteristic of vehicular and other non-computerized systems.

Nonetheless, although computer-human dialogue is what distinguishes a computerized system from one that is not, there may still be many non-computer aspects of that system. It will still be necessary for the human engineer to be concerned about control/display layout, anthropometry, display visibility, etc. The natural inclination of the manager who is responsible for the design of the computerized system may be to attempt to restrict the human engineer's activities to these more traditional aspects. He will argue that design of the C-HI is a highly specialized activity which only a computer specialist can deal with effectively, and that since HFE has traditionally been concerned with hardware (not software), this is where the human engineer should direct his efforts. The basis for hypothesizing this inclination is that the well known tendency of managers and equipment design engineers to constrain behavioral design inputs will be continued by computer design managers and engineers. This tendency must be resisted strenuously.

Of course, software programming to achieve system requirements is complex and we would not suggest that anyone unfamiliar with computers attempt to influence software design. The human engineer is assumed to have at least minimal understanding of how computers work and familiarity with programming processes. Our argument assumes also that the average software manager/ designer will be unlikely consciously to include behavioral considerations in his programming. If this last assumption is correct, and if the human engineer is prevented from making inputs to software design, the C-HI will lack any "user-friendly" qualities.

We must also distinguish between standards and design guidelines. A standard is a description of a hardware/software system characteristic (design feature) that is either required or desired. A design guideline is a description of how to incorporate that characteristic into design, how to implement the standard. Equipment/system standards exist, most notably MIL-STD 1472C (Department of Defense, 1981), and in the case of software design, Smith and Aucella (1983), but as will be pointed out in more detail later, these documents and similar ones are not design guidelines and do not substitute for design guidance. It is the design guideline that will permit the human engineer to make meaningful inputs to C-HI design.

COMPUTERIZED SYSTEM DEVELOPMENT

There is no reason to believe that the development of computerized systems will follow a course different from that of non-computerized systems. In the course of that development the human engineer will attempt to answer the following questions (based on Meister, 1982): (1) What are the behavioral implications of the system requirement or of any software program developed to implement that requirement? (2) Of the alternative software programs that could satisfy the system requirement, which is most effective from a user performance standpoint? (3) Will operators/users be able to respond effectively to the presentation of C-HI information and perform the cognitive operations required by the software program? (4) What workload will personnel experience in responding to a software program and will workload and operator error be acceptable? (5) What aptitudes and training must operators/users have in order to function effectively in the new system? (6) Does the new system (including its software) satisfy behavioral requirements? (7) What behavioral inadequacies does the new software/system have and how can these be remedied?

These questions, which also arise in the design of non-computerized systems, assume that some set of requirements has been levied on the computerized system and that the human engineer will be required to analyze these to determine their implications for the user. The software designer will conceptualize a programming strategy to satisfy these requirements and the human engineer will analyze that strategy in terms of its effect on the operator (e.g., error probability, time to perform, ease of performance). For reasons that will become clear later, we would expect the human engineer working with the software designer to enter into the design process further than he has in working with non-computerized systems. For each software program suggested by the designer the human engineer must ask whether the operator/user can function with that program to the level desired. He must analyze software programs in terms of their demands on the operator/user: workload; special aptitudes needed; training. Individual software programs and ultimately the total system must be tested; the human engineer must collect user performance data that will enable him to say that the programs and the system as a whole satisfy behavioral requirements or they do not; and where they do not, he must suggest remedies.

All of these functions require certain information to be already available: average user performance with different types of C-HI functions and software programs; variability in performance by different types of users (experienced, novice, men, women, children, etc.); different programming mechanisms that can be utilized to implement various C-HI functions; the limits of operator performance (e.g., maximum speed of response); the determination of what constitutes workload in the C-HI context, how it can be measured and predicted and how it is related to various software processing mechanisms; how one can evaluate the effectiveness of the C-HI and how C-HI performance can be related to terminal system output; the aptitudes and training needed to be effective in functioning as a computerized system operator. This list of required information can serve as an outline of the behavioral research that is needed. To deal effectively with the C-HI it is to be hoped that C-HI research requirements will be more adequately satisfied than traditional man-machine interaction research needs have been.

The function of HFE in system development is to translate system requirements into behavioral mechanisms that permit accomplishment of these requirements. Hardware systems have almost always defined their mission/goals in terms of physical parameters, e.g., to fly X distance or to produce Y components. The human engineer has had the task of determining what these physical requirements meant in terms of behavioral implications and then of specifying the mechanisms that would implement those requirements.

This transformation process is required also in the design of the C-HI and it is at one time both more direct and yet more complex. It is more direct because the C-HI system functions to be implemented are already quasi-behavioral, e.g., to secure access to information, to intergrate data, to make choices, etc.; there is no need to go through an intermediate state of translating physical requirements (e.g., fly from X to Y) into behavioral ones, and then finding an implementation mechanism. On the other hand, the computer-human dialogue is largely cognitive and cognitive functions are more complex than others; much less is known about them. Because of this cognitive aspect it is too much to expect software designers on their own to incorporate behavioral provisions in the C-HI. If, as Pew, Rollins and Williams (1976) suggest, there will never be enough properly trained/qualified human engineers to assist the software designer, we are indeed in a great deal of trouble.

The record of behavioral practitioners in system design has not been a very successful one. There are many reasons for this, among them our very inadequate knowledge of human behavior, but even more important is the engineer's well known indifference to human factors (Meister, 1971). The result is that it is very difficult to get the designer to consider and implement mechanisms designed to improve operator/user performance.

The best way of countering this indifference is to write into a contract or specification for a new system a behavioral requirement parallel to that for the equipment. The starting point for all system design is the system requirement. It has the highest priority among the criteria the designer considers when he evaluates competing design inputs. Unfortunately, developers have almost never attempted to specify behavioral requirements except in such bland and useless terms as "system should be operable with minimum difficulty." Where behavioral requirements exist, they are inferential, like ensuring that the pilot of an aircraft has no impediments to his external cockpit visibility. There is a general implied system requirement which underlies HFE in system development: that is, to create a system which produces minimal effort and error, quick operator response time, etc. The trouble with such a behavioral requirement is that it is excessively inferential and too unobtrusive to help in influencing the designer. Ultimately the failure to develop behavioral requirements has been that of the HFE community because it has avoided doing the hard thinking needed to develop such requirements. This is another item on the C-HI research agenda. One of the first topics on that agenda should be what we mean specifically by a behavioral requirement.

When the operator is the focus of the system, when the system absolutely fails to perform unless the operator does his job effectively, much more attention is paid to human factors. So, for example, if we contrast the attention paid to HFE in aviation development with that paid to HFE in surface ship development, the contrast is startling because when the pilot fails, the aircraft crashes, but ship performance does not depend directly and immediately on any single operator. In truly computerized systems the C-HI, the software, exists to assist the operator/user to do something; the user is at the center of the system universe, perhaps not as dramatically as the aircraft pilot but as much in fact. The "fifth generation" of computer

systems (Feigenbaum and McCorduck, 1983) will accentuate this tendency but it
must be emphasized repeatedly to the software designer because he is more apt
to think of his work as the manipulation of abstract symbols than as the
development of a human-computer communication language. Much of the activity
in traditional HFE practice has been oriented around the human engineer's
need to propagandize and persuade the hardware designer to take the human
seriously in his design; a comparable effort will be necessary for the human
engineer working with software design--but what a waste of time and energy!
It is possible of course that computer schools will include behavioral aspects
of software design in their curricula, but if this occurs, it will probably be
far in the future.

THE ROLE OF THE HUMAN ENGINEER

The human engineer participating in the development of non-computerized
systems has had difficulty making his participation effective because in most
cases he has been a psychologist with little or no knowledge of hardware
engineering. He has had available to him a set of standards promulgated by the
government (MIL STD 1472C, Department of Defense, 1981) but, lacking an engineering background he has usually been at a severe disadvantage in his interaction with the designer. Absent a common knowledge base with the designer,
he has typically been more passive than he should have been; he has usually
waited for the designer to produce an output which he--the human engineer--
could critique. The designer has viewed the human engineer largely as a critic
of engineering design, with all this connotes of negativism. Many, if not most
of the human engineer's behavioral inputs have been ignored because the
designer's attitude toward human factors has been quite negative (Meister,
1971; 1979).

It is too much to hope that the designer of computerized systems, in particular the software designer, will be significantly more interested in HFE
than his hardware colleague, especially if there are financial and time pres-
sures during development (as there always are). It will be easier for him to
extract a software program with which he is already familiar and to apply it
to a new system without considering whether it is best for the system. If
the C-HI designer follows his hardware colleague, he will not even consider
the range of available alternatives for the design of the C-HI. (On the other
hand, considering that computers are relatively new, it is possible that software designers will be somewhat less conservative than their hardware colleagues, but this may be overly optimistic.)

The younger, computer-oriented HFE practitioner is less likely to accept
this situation passively; he is a far different proposition from his older
colleagues and perhaps a better one. That is because his training has to a

large extent been founded on computers. Today's graduate of a university behavioral curriculum has found it necessary to become proficient in one or more computer languages; he has utilized computers extensively for statistical analysis and probably has done at least some simple programming. As a consequence the computer is a familiar part of his technological inventory and he will experience fewer of the language difficulties that have bedeviled the interaction between the older generation of HFE specialists and hardware engineers.

Although the younger HFE practitioner will lack the software designer's depth of technical knowledge, he should be able to enter into the details of the latter's design much more than could the older generation of practitioners. He is therefore less likely to be as passive as the older generation was and is. Software designers may find it somewhat less easy to fob off behavioral suggestions by retreating into engineering technicalities. In consequence the potential for enhanced consideration of behavioral inputs has increased.

This of course assumes one crucial factor: that the practitioner has available better tools than he now possesses. Until now HFE research has not typically addressed the solution of the developmental research questions listed previously. Although HFE studies have dealt generally with the subject matter of HFE practice, they have not done so specifically. Application of research results has been left to the individual practitioner, making HFE practice an art rather than a science (Meister, 1979). Application requires research just as much as theory does. Whether the new HFE opportunities in computerized system design are actually implemented depends on whether this research/ practice gap is bridged.

This gap is likely to be particularly great in the case of research performed by cognitive scientists (e.g., Oberquelle, Kupka and Maass, 1983; Jajodzinski, 1983; Hollnagel and Woods, 1983) that attempt to model the mind of the computer user and organize software architecture according to that model. More meaningful research is that which specifically seeks to answer design questions, e.g., Ehrenreich's on the design of query languages (1982) and the work of Card, Moran and Newell (1983) on the text editors. More specific design research is needed to develop HFE guidelines for software design.

HFE GUIDELINES FOR SOFTWARE DESIGN

A design guideline is a prescription for incorporating desired features into hardware or software form. It is a symbolic (verbal/graphic) description of the transformation discussed previously. Table 1 lists what the design guideline should optimally contain.

TABLE 1

Contents of the HFE design guideline

1. Description (verbal/graphic) of a hardware/software requirement to be incorporated into design (e.g., provide a means of allowing the operator to make choices among data topics).
2. Alternative ways of incorporating the requirement into design of the C-HI, e.g., a table of contents, a menu, a hierarchical series of decision-choices).
3. If applicable, limits within which a design feature will function and which it will not exceed, e.g., shortest interval in which a visual stimulus can be recognized.
4. The expected performance of the operator in utilizing the design feature or the effect of the feature on operator performance.
5. The variability of that performance (e.g., standard deviation of mean response time).
6. Advantages of incorporating the design feature.
7. Cost of not incorporating the design feature.
8. Empirical evidence for (6) and (7).

Table 1 represents an ideal, of course. Only item (1) in that table is routinely incorporated into standards like MIL-STD 1472C (Department of Defense, 1981), rarely item (2). Item (1) by itself provides us merely with a standard, not a design guideline. The designer may not know how to incorporate that standard into his design. The few "design guidelines" that do exist are in general reference books like Gilb and Weinberg (1977) and Weinberg (1971) which few designers read (Meister and Farr, 1967).

The reader may ask why items 2-8 in Table 1? What is their value? Item (2) is indispensable because it tells the designer how the desired hardware/software feature can be implemented. Item (3) prevents us from imposing an unacceptable burden upon the operator by requiring him to exceed certain limits on his performance (this is related to workload). Item (4) tells us what user performance level we can anticipate when the design feature is incorporated; this permits us to determine whether overall system requirements will be satisfied if this feature is incorporated in design. Item (5) indicates the range of performance we can expect. Items (6-8) permit the HFE practitioner to perform a cost/benefit analysis of the desired software feature.

With regard to items (6-8), the advantage of a design feature from a behavioral standpoint is the increase in performance that will accrue to the operator/user, e.g., faster data "look up" time or reduction of input errors. There are two types of cost: the actual cost in terms of programmer time to implement the standard in the form of a software program, and the cost of not implementing the design feature: longer performance time, increased error, failure to acquire needed information, etc. The human engineer is interested mainly in the latter but it is helpful if he has data on programming cost.

Cost/benefit data are extremely important because of many designers' tremendous resistance to the concept of behavioral inputs in design. Unless one has been exposed to that resistance, it is difficult to imagine the barriers that designers often erect. The designer's rationale is, first, that the input will be too expensive (in terms of programming costs), second, that the feature is unimportant because it will produce no special benefit to the operator/user. The only way to counter this argument is for the human engineer to demonstrate by empirical data that the design feature or method of programming he suggests is worth implementing as against some less applicable but more familiar design practice. Such data do not presently exist; they must be developed by performing research, specifically to provide them. HFE research has generally been directed by the idiosyncratic interests of researchers and sponsors; the relevance of that research to the general design questions listed previously has been fortuitous at best. Indeed much of the material in MIL-STD 1472C and Smith and Aucella's (1983) compilation of 580 standards has been the result of experts' experiential judgment rather than of directly applicable research. The result is that MIL-STD 1472C and similar documents do not impact strongly on design. Indeed, MIL-STD 1472C, which is the major behavioral standard for all military systems contains only a few pages devoted to the special problems of the C-HI. Smith and Aucella (1983) divide their standards into six areas: data entry; data display; sequence control; user guidance; data transmission; and data protection. Most of their items relate to characteristics of the C-HI that are hardware related. (This is hardly their fault; they simply report the state of the research available.) There is little that deals with the user's preferred strategies or his conceptual functioning, the sort of thing that cognitive psychologists have been writing papers about, which makes one wonder (without wishing to be unduly critical) about the practical outputs of cognitive science. There are also textbooks (e.g., Gilb and Weinberg, 1977) that contain some of the information needed for design guidelines. In general, however, the most noteworthy characteristic of military standards and other behavioral design references is that they do not tell the designer how to translate a behavioral requirement into either hardware or software.

Although it is somewhat unfair to extract a single entry from their report and suggest that it is completely representative of all 580 items, the following from Smith and Aucella (1983) provides some flavor of what is available:
"   --- 14 Distinctive Labels

Labels for data fields should be distinctively worded, so that they will not be readily confused with data entries, labelled control options, guidance messages or other displayed material" (Smith and Acuella, p. 36).

If the software designer is at all typical he will say that it is not the responsibility of either the HFE practitioner or the design guideline to tell him how to design: a standard levies a requirement on the designer and it is the latter's responsibility to find a way to satisfy that requirement. Unfortunately, all our experience suggests that without providing the engineer with very specific design guidance, he will usually ignore the standard, if only because he will see no feasible way of incorporating it into his design. Designers left on their own with MIL-STD 1472C do not apply its standards effectively.

NEW OPPORTUNITIES

One of the most exciting opportunities available to the HFE practitioner and to the design engineer is that the computer provides them with expanded opportunities for gathering data and for testing alternative design confugurations before one is selected. Compared to the difficulties experienced in developing physical mockups and situations to test hardware configurations, it is easier (although only in a relative sense) to develop alternative software programs and to compare their efficiency by testing subjects. Consequently, the choice of software routines in computerized system development can be much more systematic and sophisticated than it is with hardware. An objection that will be raised to the testing of alternative software programs is the programmer cost involved in developing alternatives to the point that they can be tested. We do not take this objection lightly, but it should not be used simply as an excuse to avoid systematic consideration of alternatives.

Performance data are at the heart of behavioral design. If we know how people characteristically perform, we can inventory the software design mechanisms that do not work or work less well than desired and avoid using them in the future. The gathering of objective performance data is much simpler with computerized than with non-computerized systems. All it requires is development of a special program which records the operator's keyed inputs and stores them; even the machine's responses to the operator can be recorded, so that in fact it is possible to replay the entire C-HI dialogue. This can be done routinely in any system (see Sackman, 1970) at slight cost; it can even be done without the user's knowledge, so that measurement is completely unobtrusive. This capability is already routinely employed in computer-managed instruction. Someone will of course raise the question of user privacy, but the data being collected are hardly sensitive. The ease of gathering personnel performance data in computerized systems contrasts with measurement of operator performance in non-computerized systems which may require observers, obtrusive measures and overcoming many logistical problems.

The capability of recording and reproducing CHI dialogue will be of value not only in comparing and testing design alternatives but also (and just as importantly) in gathering normative data to answer the questions: what is the

average operator's responses in utilizing various types of software routines;
what is the range of individual variability? Two questions the answers to
which are an essential part of an effective design guideline.

PROSPECTUS

All in all, there are indeed new opportunities for the HFE of computerized
systems, providing the effort is made to take advantage of these. However, if
traditional modes of dealing with the problems we have discussed are followed,
these opportunities will be disappointed. HFE for computerized systems is of
course relatively new and therefore turbulent; for that very reason its opportunities are greater. At the same time, traditional forces are very powerful.
If more conservative managers and designers are allowed to have their way, the
promise of an effective HFE for computerized systems will be dimmed. If
research on C-HI remains fractionated, idiosyncratic, overly academic, it is
likely that the research/application gap will continue to be very wide.
Designers of computerized systems and HFE specialists must work together to
break out of the old and unsatisfying mold. If the suggestions made here are
followed up, even in part, it will be possible to grasp the new and exciting
opportunities for HFE design.

REFERENCES

Card, S.K., Moran, T.P., and Newell, A., 1983. The psychology of human-
    computer interaction. Hillsdale, New Jersey: L. Erlbaum Associates.
Department of Defense, 1981. Military Standard 1472C. Human engineering
    design criteria for military systems, equipment and facilities.
Ehrenreich, S.L., 1980. Design recommendations for query languages. Report
    TR 484, U.S. Army Research Institute, Alexandria, Virginia.
Feigenbaum, E.A., and McCorduck, P., 1983. The fifth generation. Menlo Park,
    California: Addison-Wesley Publishing Co.
Gilb, T., and Weinberg, G.M., 1977. Humanized inputs: techniques for reliable
    keyed input. Cambridge, Massachusetts: Winthrop Publishers, Inc.
Hollnagel, E., and Woods, D.D., 1983. Cognitive systems engineering; new wine
    in new bottles. Inter. J. Man-Machine Studies, 18: 583-600.
Jajodzinski, A.P., 1983. A theoretical basis for representation of on-line
    computer systems to naive users. Inter. J. Man-Machine Studies, 18: 215-252.
Meister, D., 1971. Human factors; theory and practice. New York: Wiley.
Meister, D., 1979. The influence of government on human factors research and
    development. Proceedings, Human Factors Society Annual Meeting, 5-13.
Meister, D., 1982. The role of human factors in system development. Applied
    Ergonomics, 13.2: 119-124.
Meister, D., and Farr, D.E., 1967. The utilization of human factors informa-
    tion by designers. Human Factors, 9:71-87.
Oberquelle, H., Kupka, I., and Maass, S., 1983. A view of human-machine com-
    munication and cooperation. Inter. J. Man-Machine Studies, 19: 309-333.
Pew, R.W., Rollins, A., and Williams, G.A., 1976. Generic man-computer
    dialogue specification: an alternative to dialogue specialists. Proceed-
    ings, 6th Congress, International Ergonomics Association, 251-254.
Sackman, H., 1970. Man-computer problem solving. New York: Auerbach Publishers.
Smith, S.L., 1982. User-system interface. Human Factors Society Bulletin,
    25:1.

Smith, S.L., and Aucella, A., 1983. Design guidelines for the user interface to computer-based information systems. Report ESD-TR-83-122, MTR-8857, Mitre Corp., Bedford, Massachusetts (AD A127 345).

Weinberg, G.M., 1971. The psychology of computer programming. New York: Van Nostrand.

Human—Computer Interaction, edited by G. Salvendy
Elsevier Science Publishers B.V., Amsterdam, 1984 — Printed in The Netherlands

THE IMPORTANCE OF KNOWING WHAT IS IMPORTANT

E. Jeffrey Conklin

RCA Liaison, M.C.C., 9430 Research Blvd, Austin, Texas 78759-6509   (U.S.A.)

INTRODUCTION

As the size of data and knowledge-bases in computing systems grows and the interactions with users become more complex, it will become increasingly important to develop techniques for rapid and natural processing on these databases. This paper proposes "salience" as one heuristic for doing this. By salience I mean a numerical encoding of the relative importances of facts in a database with respect to some context. For example, in the database representing a visual scene the main object in the scene would have the highest salience in the database. Annotated onto each database item, either manually or automatically, salience has the effect of providing a partial ordering of a data base. Metaphorically speaking, if all of the facts in a data base are of equal significance the data base can be thought of as flat. Adding salience gives the data depth: instead of having to work with the whole data base at one time, a system can view it in "layers" of diminishing salience. This has been shown to be effective in the domain of generating descriptions of pictures, and may find application in other domains where search, reasoning, or planning are used.

WHAT IS SALIENCE?

The need for a notion of salience presented itself during the design of a system for generating natural language scene descriptions from a database representing a visual scene (Conklin, 1983). A central issue in the process of natural language generation is the problem of selection: how to determine what to say, and (equally important) what not to say. It is clear that people start their descriptions with the most important object in the scene, and that they use the salience of objects to guide their selection process throughout the description. The problem, then, was to study empirically what made things salient in pictures, to add salience information to the visual representation, and to add the ability to use that salience information to the planning stage of the description system.

A series of psychological experiments was performed to study both the perceptual phenomenon of salience and its effects on the process of writing descriptions (Conklin, Ehrlich, and McDonald, 1983). Briefly, groups of subjects rated the salience of items in color pictures of outdoor scenes. For each picture each subject had a form listing all of the major items in the scene, and their task was to rate the salience of each item on a zero to seven scale. In several experiments the subjects were given a second task: writing a description of these same pictures. In the analysis of the first task all of the subjects ratings of a given object in a given picture were averaged and that value was termed the object's "visual salience". We then studied the shifts in visual salience between similar pictures as a way of getting at the factors composing salience. In the analysis of the second task the point at which an object was first mentioned in the text was compared with that object's visual salience rating.

The experiments showed that our measure of salience was fairly stable and consistent between subjects, and showed a moderate consistency between the salience an object was assigned and the point in the description where it was mentioned. (The confounding factor here was that people select what object to mention next based both on relating it to what was just mentioned, in addition to its salience.)

The experiments also allowed us to elaborate an account of the factors that composed salience. Firstly, it was useful to separate the properties of the objects pictured ("high-level properties") from properties of the images of the objects in the picture ("low-level properties"). Our use of the terms "high-level" and "low-level" is borrowed from the field of computer vision, in which low-level processing seeks to identify and label regions in the image, while high-level processing seeks to match these regions with knowledge about objects and how those objects appear. Secondly, it is also important to distinguish between an item being salient just because it always is (e.g. UFO's, explosions, nudity, etc.) versus being salient because of the setting or context in which it occurs. We termed this distinction intrinsic versus extrinsic salience.

The primary factors determining the visual salience of an object were observed to be: the object's size and centrality (degree of centralness) in the image (low-level extrinsic factors), the item's a priori salience to the viewer (high-level intrinsic factor), and the degree to which the object was

in an unusual setting (high-level extrinsic). Low-level intrinsic factors
(i.e. brightness, shape, or color) were found to have less influence.

THE GENERATION SYSTEM

   The process of natural language generation is commonly divided into two
pipelined stages. This first is responsible for deciding what information the
text should contain as well as its thematic stucture and stylistic tone. We
called this stage deep generation; it is responsible for the interface to the
non-linguistic data base from which the information comes. The second stage,
realization, is responsible for the actual production of the text based on the
first stage's specification. This stage is where the grammatical and
morphological rules of the language are imposed.

   In the present instance, the A.I. system consists of three components: (1)
a simulated perceptual representation of a picture, structured as it would be
by a computer vision system like the UMass VISIONS system (Hanson and Riseman,
1978); (2) a deep generation component, the subject of Conklin's Ph.D.
dissertation; and (3) a
realization component, already developed by McDonald (McDonald, 1980).

   The perceptual representation simulates the kind of complete internal
perceptual model that a successful computer vision system would construct,
both for its own internal processing needs, and to represent its
"understanding" of the image so that it could be used by other parts of the
total cognitive system. It is a hand-built KL-ONE network (Brachman, 1978)
that represents the objects in the scene, their attributes, and the
relationships between them, as well as an annotation of the objects' salience
as derived empirically from the experiments.

   The deep generation component, GENARO (Conklin, 1983), contains the
thematic and rhetorical knowledge of the system, embodied in a set of
production-style rhetorical rules. GENARO is data-driven: it uses the
salience annotation in the data base to select what object to mention next,
how much detail to use describing it, and when to stop the paragraph. By
data-driven we mean a style of planning that uses information in the data, and
not some explicit goal. GENARO also does not look-ahead or backtrack --
instead the rhetorical structure is "read out" directly from the data base
under the control of locally-operating rhetorical rules, with the result that
the text can be generated in time linearly proportional to its length.

Basically, GENARO takes objects in order of decreasing salience (down to a threshold), builds a high-level specification for their textual description, and passes them sequentially to the realization component, MUMBLE. MUMBLE constructs a linguistic surface structure tree from the "rhetorical specification" in one depth-first traversal, with the words of the text printed out as they are reached (thus it also does its processing in linear time). The resulting text is generated quickly and compares favorably with human-generated descriptions, demonstrating the power of salience in planning a descriptive paragraph.

CONCLUSIONS

While it is clear that salience is not only effective but necessary in the domain of generating scene descriptions, we can only speculate about its more general usefulness. However, it seems likely that as knowledge bases grow it will become necessary to provide the user with staged responses to questions, initially providing minimal information, but being able to provide more detail if it is requested. In this regard salience annotation of the knowldge base, along with sophisticated models of the user and knowledge about the rhetorical conventions of dialog, promises to provide much more flexible and natural interaction.

Also, the GENARO/MUMBLE system demonstrates that a dramatic reduction in computational complexity is available when a localized, data-driven style of planning can be exploited. This is not to say that humans do not do goal-based planning; however, people often have multiple, competing goals which are related only by their relative priority. The process of resolving that conflict, if it is not arbitrary, will involve using salience in some form.

In what domains is it possible to compute the salience of data base items? In the domain of computer vision, it was determined that each of the factors that composed salience would be a byproduct of the complex process of analysing and interpreting the image, and thus would require no extra processing (Conklin, 1983). It appears that this could be a general property of systems complex enough to be doing significant cognition. For example, the process of resolving the competition between closely related schemas, a fundamental issue in A.I. interpretation, requires keeping close track of

which schema has the best "fit" with what is known about the world. This
amounts to a measure of unexpectedness, one of the primary factors (high-level
extrinsic) in computing salience. It is still too early to say, however,
whether the computation of salience values is in general nearly "for free", as
it appears to be in computer vision, or whether it will require extra
computational effort.

REFERENCES

Brachman, R., 1978. A Structural Paradigm for Representing Knowledge,
    Report 3605; Bolt, Beranek, and Newman, Cambridge, Mass.
Conklin, E.J., 1983. Data-driven, Indelible Planning in Discourse using
    Salience;   Ph.D. dissertation, COINS, U. Mass., Amherst, Mass.
Conklin, E.J., Ehrlich, K., McDonald, D., 1983. An Empirical Investigation
    of Visual Salience and its Role in Text Generation. In: M.H. Ringle and
    M.A. Arbib (Editors), Cognition and Brain Theory. Hillsdale, New
    Jersey.
Hanson, A.R. and Riseman, E.M., 1978. "VISIONS: A Computer System For
    Interpreting Scenes", in Computer Vision Systems, Hanson, A.R. and
    Riseman, E.M. (Editors), New York, pp. 449-510.
McDonald, D., 1980. Language Production as a Process of Decision-Making
    under Constraints, Ph.D. dissertation, MIT.

Human—Computer Interaction, edited by G. Salvendy
Elsevier Science Publishers B.V., Amsterdam, 1984 — Printed in The Netherlands   61

Perspectives of a Modern User-Interface Designer

Teresa L. Roberts
Xerox Office Systems Division, 3333 Coyote Hill Road, Palo Alto, California 94304, U.S.A.

Abstract

This paper discusses two aspects of the state of the art in user-interface design: the process of doing the design, and the product we have been delivering recently.

User interface design methodologies which have been described in the literature fall into basically two categories: those which list the features of a good user interface, and those which present tools for evaluating a user interface once it's designed. None addresses the process of creating the design, which is currently a mixture of learning about the user's tasks and inventing possible designs. It is a very iterative process, for which the emerging UIMS prototyping tools are a promising development.

The new direct-manipulation user interfaces are very compelling: their rich display screen and direct methods of pointing out objects to be manipulated greatly increase the bandwidth of communication between human and computer. But many of these systems today share certain problems: (1) awkwardness in handling structures that are not visible, (2) difficulty in user programming, and (3) a tendency to overuse menus. Responding to these problems in a way that retains the attractiveness of these systems will be the user-interface designers' challenge in the next few years.

Introduction

The conferences on Human Factors in Computer Systems in the last two years have been excellent forums for bringing together a variety of people who are interested in the problems of making machines easy and efficient for people to use, so that the human-computer combination is as effective as possible. But most of the voices at the conferences have been those of researchers who are doing their best at telling us designers what to do. In some cases their work has been helpful; in some cases it's in the right direction but at such a low level that considerably more information must be amassed before it is applicable; and in some cases it's hard to figure out how the work might be applied in a real project at all.

I'm here today to present the other side of the story, that of the practitioner, a user interface designer. First I will talk about our process. I will review what a user interface designer does, contrasting various published design "methodologies" with how it really goes. And then I will go on to talk a little about our product; I will discuss the contrast between the old typing-oriented computer-user interfaces and the new bitmap-display-and-mouse interfaces, describing the advantages of the new but pointing out their catches also.

Design Methodology

Scenario: Your company has decided to build a new computer product, somewhat related to what they've done before, but targeted at a different audience. You're put in charge of the design of the user interface. Of course, you have limited time and resources; the management is willing to be flexible with you, but within reason. What do you do? How do you get started, and where will you expect to concentrate your effort? Let's first look at some suggestions from the literature:

Components of a good user interface

Newman and Sproull's book on interactive computer graphics (1979) has a chapter on user interface design, which applies to more than just computer graphics systems. They list several components which are necessary to a good user interface:

> a clear user's model of the system's objects and processes
> a command language
> responsive feedback to the user's actions
> a rich information display which informs the user of the state
> > of the system, and
> > of the objects being manipulated

Task analysis, a study of the user's requirements, both in terms of *output* and in terms of the *process* of generating the desired output, is the basis from which all of the above are built. Newman and Sproull mention task analysis, but regard it as something given to the designer, which the designer then proceeds to work from.

In my experience, reference to the user's task, both the end product and the process of achieving that end product, is a continual aspect of the job of creating the user interface. It's something which the user interface designer must be intimately in contact with throughout the design process. After all, how well the proposed user interface fits the task is the criterion for the quality of the user interface.

Card, Moran, and Newell in their book on *The Psychology of Human-Computer Interaction* (1983) also include some tips for designers. Their principles for user-interface design are, in fact, heavily oriented toward knowing the users and their tasks. They suggest explicit analysis of the methods that the user will employ in the computer system to accomplish the tasks, in order to maximize efficiency.

Evaluation/comparison of proposal(s)

In the process of creating those four aspects of a user interface which are listed above, the designer needs a check on the goodness of the current stage of the design: Is feature x really necessary? Would feature y be useful if we could incorporate it easily? Should the command language be regular, or should we put in a special command to shorten a common, multi-step process? Do we take up valuable screen real estate with a display of a certain part of the machine's state, or do we leave the space available to the objects the user is working with? Do we add complication to the system's objects and to the command language by giving the user the means to customize the system to his or her own preferences?

Card and colleagues provide a specific tool that I have found very useful in my own design work. That's the Keystroke-Level Model (Card, Moran, and Newell, 1980), a mathematical model that allows one to estimate the amount of time an expert user will take to perform a task. Not only does it give me a quantitative idea of how well a proposed interface will perform, but, more importantly, its separate terms provide guidance in figuring out both which aspects of the interaction are unwieldy and which are approximately as fast as they can be made. Bravo!

Phyllis Reisner (1981) and Tom Moran (1981) independently created formal grammars for describing user-computer interaction. In theory, once a command language has been described by such a grammar, the result can be analysed for conciseness and consistency. Unfortunately, such grammars are cumbersome; any attempt to describe a system of a realistic size quickly becomes bogged down. I know of no use of these tools subsequent to their validation.

Another tool which has excited general comment is a methodology for evaluating text editing systems which I developed with Tom Moran (Roberts and Moran, 1983). It involves running both experts and novices through benchmark tasks to determine editing speed and error behavior; it also analyzes the range of functionality supported. It gives overall performance scores, but is weak on pointing out places where the system can be improved.

The design process, and user evaluation

The "design methodologies" described above are mostly good for enumerating the different aspects of an interface which must be designed, for giving some kind of evaluation of the quality of a design once we've created it, and for looking in an orderly manner for likely problems. But they don't really help with the design process itself. That remains an essentially creative endeavor. We learn all we can about the task we're automating: by training ourselves in the task domain, by employing as consultants professionals in that area, and by familiarizing ourselves with the systems which already exist for this set of tasks. But in the end, we often come up with ideas out of the air (or, more likely, by building on our experience with similar systems) without any *a priori* direction about how good each idea will turn out to be. We evaluate the proposed design with the checklists and tools we now have for use in the laboratory. And, most important, we try it out on potential users to see how well it fits their task and their work processes.

The bottleneck in this design/evaluate iterative loop is putting the design into a form which is suitable for evaluation by end users. All too often, especially in the fast-moving computer world, the software which implements the user interface is not available until just before it is due to be shipped, hardly a time for iteration of the design. Prototyping is costly, and often difficult for people whose expertise is more in psychology than in programming. For this reason I see the budding emergence of User Interface Management Systems as a very useful, promising development. A UIMS allows a user-interface designer to draw system objects on the screen, describe user actions which the system is to interpret as commands, and specify what the system is to do to its objects in response to the user's actions. The designer still must do some programming to specify the results of commands, but if the UIMS is appropriate to the task, the programming is at a much higher level than it would be if the prototype were being created from scratch. Examples of UIMSs which were shown at Boston's CHI'83 conference were Austin Henderson's Trillium and Bill Buxton's Menulay (1983). Each has a long way to go before it is usable to make substantially novel user interfaces or very large and complex systems, but this is a very exciting development in the aid of hard-pressed designers.

The New Direct-Manipulation Interfaces

Since 1981 we have seen the release of a new class of user interface, which is based on having a high-resolution flexible display screen and a pointing device with which the user easily points out the objects to be acted upon. Such machines started coming out in a trickle, with little more than Star and Lisa in the first years, but announcements of new machines are accelerating. There is every reason to believe that, except perhaps at the very low end, most new "personal" computers in the next few years will feature these high-bandwidth media for communicating with the user.

The style of user interface which is being built for these new machines has been described by Ben Shneiderman as being a "direct-manipulation" interface. That is, users feel more like they're touching the system's objects and doing things to them directly, rather than verbally instructing an intermediary to perform the operations for them. (By the way, expensive hardware isn't at all necessary for a direct-manipulation interface, as VisiON and MicroSoft Windows demonstrate. But the flexibility of a bit-mapped screen does help.)

I personally am sold on direct-manipulation user interfaces. They allow me to view the objects I'm working with, the context around those objects, and my general work environment. Second, they let me do what I want and see the effect happening before my very eyes. The difference can be seen, for example, between typing the mathematical formula

$$1 + \left(\frac{1}{1-x^2} \right)^3$$

using a system that allows direct type-in and maintains a properly-displayed equation at all times, as opposed to using one which requires the user to type

```
$$1+ \left( 1\over1-x↑2 \right) ↑3$$
```

as it is done in the well-respected formatting system TEX, which was created for publishing technical text (Knuth, 1984). The difference makes me feel as if I've regained the use of my eyes and of my hands after a long time without them.

But this large advance in user interfaces has not come without some drawbacks; it will be the task of user interface designers in the next few years to figure out how the direct-manipulation designs can be as elegant as some of the older designs in certain specific ways:

Hidden structure

Some direct-manipulation systems are often described as What-you-see-is-what-you-get (or WYSIWYG) systems. That's because, for systems where the primary emphasis is on creating something that will be printed, the screen displays to the best of its ability exactly what the hardcopy will look like. The direct manipulation is directed toward the look of the result. The cost of this is that since the user and the computer communicate mainly in terms of looks, there is much less emphasis on structure. If the user puts one object near another, the system has no way of discerning the intent behind the move. In later manipulations, are the two objects meant to remain near each other? If so, do they remain a fixed distance apart, or is their distance relative to something else? And so forth. In systems such as TEX shown above, the user has no choice but to instruct the system in terms of structure, so such problems never arise. The result of this problem is either that users have to manually touch-up problems that the system causes every time and every place it unknowingly violates the user's notion of the relationships which are desired. The alternative is an additional level of structure information that is carried along with the objects and is displayed at the user's option. Such an approach greatly complicates the user's model of what he or she is interacting with, and manipulating it removes the user from the direct-manipulation paradigm. But to the extent that the results of such manipulation are interactively visible, the result can still be a compelling interface, especially for dedicated, expert users.

User programmability

A convenient feature of interacting with a system through typed command languages is that such languages are easily converted to programming languages. So if the user wants to invent a new command which performs the action of several old commands, the program can be written in a language with which the user is familiar. On the other hand, if a language is based on pointing to objects and on pointing to (possibly graphic) indications of what is to be done to the object, it is much less easy to program in. Without a user programming language, the user cannot tailor the environment to his or her own tasks to the extent that many users would like. A programming-by-example scheme in which the system converts user actions to a conventional programming language is a promising solution to this (Halbert, 1984).

Arrays of choices

The people who create direct-manipulation systems often apply other psychological principles to their system design, with the result that direct-manipulation systems often share features that aren't direct manipulation as such. One such principle is "recognition is easier than recall", also worded as "seeing and pointing is better than remembering and typing". This has led to designs that include menus for commands, property sheets for specifying objects' attributes, and visible "folders" for filing. Such menus lead to several problems: they can overwhelm novices with their large array of choices; progressive-disclosure schemes which attempt to minimize the overwhelming aspects sometimes make a multi-step process out of what is just one operation to the user; and they require waiting for a display of information and pointing to a place which might be far from the user's primary focus of attention. For an expert, such a style of interaction might be much slower than just typing a few remembered characters. "Seeing and pointing" interfaces need to be designed carefully so that either they're extremely efficient in their context, or they provide bypasses for users who don't require their full richness.

In summary, while I strongly believe in the new visually rich, easy to interact with, direct-manipulation systems, they have not yet matured. They require considerable more work to solve certain problems in ways that still make full use of their advantages. This will be the challenge for us user interface designers in the next few years. And any improvements in our design methodologies or tools to perform this exciting task will be welcome.

REFERENCES

Buxton, W., Lamb, M.R., Sherman, D., and Smith, K.C. Towards a Comprehensive User Interface Management System. *Computer Graphics (SIGGraph '83 Conference Proceedings) 17*, 3 (July 1983), 35–42.

Card, Stuart K., Moran, Thomas P., and Newell, Allen. The Keystroke-Level Model for User Performance Time with Interactive Systems. *Communications of the ACM 23*, 7 (July 1980), 396–410.

Card, Stuart K., Moran, Thomas P., and Newell, Allen. *The Psychology of Human-Computer Interaction*. Lawrence Erlbaum Associates, Hillsdale, NJ (1983).

Halbert, Daniel C. *Programming by Example*. Ph.D. dissertation, University of California at Berkeley (1984, in preparation).

Knuth, Donald E. *The TEXbook*. Addison-Wesley Publishing Co., Reading, MA (1984).

Moran, Thomas P. The Command Language Grammar: A Representation for the User Interface of Interactive Computer Systems. *International Journal of Man-Machine Systems 15* (1981), 3–50.

Newman, William M., and Sproull, Robert F. *Principles of Interactive Computer Graphics, 2nd ed.* McGraw-Hill, New York (1979).

Reisner, Phyllis. Using a Formal Grammar in Human Factors Design of an Interactive Graphics System. *IEEE Transactions on Software Engineering, SE-7* (1981), 229–240.

Roberts, Teresa L., and Moran, Thomas P. The Evaluation of Text Editors: Methodology and Empirical Results. *Communications of the ACM 26*, 4 (April 1983), 265–283.

Human—Computer Interaction, edited by G. Salvendy
Elsevier Science Publishers B.V., Amsterdam, 1984 — Printed in The Netherlands

THE CRUCIBLE OF A NEW DISCIPLINE

Bill Curtis

Microelectronics and Computer Technology Corporation (MCC)
9430 Research Blvd., Echelon #1
Austin, Texas 78759

The ordeal of improving how humans interact with computers is creating a new breed of scientists. Although a few pioneers like Alphonse Chapanis have tilled this field since the early 1970's, their efforts have only been recognized as a field since 1981. Because the field is young, most of its surveyors are young also. They are, by their choice of research, multi-disciplinary.
They will espouse a major discipline, but their best work will not be performed until they have mastered several. They must be equally at ease in the company of behavioral scientists, mathematicians, or engineers. They must be eclectic, because as many advances will be made through synthesizing the contributions of several fields as by logically deducing the secrets of a one. Finally, they must be courageous, since they are the bastard children of many disciplines whose bloodlines are purified through the denial of tenure.

Programmers galore had poured out software for fifteen years when Friedrich Bauer hosted his famous NATO conference in Garmisch, West Germany in 1968. Here many of computer science's best thinkers gathered to discuss their problems and solutions. Their collective concern about more productive ways to produce reliable software christened the discipline of software engineering. This discipline was recognized because the size and complexity of the software required to run increasingly large com-

puter systems outmoded the idiosyncratic programming techniques
of the day.

So it was at the dawn of the 1980's. The onslaught of personal computers and end-user systems had begun to contaminate
even the innocent observers of the information revolution. The
demand for user interfaces engineered for non-programmers was
growing exponentially. The hunches played by system designers at
the user interface were growing more intolerable as the fiefdom
of data and information processing was overrun by hordes of naive
users. The most successful user interfaces were those which
coaxed adolescents to spend their life savings in a video arcade.
The design of user interfaces needed to be guided by a science
rather than intuition.

For several years a small group of us, the Software Psychology Society--Potomic Chapter, had gathered monthly in Washington,
D.C. to discuss our experiments on the user interface. At one of
these meetings, Ben Shneiderman, Mike Schneider and I decided
that we should offer our collegues a chance to compare notes on
their work. The Washington D.C. Chapter of the ACM and the
National Bureau of Standards backed us, gambling that we would
attract between two hundred and three hundred people, the majority probably from the D.C. area. We were unprepared for the
response. Nine hundred and seven kindred souls, some crossing
oceans, came to discuss their work with a sympathetic audience.
From this initial gathering has emerged a highly successful and
growing series of conferences, a renewed vitality in the Special
Interest Group on Computer Human Interaction of the ACM (SIGCHI)
and, most important, the debut of human-computer interaction as a
field of legitimate scientific study in its own right.

Why was it so important that human-computer interaction
emerged from Gaithersburg as a discipline, much as software
engineering had emerged from Garmisch thriteen years before?
First, because those who buy and use computers demand some recognition by the computer industry of their ordeal at the terminal.
Second, because it needs sources of funding which are not tied to
the coattails of some other field of study. Finally, because
those who ply this trade need to be recognized as legitimate

scientists developing theory and a base of empirical knowledge in
their chosen area of interest. Let us consider these underlying
factors in turn.

   Although once reduced to crying in the wilderness of a users
group meeting, users have made their concerns a sales issue.
Always quick to react to the real issues in the marketplace, IBM
has responded with a major initiative in system usability. IBM's
Chief Scientist, Lewis Branscomb, in his invited address at last
fall's World Computer Conference in Paris, chose to deliver a
clarion call for this new emphasis. Madison Avenue has elevated
the phrase "user friendly" to the fad that we were afraid it
would become. These days, all systems are "user friendly", as
least for the first few hours. After several decades of
employing them, AT&T has finally brought psychologists out of the
closet and put several of them, who look nothing at all like Tom
Landauer, in television advertisements. Thirty years of
experience has proven that software engineers are rarely
sensitive to how people try to use computers. Professionally
trained experts are now needed as much at the user interface as
at the module interface.

   Adequate sources of funding are needed to support a serious
attempt to develop theory and a base of empirical data in this
field. In the past there have been two sources of funding for
user interface research. The first was from the R&D labs of
large companies such as AT&T, IBM and Xerox. The gravest threat
to this sort of funding is the failure of technology transfer
from the research lab into product lines. Managers of research
always felt a bit powerless facing a product manager (usually a
former hardware engineer) and trying to convince him that a soft
science could make a hard contribution to the sales of his product. Fortunately, the marketplace is changing all that. The
product manager now wants user interface technology faster than
it can be developed and evaluated. Most behavioral scientists,
having been reared with academic caution, will emphasize that an
unevaluated interface is still a hunch. At least, over the past
four years we have improved the educational background of the
hunch.

The second source of funding has been through government research grants and contracts. There have been a few sources of direct funding for user interface research, such as Engineering Psychology Programs in the Office of Naval Research. However, much of the funding for user interface research has come from research programs whose primary interests were in a different area, such as cognitive phsychology, training methods, or systems design. Too often the user interface was merely a vehicle for investigating some other theoretical or research issue.

The Department of Defense, in its Software Technology for Adaptive Reliable Systems (STARS) program, identified human engineering as one of the critical areas for research, thereby providing funding for this field independent of other disciplines. We must insure that the political fate of the STARS program does not impair independent funding of user interface research. In the United States, we must continue to encourage funding support from the National Science Foundation, the National Bureau of Standards, the National Aeronautics and Space Agency, the Federal Aviation Agency, the Nuclear Regulatory Commission, the various funding arms of the Department of Defense, and other agencies who oversee functions that are increasingly under the control of computer equipment.

One of the most important spurs for funding of user interface research was the announcement by Tohru Moto-oka and Kazuhiro Fuchi of plans for Japanese research on fifth generation computer systems. The outline for an intelligent man-machine interface presented by Hozumi Tanaka and his colleagues clearly identified this area as a focus of advanced computer research. In following suit, Microelectronics and Computer Technology Corporation has identified the user interface as the focus of one of the four research programs constituting its Advanced Architecture Program. The pioneering work of groups such as that of Nicholas Negroponte and Richard Bolt at the Massachusetts Institute of Technology and Phil Hayes, Raj Reddy and Allen Newell at Carnegie-Mellon University are now seen as the blueprints for increasing the bandwidth between the ordinary user and commercial computer systems.

As funding for human-computer research grows, the legitimacy of a scientific career in this field will also increase. Tenure has been denied to several researchers who had both publications and grants, because their reserach was seen as too applied by departments of either computer science or psychology. Fortunately, in the last year this has begun to change. MIT has announced the formation of a new Media Technology Center and accompanying graduate program and Carnegie-Mellon has announced the formation of a graduate program in human-computer interaction. Other universities have less formal programs in this area, allowing students to take an interdisciplinary doctorate. The creation of these programs at universities with world class reputations in psychology and computer science insures the foundation of the discipline.

What is the model of the new scientists who will emerge from these programs? First, they will be firmly grounded in the fundamentals of computer science, likely specializing in artificial intelligence. They will also plumb the depths of cognitive and engineering psychology. Those who would study computerized group interaction must also study social and organizational psychology.

For those who would perform research on the forefront of human-computer interaction, the study of computer science and psychology is not enough. Currently, the serious student of human-computer interaction should go to the department of electrical engineering and take courses in signal processing, especially speech and image recognition. Having recognized speech signals, they must be processed and understood. This requires training in computational linguistics. General training in linguistics will aid not only the recognition and understanding of speech, but also the construction of interface languages. If one further wants to design the hardware that constitutes the computer side of the interface, some time must be spent in a combination of electrical and industrial engineering courses. Finally, a knowledge of experimental design and statistics is required for producing and analyzing the data on which the scientific aspects of this field must be built.

It is unrealistic to expect that a single individual will master the breadth of disciplines described above. Hopefully, students of human-computer interactionwill emerge from their studies conversant in all of these fields and capable of doing original research in one or two. Their creative thoughts will be synergized by ideas and principles from the various disciplines which contributed to their education. Research programs in human-computer interaction must be formed around interdisciplinary teams whose members are conversant in each other's disciplines, but each of whom brings a specialty to the scientific party.

The future of this field requires far more than the preparation for entrance described above. As we learn more about brain theory and bioelectronics, we may discover powerful ways of communicating between humans and machines which far outstrip our current meager bandwidths. The vitality of this new field must be insured through adequate research funding and the sound interdisciplinary training of research scientists and human interface engineers. The payoff for our efforts is simply this: that we will have pioneered a revolution in human capability. While previous generations of scientists gave wings to the body, we gave wings to the mind.

Human—Computer Interaction, edited by G. Salvendy
Elsevier Science Publishers B.V., Amsterdam, 1984 — Printed in The Netherlands

TO IMPROVE M.M INTERFACE

Yasuo Watanabe

Fujisawa Development Laboratory

IBM Japan

ABSTRACT

This paper is described the some concerns relating the current approaches to VDT problems which will be occurred by the mismatch between Human and Artificial object's ability, because of that evolution of artificial objects is marvelous but of human side will be pesmistic, except the speciallist and a genius man. So that, the revolution of human side must be a mandatory for human life in future.

In current, human problems with the artificial objects are being aggravated and then the many discussions about the problem solving are being done in world wide.

However, the direction of recommendations as rusult of the heated discussions apts to direct to only the modification and improvement of the object including some portions of improvement of Environment such as Lighting, Rest hour, and etc. Through the works for problem solving, the strange and apprehension feelings about the current approaches are swelling in my mind, such as the approach may brush only the phenomenon of problem and may not be the solution on fundamental problems. Therefore, my concerns and hints for achieving the fundamental one are described.

Can human ability adapt the progress of Technology? To drag out the answer for this question, the approach with a few area of Knowledge will be applied. About 50 million years old, the mammalia evolved rapidly to many sort of species in short period, but prior to reach the marvelous evolution point, many invisible and unprogrammed evolutions would be progressed continually. In case of 100m running, the oldest record was 11 sec. by English in 1867 and was not broken until the record of 10.8 sec. by L. Kelly of American in 1881 for 24 years. This 11 sec. will be broken easily by the high school student in current, and the latest record is 9.93 sec. by Smith of American.

To reduce 1 sec. at 100m running, peoples are running continually for 100 years.

The running speed is about 33 Km/Hr. in 1867 and about 36 Km/Hr. in current and will increase about 0.8 times. Meanwhile, speed of automobile might be 10 Km/Hr and was slower than human speed in 1960s and will be about 200 Km/Hr in 1980s.

So, within 120 years, the speed would increase about 20 times.

Data/information processing speed using the artificial brain also is being increased with uncountable range, but no. of brain cells and processing speed in brains may not increase within 50,000 years, except the speciallist and genius man, and unluckly, it is said that no. of brain cells of peoples after 20 years old may disappear year by year.

However, the volume of the data and information to be processed imme-diately are swelling rapidly.

As an answer to the question, it is regret to say that the basic por-tion of human ability cannot adapt the progress of Technology.

As one of matters to be supposed with the answer above, the many kind of problems with the misadaptation to the artificial object will occur in human side.

When the research on problems will be done for VDT user, and Car drivers, almost the same symptoms are observed. Physical problems such as Fatigue, Pain, Stiffness and etc. at Eyes Head, Neck, Back, Arms, Lumbar and Mental problems with Anxiety,Continual tension, Monotony, Solitude and etc. are complained by both peoples.

Therefore, if Car driver will use VDT after driving, the double effects to problem solving may be necessary.

Causes of the occurrence

To search the causes, the character of artificial objects such as com-puter as one of the mental objects and automobile as one of the physical objects must be clarified. The question -

What is a computer for human, when the computer will be used at the working place? come out.

As one of answers, the computer is a tool with the intellectual facility and will have the more abilities than human ones in the many parts of Data & information processing.

However, except the computer specialist and peoples with much inter-esting on computer, almost of the people will feel the pressure with the unmatch between human and computing/processing pace, if they are educated only How to operate.

Meanwhile, the automobile is a tool with the more physical power and facility to transport the man to the objective place easily and speedy.

However, almost of driver will feel the pressure with the unmatch between human and automobiles pace.

Next, the question about what is the tool will come out. Tool is a major element to distinguish between man and other animals, and will have the characteristics described bellows

1) Indispensable article for human life

2) To be used for making new tool

3) To be used to make it for other peoples

Therefore, to human life,

To master the use of tool is a mandatory clause, however, each people will have the born restriction to master the matter and will not be enlightened their own facilities enoughly.

Hints for the problem solving

As one of hints, M.M interface must be improved but M.M have to have 2 kind of meaning as that.

At first, you well know M.M is Man-Machine. Man-Machine interface will be technical oriented and may include some techniques that will be imaged as a sort of tricks. The solution for problem with the object which will be occurred with the misadaptation, will have restriction and will be cause of new problem. Of course, the effectiveness and importance on Man Machine interface never forget. Now, another M.M is a new term, an abbreviation of Man-Man and can be used for checkmate. Man-Man interface is humanity oriented and is enhanced by the higher reliance among humans.

According to the experiences in past years, even if, the improved man machine interface would be offered, peoples with disorder at fingers, hands, arms,shoulders in the lacked reliance condition between employee and employer would not recover completely.

Practical applications of Man-Man interface is that

1) Pay many times of a few seconds attentions to the people through the careful and heartiful consideration for finding only good points. It is said that activity to find good points needs the more ten times efforts than to find bad points.

2) Reconsider the education practice as that.

In Japanese term, KYOIKU meaning education consistes 2 basic words KYO meant teaching and IKU meant culivation.

The current practice will focus only the teaching in a group. However, as each peoples have an unique own face, each one have an unique ability to understand and to master the matter, so the combination of KYO and IKU to meet to indivisual character is another effective method to solve the problem in future.

Adaptive User Interfaces for
Distributed Information Management

Lawrence H. Miller
Gilbert Devillez
Jacques Vidal

University of California
Los Angeles, California

1. Introduction

High-level "knowledge workers" can increase their personal productivity by relying on computers and computer networks in their daily work. Daily activities span a wide variety of activities, includeing professional work, research, communication, personal records, all the way to entertainment and hobbies. The necessary software tools for such a spectrum of activities fall into broad classes such as document preparation, communication through local and long distance networks, programming, data base interrogation and updating, computer assisted decision making, action planning, etc. Importantly, switching from one type of activity to another is a frequent occurrence as is the nesting of activities within each other.

The description above implies work that thrives on the resources of a fairly complex support system. A flexible operating system with good interactive features is a prerequisite. Hardware should include a personal "work station" equipped with considerable computing power. Special I/O devices such as lightpen, mouse, voice interface, phone dialers, etc., are desirable options. Finally, a fairly large host system or multi-computer network should be in the background.

With such an array of capabilities, computer assisted intellectual work can take off. Unfortunately, the human interfaces to existing systems are generally geared to programmers rather than to executives or other knowledge workers. For instance, to operate many systems at even a modest level, users have to constantly keep in mind a complex file structure and memorize the name, function and syntax of all commands and utilities. The difficulties are compounded in heterogeneous network environments. For instance, if the tasks at hand require fetching information from remote data bases, the user has to understand network access protocols and must have mastered all relevant query languages. There is an endless list of similar obstacles which, more often than not, amounts to an intolerable burden, discouraging to all but the most determined.

1.1 Overview

We have implemented a user's Agent: a front-end software layer supported (initially) by a relational data base and capable of accessing system files, i.e., the entire panoply of available Unix/Locus facilities (Figure 1).

The central function of the Agent is to give the user the means to operate on a personal information store in a meaningful, mnemonic way. This is made possible by allowing the user to arrange complex data objects (user defined entities) and meaningful operations into a graph structure labeled by keywords and supported by the data bases. Labels and relations can be set to reflect the user's entities and opera-

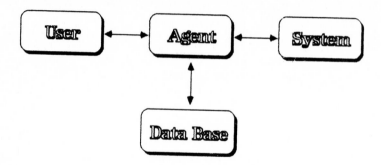

FIGURE 1:   User-Agent-System interactions

tions or else are borrowed from common sensory perception and private experience. In this fashion, entities could be, for example, arranged along some imaginary 2-D or 3-D spatial structure, given texture or
color etc., and be accessed by location. In such a process, a "virtual workspace" is created where names
are collections of keywords chosen to evoke and emulate a *mental representation* private to the user. Retrieval is interactive and will normally be non-unique. The Agent's assistance is directed toward helping
the user cope with the complexity by reducing the memory burden.

In interacting with the user, the Agent software translates commands, issued in terms of keywords, to
the format demanded by the operating system, and performs the inverse interpretation for system replies
and error messages. Thus, whenever the request implies a call to system resources, the Agent must act as
a system expert and insert the proper access paths. A "System Model" is available to the Agent in the
form of a rule-based decision program that embodies knowledge about system resources. Currently these
rules are hard wired into the program through Ingres relations. The model also enables the use of the
Agent as a much needed guide and assistant into the existing "help" facilities in the system.

2. System Description

2.1 User's Roles

The user-system interactions are conducted along three basic *modes* in which the user can be respectively *Supervisor, Learner* or *Actor*. In the Supervisor mode, relations are set. In the Learner mode the
Agent displays information to the user that results from implications of a request and a set of keywords.
In the Actor mode, the user issues action requests that are passed on to the executive after interactive
confirmation by the user. In this respect, the Agent dilemma is alleviated in part by noting that the
user-Actor plays a number of different "roles." For periods of time, he is a Communicator, reading and
sending messages via the computer-based electronic mail system; filing and retrieving messages; discover-
ing network addresses; using teleconferencing facilities, etc. Then he may find himself in the role of Author, making use of the system's various text editors, formatters, spelling correctors, style analyzers or
other document creation tools available. At still another time, he will act as a Programmer, where he
makes use of some of the Author tools (text editor, program formatter, etc.), but also must use the additional programming oriented tools: compilers, linking loaders, run-time (execution) handlers, debuggers,
profilers, etc. In addition, if the programming project involves the use of a programming team, then the
Programmer role interleaves with that of Communicator, etc.

The likelihood of requesting a given software tool varies from role to role and can be used by the Agent to disambiguate requests. Similarly, when the Learner ("help") mode is invoked, certain canonical requests, "HELP," "WHO," "WHAT," "WHERE," "WHEN,". may take different meanings with respect to the most recent role setting. The rules for assigning and taking advantage of these roles are essential components of the "User Model." In time, the Agent system will incorporate further predictive notions of how users behave within a given role. One promising approach is to introduce "Role Models" in a manner similar to Rich   who defined a set of personality stereotypes for a book recommendation system.

2.2 High Level Command Language

As shown in Figure 1 previously, there are four basic entities between which dialogue or information transfer takes place: the user, the Agent, the relational data base, and the system command processor, here the Unix shell.

The pilot implementation of the Agent language consists simply of keyword lists with positional and parenthesis conventions to assign them a syntactic type: input-subject, action-verb, output-object or qualifier. More flexibility is being added with appropriate parsing, in order to provide more of a natural language interaction. The natural language front end is written in Prolog.

2.3 The Data Bases

Data bases are maintained for the benefit of the Agent, to hold relations spanned by user-provided keywords and to store information needed to translate virtual commands and generate appropriate screen formats. This information can be subdivided into system information (the system model) and user related information (the user model). The user model subdivides further, into relations created dynamically by the Agent and relations entered by the user in naming private entities in the virtual workspace. An existing general-purpose relational data base system, Ingres   operating under Unix, has been used initially.

After following all relevant relation chains triggered by the keywords in the user request, the Agent is able to infer an action (after role disambiguation). The Agent keeps track of the current user role and workspace status to decode requests efficiently and to generate screen formats appropriate to the user's current preoccupations. (In the prototype implementation, the Agent is placed into one particular role by the user; all role changes are requested by the user.)

Producing the desired result generally requires multiple accesses of the data bases to ₁access the relevant relations. Some of these are structures with special missions such as a people directory, a calendar or a user Scratchpad file. In the process the Agent may also need to issue calls to system utilities and help files. This concept of personalized database use is novel because it is user oriented and it is not designed to be highly integrative.

Finally one may observe that the use of tags to characterize relation domains amounts to exploiting semantic information about the user workspace. This information must be entered when the relations are established and to some extent represents an additional burden, since, in general, the semantics of a personal file systems are kept exclusively in the user's head.

2.4 The System and System Model

The Unix operating system includes strong components in support of office automation and of network use, and is quite typical of the type of rich environment for users and their changing roles as described above. However, as Norman   has pointed out, Unix still suffers from a number of failings from the point of view of the user interface which alone makes the Agent approach worthwhile.

Unix is addressed through a command interpreter, the shell. In most instances, the Agent translates requests into shell language with the combined help of the user and system models. The central mechanism for implementations of this translation is a rules based inference program (under Prolog) that embodies production rules for Unix command sequences. It complements the existing Agent utilities, and will provide for the incorporation of additional utilities necessary to create and maintain the system knowledge base without the (currently painful) manual intervention of the user in Supervisor mode.

3. Existing implementations

There have been several implementations of the Agent in the course of this research. The first deals with the interface between Ingres and the Agent or the user. Through a set of specific functions presented via menus, one can create new data bases, create new relations, add new tuples, and display or print the content of some relations. One can perform several basic Ingres commands without knowing anything about the system itself and its query language.

The second implementation analyzes in further detail the aspects of user-defined command translations. Simple commands are defined by the user in terms of keywords and corresponding Unix syntax. The distinction between "subjects" and "object" is made here through the sequence of the given keywords. The translation is performed by a one-to-one mapping of the keywords to their corresponding portion of a Unix command, which is retrieved from the data base. The global result is then passed on to the shell.

The third implementation has been performed with the concept of set of canonical requests in mind. Here, the system relations are taken into consideration in order to permit a later execution of these requests.

4. Discussion

In order to implement the Agent's knowledge, the user has to specify his own workspace perception through the use of entity structure definitions as well as entity content definitions. This is done in the Supervisor mode. One can create new entities or modify existing entities so that the model stored in the data base can grow and evolve according to the development of the user's real workspace. Currently it is the user who has to keep the model up to date. In further developments, the Agent assumes a more active role. The Agent will learn about the user's environment and current concern through the type of interactions requested, as well as through their sequence and frequence. For example, if the user makes a great use of a specific (but long) request, the Agent could assume that whenever a request starts like the only usually specified, the user actually wants to repeat that request. The Agent could then anticipate the user's action and define the request for the user.

We are investigating the progressive learning process of the Agent. Although the Actor mode has only been introduced in this paper and needs more refinement before implementation, it is obvious that the Agent data base needs a considerable amount of data directly related to the computer system supporting the Agent. This data will be retrieved for a progressive learning process.

5. Future Directions

Continued work points towards a progressive evolution of these systems into "super-terminals" equipped with innovative displays and controls to enhance the verisimilitude of the mental workspace. Voice I/O, for example, is well adapted to terse, keyword based, dialogues.

In its present form the relational data base implementation is lacking in performance. Certain components, primarily a command language parser, have been recoded in Prolog. We have been using the Ingres system because the relational model is a reasonable one for human memory associations. None-the-less, Ingres is substantial overkill for needs of the Agent, while not providing an opportunity for natural language interaction, nor a reasonable programming environment.

Finally, this work contributes to the modeling of general expert systems, in a way that separates the system structures from the particular task implemented. In addition, it leads to a better understanding of the potential of model-assisted, context dependent human-machine

References

Epstein, Robert, "A Tutorial on Ingres," Memorandum No. ERL-M77-25, U.C. Berkeley, Berkeley, CA. (1975).

Norman, Donald A., "The Trouble with Unix," *Datamation* **27**(12), pp.139-150 (November, 1981).

Rich, Elaine, "Building and Exploiting User Models," Report CMU-CS-79-119, Carnegie-Mellon University, Dept. of Computer Science, Pittsburgh, PA. (April, 1979).

II. TAXONOMIES, STANDARDIZATION AND EVALUATION OF
HUMAN-COMPUTER INTERACTION

NATIONAL STANDARDS AND THE PRACTICE OF HUMAN FACTORS

RICHARD S. HIRSCH
International Business Machines Corporation, Old Orchard Road,
Armonk, New York 10504

ABSTRACT

Hirsch, Richard S., 1981. National Standards and the practice
of Human Factors.

At least five countries have set specifications for the design of
computer terminals. These specifications refer mainly to hardware
designs and a number of the recommendations have required that
relatively fundamental design studies be conducted to validate the
requirements. In addition to the hardware specifications, a number
of states of the United States have proposed legislation governing the
use of computer terminals. As a consequence of the national and international activity, the nature and scope of the practice of human factors
in industrial organizations has been profoundly affected.

INTRODUCTION

During the past decade or so, the practice of human factors has
undergone certain profound changes. For example, what used to be
primarily the evaluation of man-machine hardware has in recent years,
become concerned with questions of man-machine software and instructional documentation. Until about 1970 human factors work in IBM
was mostly hardware oriented. Since then the emphasis has shifted
to the point where today it is at least fifty percent software and
another ten to twenty percent is dedicated to documentation. These
changes reflect the fact that systems are now being developed for
a broader, less computer-sophisticated base of users. Hardware, from
a human factors viewpoint, has become relatively simple, while the
major interfaces now between the system and the user are the system
software, the applications software, and the documentation that tells
the user how to operate the system. A recent article by Neal and Simons
(1984) describes a methodology developed to evaluate the usability of
software and its documentation. System software is virtually transparent to the user, although it profoundly affects the design of the
application software. It is the application software that the user
interacts with directly; hence, so far as the user is concerned, it is
the application software that makes the system easy (or hard) to use. For
that reason, human factors practitioners have been placing increasing

emphasis on application software. Meanwhile, it is recognized that system software does require human factors attention. The complexities of system software are such that an effective study methodology has not yet been developed. The importance and complexity of the work was most clearly stated in a paper by Branscomb and Thomas (1983). Thus, one major change in the practice of human factors has been the emergence of software (and instructional documentation) as a subject requiring evaluation. As will be seen, they are now also the subject of national and international standards and regulations.

Another item that should be mentioned in this Introduction is what is covered by the term "standards." First, of course, are those pronouncements by individual countries that govern the design and use of products manufactured and marketed both internally and externally of the consuming country. For the purposes of this paper, however, the scope of "standards" has been broadened to include such requirements as those proposed by trade cooperatives and that result in "regulations" that, for all practical purposes, have the force of law. Also included here are those deliberations by various state legislatures in the United States.

NATIONAL STANDARDS AND REGULATIONS

A paper by Rupp (1981) reviews in some detail the many issues raised by visual display standards. The hardware issues covered in the review include the following:

Workstation dimensions	Symbol contrast
Workstation reflectivities	Symbol size
Per cent active area	Character format
Character line/column spacing	Image distortion
Ambient light levels	Height of display
Keyboard factors	Viewing distance
Keyboard slope	Symbol luminance
Feedback	Acceptable color
Key travel	Glare control
Keytop dimension	Phosphors
Keyboard height	Image Polarity
Actuation force	Refresh rate
Key spacing	Screen orientation
Numeric block	

The Rupp review covered material obtained from seven source documents, three German in origin, the other four originated in Canada, Sweden, England, and France. Rupp's clear-cut review of

the issues will not be repeated here, but it should be pointed out
that the list consists mainly of items that, to varying degrees of
reliability, can be put to empirical test and evaluation.

The principal effect of the recommendations emerging from discussions
of those issues has been another significant shift of emphasis in the
practice of human factors in many industrial organizations. Many of
those concerned with the design and manufacture of display terminals
have had to undertake the conduct of "basic" or "fundamental" experimental studies dealing with the various issues. Few human factors
practitioners are likely to be upset by that development. Usually
constrained to studies that are narrow in scope and product-specific,
many in the human factors community have frequently longed for
opportunities to investigate some of the issues more broadly. The
national and international discussion of standards has literally made
definitive investigations of the issues mandatory. As a consequence,
a number of organizations have built or acquired equipment enabling them
to conduct quite sophisticated evaluations. The IBM Human Factors Center
(San Jose, California), for example, has acquired from Stanford Research
Institute International an optometer and eye-tracker of advanced design
that enables the collection of very detailed and sophisticated data in
the field of physiological optics. In a sense, then, human factors
practitioners have been engaging lately in studies that in the past were
conducted mainly in the laboratories of academia.

Meanwhile, in the United States, ten states have had legislative
Bills under consideration dealing with many of the same issues raised
in the national and international standards proposals. The states are:
California, Connecticut, Illinois, Maine, Massachusetts, New York, Ohio,
Oregon, Rhode Island, and Washington. As of this writing, no state has
passed a Bill governing the design and use of (visual display) computer
terminals.

An article by Abernathy (1984) indicates that there is very little
difference from state to state in the issues being discussed in their
legislatures. In almost every case, the Bills are modelled after one
provided by certain proponents of legislation. The issues covered in these
state Bills include, among others, items relating to the workstation and
to a variety of employer-employee relationships.

The Workstation

The workstation in these Bills includes the actual terminal hardware and the area immediately surrounding the operator. For example,
they call for chairs with fully adjustable backs, seats and heights;

tables must also be adjustable as to height; the ambient light must
not exceed 700 lux; noise levels must be below 65 dB; and "excessive"
heat is to be avoided.

As to the hardware the operator uses, the Bills specify that keyboards shall be detached from their associated displays; the displays
must be tilt-adjustable and possess tilt-adjustable "screen surfaces;"
and brightness and contrast controls shall be provided.

A major concern in the Bills is the control of glare. Accordingly,
the Bills specify that windows should be draped and overhead indirect
lighting louvered. In addition, antiglare filters should be made
available. Underlying those requirements is an assumption, that the
computer terminals are a source of glare and are therefore, a hazard to
the health and safety of the operators.

Even the "operator" is not well defined; in most Bills an operator
is anyone who uses a terminal for some minimum period of time, usually
set at two hours. Having thus stated who users are and having assumed
that the terminals are a hazard to them, the Bills further assume, again
without proof, that the above requirements will eliminate the hazards to
alleged health and safety. The human factors practitioner who engages in
the legislative discussions is frequently placed in an awkward position.
Generally speaking, most of the requirements are "goodness." Accordingly,
the practitioner of human factors, testifying at legislative hearings,
argues that the requirements are not unique to computer terminals,
especially not to visual display terminals. As a consequence, the
human factors experts appears to be opposed to goodness. A position
both uncomfortable and unjustified.

Employer-employee relations

All state Bills address, at a minimum, four industrial relations
issues. One deals with eye examinations (as an employer expense).
Another specifies schedules of rest breaks. A third, relating to
concerns about alleged harmful radiation from the terminals, calls
for pregnant operators to be given work away from the terminals. The
fourth issue prohibits employers from using the facilities of the
computer terminal to monitor operator productivity and performance.

Each of these issues are presented by their proponents with considerable vigor and detail. What is not presented, however, is evidence
that they are truly problems unique to computer terminals. On the
contrary, these industrial relations issues are presented as being in
some way coupled, on the one hand, to the hardware and workstation
specifications and, on the other hand, to the items of goodness. As

a consequence, the human factors practitioner, testifying about man-
machine relationships, is thus assumed to be addressing also the
industrial relationships to which they have been arbitrarily coupled.
Proponents of legislative action in this way broaden the scope of
human factors to include matters of a largely sociological nature and
call it "ergonomics." Thus, the practitioner of human factors -- who
knows that "ergonomics" is essentially the European equivalent of
North American "human factors" -- is frequently forced to walk in the
field of social psychology. Seasoned workers in human factors find
this also uncomfortable. Human Factors credibility stems from reliance
on empirically derived, scientifically controlled objective data, but
in dealing (or appearing to deal) as well with those largely subjective
matters there is risk of compromising that credibility.

A further consequence of state legislation and national standards
has been the establishment of several official bureaucracies that have
required participation by human factors practitioners. For example,
the American National Standards Institute (ANSI) recently requested
the Human Factors Society to establish a Technical Advisory Group
(TAG) to deal with standards being considered by the International
Standards Organization (ISO) as proposed by its various national
members. A meeting of the ISO Technical Committee was held in May 1983
in Manchester, England, and further established three major work
groups (WGs) to define ergonomic functional standards and user-oriented
scientific test methods in the field of visual information processing in
office tasks. The WGs are to concern themselves with:

   (a) visual display requirements,
   (b) control, workplace and environmental requirements,
       and
   (c) task requirements.

The organization (CCITT) dealing with international telecommunications has also established committees, subcommittees, working parties,
task forces, etc., to look into questions of ergonomic standards.

The members of all those many deliberative bodies must obviously
include human factors practitioners qualified in the specialized areas
of consideration. Accordingly many workers in human factors now find
themselves engaged in such activities. The challenges in those
activities are truly formidable, both intellectually and logistically.

The primary challenge is for the human factors practitioner to
develop an awareness of the issues sufficient to be able to take
positions about them that will withstand scientific scrutiny.

SUMMARY

The practice of human factors has undergone changes in recent years as a function of changes in the user population which dictate that not only must the man-machine relationship be well designed, but also the man-system interface, that is, software and documentation must be easy to understand and use. To that essentially technical enhancement of the human factors role, proposals for national and international standards and regulations have presented the human factors practitioner with even greater challenges.

Disagreement with, uncertainty about, and challenges to a number of the proposed standards and regulations have resulted in the human factors practitioner now engaging in more fundamental studies than was the case in the past.

Discussions in state legislatures of proposed Bills governing the design and use of computer terminals have called for testimony from human factors practitioners. This has become a non-trivial challenge in order not to appear opposed to "obvious goodness." As much of the proposed legislation deals, moreover, with employer-employee relationships, the challenge to the human factors practitioner is to retain his scientific credibility by avoiding dealing with what are primarily sociological issues.

Finally, the establishment of national and international bureaucracies for dealing with standards and regulations has also imposed an additional burden on the human factors community who have been called on to participate in the work of those deliberative bodies.

REFERENCES

Abernathy, C.N., 1984. VDTs and the Human Factors Society: A double-edged sword. Human Factors Society Bulletin, Vol. 27 (4), 1-2.

Branscomb, L.M. and Thomas, J.C., 1983. Ease of use: a system design challenge. Paper presented at IFIP '83 Ninth World Computer Conference (Paris).

Neal, A.S. and Simons, R.M., 1984. Playback: a method for evaluating the usability of software and its documentation. IBM Systems Journal, Vol. 23 (1), 82-96.

Rupp, B.A., 1981. Visual display standards: a review of issues. Proceedings of the Society for Information Display, Vol. 22 (1), 63-72.

Human—Computer Interaction, edited by G. Salvendy
Elsevier Science Publishers B.V., Amsterdam, 1984 — Printed in The Netherlands

HUMAN PROBLEMS IN STANDARDIZED AND HABITUATED COGNITIVE ACTIVITY--READING AND WRITING IN JAPANESE LANGUAGE

S. SUGIYAMA[1] and M. OHNO[2]

[1]Faculty of Sociology, Kwansei Gakuin University, Nishinomiya, Hyogo, Japan
[2]Fujisawa Development Laboratory, IBM Japan, Ltd., Fujisawa, Kanagawa, Japan

INTRODUCTION

Now the computer is used all over the world by different peoples who have different cultural backgrounds. Different peoples speak different languages and indeed it is said that in the world today there are about 2,800 different languages, which is roughly twenty times the number of currently existing countries. Moreover, many of those languages are written, printed and read in different ways.

Majority of languages, including English, for example, are written, printed and read from left to right in lateral lines, while Japanese used to be and still is written and read from top to bottom in vertical lines moving from right to left.

Traditionally, Japanese language used to be written and never laterally until the late 19th century, when Japanese culture itself came to undergo radical changes under the western influence. Then in 1949, lateral writing and printing began to be used officially for the governmental correspondence. Since then, this practice has come into wide use in every sector in the society. It is said at present that Japanese, especially younger generations, do not feel any psychological resistance to those two ways of manipulating their language.

The computer is certainly closely related to our reading and writing behaviors. On the CRT display, symbols, numerals and sentences in English or in Japanese appear and disappear, which we must recognize, is truly a newest type of human language manipulation created by computer technology. Thus our laboratory came to be interested in an important factor of reading and writing Japanese in relation to the computer use. We concentrated on the problems arising from the basic differences in reading vertical printing and the lateral one.

Previous researches reported in Japan.show that the speed and accuracy of reading is greater in lateral.writing than in the vertical one, because human visual field is greater in lateral axis than in the vertical one and because of the easiness of lateral eye movement. However, since the Japanese are more used to books printed vertically, they are supposed to be faster when reading vertically. The fact is that there has been a gradual change in reading and printing habits in Japan during the last 100 years, and surveys conducted successively prove the change from preference for vertical reading and writing to that of the lateral.

Here, we would like to show briefly the results of our survey and experiments.

EXPERIMENTS

The first is about a survey given to college students concerning what kind of images or ideas they have about the vertical and lateral printings of Japanese language. The subjects were chosen from students majoring sociology and those majoring Japanese literature, because we supposed they might have different habits of reading: the former usually read textbooks printed laterally in Japanese as well as other languages, while the latter are used to reading Japanese language printed vertically and writing it vertically in their notebooks. The results of this study will be seen in Figure 1.

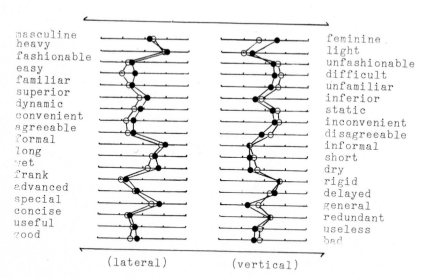

Fig. 1. Images about lateral and vertical printings of students majoring sociology (o) and majoring Japanese literature(●).

The profiles of the images obtained from lateral printing and from vertical one are almost symmetrical. Differences between the two groups concerning their respective impressions of lateral and vertical printings are very slight. Thus, we can conclude that their impressions are almost the same and that their ways of reading either vertically or laterally in their daily life is into related with their impressions of them.

In the second study, we asked the subjects to respond to 13 different questions by choosing one of the five categories on the scale. Among them seven questions are related to their writing practice and six to their reading experience in daily life. The purpose of this survey is to see the degree of familiarity the subjects feel with those two types of expression, that is, the vertical and lateral types of printing and writing.

The scores of reading and writing were calculated. The results are shown in Figure 2. What is noticeable in case of sociology major students is that the writing score 3.70 (SD 0.84) is significantly higher than the reading score 2.84 (SD 0.89). As far as the students majoring Japanese literature are concerned, despite the fact that they are obliged to use vertical writing and read materials printed vertically, the profile does not show much difference from that of the sociology students. The writing score 3.30 (SD 0.80) is also significantly higher than the reading score 2.64 (SD 0.76). From these results, we can say that the students of both majors think of lateral writing as convenient and use it much oftener than vertical writing whenever they write.

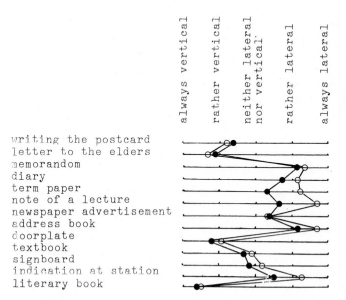

Fig. 2. Degree of familiarity with lateral and vertical types of printing and writing of students majoring sociology (o) and majoring Japanese literature (●).

On the other hand, it can be noted that they do not use lateral writing all the time in every case. All of them practice quite often the traditional vertical writing for letters and postcards to elders as well as superior people due to both formality in writing and a prescribed form used. It can be concluded that young Japanese students always choose freely either vertical or lateral way of writing according to the purpose of writing.

In the third study, we tried to investigate about the necessary time required for reading the sentences printed in ordinary and reversed ways in Japanese printed in lateral and vertical lines. On the stimulus cards, sentences in Japanese hirakana were printed vertically (ordinary-reverse) and laterally (ordinary-reverse), each containing 114 to 117 letters. Three cards were presented to the subjects successively with the following orders; (1) ordinary-

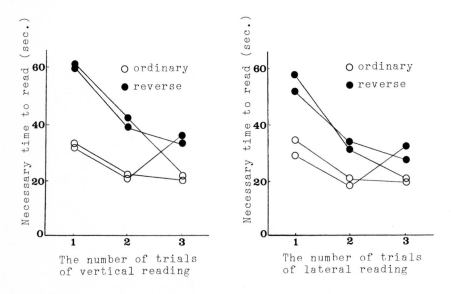

Fig. 3. Necessary time required for reading the sentences printed in ordinary and reversed ways.

ordinary-ordinary, (2) ordinary-ordinary-reverse, (3) reverse-reverse-reverse, and (4) reverse-reverse-ordinary. The results will be seen in Figure 3. Generally speaking, it can be stated that with each lateral and vertical printing, if the sentences with ordinary-only or reverse-only cards were presented, the necessary time required for reading decreased as the trials proceeded as the result of learning. In the cases of "ordinary-ordinary-reverse" and "reverse-reverse-ordinary" cards successively presented, the tendency of decrement of necessary time for reading was disturbed by this change and in those cases the necessary time required for reading the third card seemed to reach the time which was originally required. Another obvious fact was that reading the laterally printed material requires less time than reading the vertically printed one. It may suggest that for the reader the lateral way is easier to be habituated than the vertical one. Therefore, one can not attribute the students' easy adaptation only to their familiarity with the traditional vertical printing.

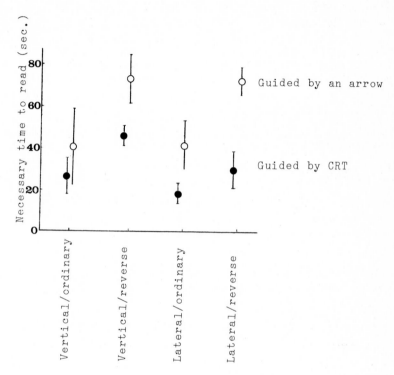

Fig. 4. Reading speed in four different conditions, when reading direction is guided by two different methods.

The fourth experiment tested whether the successively presented letters at a constant pace to one direction shown on the CRT display had any effect in improving the reading speed or not. The guidance implied to indicate the direction of reading was made by the following two methods: (1) a single red arrow printed on the stimulus card showed the direction for reading; (2) the subjects were asked to read silently the trial sentences on the CRT display in Japanese katakana letters one by one, before actual stimulus sentences were shown. Figure 4 shows the difference between he result of showing the direction with an arrow and that of reading the sentence in katakana appearing on the CRT display. In all cases, the effect of guiding the direction by the second method was greater than the first one. Reading speed was about 1.5 to 2 times greater by the CRT method, due to the fact that it not only guided the direction of reading but also speeded up the pace of reading. Remarkable effect was seen in variance as shown in the figure. The effects of shortening the time necessary for reading and of converging the variance were greater in lateral and ordinary reading than in vertical ordinary reading of the sentences appearing on CRT display.

FURTHER PROBLEMS

We have summarized here the results of our experimental studies carried out recently in our laboratory. Those results seem not to be directly related to the concept of "standardization" which has been commonly used in ergonomics. All of our experiments are concerned with human psychological responses to vertical and lateral printing of Japanese language and with our habit of writing either vertically or laterally.

What we would like to show here is the fact that people do get used to either ways of reading and writing until they come to use it uncritically and manipulate it unconsciously. Japanese language has obtained two methods of reading and writing during the past one hundred years. What seems so amazing is that people do not feel this dramatic change of habit unnatural, nor they are having no trouble with it. This shows human's great adaptability not only to the physical object or to other values but also to the way of manipulating their language. However, it should be noted that these changes are not directly and basically concerned with human thoughts and ideas, but have to do simply with the techniques for daily communication.

However, we are skeptical about whether such communication techniques which are used daily might affect the substance of human cognitive activity and the ways of thinking or not. With the introduction of the computer into our daily life, despite the fact that symbols and sentences appearing on the CRT display are quite logically constructed, this type of logic is less redundant as compared with the one used in our daily life.

The fact is that human is capable of too easily naturally getting used to this kind of manipulation of simple logic. It might create a human being who tends to manage everything only with a given logic in the long range of time. What has to be considered seriously is the influence brought repeating the same pattern of human cognitive activity with standardized procedure. We feel that this repeated simple cognitive activities patternize in a long run the human cognitive function.

Human—Computer Interaction, edited by G. Salvendy 97
Elsevier Science Publishers B.V., Amsterdam, 1984 — Printed in The Netherlands

Economic Modeling Languages: The DRI Experience
by
William Raduchel and Otto Eckstein
McGraw-Hill, Inc.

The DRI economic modeling languages have evolved over thirteen years of heavy use. New needs have been identified, and experience has lead to numerous adaptations of detail which, taken individually, may seem trivial but which, when cumulated over the full period, add up to a very significant learning experience. The initial generation of DRI software consisted of a large model program suited for easy solution of macroeconomic models running into hundreds of equations, plus EPL, an econometric package initially adapted from the well-known academic program TSP, pioneered by Robert E. Hall. The second generation of DRI software embodied in EPS a very considerable generalization in terms of the range of features offered and the efficiency offered.[1] The third generation of software, on which this paper focuses, is EPS Plus: While EPS was largely an econometrics language in which you could perform some more general programming, EPS Plus is a general programming language with special features to facilitate econometric analysis.

This paper is about EPS Plus and more generally about the modeling process. Software is a unique product, representing congealed logic written in a precise, unambiguous fashion. Proper design of any software reflects the requirements of the process it supports; as important, however, is that the software itself changes the nature of the process. It is impossible to discuss one without the other, because, if the powers of the software are increased, the new options provided to the model-builder will surely change the final model.

A consistent theme of this paper is that model-building and software creation are highly similar processes. Some basic principles of software engineering will be argued to apply as well to model-building. The implications of this for economic modeling languages are substantial, as concerns over estimation

98

and solution techniques, while still important, are secondary to the concerns of supporting the creative mental process of modeling.

A. Modeling and Forecasting

Economic modeling is a complex process involving interrelated, creative tasks in at least eight areas:

1. **Economic Theory.** Econometrics is the science of merging theory and data. As is taught in every statistics course, correlation does not establish causality. Thus, the first step in every modeling effort results in a proper abstraction of the economic process to be studied. Although conceptually this abstraction is purely theoretic, in practice severe constraints exist on both the availability and accuracy of data and on the functional forms which feasibly can be estimated. Thus, even in this early stage, the modeler usually must compromise between what is theoretically correct and what is feasible in practice.

2. **Data.** Raw data is available from a wide range of originating agencies. Even within the same department of the U.S. government, widely different conventions and practices may be applied. Preliminary, revised and seasonally-adjusted data all pose their own problems to the economist--and to the data professional. Having chosen a preliminary specification of the model, the economist must then match actual data series to the included concepts. These series may not match the desired frequency or may ·be seasonally-adjusted or not with little consistency between series. Collecting the data may be an enormous task; manipulating it into useful form may be an even larger data processing task.

3. **Estimation.** The model-builder next needs to estimate individually or jointly each of the equations included in the model. In practice, of course, this usually is a complex, iterative specification search[2] where each estimation suggests a revised specification. A wide variety of estimation techniques may be necessary. Ideally, these should be straightforward options for the modeler.

Estimation becomes more important in terms of computer resources as more mechanical time series methods (such as ARIMA) are increasingly employed as components or alternatives to traditional modeling.

4. **Model Formation.** The individual equations must be combined into a model. Accounting identities must be added. In practice, equations must often be reordered to make the model solution cost-effective, as numerical solution algorithms can be sensitive to the order in which equations are evaluated.

5. **Model Solution.** This is the most mechanical task in the entire process: the model must be simulated either historically or over the desired forecast range. This is primarily a problem in numerical methods. Solution algorithms are well-known and have been the subject of much study. Nevertheless, because each and every model has its own numerical properties and because all finite-length arithmetic algorithms can only be approximations, any given solution technique may not work for any specified model. When this does occur, the model-builder may face significant frustration.

6. **Report Generation.** Having obtained a model solution, the builder then needs to present the results. This in itself may be a data processing task involving not only report writing and graphics but also significant data manipulation. Many reports will involve comparisons between alternate solutions or between solutions and history.

7. **Model Maintenance.** Models change over time and must be adapted to new information. New equations must be tested and evaluated. The model must be periodically reestimated. Changes must be made to accommodate changes in the availability of data, as when, for example, a series is no longer reported.

8. **Model Management.** With very few exceptions, almost all real-world models are managed in two ways: (1) in specifying the future values of exogenous variables and (2) in establishing add-factors to incorporate information

recently obtained or relating to forces not modeled. The
modeler needs not only an easy means of entering these items
but also ample analytical tools by which to forecast their
values.[3]   Good forecasting requires careful tracking of
hundreds, even thousands, of underlying data series, and the
analyst needs substantial aid in doing this task well.

B. Software Engineering

The idea that software is a discipline in itself, a discipline
quite different than others, began in the early 1970s.   Two
books, The Mythical Man-Month[4] and The Psychology of Computer
Programming[5], were instrumental in this regard, in large part by
establishing that successful programmers had unusual skills.
Indeed, a key contribution of this movement has been the
recognition that software creation actually consists of two
complementary but quite different processes: the selection and
design of algorithms and the coding of those algorithms into
computer-readable languages.

It is probably now well-understood that computers are not
intelligent machines; whatever attributes of intelligence they
may possess derive from the algorithms controlling them and not
from their capability for manipulating bits.   It is the
algorithms that tell the processor what to do. Whether or not a
particular program is efficient depends first and foremost on
whether the algorithms controlling it are efficient.

Coding is the process of translating an algorithm into a form
mutually understood by human beings and computers.   It is the
classic concept of programming.   However, while nearly all
software creators are also skilled at coding, all coders are not
skilled in design.   Algorithmic design and selection is a
creative process far more akin to creative writing than to
indexing, and just as most persons can be taught to index or
code, only a few prove to have real talent at creative writing or
software creation.

Of the many principles of software engineering, the following
four are appropriate to this paper. As with most basic truths,
these maxims are in retrospect apparent and applicable generally
to intellectual engineering endeavor.

1. **The only way to adequately design a system is to build it.**
    Brooks first established this point in <u>The Mythical Man-Month</u>[4] as his "throwaway one" rule. Essentially, it is a statement on the limits on human intelligence, or a more academic version of Murphy's Law (if something can go wrong, it will). It implies, however, that software creation is an inherently iterative process.

2. **Individual programmers have enormous differences in productivity.** Although an imperfect measure, lines of code produced per day is an obvious means of evaluating output, and by this measure up to 1,000 to 1 variations in output have been observed within the same shop between people of similar background! Clearly, such differences all cannot reflect learned behavior.

3. **The human brain has intrinsic limits on the complexity of problems with which it can efficiently deal.** Using elegant yet simple measures, Halstead, in <u>Elements of Software Science</u>[6], introduced concepts of redundancy and length now associated with his name. Tests have shown that for optimal absorption of information there is a desired level of redundancy; being either too concise or too verbose inhibits understanding. More importantly, perhaps, is the concept of Halstead length.

    The details are irrelevant here, but Halstead length is a concrete way of measuring the interactions of complexity and length. The key result is that humans have an upper limit to the Halstead length they can handle. To deal with a problem requires reducing it to modules of acceptable Halstead length. This is a given: it must and does occur with every problem. This can be done by simply ignoring details or by subdividing a problem into pieces, although this latter raises new, possibly very large costs of coordination.

4. **Group and individual behavior are very different.** This observation is the title tenet of <u>The Mythical Man-Month</u>[4]: six programmers for one month are not the same as one programmer for six months. This result should not surprise

economists familiar with the transaction costs of coordinating efforts. Subsequent results have established extreme tradeoffs between complexity and elapsed time (an 8% increase in complexity requires a doubling of staff, for example, according to one accepted rule).

The thrust of these findings is that tools are very important. The best software is developed by applying leverage to one of those unusually productive individuals that do exist. Software creation is a creative process. Not everyone can be made or can become a software wizard. There are very real, if intangible, limits on the process that derive from the nature of the human thought process.

Not surprisingly, one solution people have developed is to use software to support the writing of software. The Source Code Control System or Programmer's Work Bench option of the popular UNIX[tm] operating system provides software creators with an easy mechanism for tracking versions, for manipulating the code and for modifying it. Large productivity gains are said to result.[7]

Importantly, none of these findings place any absolute limit on software. Instead, they define rules on the amount of resources and on the amount of elapsed time necessary to produce good software. At some point a grand architect must lay out the component pieces and show how they are to interrelate. Each component in turn must be similarly divided until the resulting parts are doable by single individuals. The algorithms to be used for each piece must be selected or developed, and then these are coded.

Brooks and others have reached very similar conclusions: the way to maximize productivity is to use chief programmer teams who lever the unusual design and conceptual talents of the chief programmer by supporting his or her work by, for example, maintaining a full history of versions or finding the optimal means of coding an algorithm for a particular system. Software, good software, cannot be produced either quickly (by applying more staff) or mechanically.

C. Modeling in Software Engineering Terms

It will be useful now to recast the modeling process along different lines than done above. As follows, there are some very real parallels between "model engineering" and "software engineering":

1. **Every good model is a properly specified model.** No matter how facile with statistics or software, a modeler can produce a model no better than its underlying theoretical specification. Just as the several modules of a software system interact, so do the blocks of an economic model.

2. **Tools are vital to good modeling.** The information management task involved in modeling is incredibly large. With a model of the U.S. economy, or even a part of it, the builder must deal with thousands of names of endogenous and exogenous variables, equations, lag structures, seasonal factors and other such items, any or all of which may exist in several versions. Compounding this is that data often exist at multiple frequencies and may be both seasonally-adjusted and not seasonally-adjusted.

3. **The tasks of implementing the estimation and solution techniques are no longer central to modeling.** Today, these techniques are easily available in a wide range of software packages. There are few excuses for not using the best available technique. At the same time, these techniques must be implemented in a way that recognizes the limitations of their potential users. Full documentation and error-checking are critical.

4. **Modeling is usually a dynamic process with ongoing maintenance and management required.** Thus, facilities must exist for easily modifying a model and for easily testing these changes. It must be easy to document alterations and to keep their history. The model must be stored in a form that easily permits full and partial reestimation.

5. **The only way to adequately specify a model is to build it.** As with software, modeling is an iterative process. Each set of results suggests new modifications to the builder.

Even the most well-considered specification will prove to have failings when estimated and simulated.

6. **Individual model-builders have tremendous variations in productivity.** If equations per day is an equivalent measure to lines of code today, this is clearly the DRI experience. Some people are exceptionally good model-builders; others-- even though equal in statistical, economic and software skills--are not. Good models or model components tend to have guiding gurus.

7. **Few, if any, individuals can comprehend all the detail of a large model.** The same limits identified by Halstead apply to models as to software. Humans have limits to the size of the problem with which they can deal. Identifying and managing blocks as "financial" or "investment" is essential to keeping the task in bounds. No matter what the underlying theories, the detail in a thousand-equation model with thousands of coefficients and variables is overpowering.

8. **Group modeling efforts are very different from individual efforts.** Coordination and communication costs are as real for modeling as for software, and when a task becomes so large that it is no longer possible for one individual alone, very different rules govern the process. Doubling the size of a model may literally require eight or ten times more staff, although there is no direct evidence on this point. In economic terms there are very large diseconomies of scale in the modeling process.

The obvious conclusion of the above analysis is that the tools and techniques of software engineering can yield equally large benefits when applied to model engineering. While "chief modeler teams" may not be the formal name, most successful models have such a proprietor. A corollary conclusion is that building a large model is proportionately a many, many times larger task than the increase in number of equations or data series.

D. EPS Plus

As noted earlier, DRI began with an outgrowth of TSP as its
basic software. Known as EPL, this software served DRI until
1977, but from the beginning it was surrounded by auxiliary
software. One family of this ancillary software provided time-
series databanking capabilities, while another supported model
simulation and report writing. Still another provided graphics
capabilities. Introduced in 1977 as the Econometric Programming
System, EPS became an instant success by replacing not only EPL
but also most of this auxiliary software. The "Plus" has been
added recently to recognize the large and growing capabilities of
EPS in areas outside econometrics.

EPS Plus can be distinguished from other languages on many
counts, of which nine are most important:

1.   **EPS Plus is a complete programming language, a system for
     implementing both software and models.** This is in explicit
     recognition of the fact that modeling cannot be isolated
     from the antecedent, included and subsequent data processing
     tasks.

2.   **EPS Plus provides an <u>environment</u> for the model builder.** The
     EPS Plus workspace functions as an extension of the user's
     brain; the modeler can use it to hold all the data,
     equations, models, reports and graphs in one place.
     Importantly, all these capabilities are directly available
     to the user. Extensive memory management features aid the·
     user in managing the workspace. The workspace means that
     all the modeler has to remember is a name. Documentation
     can be stored with every item and name.

3.   **EPS Plus handles details for the user.** Conversion between
     frequencies is handled automatically. Not available
     datapoints are so marked. Multiple versions of a model can
     exist in one workspace and be accessed simultaneously. A
     model is simply a list of the names of the included
     equations; equation ordering to minimize solution time and
     cost is automatic. By using default values for options,

reports and plots can be one-line commands. This list can be continued, but the central point should be clear.

4. **EPS Plus is prepared to handle even very large problems.** Models grow over time and the support environment must grow with them. The user need not specify in advance the size of a problem. The limits on EPS Plus are only those of the system on which it runs, and to push these to their limits EPS Plus has been expressly designed to use virtual memory.

5. **EPS Plus provides easy access to all DRI data.** The modeler has data available on demand in the format required. To permit effective use of the hierarchical structure of many DRI mnemonics EPS Plus includes a complete set of operators and functions to operate on names. This allows maximal use of looping and similar capabilities to operate efficiently on a set, given the regular nature of DRI naming conventions.

6. **EPS Plus provides data management, estimation, simulation, forecasting, report writing and graphics in one unified environment.** This eliminates the need to transfer data among applications. More importantly, it minimizes the need for interruptions to the thought process central to modeling.

7. **EPS Plus facilitates interaction with the modeler.** DRI pioneered the use of add factors to incorporate prior knowledge into forecasting, and EPS Plus automatically recognizes and includes add factors as specified, with no requirement that they be present or absent.

8. **EPS Plus allows the user full access to all results.** Statistical operations in EPS Plus <u>always</u> result in synopses; they may result in a printed report. By returning all results in one data structure, the user can both interactively control the printing of results and operate on the results to form other data.

9. **EPS Plus incorporates an extensive matrix capability.** Matrices are an exceptionally powerful way to store, manage and manipulate data. Not only does EPS Plus include a full

provides matrices that can be mapped by names, strings and dates as well as the conventional sequential integers.

Wherever and whenever possible, these capabilities minimize the need to know about software details. For example, to create and solve a simple two equation macroeconomic model takes only a very few steps:

1. LEASTSQUARES C, GNP, GNP\1   ...estimate the consumption
    function using current and lagged GNP

2. FORMEQUATION ONE   ...form an equation from the results

3. EQUATION TWO, C = I + G   ...form an identity;

4. M = NL (ONE,TWO)   ...define the model

5. LONGNAME (M) = "Test Model"   ...attach a longname to M

6. MEMO DOC(M)   ...more complete documentation

    1> as many lines as

    2> desired can be done

    3> ;

7. SOLVE M   ...solve the model

Of course, there are many options and features besides; the latest reference manual, in fact, has nearly five hundred pages.[8]

It is important to recognize the three interrelated services EPS Plus provides to the model-builder:

1. **EPS Plus does the work.**   Estimation, model solution, seasonal adjustment and all the other analytical techniques would be impossibly tedious to do by hand, and through EPS Plus the modeler can have a computer do them.

2. **EPS Plus augments the model-builder's memory.**   EPS Plus stores, retrieves and manages all the information necessary to the modeling effort.

3. **EPS Plus expands the scope of techniques available to the modeler.**   Few persons have good statistical, software <u>and</u> modeling skills.   Many more persons know how and where to correctly apply techniques (and interpret the results) than

know how to implement them. EPS Plus provides state-of-the-art, sophisticated techniques through simple, English-language commands.

Thus, EPS Plus allows one individual to do exceptionally large modeling tasks using state-of-the-art techniques, while also facilitating the integration and management of pieces done by several individuals.

E. Concluding Remarks

DRI data suggest that well under 10% of computer resources used in modeling are actually used in model solution. More interestingly, only 10-15% appears to be used in estimation. Seventy-five percent or more of the computer resources are used in data management, data manipulation, report writing and graphics--even for users whose primary work is modeling (this percentage is higher obviously for the many users who rely on DRI primarily as a data source). This percentage would be far larger were it not for the substantial investment in structuring the DRI databanks, in converting those data into information. Thus, the available data strongly support the arguments of the second section that, as a process, modeling is dominated by information management and data processing.

Supporting this conclusion is the anecdotal evidence from hundreds of users inside and outside DRI on what they like about EPS Plus. While some do cite the latest statistical techniques, the overwhelming majority cite convenience and the information management capabilities of EPS Plus.

An important additional reason for the importance of convenience is that attention spans are limited. Whether for reasons of physiology or psychology, the average session length on the DRI system has remained remarkably constant over time. There are clearly overhead costs involved in continuing any analytical process, so allowing more in each session can disproportionately increase productivity.

A final empirical lesson is that modeling problems persist. Workspaces in EPS Plus were originally designed around the problem of "lunch": they allow a worker to interrupt work and resume later exactly at the same point. Despite the fact that other storage formats are cheaper, users continue to rely upon workspaces because they value having the full context. Indeed, some workspaces are as old as EPS.

Notes

[1] EPS was designed by Robert E. Hall and Robert P. Lacy and implemented by Robert P. Lacy with major contributions from Paul R. LeCain and Peter W. White.

[2] Edward E. Leamer, **Specification Search**, John Wiley and Sons.

[3] This need is so pressing that DRI has developed an entire service including many software tools.

[4] Frederick P. Brooks, Jr., **The Mythical Man-Month**, Addison-Wesley Publishing Company.

[5] Gerald Weinberg, **The Psychology of Computer Programming**, Van Nostrand Reinhold Company.

[6] Maurice Halstead, **Elements of Software Science**, Elsevier North-Holland, Inc.

[7] Frederick P. Brooks, Jr.

[8] **EPS Plus Reference Manual**, Data Resources, Inc., 1981.

Human—Computer Interaction, edited by G. Salvendy
Elsevier Science Publishers B.V., Amsterdam, 1984 — Printed in The Netherlands

A TAXONOMIC APPROACH TO CHARACTERIZING HUMAN-COMPUTER INTERFACES

D.R. LENOROVITZ, M.D. PHILLIPS, R.S. ARDREY, and G.V. KLOSTER

Computer Technology Associates, 5670 S. Syracuse Circle, Suite 200, Englewood, CO 80111 (USA)

INTRODUCTION

Task analysis has long been a basic tool of Human Factors Engineering. The literature is replete with descriptions of techniques which have been used to achieve the common objectives of documenting and and analyzing the actions and activities of humans in man-machine systems. Task analysis is equally as valuable in analyzing and upgrading existing systems as it is in analyzing and deriving the human interface requirements of new systems or components--ones having no viable legacy of on-line user experience upon which to build. In either case, the motivations behind task analysis are invariant--to better understand the intended role of the user within the system. This enhanced understanding, in turn, is instrumental to making intelligent design trade-off decisions, providing effective communication between implementation team members and user population representatives, and affording earlier establishment of appropriate user training objectives and criteria. User task analysis is (and always has been) strongly correlated to the probability of success in developing effective man-machine systems.

What has significantly changed over the years, however, is the nature of the man-machine systems being produced. Of particular interest are interactive computer-based systems--systems in which there is not only a physical man-machine interface but also a complex logical interface between users, the information being displayed, and the user input "language" being employed. If we collectively refer to these various interface components as the overall user-system interface (USI) then the question arises as to whether a concise set of logically related terms, a taxonomy, can be devised so as to properly characterize USIs for task analytic purposes. Clearly, time and motion study "therbligs" (Niebel, 1967) are not entirely suitable for current purposes, nor do some of the frequently cited taxonomies of behavior evaluation (Berliner, Angell, and Shearer, 1964) adequately capture the range of actions and activities common to many of today's complex USIs.

TAXONOMY DEVELOPMENT AND USE

In analyzing the needs and specifying the USI requirements for a very

large and complex human-computer interactive system[1], the authors have
developed and are continuing to refine a taxonomy of terms (verbs) which we
believe to be well-suited to characterizing the activities and actions of
users in a wide range of user-computer interactive applications. As is
shown in Figure 1, we believe that such a comprehensive USI Action Taxonomy
actually entails four major sub-taxonomies, each of which is functionally
distinct. First, there is what we have termed a Computer-Internal Taxonomy.
This taxonomy is concerned with actions which are central to the automated
portion of the USI, but are totally transparent to the user (e.g., internal
computer hardware, operating systems software). As this taxonomy deals with
issues totally within the established domain of Computer Science, we will
not address it further within the scope of this paper.

Second, continuing on the computer system side of Figure 1, we have
identified the need for a Computer-Output Taxonomy. As its name implies,
this taxonomy deals with the various ways and means by which a computer can
present or display information to a user. This taxonomy is closely tied to
the fields of computer graphics and information display technology. To be
maximally useful a Computer-Output Taxonomy needs to be device independent
so as to support mappings to a variety of implementation technologies. We
believe that some of the work reported by Foley, Wallace, and Chan (1981)
represents a good baseline upon which to build, and we will be focusing
future energies in that direction. For the present however, we have
concentrated on the user-side of the USI, trying to establish terms which
capture the human perceptual, cognitive, communicative, and logical-level
input activities of computer interaction.

In a manner analogous to the Computer-Internal Taxonomy, the User-
Internal Taxonomy deals with actions central to the user, but transparent to
the computer system. As is shown in Figure 1, we have devised an hierarchical structure with three major classes of behaviors which users exhibit
independently of the computer system--"Perception", "Mediation", and (inter-
personal) "Communication". Perception deals with the process of getting
information into the (human) system, as well as some initial level of
recognition/classification/identification of that information. Mediation
(or, alternatively, cognition) is concerned with the human information
processing activities which users perform upon the information once it has
been perceived. Finally, communications between people (via either some
indirect telephonic medium or direct personal interchange) have been

---

[1]This work was performed in association with an effort underway to define
and document the USI requirements of the Sector Suite Workstations of the
Federal Aviation Administration's Advanced Automation System for Air
Traffic Control.

USI ACTION TAXONOMY

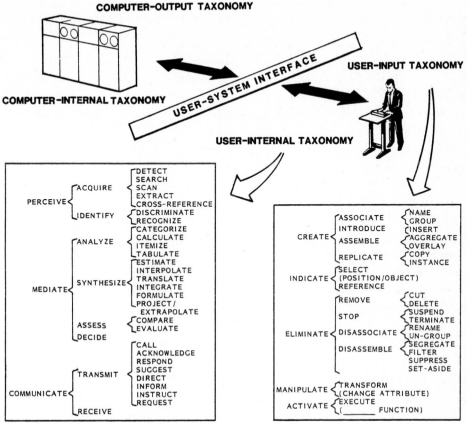

Fig. 1. Four major sub-taxonomies of overall USI taxonomy, and hierarchial structures of the User-Internal and User-Input taxonomies.

included here because: such communication links are critical components of many real world human-computer interactive systems; they frequently impact the system's USI design (especially when source data capture is one of the system's principle functions); and finally, as an activity class, they share the characteristic of being transparent to the computer.

Our User-Internal Taxonomy builds upon the earlier work of Berliner, et al. (1981), and directly incorporates many of their terms. However, an important addition is that we have explicitly defined each and every term we have used (see Table 1). This difference is key because one of the major benefits of a taxonomy should be its ability to support clear and consistent communication between its users. The taxonomy's precision of meaning and consistency of application across analysts and implementors are crucial to assuring traceability and completeness when analyzing and engineering a complex USI.

TABLE 1
Dictionary of USI action taxonomy terms

Term	Definition
Detect	Discover or notice an occurrence (usually unsolicited).
Search	Purposeful exploration or looking for specified item(s).
Scan	Glance over quickly, usually looking for overall patterns or anomalous occurrences (not details).
Extract	Directed, attentive reading, observing, or listening with the purpose of gleaning the meaning or contents thereof.
Cross-Reference	Accessing or looking up related information usually by means of an indexing or organized structuring scheme set up for that purpose.
Discriminate	Roughly classify or differentiate an entity in terms of a gross level grouping or set membership--frequently on the basis of only a limited number of attributes.
Recognize	Specific, positive identification of an entity.
Categorize	Classify or sort one or more entities into specific sets or groupings, usually on the basis of a well-defined classification scheme.
Calculate	Reckon, mentally compute, or computationally determine.
Itemize	List or specify the various components of a grouping.
Tabulate	Tally or enumerate the frequencies or values of the members of an itemized list or table.
Estimate	Mentally gauge, judge, or approximate, often on the basis of imcomplete data.
Interpolate	Assign an approximate value to an interim point based upon knowledge of values of two or more bracketing reference points.
Extrapolate/ Project	Assign an approximate value to a future point based upon the value(s) of preceding point(s).
Translate	Convert or change from one form or representational system to another according to some consistent "mapping" scheme.
Formulate	Generate and put together a set of ideas so as to produce an intergrated concept or plan.
Integrate	Pull together, and mentally organize a variety of data elements so as to extract the information contained therein.
Compare	Consider two or more entities in parallel so as to note relative similarities and differences.
Evaluate	Determine the value, amount, or worth of an entity, often on the basis of a standard rating scale or metric.
Decide	Arrive at an answer, choice, or conclusion.
Call	Signal to a specific recipient or set of recipients that a message is forthcoming.
Acknowledge	Confirm that a call or message has been received.
Respond	Answer or reply in reaction to an input.
Suggest	Offer for consideration.
Direct	Provide explicit authoritative instructions.
Inform	Pass on or relay new knowledge or data.
Instruct	Teach, educate, or provide remedial data.
Request	Solicit, query, or ask for.
Receive	Get, obtain, or acquire an incoming message.
Name	Give title to or attach label to for purposes of identification/reference.
Group	Link together or associate for purposes of identification.
Introduce	Originate or enter new data into the system (e.g., type in a free-form message).
Insert	Make space for and place an entity at a selected location within the bounds of another such that the latter wholly encompasses the former, and the former becomes an integral component of the latter.
Aggregate	Combine two or more components so as to form a new composite entity.
Overlay	Superimpose one entity on top of another so as to affect a composite appearance while still retaining the separability of each component layer.
Copy	Reproduce one or more duplicates of an entity (no links to "master").
Instance	Reproduce an original ("master") entity in such a way as to retain a definitional link to the master--i.e., such that any subsequent changes or modifications made to the master will automatically be reflected in each and every "instance" created therefrom.
Select	Opt for or choose an entity (e.g., a position or an object) by "pointing" to it.
Reference	Opt for or choose an entity by invoking its name.
Delete	Remove and (irrevocably) destory a designated portion of an entity.
Cut	Remove a designated portion of an entity and place it in a special purpose buffer (residual components of the original entity usually close in around "hole" left by "cut-out" portion).
Set-Aside	Remove entire contents of current (active) work area and store in a readily accessable buffer (for future recall).
Suspend	Stop a process and temporarily hold in abeyance for future restoration.
Terminate	Conclude a process such that it cannot be restarted from the point of interruption, only by complete re-initiation.
Suppress	Conceal or keep back certain aspects or products of a process without affecting the process itself (i.e., affects appearance only).
Rename	Change an entity's title or label without changing the entity itself.
Un-Group	Eliminate the common bond or reference linkage of a group of entities.
Segregate	Particion and separate an entity into one or more component parts such that the structure and identity of the original is lost.
Filter	Selectively eliminate one or more layers of an overlayed composite.
Transform	Manipulate or change one or more of an entity's attributes (e.g., color, line type, character font, size, orientation) without changing the essential content of the entity itself.
Execute	Initiate or activate any of a set of predefined utility or special purpose functions (e.g., sort, merge, calculate, update, extract, search, replace).

In a similar manner, Figure 1, and the corresponding definitional entries in Table 1, present our Computer-Input Taxonomy. Again, in the interest of generalizability, we focused on the "logical" level of input activity description, rather than a more "physically-oriented" scheme (i.e., one which would have been more dependent upon particular hardware/software implementation technologies). The approach taken was patterned in part after some of the user modeling concepts of Card, Moran, and Newell (1983), in that we initially tried to identify a set of exhaustive, yet mutually exclusive, goals or objectives that users might have in conveying information to a computer system (i.e., the top level "Create", "Indicate", "Eliminate", "Manipulate", and "Activate" terms in Figure 1). These terms were then refined to lower levels of detail, by first identifying sub-goals or objectives and then defining generic methods which might be utilized to achieve those objectives. Again, the hierarchical terms are just the structural skeleton of the taxonomy, and the supporting definitions in Table 1 are needed to properly apply the overall classification scheme.

These taxonomies represent tools which we have used to facilitate the overall human-computer systems analysis and design process. In the interest of clarity and generalized usability we have restricted any unnecessary growth of the taxonomy. In several cases when a new term seemed desirable, we first checked to see if the concept could be defined via a combination of existing terms--e.g., we defined "Determine" to be a combination of an (optional) "Analyze", (optional) "Synthesize", an "Assess", and a "Decide". By using the higher level hierarchial terms, and/or constructing composite terms (such as Determine or Edit), we found that we could account for a great many types of USI activities without substantial expansion of the set of elemental terms. Also, we found that by combining these taxonomic verbs with a set of well-defined (application specific) objects, forming a series of brief structured-English "sentences" or task element statements, we can concisely and clearly convey the intended workings of a complex USI to a very diverse population of highly experienced (but computer-naive) applications users, system engineers, hardware architects, and software engineers.

CONCLUSION

We have found the above taxonomies to be very servicable tools which facilitate human-computer task analysis and USI requirements specification. Further, we see these taxonomies as components of a comprehensive, integrated toolbox (Kloster & Tischer, 1984 and Phillips & Tischer, 1984) to be used by the systems engineer/ analyst in producing more effective and efficient human-computer interactive systems.

REFERENCES

Berliner, D.C., Angell, D., and Shearer, J.W. Behaviors, measures, and instruments for performance evaluation in simulated environments. Proceedings of the Symposium and Workshop on the Quantification of Human Performance, University of New Mexico, 1964.

Card, S.K., Moran, T.P., and Newell, A. The Psychology of Human-Computer Interaction, Hillsdale, New Jersey: Erlbaum, 1983.

Foley, J.D., Wallace, V.L., and Chan, P. The human factors of graphic interaction techniques. George Washington University Technical Report GWY-IIST-81-3, January 1981.

Kloster, G.V. and Tischer, K. Man-machine interface design process. Paper submitted to INTERACT '84, First IFIP Conference on Human-Computer INTERACTION, in Press.

Niebel, B.W. Motion and Time Study, Homewood, Illinois: Richard D. Irwin, 1967.

Phillips, M.D. and Tischer, K. Operations concept for next generation air traffic control systems. Paper submitted to INTERACT '84, First IFIP Conference on Human-Computer INTERACTION, in Press.

ACKNOWLEDGEMENTS

The authors gratefully acknowledge the contributions of J.D. Foley, H. E. Price, S. Seidenstein, H.P. Van Cott, and R. C. Williges in critically reviewing earlier versions of the taxonomies; and A. Zellweger, R. Bourne, and D. Weathers of the FAA for their motivation and support in developing the taxonomies.

Human—Computer Interaction, edited by G. Salvendy
Elsevier Science Publishers B.V., Amsterdam, 1984 — Printed in The Netherlands

HUMAN-COMPUTER INTERFACE EFFECTIVENESS EVALUATION

Thomas B. Malone, Mark Kirkpatrick, and Christopher C. Heasly

Carlow Associates Incorporated, 8315 Lee Highway, Fairfax, VA 22031 USA

INTRODUCTION

The objective of this paper is to describe and discuss the more important issues in evaluating the effectiveness of human-computer interfaces. In the development of a software system, evaluation of the human-computer interface is usually limited to an evaluation of the adequacy of information displays after the program has been designed, developed, written and debugged. It is usually typified as being too little, and too late!

First of all, evaluation of human-computer interface must address <u>all</u> interfaces between the human and the computer and not just the display interface. Secondly, an evaluation, to be effective in producing an improved system, must begin earlier than when the program is completed. The earlier that the human-computer interface can be evaluated, the more likely that the final interface will be effective.

The major issues in the evaluation of the human-computer interface are: 1) what constitutes the interface? 2) what constitutes the evaluation?, and 3) how can human-computer interface evaluations be conducted early in the software development process?

The Scope of Human-Computer Interface

In identifying the scope of the human-computer interface it is well to keep in mind that what we are discussing here is an interface - a link or connection, between two elements, in this case the human, and the computer. The interface can then be addressed on the machine side, and also on the human side. The machine side of the interface includes:

- Information displays - the information displayed and the display format
- Display characteristics - symbol size, shape, color, density, etc.
- Data organization - the architecture producing hierarchical levels of data specificity
- Dialogues - command modes, error messages, prompts, alerts, queries, etc.
- Procedures - task sequences, decisions, and decision rules
- Data entry devices - for data entry, manipulation, and designation

● Documentation - hard copy manuals and aids.

The human side of the interface includes:

● Personnel availability - manning levels and work levels
● Personnel capability - skills and skill levels
● Personnel performance - completion of assigned tasks
● Personnel productivity - quantity produced per unit time
● Personnel safety.

From this list it is apparent that the human-computer interface is not limited to the physical control and display interfaces usually encountered in human factors hardware applications. Rather, a significant portion of the interface is at the cognitive level.

The Scope of Human-Computer Interface Evaluation

The conduct of an evaluation of human-computer interface effectiveness should parallel the conduct of any human factors evaluation. The specific steps comprising an evaluation of human-computer interfaces include the following:

1. Identify the objectives of the evaluation

2. Identify the specific aspects of the human-computer interface to be evaluated, including a sampling plan for selecting test participants or subjects

3. Select missions, operations and tasks to be used in the evaluation

4. Select operational conditions to be included in the evaluation, including quantity of information to be processed, time constraints, equipment, condition of readiness, etc.

5. Select test methods:
   - analysis including application of standard analytical techiques, such as task analysis, decision analysis, error analysis, link analysis, etc.
   - experiment - controlled experimental evaluation of limited aspects of the system
   - simulation - part-task or full-task simulation of system operations
   - observation and measurement of actual system performance
   - measurement through embedded evaluation techniques
   - human operator report - through interview, survey and questionnaire

6. Select test measures, including measures of:
   - program user friendliness - extent to which it directs the user on what to do next, keeps him informed as to where he is in the process, and what the computer is doing, is responsive to his needs, and provides procedures which are logical and efficient
   - information quality, including availability when needed, currency, and accuracy

- display quality, including readability and coding
- display characteristics - compliance with standards
- data organization - meaningfulness of the architecture
- dialogues - system response time, adequacy of command modes, etc.
- procedures - accuracy, internal consistency, and sequencing
- data entry device characteristics
- documentation - correspondence with software, coverage, clarity, currency, correctness, compatibility with user skills, and compliance with criteria
- human performance - error rates, time to respond, time to perform
- human productivity - quantity produced per unit time
- human workloads, and workload distribution
- program learnability - time to train

7. Identify evaluation criteria
   - standard human factors design criteria
   - system specific performance criteria

8. Identify requirements for data collection and recording

9. Identify data validation requirements, assessment of:
   - data validity, based on the fidelity of the test situation to the real world situation
   - data reliability, based on the experimental controls imposed on the data collection process
   - data usability, based on the selection of evaluation data

10. Identify requirements for data analysis.

Conduct of Human-Computer Interface Evaluation Early in the Development Process

One reason why it has been the common practice of evaluating human-computer interfaces after the system has been designed and developed is that the product to be evaluated is readily identifiable. The advantage of evaluating the interface after it has been designed and implemented is that the interface is then available for evaluation in all its aspects. The disadvantage is that, having waited until the design process is completed, it will be much more difficult to get changes made. Clearly the evaluation should begin earlier; as early as possible. The question is, how?

The software development process can logically be reduced to a series of four major stages: system analysis, system design, code development, and program integration and verification. The products which are available for evaluation at each stage are: requirements, specifications, computer code, and the completed program. Can human-computer interface evaluations be conducted at the initial (system analyses) stage where not only is a human computer interface not yet available but the concept for the interface has not even been developed? The answer is - an evaluation should be conducted of the human-computer interfaces within a system which currently exists and which most closely represents the new system in terms of objectives, tasks, operating conditions, and constraints. This system is designated the baseline comparison system (BCS). Through a human factors evaluation of the BCS, significant problem areas can be identified and avoided in the new system. The BCS evaluation should also identify positive aspects of the human-computer interface which should be implemented in the new system. Finally, the evaluation of the BCS provides the data base from which human-computer interface effectiveness criteria can be developed.

Human—Computer Interaction, edited by G. Salvendy
Elsevier Science Publishers B.V., Amsterdam, 1984 — Printed in The Netherlands

A TAXONOMY OF HUMAN-COMPUTER INTERACTIONS: TOWARD A MODULAR USER INTERFACE

ROGER SCHVANEVELDT, NANCY COOKE, FRANCIS DURSO[1], LISA ONORATO, AND GREGG BAILEY

Computing Research Laboratory and Department of Psychology, New Mexico State University, Las Cruces, NM 88003 (U.S.A.)

[1]On leave from the University of Oklahoma

The user interface refers to the aspects of a computer system that are directly involved in interactions between a computer system and users of the system. The interface embodies assumptions about the knowledge and skill of the user as well as the physical makeup of displays and data entry devices. The transactions at the interface involve presenting information to users and obtaining information from users. The nature of the user interface is a primary determinant of the "friendliness" or "usability" of the system.

In many computer systems, the user interface has been the result of individual programmers using intuition about the best way to interact with users. There are several possible reasons for the failure of this approach to produce effective interfaces. First, programmers are not particularly representative of the people who will use the programs. Second, many systems are developed by several programmers leading to a motley blend of different intuitions. Third, solving the technical problems involved in developing software often leaves little time for working on the user interface. Fourth, programmers usually have little systematic understanding of the information processing capabilities of people. Finally, programmers often have a system-oriented view of the problems they are trying to solve, leading to a precedence of system convenience over what is convenient for the user.

With increased attention to user interface issues, there have been some noted improvements in interface design, but the work has just begun. Much of the research on the user interface leads to guidelines for programmers and system designers. These guidelines must be accepted and correctly interpreted before they have a real impact on the quality of systems. It is reasonable to be pessimistic about the quality and consistency of interfaces that result from guidelines. A better approach would be to make it possible for specially trained people to design interface (cf. Norman, 1982) and allow programmers to specify user interactions in formal terms. Modularizing the user interface would promote such a division of labor.

As we conceive it, a modular user interface consists of two major sections. A user knowledgeable section is responsible for directly interacting with users. This component should embody the best techniques of interacting with users at particular skill levels. The translation section is responsible for interacting with a computer system. This component embodies the formal specifications of user interactions and accomplishes the translation between the system-oriented definitions of user interactions and the user-oriented forms of the interactions.

Advantages of modularizing the user interface include: (a) independence of systems and the interface allowing for portability; (b) different interfaces for different users; (c) research on the user interface with a constant system; (d) programmers specify user-transactions in formal terms rather than worrying about effective methods of communicating with people; (e) interface design by trained experts; (f) correct implementation of effective interfaces; and (g) implementation of new interface technology without modification of applications programs.

Lacking space to review related work, we have listed some relevant papers in the references. The major objectives of our research are; (a) to define a modular user interface using both psychological computer system constraints; (b) to use this definition to organize and direct empirical research on the most effective methods for interacting with various types of users; and (c) to implement the interface resulting from this work for use in systems and applications programs. To date, our work has focussed on the input side of user interactions. We will summarize our approach, initial results, and an initial implementation.

TAXONOMY OF INTERACTIONS

We have analyzed both operating systems and application programs in terms of the type of information exchanged and the method of exchange in individual interactions. In the process, we have attempted to identify information exchange at an abstract level as distinct from the particular methods used by particular programs. For example, the distinction between menu-driven and command-based systems represents a style difference. This distinction could appear in a taxonomy of interactions as selection vs. specification, but such a taxonomy would reflect methods of interaction. We are in search of abstractions that are less dependent on methods and yet provide constraints that could be exploited by the user interface. While it would be informative to trace the false starts we have made, space will only allow an outline of the major elements of the taxonomy for user input interactions, along with examples of subtypes.

Our work on a taxonomy has been importantly influenced by a desire to design specifications of user-computer interactions. These specifications should: (a) have the form of a subroutine or function call in the context of a program; (b) provide sufficient information to the interface module to allow for effective implementation of an actual interaction with a user; (c) approach an optimum balance between specification of detail and brevity. From the perspective of the specifications, we must explore ways of classifying information exchanged between users and computers so that specifications can be defined in terms of the classification.

Class. This element of the taxonomy covers a wide range and probably deserves further subdivision. However, the class of the interaction serves to identify the interaction in the context of the program or system. It includes such frequently occurring things as dates, times, file names, positions, and commands as well as more rare categories such as furniture, heights, and dogs. The user interface would presumably be prepared to deal specifically with frequent classes. With the less frequent classes, it could at least use the class name to refer to the desired input. By keeping a history of class use, the interface could help to identify classes that need special attention.

Data Type. Data types include numbers (integer, real, complex), character strings, and special record structures. The data type constrains interactions without determining the actions to be performed by the user. The data type can also specify the form of data expected by the system.

Specific Constraints. While the class and data type provide constraints on the desirable input, there are often specific constraints that provide further limits. Such constraints include lists of alternatives, units of measurement, ranges of values, length of character strings, and status of system elements (e.g., old vs. new files). The set of constraints also defines the uncertainty of the interaction, i.e., the number of alternative acceptable inputs.

Default. Default input can be used to protect users from serious mistakes, to speed selection of frequent choices, and to direct novice users.

Description. The description is used to characterize the desired input in more detail than the class specification. The description is a phrase or sentence describing the desired input or its function.

Interaction Identification. While identifying particular interactions is relatively uninteresting, identification can be used to simplify repetition of interactions, to customize an interface for particular interactions, and to maintain a history of interactions.

124

SYSTEM-INTERFACE COMMUNICATION

Using the elements outlined above, a request for user input would have the following form in a Pascal-like language:

USERIN(IDENTIFICATION;CLASS;DATA TYPE;CONSTRAINTS;DEFAULT;DESCRIPTION)

Some specific examples are:

USERIN(7;"decimals";INTEGER;(0..9);2;"digits in decimal fractions")
USERIN(43;"confirmation";STRING;Yes/No;No;"Remove all files?")
USERIN(22;"file name";STRING;OLDFILE,LENGTH ≤15;;"name of data file")

We have begun to implement an interface based on this analysis of input interactions. The specifications do provide useful information in directing possible interaction styles. It is likely that future developments will take us in the direction of artificial intelligence techniques to handle some of the problems that arise. It seems likely that intelligence will be required to deal with problems of presenting complex information to users. We are encouraged by the direction our own thinking has been given by the attempt to define a modular interface. We speculate that we may learn a great deal about human-computer interaction by learning what is easy and what is difficult in the modular interface.

REFERENCES

Ball, E. & Hayes, P. A test-bed for user interface designs. Proceedings of Human Factors in Computer Systems, 1982, 85-88.
Geiselman, R. E. & Samet, M. G. Personalized versus fixed formats for computer-displayed intelligence messages. IEEE Transactions on Systems, Man, and Cybernetics, 1982, 12(4), 490-495.
Hayes, P.J. & Szekely, P.A. Graceful Interaction Through the COUSIN Command Interface. Department of Computer Science Publication No. CMU-CS-83-102, Carnegie-Mellon University.
Jacob, R.J.K. Using formal specification in the design of a human-computer interface. Communications of the ACM, 1983a, 26(4), 259-264.
Jacob, R.J.K. "Executable specifications for a human-computer interface," NRL Report, Navel Research Laboratory, Washington, D.C. (1983b).
Kaiser, P. & Stetina, I. A dialogue generator. Software-Practice and Experience, 1982, 12, 693-707.
Norman, D. A. Steps toward a cognitive engineering: design rules based on analyses of human error. Proceedings of Human Factors in Computer Systems, 1982, 378-382.
Treu, S. Uniformity in user-computer interaction languages: a compromise solution. International Journal of Man-Machine Studies, 1982, 16, 183-210.

Human—Computer Interaction, edited by G. Salvendy
Elsevier Science Publishers B.V., Amsterdam, 1984 — Printed in The Netherlands

A TAXONOMY OF USER-COMPUTER INTERFACE FUNCTIONS

L. F. COHILL
AT&T Communications

INTRODUCTION

New computer systems are being developed every day. Most of these systems involve human operators or users. Therefore, they include user interfaces. Unfortunately, these user interfaces vary greatly from system to system, whether due to independent development, tailoring to different functions, or varying availability of new technology.

Because of these differences, users who must deal with more than one user-computer interface are frequently confused and frustrated. This ever-growing number of multiple-system users is forced to learn the idiosyncracies of each system; a difficult task that can easily defeat even the most enthusiastic user.

At AT&T Communications, work is currently under way to develop a common customer interface for computer systems planned for direct customer access. This includes all systems in which the customer will be making control input and/or database changes directly to the system via a user-computer interface. As the first step in this development, a list of interface functions and sub-functions was compiled. The main objective of this project was to comprehensively list and define the functional needs of the user-computer interfaces concerned, so that the common interface would cover all these needs.

INITIAL FUNCTION LIST

The initial functional model was adapted from Hansen (1978), who originally developed the model to describe engineering systems for use by telephone personnel. Hansen listed thirteen functions: access, security, menus, news, help, inquiry, update, linkage, temporary hold, error and message handling, statistics, training, and testing. His model is given in Figure 1.

In order to determine the applicability of these thirteen functions to customer interfaces, the functions were defined at a highly detailed level. Each function was also divided into an appropriate set of sub-functions to more clearly define the specifics of its application.

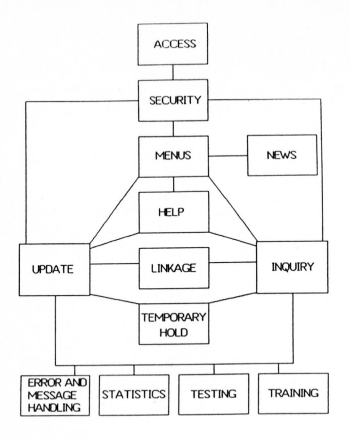

Figure 1. Initial Function Model

SYSTEM REVIEW

Nine existing computer systems were evaluated based on the adapted Hansen model of functions. The systems surveyed were all AT&T Communications systems which currently, or could in the future, allow direct customer access. The systems surveyed all used CRTs with a keyboard for user input. System purposes ranged from teleconferencing call set-up to remote circuit testing.

RESULTS

Each system's implementation of each function and sub-function was summarized. Wide differences were found among the systems. For example, the MENUS function was implemented very differently in the various systems.

The menus across systems varied not only in hierarchical structure, but in layout, selection method, and time of presentation. Some systems supplied only a single menu; others had multiple levels. Some menus were displayed as a vertical list on the full screen, others were compacted into a serial list of choices next to a prompt or at the screen bottom.

Similarly large differences were found in the access, security, help, linkage, temporary hold, and statistics functions. Based on this system summary, the function model was revised.

REVISED FUNCTION LIST

The functions were regrouped (and some added or deleted) so that the function list would better match the system interfaces reviewed, and the user view. The new function list contained ten functions: access/security, menus, news/mail, help, inquiry, temporary hold, update, error and message handling, statistics, and linkage, as illustrated in Figure 2. Access and security were combined because security is really a component of access, and is hidden from direct customer involvement. News was expanded to include messages sent between users (mail), not just messages sent from the system administrator to users. The on-line training package function was deleted because a tutorial can be considered separate from the actual system operation, and because none of the systems reviewed included any type of on-line training. The on-line testing function was deleted from the function list because testing of the system software and hardware is the responsibility of developers, not end-users.

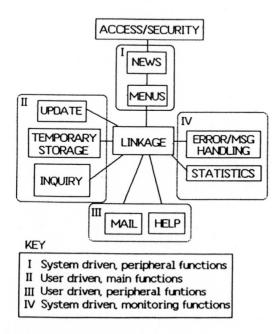

Figure 2. Revised Function Model

SUMMARY

This revised function list has several uses. In this particular case, it was used to outline the capabilities that need to be included in the common customer interface. By summarizing and defining functions common to all customer interfaces, the way is prepared for the design of a common customer interface.

In addition to its use for this particular customer interface design project, the function list can be used in the design of other interactive systems. Since it covers all areas of the human-computer dialogue, the system designer may use it as a checklist.

The interface function list can also be used, as in this case, to evaluate existing systems in terms of (1) the functions they include, (2) whether omitted functions should be included for the particular application, and (3) how the interfaces handle the listed functions. Each user-computer interface's handling of a given function can be compared and evaluated in terms of user performance, user satisfaction, and ease of implementation. In this way, a recommended handling of a given function for a given type of system may be developed. These approaches can then be applied to systems under design, saving time, money, and effort.

The function classification can also be used as a means of systematically exploring the issues and options with respect to human-computer interaction. It can serve to point out gaps in research knowledge. If several systems handle a particular function differently, this points out a need for research to explore options for the treatment of that function.

This function model provides an outline of the functions to be included in a common customer interface. It also provides the basis on which human-computer dialogues can be evaluated and designed.

REFERENCES
Hansen, J. A. Design guidelines for on-line human machine interface. Kansas City, Missouri: AT&T Long Lines, August, 1978.

Human—Computer Interaction, edited by G. Salvendy
Elsevier Science Publishers B.V., Amsterdam, 1984 — Printed in The Netherlands

EVALUATING USABILITY OF APPLICATION INTERFACES

C.A. SCHNEIER and M.E. MEHAL

Product Usability Dept., IBM, P.O. Box 28331, Atlanta, GA 30358 USA

INTRODUCTION

Once user requirements are understood and the external design of system
interfaces are formulated, two design principles are necessary to insure these
interfaces will be easy to use (Gould and Lewis, 1983).

1. User Testing - Early in the development process intended users should
   actually use simulations and prototypes to carry out real work.
2. Iterative Design - When problems are found in user testing, they must be
   fixed.

IBM's Information Programming Services has a development facility for application products in Atlanta, Georgia. To facilitate user testing and iterative
design, developers have access to a Usability Laboratory. This paper will
describe lab facilities and users.

WHAT IS TESTED

The lab allows testing of a total system. Hardware and software jointly
determine the user's impression of the system. Software includes screens with
which the user interacts, along with its supporting documentation. This can
be hardcopy manuals, messages or help displayed on the screen, learning packages, and/or customer response line support. A test can focus on all aspects
of the user interface, or a subset. For example, a small test might compare
online help with hard-copy help.

WHERE THE TEST TAKES PLACE

The lab consists of four test modules. Movable walls separate the modules,
to allow a maximum of flexibility. A module consists of a test area of
approximately 17 by 20 feet, and a control room, as shown in Figure 1.
One-way glass separates the two areas. Test subjects work in an area furnished
similar to a typical business office. They are asked to perform typical tasks
using the product.

Product developers, planners, and information developers observe the subject
from within the control room. The monitoring team is busy collecting data
simulating customer response line support, and recording the test. The control

room is divided into a console area and an observation area. The console area contains video displays, the sound system, and a mini computer. The monitoring team keeps a log of the evaluation on the mini computer, and videotapes the entire session for future reference. Additional observers can peer "over the shoulders" of the monitoring team from the raised observation area. There are desks to facilitate note taking.

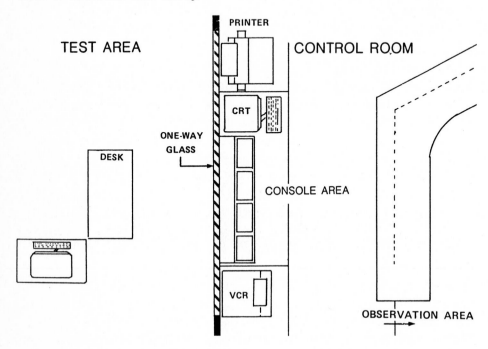

Figure 1. A typical Module in the Atlanta Usability Lab

WHAT IS MEASURED
   Usability has the following measureable aspects:
   1. Easy to learn
       The effort to learn or relearn a task should be minimized.
   2. Useful
       The effort to perform a task should be minimized. The system should fit well with the task at hand.
   3. Tolerant of errors
       It should be difficult to make errors. When errors are made, it should be easy to recover.
   4. Pleasant to use
       Users should have a positive attitude.

Test subjects are asked to perform typical tasks which are laid out in a scenario. The scenario is oriented towards the user. It tells the user <u>what</u> to do (for example, enter an invoice into a business application) but not <u>how</u> to do it. Sometimes the users are asked to "think aloud" (Lewis, 1982). With this method the subject makes spoken comments as he works on a task. Another testing methodology is to mimic an office environment more closely by requiring the user to work straight through the task. In this case intervention is kept to a minimum so that task timings will be accurate.

Observers collect the following data during a test.

* Quantitative variables
    - Time to learn
    - Successful completion of the task
    - Time to complete the task
    - Number/severity of customer response line calls
    - Number/severity of errors
    - Error recovery time
* Qualitative variables
    - User perceptions
    - Observations of the test team
    - User preferences on questionnaires

WHO DOES THE TEST

During a usability test, a number of people are involved, representing a variety of interests. This can include the following people.

* Product usability specialists to advise on testing methodology and teach the team how to use the lab equipment and capture data.
* Planners who are familiar with the user requirements.
* Programmers writing the code for the product.
* Information developers writing the associated documentation.
* Testers overseeing product quality.

We believe an interdisciplinary test team results in a higher quality tests, since each individual brings their own perspective. In addition, we have fewer problems negotiating fixes for observed problems when members of the affected areas are participating on the test team.

Test subjects are selected based on the audience requirements for the product. We try to fit the profile of a typical user as closely as possible. Demographic categories can include:

* Age
* Education
* Computer experience
* Business background (e.g., accounting)

WHEN PRODUCTS ARE TESTED

Although Usability testing can be done anywhere in the product development cycle, we recommend doing it as early as possible. Developers can compare design alternatives using a prototype version of an interface. If usability testing is not done until system test time (or later) it may be difficult to fix problems without impacting development schedule or resources. The lab is versatile, supporting anything from a prototype version of an interface, through component and system test, to a final product checkout right before it is shipped.

When problems are found, fixes may impact the code being developed, or the associated documentation (or sometimes both). If time permits, the fixes are evaluated again, to be sure they have indeed solved the problem. This iterative design results in better ease of use of the product.

SUMMARY

The Atlanta Usability Lab is a place where developers can watch typical users use a product. As soon as possible in the development cycle, external inter-faces are tested with intended users doing realistic tasks. The user interacts with entire system, including hardware, software, and associated documentation. Test subjects perform typical tasks while they are observed by the monitoring team. Usability data includes task timings, error counts, customer response line calls, documentation usage, user preferences, questionnaires and inter-views. When developers observe usability problems themselves, they can more easily fix them. The result is a higher quality product in the market place.

BIBLIOGRAPHY

Gould, J.D., Lewis, C., 1983. Designing For Usability--Key Principles and What Designers Think. In CHI'83 Human Factors in Computing Systems (Boston, December 12-15, 1983), ACM, New York, pp.50-53.
Lewis, C., 1982. Using the "Thinking-aloud" Method in Cognitive Interface Design, Research report RC 9265 (#40713) 2/17/82. Available from IBM Thomas J. Watson Research Center, Yorktown Heights, NY 10598.

III.   SOFTWARE DESIGN AND USE

Human—Computer Interaction, edited by G. Salvendy
Elsevier Science Publishers B.V., Amsterdam, 1984 — Printed in The Netherlands

CORRECT, COMPLETE OPERATIONS AND OTHER PRINCIPLES OF INTERACTION

BEN SHNEIDERMAN
Department of Computer Science, University of Maryland, College Park, MD 20742

ABSTRACT

Too often the users of interactive computer systems find that they have made an
error. Three techniques are proposed to reduce error rates: correct matching
pairs, complete sequences, and correct commands. Further principles of interface
design are offered for data display, data entry, distinctions across user
communities, and the balance of automation and human control.

INTRODUCTION

In many contemporary systems there is a grand opportunity to improve the human
interface. The cluttered and multiple displays, complex and tedious procedures,
inadequate command languages, inconsistent sequences of operations, and
insufficient informative feedback generate frustration and debilitating anxiety
which lead to poor performance, frequent minor and occasional serious errors, job
dissatisfaction, and occasional nervous breakdowns.

It is easier to be a critic than a designer; finding flaws is easier than
correcting or avoiding the design failures. Other papers (Gaines, 1981;
Shneiderman, 1984; Smith and Aucella, 1983) offer constructive guidance for
design of menu selection, command languages, etc., but this paper is an attempt
to present some underlying principles of design which are applicable in most
interactive systems.

The initial principle, developed in detail in this paper, is that operations
should be correct and complete so as to reduce the number of errors of commission
and omission that a user can make. Subsequent principles provide guidance in the
design of task sequences, data display, and data entry. No set of principles is
complete, but the explicit statement of principles is necessary to transmit the
ideas and provoke experimental validation, refutation, or qualification.
Scientific progress emerges from the sequence of increasingly specific hypotheses
which reflect a deeper theory and yet offer more practical advice.

CORRECT AND COMPLETE OPERATIONS

The problem

Users of text editors, database query facilities, air traffic control systems,
and other interactive systems often make mistakes. Ledgard et al. (1980) found
that novice users of a 15-command subset of a text editor were making mistakes in
19% of their commands. Experienced users were making mistakes in 10% of their
commands. In a more demanding environment Card et al. (1980) reported that
experienced professional users of text editors and operating systems were making
mistakes in 31% of the tasks assigned to them. Barber (1979) found that
professional workers in a challenging decision making job made errors in 7% to
46% of their transactions, depending on the response time of the computer system.
Other studies are beginning to reveal the magnitude of the problem and the loss
of productivity due to user errors.

One direction for reducing the loss in productivity due to errors is to
improve the error messages provided by the computer system. Shneiderman (1982)

reports on five experiments in which changes to error messages led to improved success at repairing the errors, lower error rates, and increased subjective satisfaction. Superior error messages were more specific, positive in tone, and constructive (telling the user what to do, rather than merely reporting the problem). Rather than vague and hostile messages such as SYNTAX ERROR or ILLEGAL DATA, designers are encouraged to use informative messages such as UNMATCHED LEFT PARENTHESIS or MENU CHOICES ARE IN THE RANGE OF 1 TO 6.

But improved error messages are only helpful medicine. A more effective approach is to prevent the errors from occuring. This goal is more attainable than it may seem in many systems.

The first step is to understand the nature of errors. One perspective is that people make mistakes or "slips" (Norman, 1983) which can be avoided by organizing screens and menus functionally, designing commands or menu choices to be distinctive, and making it difficult for users to do irreversible operations. Norman offers other guidelines such as "do not have modes", offer feedback about the state of the system, and design for consistency of commands. Norman's analysis provides practical examples and a useful theory. The ensuing sections refine his analysis and describe three specific techniques for reducing errors by ensuring complete and correct operations: correct matching pairs, complete sequences, and correct commands.

Techniques for ensuring correct operations

Correct matching pairs. This is a common problem with many manifestations and several simple prevention strategies. Examples include the failure to provide

- the right parenthesis to close an arithmetic expression,
  If an arithmetic assignment statement such as

  CENTIGRADE = (5/9) * (FAHRENHEIT - 32)

  failed to the right parenthesis after the 32, it would result in a SYNTAX ERROR message in many compilers or interpreters, or hopefully or a more meaningful message such as UNMATCHED LEFT PARENTHESES.

- the */ to close a PL/I comment,
  The required form for a PL/I comment is /* THIS IS A COMMENT */ and the omission of the closing */ causes the compiler to treat the remainder of the program as a comment.

- the " to close a string in BASIC,
  The command 10 PRINT "HELLO" is in error if the rightmost " is missing.

- the ฿ or other markers to close a boldface, italic, or underscored text in wordprocessors such as Wordstar,
  If the text file contains ฿This is boldface ฿ then the three words between the ฿ markers appear in boldface on the printer. If the rightmost ฿ is missing, then the remainder of the file is printed in boldface.

- the termination of a centering command in a text formatter.
  Some text formatters have a pair of commands such as .on center and .off center which are to surround lines of text that are to be centered. The omission of the latter command causes the entire file to be centered.

In each of these cases, a matching pair of markers is necessary for operation to be complete and correct. The omission of the closing marker can be prevented by using an editor, preferably screen-oriented, which puts both the beginning and ending components of the pair on the screen in one operation. For example, typing a left parenthesis generates a left and right parenthesis and puts the cursor in between to allow creation of the contents. An attempt to delete one of the parentheses will cause the matching parenthesis (and possibly the contents as well) to be deleted. Thus, the text can never be in a syntactically incorrect form.

Some people find this rigid approach to be too restrictive and may prefer a milder form of protection. When the user types a left parenthesis, the screen has a visual indicator of the need for a right parenthesis, until it is typed.

Another approach is to replace the requirement for the ending marker. Many microcomputer versions of BASIC do not require an ending " to terminate a string. They use a carriage return to signal the closing of a string. Variants of this theme occur in line-oriented text editors which allow omission of the final '/' in a CHANGE /OLD STRING/NEW STRING/ command and in versions of LISP which offer a special character to terminate all open parentheses.

In each of these cases, the designers have recognized a frequently occuring error and have found a way to eliminate the error situation.

Complete sequences. Sometimes an operation requires several steps or commands to reach completion. Since people may forget to complete every step of an operation, designers attempt to offer a sequence of steps as a single operation. Putting on the left turn signal in a car causes three or more lights to flash. When a pilot lowers the landing gear, hundres of steps and checks are invoked automatically.

This same concept can be applied to interactive uses of computers. For example:

- programming language loop constructs require a WHILE-DO-BEGIN-END or FOR-NEXT structure, but sometimes users forget to put the complete structure in or delete one component but not the other components. One solution would be for users to indicate that they wanted a loop, and the system could supply the complete and correct syntax, which would be filled in by the user. This approachs reduces typing and the possibility of making a typographical error or a slip such as the omission of one component.

- conditional constructs require an IF-THEN-ELSE or CASE-OF-END structure, but again users may forget a component when creating or deleting. Here again, if users could indicate that they wanted a conditional construct the system could provide the syntactic template and prompt for the contents to be filled in (Teitelbaum, 1980).

- programming plans (Soloway et al., 1982) may contain several components which must be created and deleted one component at a time. The counter plan requires a a data declaration of the integer variable, initialization to zero, incrementation, and a test. If the user could indicate that a counter plan is desired then the system to provide the complete template, or prompt the user for inclusion of each component, or merely remind the user of the need to complete the plan.

- a user of a text editor should be able to indicate that section titles are to be centered, in upper case, and underlined without having to issue a series of commands each time a section title is entered. Then if a change is made in style, for example to eliminate underlining, a single command would guarantee all commands were made correctly.

- air traffic controllers may formulate plans to change the altitude of a plane from 14,000 feet to 18,000 feet in two steps, but after raising the plane to 16,000 feet, the controller may get distracted and fail to complete the operation. The controller should be able to record the plan and then have the computer prompt for completion.

The notion of complete sequences of operations may be difficult to implement because the users may need to issue atomic operations as well as complete sequences. In this case users should be allowed to define sequences of their own — the macro or subroutine concept should available at every level of usage.

Designers can gather information about potential complete sequences by studying sequences of commands actually issued and the pattern of errors that people actually make.

Correct commands. Industrial designers recognize that successful products must be safe and must prevent the user from making incorrect use of the product. Airplane engines cannot be put into reverse until the landing gear have touched down and cars cannot be put into reverse while traveling forward at faster than five miles per hour. Cameras prevent double exposures, even though this is sometimes desired, and appliances have interlocks to prevent tampering while the power is on, even though expert users occasionally need to persorm diagnoses.

The same principles can be applied to interactive systems. All too often the users of computer systems invoke a command that is not available, make a menu selection choice that is not indicated, request a file that does not exist, or enter a data value which is not acceptable. These errors are often caused by annoying typographic errors such as using an incorrect command abbreviation, pressing a pair of keys rather than a desired single key, misspelling a file name, or making an minor error or omitting, inserting, or transposing characters. Error messages range from the annoyingly brief "?" or WHAT? to the vague UNRECOGNIZED COMMAND or SYNTAX ERROR to the condemning BAD FILE NAME or ILLEGAL COMMAND. The brief "?" is suitable for expert users who have made a trivial error and can recognize it when then see the command line on the screen. But if an expert has ventured to use a new command and has made a mistake of understanding, then the brief message is not helpful even for experts.

Whoever made the mistake and whatever were its causes, the user must interrupt their planning to deal with the problem and their frustration in not getting what they wanted. As long as a command must be made up of a series of keystrokes on a keyboard, there is a substantial chance of making an error in entering the sequence of keypresses. Some keypressing sequences are more error prone than others, especially those that require shifting or unfamiliar patterns. Reducing the number of keypresses can help, but it may place a greater burden on learning and memory since an entry with reduced keystrokes, e.g. "E" for "ERASE", may be more difficult to remember.

Another approach is to have the computer offer the permissible commands, menu choices, or file names on the screen and let the user select with a pointing device such as a mouse, lightpen, or arrow cursors. This is effective if the screen has ample space, the display rate is rapid, and the pointing device is fast and accurate. When the list grows too long to fit on the available screen space, some approach to hierarchical decomposition must be used.

Imagine that the twenty commands of an operating system were constantly displayed on the screen. After selecting the PRINT command (or icon) the system automatically offered the list of thirty files for selection. Two lightpen, touchscreen, or mouse selections can be done in less time and with higher accuracy than typing the command PRINT USA-JAPAN-PAPER.

In principle, a programmer need type a variable name only once. After it has been typed, the programmer only selects it, thus eliminating the chance of a misspelling and an UNDECLARED VARIABLE message.

It is not always easy to convert a complex command into a small number of selections and reduce errors. Pointing devices are often crude, slow, and annoying to use. The Apple LISA 2 and the Macintosh are successful and practical applications of these concepts, but there is still room for further invention and application of this concept.

FURTHER PRINCIPLES

Fundamental principles of interface design include:

1. Offer informative feedback - for every operator action there is some system feedback. For frequent and minor actions the response can be very modest, while for infrequent and major actions the response should be more substantial. Every keystroke or cursor movement should be immediately (less than 100 milliseconds) shown on the screen. When a file is printed, copied, or deleted, the user should be given some feedback about the size of the file to confirm that the correct file was used. Thus, if a file is deleted the user should a message like FILE FINALREPORT DELETED - 127 PAGES. As much as possible show the user the state of the machine in the context of a cognitive model of the user's activity. This is a central concept in direct manipulation (Shneiderman, 1983).

2. Design transactions to yield closure - sequences of actions should be organized into groups with a beginning, middle, and end. The informative feedback at the completion of a transaction gives the operator the satisfaction of accomplishment, a sense of relief, the signal to drop contingency plans and options from his/her mind, and an indication that the way is clear to prepare for the next transaction.

3. Offer simple error handling - as much as possible design the system so that the user cannot make an error. If an error is made, try to have the system detect the error, and offer simple, comprehensible mechanisms for handling the error. The user should not have to retype the entire command, but only need repair the faulty part of it. Erroneous commands should leave the state of the system unchanged or give instructions about how to restore the system to a safe state.

4. Permit easy reversal of actions - as much as possible, actions should be reversible. This relieves anxiety since the operator knows that errors can be undone and encourages exploration of unfamiliar options. The units of reversibility may be a single action, a data entry, or a complete transaction.

5. Support internal locus of control - experienced operators strongly desire the sense that they are in charge of the system and that the system responds to their actions. Surprising system actions, tedious sequences of data entries, incapacity or difficulty in obtaining necessary information, and the inability to produce the action they want build anxiety and dissatisfaction.

6. Reduce short-term memory load - the limitation of human information processing in short-term memory ("seven plus or minus two chunks") requires that displays be kept simple, multiple page displays be consolidated, frequent window motion be reduced, and that sufficient training time be permitted for codes, mnemonics, and sequences of actions. Where appropriate, online access to command syntax forms, abbreviations, codes, and other information should be provided.

7. Provide rapid system response - most operator actions should produce a response within 300 milliseconds (this is a good target but there is only

controversial data about the exact time) although some processes may be designed
to take longer. Consistent response times (never less than one quarter the mean
or more than twice the mean) should be provided to support the experience of
predictability. Rapid response facilitates operation since delays force the
operator to waste effort in repeatedly reviewing a sequence of actions retained
in short- term memory. Slower response may be designed for costly, complex, or
dangerous operations.

These underlying principles must be interpreted, refined, and extended for
each environment. The principles presented in the ensuing sections focus on
increasing the productivity of users by providing simplified data entry
procedures, comprehensible displays, and rapid informative feedback which improve
the feelings of competence, mastery, and control over the system.

DATA DISPLAY

Guidelines for display of data are being developed by many organizations.
Smith and Aucella (1983) offer five high level objectives for data display (my
comments follow each objective):

1. Consistency of data display - this principle is frequently violated, but it
is easy to repair. During the design process, the terminology, abbreviations,
formats, etc. should be standardized and controlled by using a written (or
computer managed) dictionary of these items.

2. Efficient information assimilation by the user - the format should be
familiar to the operator and related to the tasks required to be performed with
this data. This objective is served by rules for neat columns of data, left
justification for alphanumeric data, right justification of integers, lining up
on decimal points, proper spacing, comprehensible labels, and appropriate use of
coded values.

3. Minimal memory load on user - do not require users to remember information
from one screen for use on another screen. Arrange tasks such that completion
occurs with few commands, minimizing the chance of forgetting to perform a step.
Provide labels and common formats for novice or intermittent users.

4. Compatibility of data display with data entry - the format of displayed
information should be closely linked to the format of the data entry.

5. Flexibility for user control of data display - users can get the information
in the form most convenient for the task they are working on.

This compact set of high level objectives is a useful starting point, but each
project needs to expand these into application-specific and hardware-dependent
standards and practices. For example, these detailed comments for control rooms
design come from a report from the Electric Power Research Institute (1981):

- Be consistent in labeling and graphic conventions.

- Standardize abbreviations.

- Use consistent format in all displays (headers, footers, paging, menus,
etc.)

- Present a page number on each display page and allow operators to call a
page by entering its page number.

- Present data only if they assist the operator.

- Present information graphically, where appropriate, using widths of lines, positions of markers on scales, and other techniques that relieve the need to read and interpret alphanumeric data.

- Present digital values only when knowledge of numerical value is actually necessary and useful.

- Use high resolution monitors and maintain them to provide maximum display quality.

- Design a display in monochromatic form, using spacing and arrangement for organization, and then judiciously add color where it will aid the operator.

- Involve operators in the development of new displays and procedures.

Attention Getting

Since substantial information may be presented to users for the normal performance of their work, exceptional conditions or time dependent information must be presented so as to attract attention. Multiple techniques exist for attention getting:

1. Intensity - use two levels only.

2. Marking - underline, enclose in a box, point to with an arrow, or use an indicator such as an asterisk, bullet, dash, or an X.

3. Size - use up to four sizes.

4. Choice of fonts - use up to three fonts.

5. Inverse video - use normal or inverse.

6. Blinking - use blinking or non-blinking (2-4 hertz).

7. Color - use up to four standard colors, with additional colors reserved for occasional use.

8. Audio - use soft tones for regular positive feedback, harsh sounds for rare emergency conditions.

A few words of caution seem appropriate. There is a danger in creating cluttered displays by overuse of these techniques. Novices need simple logically organized and well labelled displays which guide their actions. Expert operators do not need extensive labels on fields, subtle highlighting or positional presentation is sufficient. Display formats must be tested with users for comprehensibility.

Similarly highlighted items will be perceived as being related. Color coding is especially powerful in linking related items, but then it becomes more difficult to cluster items across color codes (Robertson, 1980). Operator control over highlighting, for example, allowing the operator in an air traffic control environment to assign orange to aircraft above 18000 feet, may provide a useful resolution to concerns about personal preferences and operator familiarity with monochrome display. Highlighting can be accomplished by intensity, blinking, or other methods.

Audio tones can provide informative feedback about progress, such as the
clicks in keyboards or ringing sounds in telephones. Alarms for emergency
conditions do rapidly alert operators, but a mechanism to suppress alarms must be
provided. Testing is necessary to ensure that operators can distinguish among
alarm levels. Prerecorded or synthesized messages are an intriguing alternative
but their interference with communications among operators should be observed.

DATA ENTRY

Data entry tasks can occupy a substantial fraction of the operator's time and
are the source of frustrating and potentially dangerous errors. Smith and
Aucella (1983) offer five high level objectives for data entry (my comments
follow each objective):

1. Consistency of data entry transactions - similar sequences of actions under
all conditions - similar delimiters, abbreviations, etc. An unfortunate example
of inconsistency in an operating system command language is the requirement for a
period following the file name in some cases, the prohibition of its use in other
cases, and optional use in most cases.

2. Minimal input actions by user - fewer input actions mean greater operator
productivity and less chance for error. Making a choice by a single keystroke,
lightpen touch, finger press, etc. rather than by typing in a lengthy string of
characters is potentially advantageous. Selecting from a list of choices
eliminates the need for memorization, structures the decision making task, and
eliminates the possibility of typographic errors.

However, if the operators must move their hands from a keyboard to a separate
choice device, the advantage is defeated. Experienced operators often type 6 to
8 characters instead of moving to a lightpen, joystick, or other selection
device.

A second aspect of this guideline is that redundant data entry should be
avoided. It is annoying for an operator to enter the same information in two
locations, since it is perceived as a waste of effort and an opportunity for
error. When the same information is required in two places, the system should
copy the information for the operator, who still has the option of overriding by
retyping.

3. Minimal memory load on user - reduce the need for the operator to remember
lengthy lists of codes and complex syntactic command strings. Part of the reason
it takes so long to learn the airlines reservations systems is that operators
must memorize codes for the airports (LGA for LaGuardia in New York City, IAD for
Dulles near Washington, DC), the airlines (UA for United Airlines, AL for USAir),
the class of service (Y for coach, K for special fares), etc.

4. Compatibility of data entry with data display - the format of data entry
information should be closely linked to the format of displayed information.

5. Flexibility for user control of data entry - experienced operators desire to
enter information in a sequence they can control. On some occasions in the air
traffic control environment, the arrival time is the prime field in their mind.
On other occasions the altitude is the prime field. Flexibility should be used
cautiously since it goes against the consistency principle.

DISTINCTIONS ACROSS USER COMMUNITIES

The remarkable diversity of human abilities, backgrounds, cognitive styles,
and personalities challenges the interactive system designer. When multiplied by

the wide range of situations, tasks, and frequency of use, the state space of design parameters becomes unbounded. A preschooler playing a graphic computer game is a long way from a reference librarian doing bibliographic searches for anxious and hurried patrons. Similarly, a professional programmer using a new operating system is a long way from a highly trained and experienced air traffic controller. Finally, a student learning from a computer assisted instruction lesson is a long way from a hotel reservations clerk serving customers for many hours a day.

These portraits of users highlight the differences in background knowledge, training in the use of the system, frequency of use, goals of the user, and the impact of a user error. No single design could satisfy all these users and situations, so before beginning a design, the characterization of the users and the situation must be precise and complete.

User profiles

"Know the user" was the first principle in Hansen's (1971) list of user engineering principles. It's a simple idea, but a difficult goal and, unfortunately, an often undervalued goal. No one would argue against this principle, but many designers assume that they understand the users and their tasks. Successful designers are aware that other people learn, think, and solve problems in very different ways. Some users really do have an easier time with tables than graphs, with words instead of numbers, with slower rather than faster display rates, or with a rigid structure rather than an open ended form.

It's hard for most designers to know whether Boolean expressions are too difficult a concept for library patrons at a junior college, fourth graders learning programming, or professional electric power utility controllers.

All design begins with an understanding of the user including profiles of the age, sex, physical abilities, education, background, training, motivation, goals, and personality. There are often several communities of users for a system, so the effort is multiplied. In addition to these profiles, users might be tested for skills such as comprehension of Boolean expressions, knowledge of set theory, fluency in a foreign language, or skills in human relationships. Other tests might cover task specific abilities such as knowledge of airport city codes, stockbrokerage terminology, insurance claims concepts, or map icons.

The process of knowing the user is never ending, because there is so much to know and because the users keep changing. Every step in understanding the users and in recognizing them as individuals whose outlook is different from your own, is a step closer to a successful design.

Task analysis

After carefully drawing the user profile, the tasks must be pencilled in. Task analysis has a long, but mixed history. Every designer would agree that the set of tasks must be decided on before design can proceed, but too often the task analysis is done informally or implicitly. If another command can be added, the designer is often tempted to include the command in the hope that some users will find it helpful. Design convenience should not dictate system functionality or command features.

High level tasks can be decomposed into multiple middle level tasks which can be further refined into atomic operations which the user executes with a single command, menu selection, etc. Choosing the most appropriate set of atomic operations is a difficult task. If the atomic operations are too small, the users will become frustrated by the large number of operations necessary to accomplish a higher level task. If the atomic operations are too big, the users will need many such operations with special options, or they will not be able to get exactly what they want from the system.

The relative task frequencies will be important in shaping a set of commands, a menu tree, etc. Frequently performed tasks should be simple and quick to carry out, even at the expense of lengthening some infrequent tasks. For example, frequent editing commands, such as INSERT, should be a single letter or special key, while infrequent commands, such as CONVERT TO UPPER CASE, may require a longer name.

Relative frequency of use is one of the bases for making architectural design decisions. For example, in a text editor:

1. frequent operations might be performed by a special key, such as four cursor arrows, an INSERT, and a DELETE key.

2. Intermediate frequency operations might be performed by a single letter followed by the ENTER key or the single letter with the CONTROL key. Examples include underscore, center, indent, subscript, or superscript.

3. Less frequent operations might require going to a command mode and typing the command name, for example MOVE BLOCK or SPELLING CHECK.

4. Still less frequent operations or complex operations might require going to command mode and then entering a menu selection process, for example to change the printing format or to revise network protocol parameters.

BALANCE OF AUTOMATION AND HUMAN CONTROL

A fundamental principle of interaction should be to eliminate human actions when no judgment is required. Users should not be burdened with the annoyance of handling routine, tedious, and error-prone tasks, but should concentrate on critical decisions.

The degree of automation will increase over the years as procedures become more standardized, hardware reliability increases, and software verification and validation improves. With routine tasks, automation is preferred since the potential for error may be reduced. However, I believe that there will always be a critical human role because the real world is an "open system" (there are a non-denumerable number of unpredictable events and system failures) while computers constitute a "closed system" (there are only a denumerable number of predictable normal and failure situations which can be accommodated in hardware and software). Human judgment is necessary for the unpredictable events in which some action must be taken to preserve safety, avoid expensive failures, or increase product quality.

For example, in air traffic control, the common operations are well understood and potentially automatable, but the operators must be present to deal with the highly variable and unpredictable emergency situations. An automated system might successfully deal with high volumes of traffic, but what happens when the airport manager changes runways because of turbulent weather, causing planes to be rerouted quickly, and then one pilot calls in to request special clearance to land because of a failed engine while a second pilot reports a passenger with a potential heart attack. Human judgment is necessary to decide on which plane should land first and how much costly and risky diversion of normal traffic is appropriate. The air traffic controller cannot just jump into the emergency, but he or she must be intensely involved in the situation in order to make an informed, rapid, and optimal decision. In short, the real world situation is so complex that it is impossible to anticipate and program for every contingency, human judgment and values are necessary in the decisionmaking process.

Another example of the complexity of real world situations in air traffic control emerges from an incident in May 1983. An Air Canada Boeing 727 jet had a fire on board and the controller cleared away traffic and began to guide the plane in for a landing. The smoke was so bad that the pilot had trouble reading his instruments and then the onboard transponder burned out so that the air traffic controller could no longer read the plane's altitude from the situation display. In spite of these multiple failures, the controller and the pilot managed to bring the plane down quickly enough to save the lives of many, but not all, of the passengers.

The goal of system design in many applications is to give the operator sufficient information about current status and activities so that when intervention is necessary, the operator has the knowledge and the capacity to perform correctly. Increasingly the human role will be to respond to anomalous situations such as unanticipated situations, failing equipment, improper human performance, and incomplete or erroneous data.

The entire system must be designed and tested, not only for normal situations, but for as wide a range of anomalous situations as can be anticipated. An extensive set of test conditions might be included as part of the requirements document.

Beyond performance of productive decisionmaking tasks and handling of failures, the role of the human operator will be to improve the design of the system. In complex systems there is always an opportunity for improvement, so systems that lend themselves to refinement will evolve under the continual incremental redesign by the operator.

CONCLUSIONS

Principles and guidelines are useful in focussing attention on specific issues. Successful designers recognize that principles will often be in conflict and that tradeoffs must be made based on experimental data and good judgment. Over the next few years we can expect a profusion of principles and guidelines documents which address the diversity of users and tasks. Reliable principles will emerge for standard situations in word processing, educational applications, data entry, or programming, but the creative and bold designer will always be pushing back the borders of the familiar with an innovative idea.

Acknowledgements. This work was done with support from IBM and Control Data Corporation. The University of Maryland Computer Science Center provided computer facilities for the manuscript preparation. Linda Weldon suggested changes which improved the presentation.

REFERENCES

Barber, Raymond E., 1979. Response time, operator productivity and job satisfaction, Ph. D. dissertation, NYU Graduate School of Business Administration.

Card, Stuart, Moran, Thomas P., and Newell, Allan, 1980. The keystroke-level model for user performance with interactive systems, Communications of the ACM 23, (1980), 396-410.

Gaines, Brian R., 1981. The technology of interaction -- dialogue programming
rules, International Journal of Man-Machine Studies 14, 133-150.

Hansen, Wilfred J., 1971. User engineering principles for interactive systems,
Proceedings of the Fall Joint Computer Conference, 39, AFIPS Press, Montvale,
NJ, 523-532.

Ledgard, Henry, Whiteseide, John, Singer, Andrew, and Seymour, William, 1980. The
natural language of interactive systems, Communications of the ACM 23, 10,
(October 1980), 556-563.

Lockheed Missiles and Space Company, 1981. Human Factors Review of Electric Power
Dispatch Control Centers: Volume 2 Detailed Survey Results, Prepared for
Electric Power Research Institute, 3412 Hillview Avenue, Palo Alto, CA 94304.

Norman, Donald A., 1983. Design rules based on analyses of human error,
Communications of the ACM 26, 26, (April 1983), 254-258.

Robertson, P. J., 1980. A guide to using color on alphanumeric displays, IBM
Technical Report G320-6296, IBM White Plains, NY.

Shneiderman, Ben, 1984. Design issues and experimental results for menu
selection systems, University of Maryland Computer Science Center Technical
Report 1303, (submitted for publication).

Shneiderman, Ben, 1983. Direct manipulation: A step beyond programming
languages, IEEE Computer 16, 8, (August 1983), 57-69.

Shneiderman, Ben, 1982. System message design: Guidelines and experimental
results, In Directions in Human-Computer Interaction A. Badre and B.
Shneiderman, Eds., Ablex Publishing Co., Norwood, NJ, 55-78.

Shneiderman, Ben, 1980. Software Psychology: Human Factors in Computer and
Information Systems, Little, Brown and Co., Boston, MA.

Smith, Sid L. and Aucella, A. F., 1983. Design Guidelines for the User Interface
for Computer-Based Information Systems, The MITRE Corporation, Bedford, MA
01730, Electronic Systems Division, (March 1983), 279 pages. Available from
the National Technical Information Service, Springfield, VA.

Soloway, Elliot, Ehrlich, Kate, Bonar, Jeffrey, and Greenspan, Judith, 1982.
What do novices know about programming?, In Directions in Human-Computer
Interaction, A Badre and B. Shneiderman, Eds., Ablex Publishing Co., Norwood,
NJ, 27-54.

Human—Computer Interaction, edited by G. Salvendy
Elsevier Science Publishers B.V., Amsterdam, 1984 — Printed in The Netherlands

147

PLACE OF WORK ANALYSIS IN SOFTWARE DESIGN

A. WISNER[1], F. DANIELLOU[1], B. PAVARD[1], L. PINSKY[2], J. THEUREAU[2]

[1]
Conservatoire National des Arts et Métiers, 41 rue Gay-Lussac, 75005 PARIS
[2]
Centre National de la Recherche Scientifique, 41 rue Gay-Lussac, 75005 PARIS

ABSTRACT

Wisner A., Daniellou F., Pavard B., Pinsky L., Theureau J., 1984. Place of
work analysis in software Design in Salvendy G. Human Computer Interaction.
Elzevier, Amsterdam.

In three different situations involving text composition, line coding,
and the monitoring of ongoing processes, three teams from the same laboratory
have shown that it is necessary to proceed with a real work analysis in order
to identify possible errors in initial software design, to implement an
experiment on new software, to obtain better results when dealing with performance and workload, and to formulate rules for future software designs. Thus,
as in pre-data processing ergonomics, the analysis of the real work situation
is shown to be an unavoidable phase in designing experiments that are adequate
to answer questions raised by the nature of the work involved.

INTRODUCTION : WORK ANALYSIS

The increasing complexity of work situations in data processing leads to
stress certain basic aspects of the necessary work analysis (Wisner and
colls., 1982).

- Exhaustivity : The work analysis has got to consider all activities without
differentiating beforehand between what is primarily important and what is
secondary.

- Taking uncertainty into account : Real situations always contain a given
degree of uncertainty which is rarely taken into account when considering
designs beforehand and when considering experimental situations in the lab.
This uncertainty must be studied and then reduced to the greatest degree
possible by improving the software.

- Study of variations over time : Very often the work will consist of monitoring the appearance, development and resolution of a difficulty. It is
important to observe if the software favours or hinders this monitoring
process throughout the time covered by all the operations.

- <u>Clear showing of the various operating registers</u> : Some problems can be
easely solved with **algorithms** whereas others will require a more or less
complex heuristic activity. However in real-life situations, the operator will
often go suddenly from one level to another according to the characteristics
of the software and the operators'own past experience.
- <u>Importance of further information sources</u> : Direct and telephoned verbal
communications, **job aids** consultations, and personal documents and notes are
sources of information on what is needed and does not appear on the computer's
screen or appears in an improper way.
- <u>Conversations and verbal contacts</u> : Talking with the operators produces
comments and thus sheds further light on what has been observed before.
Furthermore, verbalizing an ongoing activity ("thinking aloud") is often possible and useful.
However, even if work analysis is an indispensable tool, it is not enough in
itself, and we will conclude by describing the characteristics of the experimental techniques and the type of theoretical progress required that can enable
the laboratory to provide data that can be put to good use by the designer.
WORD PROCESSING STUDY

B. Pavard deals with the problem of designing a word processing software
intented for use in composition tasks for written documents such as translations
text rewording, letter-writings etc...

Most researches in the subject have shown that the technical means
available influence the amount of time needed to realize the task (Gould,
1978, 1982, Card, Moran, Newell, 1983).

These authors have also shown that the software influences the organization
of composition activities over time, but they do not (or at least hardly ever)
deal with the effects on the linguistic structure of the material being
produced.

<u>Result of work analysis</u>

A work analysis dealing with the composing of new bulletins in a press
room (Pavard, 1984) has shown quite clearly that :

1) The cognitive strategies used to plan and draft the news bulletins will
change according to whether the journalist is working on a screen or with a
typewriter.

2) The linguistic structure of the news items being drafted will also be
influenced by the characteristics of the technical device being used. If, for
instance, one considers the activity of composing a narrative sentence, it can
be seen that working on a screen induces drafting strategies that can be broken
down into two successive stages :

- In the first stage the journalist formulates lexical components which give a basic description of the action, the subject and the protagonist... (1)

(1) *X was elected and his party was considered* ...

- At the second stage, the journalist inserts the non-mandatory logic or colouring which will play a locational, instrumental or qualifying role... (2).

(2) *X was elected [congressman] and his party, [the D], was considered* ...

These psycholinguistic compositional strategies were never observed when the journalist was working on a simple typewriter. One can thus formulate the hypothesis that these strategies only appear when one works on a screen terminal because in this case it is possible to insert further lexical items without considerably increasing the editing and printing costs of the operations involved.

The work analysis has also shown that the journalist will adopt similar strategies for reformulating a partially written text on the screen as he will do when resolving a problem.

The objective of this strategy will be to find the grammatical connectives (and, in order to, when he...) which can then be inserted into the available lexical material in order to come up with a grammatically correct sentence.

The hypothesis has been made that the interest of such a strategy is to limit the amount of lexical inputs needed (since they have already been put on screen). The constraints that induce this strategy for problem resolution can be attributed to the "availability" of editing operations, such as insertion and deletion of words, but the editing operation has also got to be "accessible", that is, usable without involving too great a cost of physical actions on the system.

The availability and accessibility of the editing operations thus function as constraints that either facilitate or hinder certain operations for transforming the text. These pragmatic constraints, like the linguistic constraints or the constraints involving the human operator's capacity (for instance the size of his working memory), will determine the strategies being used during composition. The designing of a word processing software will thus entail the identification of those pragmatic constraints that relate to the operational procedures, and therefore to the linguistic structure of the target text.

Can the experiment enable us to identify the pragmatic constraints ?

Various word processing systems were considered containing different characteristics of availability and accessibility for the editing operations in order to evaluate the effect of pragmatic constraints on the strategies used for text composition.

The procedures followed by the subjects as well as their performances were analysed in terms on the softwares used.

As had already been observed during the work analysis, the results thus obtained show an interaction effect between the type of editing operations available and the procedures used by the subjects.

But the experiment showed above all that performances depend on the software being used.

For instance, it is noted that the percentage of "forgotten" propositions varies between 0 and 12% if they are propositions describing the events of the narrative text, and 3 to 27% if they are defining the temporal or spacial conditions in which these events were taking place.

The software design for word processing therefore requires :

1) That the pragmatic constraints associated with the technical means or with the software being used be identified (research on real work or laboratory situation).

2) That the relationship between pragmatic constraints and performance be studied (laboratory research).

3) That the editing functions adapted to the task be defined using a model that integrates the pragmatic constraints with the cognitive system constraints.

LINE CODING STUDY

L. Pinsky and J. Theureau studied women operators whose task was to codify information from a poll. The example we will use will be the encoding of the poll subject's profession. A nomenclature was established before the polling took place : it contained heading for professions (each heading having its own code). This coding process consisted of finding a heading that corresponded to the information about the profession. There was a considerable difference between the information as provided by the poll subjects and the nomenclature headings, so that identification of an adequate code often raises complex problems.

Furthermore, this research was undertaken using an interactive data processing system which encodes the profession whenever it can, sending the message back to the operator if it cannot.

The object of the ergonomic study was as follows : since a data processing system already existed to perform the job (system 1), the question was how to design a new system (system 2) which would be better suited to the operator.

Stages of the Ergonomic Study

Analysis of Initial Work. This is the core of the study, which attempts to apprehend and explain the successive actions of the operator using the system.

What is attempted   to apprehend is the real activity in the fullness of its complexity, consisting of a description of the reasons for the operators' action, i.e. the whole process leading up to the decision of choosing a given heading following successive responses from the system. Two types of data were involved: part of the observable behaviour (actions whose result appear on the screen) and verbal comments induced during action. Interpreting such data required close collaboration from the operators themselves.

Two methods of describing the reasoning process were used based on the work of Newell and Simon (1972) and on Borel, Grize and Mieville (1983).

Elaboration of Ergonomic transformations. This is organized in two stages. The work analysis on System 1 gives us a picture of the operator's action characteristics, along with the difficulties involved and their consequences on the workload. This enables us to define the principles of ergonomic transformations. Only the principles can be involved here since the introduction of ergonomic transformations and any purely technical changes will considerably modify the work situation. Any realization of ergonomic transformations will thus require an experimental process involving System 2 prototypes.

Ergonomic experiments. The purpose of these experiments is to amass solid evidence that will enable the activities of the operators to be forseen using System 2, using this as a basis for suggesting the ergonomic changes required. The definition will be based on three essential principles :

- an experimental situation must be built that will be as close as possible to the future work situation (and futhermore, the "subjects" must accurately reflect the future population of female operators).

- an attempt will be made to apprehend the full complexity of the work being analysed in an experimental situation.

- the results must be interpreted using everything that can be known about the future work situation (which will of necessity be different from any experimental situation). Only if these conditions are fulfilled can one formulate recommendations that will be truly relevant to System 2.

It can be noted that work analysis intervenes at two different instances :

- in order to take into account the real work of coding and all the difficulties involved when using System 1.

- in order to forsee and deal with the problems that come up in System 2 by analyzing the latter system at the prototype stage.

Encoding aid and cooperative competence

The results of the work analysis called for ergonomic changes at two levels :

The operator must resolve encoding problems. The first question was whether the help provided by the system was sufficient. This defines the first level : the encoding aid.

A required (though not sufficient) condition for this aid to be effective is that the dialogue between the operator and the system be able to take place without hindrance. One can thus identify a second level : that of cooperative competence.

The following example can enable one to define these two levels :

System 1 is centered on the names of the professions.

The name denotes a particular profession. A heading will consist of a collection of names. The name of the profession will therefore not be the heading, but an intermediary.

The operator transfers a name into the system. The programme will then compare the name with those that are already in the programme on a word-by-word basis :

- if a stored name is identical to the name sent in by the operator, a heading code will be automatically attributed to the name, and no message will be sent back to the operator.

- if the name in the file have at least one word in common with the name being put in by the operator, the list of these names will be put on screen so that the operator can choose whichever one is the most suitable.

- if the stored name file does not contain the words put in by the operator, a "name unknown" message will appear.

The work analysis shows that the real activity is different to the one forseen by the design originators. The system induces the operator only to seek to determine a "suitable" name. In fact the operator is trying to attribute a heading to the name in spite of the system. In order to do this she either uses a paper list of nomenclatures or else relies on her own memory.

The consequences for the operator of the system's faults are as follows :

- reasoning is undertaken in situations where information is insufficient (i.e. uncertainty regarding the code which she is nevertheless responsible for).

- too much is expected from the operator's memory.

The first principles of ergonomic transformation relate to the encoding aid :

- providing heading information and particularly sending back the heading that has been attributed automatically.

-adapting messages that will take maximum account of the significance of the name being sent in, and not just the fact that it shares a common word with this name.

System 2 follows these principles ; and yet work analysis in ergonomic experiments has shown that this dialogue is unsatisfactory. The operator expects the system to follow certain rules of cooperation, for instance, that it makes use of all information she has put in (Pinsky, 1983). The fact that the system does not obey these rules entails the following consequences : the operator cannot be logical, since the system's response induces reasoning that puts her off track, and she will then undertake parasite activities in order to make up for the lack of information, since her memory is overload with unstructured information that gets in the way of the knowledge required for encoding.

The new ergonomic transformations are aimed at the cooperative competence of the system by means of influencing the automatic encoding programme (for instance by enabling it to take into account all information sent in by the operator), or by influencing the drafting of the messages (for instance by stating the encoding problem that the message itself has raised).

PROCESS CONTROL STUDY

F. Daniellou and M. Boel studied the control panel operators in the control room of an oil refinery, in which 600 valves are automatically regulated by a centralized system, and which enables the panel operators to benefit from automatic control aid.

Work analysis results

The work analysis is based on records of 105 hours of activity and on-job conversations.

This analysis in the field enabled us to stress three main aspects of the control panel operators' activity which cannot easily be taken into account in a laboratory simulation :
- the gradual buildup of information from multiple sources,
- the role of outside operators,
- simultaneous processing of several incidents.

Gradual buildup of information. The recordings have shown that the management of the process from the control room is not limited to the simple usage of information provided by the automatic regulation shown on screen.

First of all, it can be said that information relating to certain states of the process are never referred back to the control panel. This applies in cases such as areas which are under repair, or unusual use being made of some channels...

Furthermore, what often happens is that a sensor or a switch fails and thus causes a failure in the automatic regulation. Because of the number of regulation loops, the phenomen never leads to a high number of material breakdowns. But it would appear that an important aspect of the panel operators' activity is to record and identify any material failures in the plant equipment. The operator will do this by establishing a comparison between various different indicators, some of them being visible at the panel and others requiring outside operators examining the unit. It was noted that during this process of comparing indicators, each information component is affected by its "age" (the sensor response time) and its probability of failure.

The role of the outside team. This gradual buildup of the information will be dependant on the whole of the production team.

Each outside operator's activity will be oriented by the representation he has of the ongoing incidents. This representation is being constantly updated by listening to the conversations coming over the radio channel, and which will include those that are not adressed to the operator.

The control panel operator is in a situation that enables him to forsee and integrate all of the outside operators'time delays in gaining access to a piece of information in a given area of the refinery. The capacity of the control panel operator to do this will depend on his precise knowledge of the geographical configurations of the units.

Simultaneous processing of several incidents. The control panel operator is sometimes faced with simultaneous incidents which are taking place at different places within the unit. Observation of the way in which he consults his screens at these times suggests that he always processes these incidents in two ways :

- a "central" method, in which an incident is followed up in full detail by means of practically continuous scanning of the relevant screens. It would seem that the representation of the process that guides the control panel operator's activity deals with functionally linked groups of equipment, with a view to examining the possible consequences of the incident's further development.

- a "peripheral" method : while continuing to work according to the "central" way, the control panel operator is monitoring the development of the other wrong adjustments by means of "reference points" or "cues" that are providing summary indications about the state of the other units. When one of these "cues" arrives at a critical threshold point, the activity is then reorganized and the incident involved becomed the "central" phenomenon in turn.

Contribution of work analysis to the thinking involved in designing
centralised controls rooms for processing industries.

The above elements, which are inherent to work analysis in real-life
situations, are essential inputs when designing computerized control rooms.

Thus the design approach cannot just simply deal with the purely presenta-
tional aspects of data processing information. What is really at stake above all
is the work organization of the staff taken as a whole. A clear definition of
who will be operating in the field and who in the control room, the possibility
for control room operators to remain in touch with the updated information
coming from the equipment, along with the detection and collective diagnosis of
the equipment's breakdown.

Information presentation must be compatible, not only with the reasoning
process of the operator when he is dealing with an incident, but also with the
appearence of simultaneous incidents, which are a not-uncommon occurence in
real-life situations. These in turn induce a reorganization of activities which
can be greatly facilitated by the operators' management screens. It is therefore
necessary to take changes of operating register into account during the
designing process, since this plays a real role in the activities of the panel
controller.

The activity of each staff member will be directed by the knowledge he has
of each of his colleague's activities. This raises the question of undertaking
a common training scheme for the whole team together, as a further stage
beyond the individual training each operator is provided with at various
stages of his career.

CONCLUSIONS

The observed pattern and results of the foregoing three studies show that it
is insufficient to just enable the operator to use a data processor more
easily. The computer's layout plays a direct and determining role in inducing
the cognitive representations that will result in problem solving. This
intervention can be either favourable or unfavourable. In this latter case, the
way in which the information is being represented and processed throughout the
computer system has got to be reconsidered. It can be seen that what is now
under consideration is artificial intelligence. Thus we have now passed from
the ergonomics of the man/computer interface to the ergonomics of artificial
intelligence.

156

The experiments required for this can therefore be considered to require some very particular characteristics : they have got to be situated in conditions which approximate to real-life practice ; there must be properly-trained subjects, complex and even multiple problems to be solved, along with enough duration to take into account the whole development of a breakdown. However, the risk involved in this type of experiment is well-known ; one can set up experiments that are only adapted to a given situation and which thus become inadequate to cover situations that vary. One can in fact observe various states for the same operator and for the same device under study, so long as the period of time covered is sufficiently extensive. Since the learning periods can be very long, because there is a huge diversity of problems to be solved and because the technical and social demands can change, the operational registers are continuously changing. For each operational register, the operator will expect the calculator to help him adequately.

It is obvious that when establishing the overall software design, full account must be taken of the action's context (multiple contacts between the operator and his colleagues, documents used).

Thus the theoretical model of the necessary activity is no longer that of a more-or-less simple interrogation of a data bank, but rather that of an operator. building up his own more-or-less complex pattern of information, which can be transformed in turn, hence leading to the decision-making, problem solving, and follow up of successive events.

REFERENCES

BOREL, M.J., GRIZE, J.B., MIEVILLE, D. (1983) Essai de logique naturelle, Peter Lang, Berne.

CARD, S.K., MORAN, T.P., NEWELL, A. (1983) The psychology of Human Computer Interaction, Lawrence Erlbaum, Hillsdale, N.J.

DANIELLOU F., BOEL M. (1984) Automatized process-control : the roles of computer available, and in-the-field collected information, in Ergonomics Problems in Process Operations, Birmingham Symposium preprints.

GOULD, J.D. (1978) An experimental study of writing, dictating and speaking. In J. Requin, (Ed.) Attention and Performance VII, Lawrence Erlbaum, Hillsdale, N.J., 299-319.

GOULD, J.D. (1982) Writing and speaking letters and messages. Int. J. Man machine studies, 16, 147-171.

NEWELL, A., SIMON, H.A. (1972) Human problem solving. Prentice - Hall Englewood cliffs, N.J.

PAVARD, B., Analyses des contraintes exercées par le langage de commandes sur les procèdures de traitement de texte. Actes du Congrès d'Ergonomie et d'Automatismes de Valenciennes (à paraître NORTH HOLLAND pub.)

PINSKY, L. (1983) What kind of "dialogue" is it when working with a computer, in T.R.G. Green, S.J. Payne and G.C. Van der Veer (eds.). The Psychology of Computer Use. Academic Press (29-40)

WISNER, A., PAVARD, B., PINSKY, L., Language and computer systems (work analysis and cognitive load) in NORO K. (ed.) I.E.A. 82 Japan Ergonomics Society TOKYO 544-545.

Human—Computer Interaction, edited by G. Salvendy
Elsevier Science Publishers B.V., Amsterdam, 1984 — Printed in The Netherlands

LINE AND SCREEN TEXT EDITORS:
SOME UNIVERSITY EXPERIMENT RESULTS

H. E. DUNSMORE

Department of Computer Science, Purdue University, West Lafayette, Indiana
47907

ABSTRACT

This paper reports some experimental results obtained comparing the use
of line editors and screen editors by non–programmer computer users. Line
editors display text line–by–line and recognize a number of commands to
alter, delete, or include more text. Screen editors display about 20 lines of
text on a video screen and allow alterations or additions by simply moving a
"cursor" to a desired point and typing in the desired text (sometimes over
undesired text like misspelled words). The results of two independent
experiments conducted at Purdue University suggest that screen editors are
easier for non–programmers to learn and to use.

INTRODUCTION

Text editors are probably the most–used computer software today.
Programmers use text editors to prepare specifications, designs, programs,
data, and documentation. Other computer users (as well as programmers) use
text editors for typical word processing activities - text entry, modification,
and document preparation (Shneiderman, 1980). Editors are a part of the
standard software on large computers, minicomputers, micro– (including
personal) computers, and standalone word processors. There is general
agreement that on most computing systems text editing is the most prominent
activity - in terms of percentage of computing resource used. In recent years
text editors have undergone a metamorphosis from the classical *line* editors to
the newer *screen* editors - both of which are described below.

This change from line to screen editors has been accomplished
predominantly because of the intuition shared in the computing community
that we are more efficient editing text and programs with a screen editor.
Even if programmers work better with a screen editor and even if they like

them better than line editors (the second of which is true without a doubt), there is still the open question whether screen editors are better for non–programmers. With an eye toward the so–called "user friendly" aspects of a system, we were interested in exploring whether screen editors are superior to line editors for people who are using a computer but who are not programmers. Since the use of computers by non–programmers is on the rise (fueled by the availability of microcomputers), we believe that insight concerning editors for this class of computer users is very much needed.

In this paper we first describe and discuss line editors and screen editors. Then we present the results from two experiments conducted at Purdue University concerning the use of these two types of editors by non–programmers.

LINE EDITORS

The first text editors were those that could be used on typewriter–like terminals. They operated in what is called a "line" mode in which all lines of text as well as directives to the editor to change words, delete lines, or move lines were entered as separate lines. An example of the use of a line editor appears in figure 1. There is no line editor that performs precisely like this one, but this is an example of the way line editors usually work. Notice that there are really two modes in which lines are entered. Some lines (i.e., all those after the LINES command and before the COMMANDS command) are accepted by the text editor and stored away. They are the lines of text that are being entered. They can be altered, moved, or deleted. Later they will be printed when the user wants to see the document.

On the other hand, some lines (i.e., all those beginning with COMMANDS and including LINES) are not stored anywhere but request the text editor to do something immediately. For example, LINES indicates that all following lines are to be treated as lines of text until the COMMANDS command is given. FIND requests the editor to look through the lines of text that follow until it finds the next occurrence of some characters. The line where the character string is found becomes the "current" line. REPLACE commands the editor to replace the first occurrence of some characters on the current line with some other characters. PRINT requests a listing of the

LINES
The Department of Computer Science at Purdue University
has been giving degrees in Computer Science since 1962.
Since that time, the department has become one of the
leeding departments in the United States.
COMMANDS
FIND "giving"
--> has been giving degrees in Computer Science since 1962.
REPLACE "giving" with "awarding"
--> has been awarding degrees in Computer Science since 1962.
FIND "leeding"
--> leeding departments in the United States.
REPLACE "leeding" with "leading"
--> leading departments in the United States.
LINES
Members of the faculty serve their profession by conducting
state-of-the-art research projects.
COMMANDS
PRINT
The Department of Computer Science at Purdue University
has been awarding degrees in Computer Science since 1962.
Since that time, the department has become one of the
leading departments in the United States.
Members of the faculty serve their profession by conducting
state-of-the-art research projects.

Figure 1. This sample editing session with our line editor shows the use of the
LINES, COMMANDS, FIND, REPLACE, and PRINT commands. There are
many more including commands to delete or move lines around in the file.

entire set of lines as they now appear.

MOVE is used to pick up a group of lines and move them somewhere
else. COPY is very similar to MOVE except it leaves the original lines and
just puts a copy of them somewhere else. DELETE can be used to delete the
current line. If DELETE is followed by a number this means to delete that
many lines beginning with the current one.

Most line editors employ mnemonic commands similar to those described
here (Ledgard et al., 1980). But, some do not. For example,
REPLACE "giving" with "awarding"
might be done with some editors via something like
s.,/giving/awarding/p

It is generally agreed that editors that use terms and syntax that are more like English are easier for people to use. Many editors that have mnemonic commands allow experienced users (they might still be non-programmers, but experienced non-programmers) to enter abbreviations to save time. Thus, our system allows you to say

REP "giving" with "awarding"

or even

REP "giving" "awarding"

SCREEN EDITORS

Line editors do have some disadvantages. First, a lot of command lines have to be entered in order to do relatively-simple things (like changing the second "e" in "leeding" to an "a"). Second, to replace text you have to type the incorrect item as well as the replacement. (cf., the need to type "leeding" again in order to correct the misspelling). Third, the screen reflects a history of the work session rather than showing only the text on file. For example, in figure 1 the person using the editor employed the PRINT command at the end because it was difficult to tell what was really on file as a result of all the previous commands.

With screen editors a whole "window" (about 20 lines) of text can be seen at once. In addition to the lines of text the screen also contains an indicator called a "cursor" that indicates the current position where text will be entered when it is typed. Changes are made by moving the cursor up, down, left, or right via some special keys (these are sometimes called "cursor keys" or "function keys") or other positioning devices, and then by simply typing over existing text. Furthermore, instead of typing in commands, with a screen editor a lot of things can be accomplished with function keys (or special multi-key sequences). For example, lines can be deleted, blank lines can be added, lines can be moved, etc.

Screen editors make finding and replacing text very easy, but there are some problems associated with them. First, they usually take a lot more system resources than line editors since they must be able to address and alter any of the entire screen contents (not just the "current" line). Second, the function keys and special key sequences mentioned above frequently have little mnemonic value.

FIRST EXPERIMENT

Subjects

Eighteen Purdue University students were the subjects. The participants were all non–programmers in order to test the ease of learning to use text editors for subjects with no previous experience with them. The subjects were randomly split into two groups (9 in each group) - assigned to each of the two editors, line and screen. Each experimental session lasted approximately one hour.

Apparatus

The computing system serving the Department of Computer Science at Purdue University has editors of both line and screen types. This experiment was conducted using four video terminals located in separate rooms to minimize distractions. The study was run from 5:00 p.m. to 8:00 p.m. on four weeknights to minimize the system response time.

The experimental sessions were automated to insure objective data collection. Each subject was guided through the session via a program that presented a tutorial about the editor and then exhibited files to be edited. A copy of each file was made at the end of each session and timing information was also recorded by this program.

Procedure.

Participants were given a brief, standardized introduction to the appropriate editor. Each subject was then given a tutorial to illustrate the use of several editor commands and to allow practice with the editor. These command subsets allowed subjects to add, change, and delete characters and lines in the files. Given the commands they had been taught and the limitations in flexibility imposed by these commands, subjects were given free rein in deciding how to make each correction; i.e., the manner in which a change was made was unimportant as long as it resulted in a proper correction.

Subjects received an incorrect version of the tutorial file on their screen and were told to correct it to match a paper copy of the file. The corrections to be made were highlighted on the paper to facilitate the subjects' tasks. There were sixteen changes to be made in the incorrect tutorial file; the practice session ended when all of these corrections had been completed.

After completion of the tutorial, each subject was asked to perform similar kinds of corrections in a different, test file. Subjects were again given a paper copy of the correct file in which the changes they were to make had been highlighted. Each subject was allowed to make changes in the test file for fifteen minutes, at which time the experimental session ended. The test file contained 42 errors to be corrected. No subject was able to finish the task in the allotted time.

Results

The time the subjects required for completion of the tutorial is shown in figure 2. Subjects required about 17% more time to learn to use the line editor (i.e., to complete corrections to the tutorial file) than the screen editor. This difference is statistically significant at the .05 level.

Performance with the editors was measured in terms of the number of corrections made in the test file (see figure 3). Only complete, requested corrections were counted. Subjects made approximately 40% more corrections with the screen editor than with the line editor. This difference is also statistically significant at the .05 level.

Editor	Mean Time Spent on Tutorial
Line	28 minutes
Screen	24 minutes

Figure 2. The line editor subjects required more time to complete the tutorial than the screen editor group.

Editor	Mean Number of Corrections Made
Line	20 corrections
Screen	27 corrections

Figure 3. The screen editor subjects made more corrections in the restricted time test following the tutorial than did the line editor subjects.

163

SECOND EXPERIMENT

Subjects

Eleven non–programmer Purdue University students were the subjects. They were randomly split into two groups assigned to each of the two editors, line (5 subjects) and screen (6 subjects).

Apparatus

In contrast to the first experiment, performed on terminals using the Department's primary computing system, for the second experiment a small well–known personal computer with both line and screen editors was used. The study was run from 7:00 p.m. to 10:00 p.m. on four weeknights.

Procedure.

Participants were given a brief, standardized introduction to the appropriate editor. Each subject was then given a tutorial to illustrate the use of several editor commands and to allow practice with the editor. As in the first experiment, subjects received an incorrect version of a file on their screen and were directed to correct it to match a paper copy of the file. Each subject was allowed to make changes in the test file for fifteen minutes. No subject was able to finish the task in the allotted time.

Results

Performance was again measured in terms of the number of corrections made in the test file (see figure 4). Again subjects made approximately 40% more corrections with the screen editor than with the line editor. This difference is statistically significant at the .05 level.

Editor	Number of Corrections Made
Line	19 corrections
Screen	26 corrections

Figure 4. The screen editor subjects made more corrections than did the line editor subjects.

DISCUSSION

The results from these two experiments consistently show that for non–programmers the screen editor was superior to the line editor in terms of both ease of learning and in performance of the subjects. Possible reasons include both the fewer keystrokes required to correct most errors as well as the inherently–more–clear display of the file (rather than the history of the editing session) with the screen editor.

Although the screen editor was found to be the more efficient editor tested, it is important to realize that only a limited number of commands were included in this study. These command sets were not able to provide an assessment of the full power of either editor, because they only provided non–programmers with a working knowledge of the editors. The ease of use of line editors and screen editors should be further tested with an enlarged set of commands. Furthermore, these results may not generalize to the realm of experienced programmers. It remains to be shown that these results are programmer/non–programmer independent.

We do not suggest that these two small, University experiments settle the issue concerning the use of editors by non–programmers. Instead, it is hoped that the results of these experiments will simply inspire more investigation.

ACKNOWLEDGEMENTS

The author expresses his deepest appreciation to the students who participated in the design, conduct, and analyses of these experiments - Adkins, J., Boss, D., Brandes, M., Collins, N., Crow, J., Driscoll, P., Michtom, G., Moore, N., Notarnicola, R., and O'Keefe, B. A good deal of thanks is also due to the students who were our subjects in these experiments. Special appreciation to J. Adkins whose report on the first experiment is the basis for much of the experimental results reported herein.

REFERENCES

Ledgard, H. F., Whiteside, J. A., Seymour, W., and Singer, A., 1980. An experiment on human engineering of interactive software. IEEE Transactions on Software Engineering, 6: 602–604.

Shneiderman, B., 1980. Software Psychology: Human Factors in Computer and Information Systems. Winthrop, Cambridge.

Human—Computer Interaction, edited by G. Salvendy
Elsevier Science Publishers B.V., Amsterdam, 1984 — Printed in The Netherlands

MNEMONIC CODES FOR ENTITY IDENTIFICATION IN DATABASE SYSTEMS

E.R.F.W. CROSSMAN

Department of Industrial Engineering and Operations Research,
University of California, Berkeley, CA 94720

ABSTRACT

The concepts of entity and entity set, as used in contemporary database design, imply a need for designer-assigned identifiers serving to link each real world entity with its associated logical record(s) within the database. To date the literature does not reveal any systematic discussion of identifier construction goals and process, though several studies have dealt with the human-efficiency of particular codes. To open discussion on this practically significant topic, the paper proposes a classification scheme and a code-construction procedure for one of the four classes recognized.

Qualitative and quantitative goals are outlined and the following classes of alphanumeric identifiers are distinguished:- (1) Full-names used directly, (2) Arbitrarily assigned numeric values, (3) Fully mnemonic abbreviations, and (4) Partially mnemonic abbreviations. Attention is focussed on the fourth class and a five-step construction procedure is suggested for use by system designers and application developers.

The code-construction process and results are illustrated by reference to:- (1) A departmental nominal roll (129 entities, 7.01 bits), and (2) A city's streets (2032 entities, 10.99 bits). Both were designed to meet data recording and reporting needs of a city maintenance department and are now in regular service.

Relevant computer-efficiency and human-efficiency factors are mentioned but not discussed in depth. the difficulty of empirically evaluating candidate codes is briefly discussed.

INTRODUCTION General background and objectives

Possibly because its solution has often seemed obvious, the generic problem of data-coding for transfer of information from humans to computers and vice versa seems to have hitherto received less attention than its practical importance warrants. Optimal results in this area call for careful consideration of human characteristics in relation to those of computer hardware and software, hence it properly falls within the scope of this Conference.

I will not attempt to review the overall scope of the data-coding problem, but rather will consider a particular subclass of such problems, namely that of assigning unique identification symbols or "identifiers", themselves often called "codes", to entities whose attributes are to be stored and reported back in database systems. The conventional solution, which seems to have been adopted by default, is arbitrary numeric coding. This is certainly computer-efficient but in my opinion unnecessarily human-inefficient. I contend that with reduced hardware costs this solution should now be reconsidered, and that future identification codes should be constructed with mnemonic principles in mind, thus securing a gain in human efficiency while still preserving acceptable computer efficiency.

My approach will be heuristic. Deferring presentation of a full theoretical analysis to a later report, I will confine myself to setting out broad goals and outlining a practical code-construction procedure which I have found to work in the eight or ten cases so far considered within the framework of recent system development efforts undertaken in California cities. Because I cannot currently present formal empirical evidence to prove that my proposed solutions to the entity-coding problem are better than anyone else's, I will in effect be setting up hypotheses for future empirical test. In my opinion there is room for much experimental work in this area. I hope to report some of it, and perhaps hear others report more, at future conferences on Human-Computer Interaction.

Symbols used for Data-storage in Humans and Computers

Most commercial and industrial computer applications, as well as many engineering and scientific ones, call for entry, storage, recall and processing of symbolic data describing real world objects, events and transactions. Before this sophisticated audience I'm sure I don't need to cite examples.

Because computer-storable symbols must be expressed as bit strings, while, for the present purpose at least, humans can be considered to use words selected from the lexicon of some natural language, all such applications must provide for word-to-binary and binary-to-word translations, associated respectively with the data entry and data dislay stages of the system as indicated below.

```
Physical      External         Internal         External      Displayed Imagined
entity  Name identifier       identifier       identifier     name      entity
             (Human symbols)  (Computer symbol) (Human symbols)
O---)---(O)-->-O->------o--------O--------o---------O------->-O---->----O
recognition,
  naming,        data     data     data     data     data     name-
  association     entry   storage  retrieval decoding display  recognition
  to identifier
  value
```

Dataflow and coding processes for entity recording & reporting.

Input/output complementarity

In cases where names are entered directly as identifiers the input (en)coding and output (de)coding processes bear a reciprocal relationship to one another, so that in simple storage and recall of object-related data the words displayed will be the same as those entered, and the computer-produced output symbols will be the same as the computer-acceptable input symbols. However because of the mismatch between human and computer symbolism this seldom represents an efficient solution to the entity-identification problem.

The remainder of this paper discusses statistical design principles and methods for construction and assignment of entity identifiers used in data management systems of this generic type, which are usually though not necessarily computer based. Ideally we should consider codes used at both ends of the system, but for brevity and because the two bear a roughly reciprocal relationship to one another I will discuss only the front end, i.e. the code utilized at data-entry time. We can reasonably assume that whatever code is used for data entry will be reversed for data display.

Before proceeding I want to make clear that this is a software problem, solutions being expressed as tables either in print or stored in an application program or database. Naturally in an actual system the software, including identifier/full name tables, will be executed using familiar hardware interfaces such as keyboards and CRT screens with all their attendant problems of display/control compatibility, legibility, etc. However, for the present purpose we leave these on one side.

Literature

So far as I am aware this particular class of software problems has received no explicit consideration in the computer-science literature, though Shannon and Weaver (1949) long ago set out a very clear quantitative framework for discussion of coding problems in communication systems. A few

empirical studies have been reported in the Human Factors literature
indicating awareness that data entry and display coding problems exist, and
some tentative solutions have been developed and evaluated (Miller, 1977;
Wright et al., 1977). Aume & Topmiler (1970) in particular made a strong
empirical case for adoption of a mnemonic code for faults occurring in
certain military systems, but because they did not discuss the process used
to design the specific code tested, their report seems to have limited
relevance to problems faced by designers in other application environments.

Application goals

Because each particular application problem calls for a solution adapted
to its specific circumstances and user experience, application engineers
need generic solution procedures and evaluation tools rather than
prepackaged specific solutions. Therefore my goal will be to develop
practically useful code-construction rules and procedures rather than to
argue the merits of codes for particular cases.

Accordingly, after outlining some theoretical background and developing
needed definitions, the remainder of the paper is devoted to setting out
what I claim is a practical method of constructing partially mnemonic
abbreviation codes and presenting a couple of illustrative problems whose
solutions have been put into (so far) successful service. Naturally I will
welcome critical appraisal of the results, and suggestions for improved
methods and techniques.

Empirical evaluation

Because the performance of my suggested solutions to the stated problems
has not yet been fully evaluated, I do not claim to have constructed perfect
or even absolutely "good" codes, only that they seem to perform better than
those a conventional systems analyst or applications engineer (i.e. one
perhaps less alert to human-efficiency considerations) would have been
likely to propose.

Actually formal empirical evaluation presents significant problems,
because once installed a code rapidly becomes ingrained and thereafter users
resist change, so that alternates cannot be tested with the same user
population. In any case managers are rarely willing to risk significant
changes in currently satisfactory procedures even in the name of science.
In this respect the problem of evaluating ID codes resembles many other
Human Factors evaluation problems, and we will probably be forced to draw
somewhat less than totally watertight conclusions from comparisons across
different applications with different user populations, based on using

similar but not identical code-construction procedures.

THEORETICAL FRAMEWORK Database Systems and the Entity/Attribute/Set data model

I will assume familiarity with the general approach to data storage and retrieval that has been developed in recent years under the rubric of Database Systems (for a general review see for example Teorey & Fry, 1982). The conceptual framework that includes Entities (Martin, 1983), Entity-sets (Pasel et al., 1983), and Relationships between entities (Chen, 1978) has emerged as a major organizing principle for use in mapping real world operations and their recording/reporting needs onto logical records and larger database structures.

In brief the idea is that any operationally interesting fact or datum can be modelled as an "attribute" of some independently existing "entity", a member of a predefined entity-set, or perhaps of two or more such entities associated in a "relationship". Thus every storable attribute or descriptive variable, whose values are represented after attribute-coding in a logical data element and physically by the contents of a given field within a record, must "belong" to some logically defined entity, a member of a set of entities considered interesting (or potentially interesting) in the given database application. Each such logical record is considered as describing just one entity in a given set.

Unique Identification of entities

The entity-identification problem arises because for uniqueness of reference each entity must be operationally distinguishable, and logically distinguished, from all others in the same set. This logical distinctness is physically expressed in the database by uniqueness of values of one or more attributes stored in the physical record. These unique recorded values of course serve as "keys" for retrieval of desired records, from which the values of other attributes or variables can be read off and displayed for use in managerial decision-making, etc. Because the term "key" implies a physical search operation with which we are not directly concerned, I will use the more neutral term "identifier" for recorded attributes which permit unambiguous reference to particular entity-records within a given set.

To take a familiar noncomputer example from the campus environment, which also serves to introduce the idea of mnemonic coding of identifiers:- HUMAN-FACTORS (journal) is considered as a member of the entity set SERIAL and is recorded in our microfiche catalog as being available in ENGI, a member of the entity set LIBRARY. Other recorded attributes of HUMAN-FACTORS are its subject code, shelf location, starting year, and circulation status. The entity-set LIBRARY contains 65 members given in a printed list, each of which has recorded attributes such as building location, opening hours, etc. In this case the abbreviation ENGI serves as an identifier, and anyone given this identifier is assumed able to find the entity referenced (the Engineering Library), and hence retrieve Human Factors journal when needed. Because of a possible conflict with the English Library, etc., in this case a unique fully mnemonic identifier based on the full name requires at least 4 letters.

Computer-efficiency of identifiers

In contemporary practice computer databases are structured so that each logical record "describes" just one entity (or entity-set if the attributes of interest are aggregates). Updates are applied to single records and the most detailed type of query may call for display of the values of one (or more) attribute(s) retrieved from one such record. Some form of DataBase Management System(DBMS) software is normally responsible for retrieving the logical record corresponding to the identifier value included in an update command or query submission. this is accomplished by repeated comparison with identifier values stored in indexes, search, trees, etc.

It can be inferred from this brief description that identifier length (= number of characters) will have a significant effect on the cost of physical data entry, storage, updating and retrieval of records, and on the time taken to execute such operations, usually termed "performance". Computer cost and performance considerations therefore suggest using the shortest possible identifiers consistent with uniqueness within each given entity set.

Information content of identifiers

Following Shannon and Weaver (1949) we note that the amount of information I_r required to identify an entity within a set of N is given by $I_r = \log_2 N$ bits. The amount of information I_a available from an L-character identifier using an alphabet with S alternate symbols is given by $I_a = L.\log_2 S$ bits. Computer-efficiency of a given identifier is indicated by the ratio I_r/I_a, which I shall call Utilization, U. Its maximum possible value is unity (or 100%), which implies ideal computer-efficiency.

Full names used directly as identifiers typically show low utilization when evaluated for use in a limited application environment. To analyze the library case a little further though it actually does not involve a computer, the typical 25 characters in the full name of a LIBRARY contain $I_a = 25\log_2 26 = 25 \times 4.70 = 117.50$ bits as against a required amount

$I_r = \log_2 65 = 6.00$ bits (for libraries on the U.C. campus), indicating only 5.1% utilization. The four-letter abbreviation contains 18.84 bits, for a much better 31.3% utilization.

Human-efficiency of the identification process

Unlike computers, humans recognize entities directly, and can often identify them by name, using proper names, nouns plus adjectives, etc., to ensure uniqueness of reference. For general human discourse this uniqueness must be attained within the total field of knowledge rather than within a limited application environment, though as we are all aware abbreviations are rapidly adopted by groups of people concerned with a limited topic or situation. Because of the needed universality, full names are normally quite long in relation to the amount of entity identification information conveyed.

The identifier determination process may operate by associating (in the psychological sense) assigned values directly to recognized entities, but only if the operator "knows" the appropriate code. If he or she does not know the code it will be necessary to look up the correct value in some form of reference document. Just as within the computer, a key will be required to retrieve the correct record, and in most cases the full name, itself determined by association to the entity, serves this function, so it is a natural choice for adoption as a direct identifier within the computer.

Without going into the various ramifications of the search process, you will probably agree that external visual or other search is slower than memory recall or mental computation. Therefore human-efficiency considerations suggest assignment of identifiers that lend themselves either to rapid memorization or to online construction based on currently available data, of which the most frequently available are full names. I note in passing that strictly speaking the term "mnemonic" connotes only rapid memorization. This however I shall use here to cover both modes of functioning.

CLASSIFICATION OF IDENTIFICATION CODES

Before proceeding to suggest procedures for constructing identifiers which jointly optimize human- and computer-efficiency, I will review some code-construction options which fall into a simple taxonomic scheme that will guide us in searching for solutions.

Direct use of full names as identifiers

This approach was mentioned above and is repeated here for completeness.

Arbitrarily assigned numerical identifiers

The second option considered is the conventional approach which assigns a unique usually decimal numerical valued "code" to each entity in the given set, using as many digits as are needed to ensure uniqueness of reference. We are all familiar with this approach, which is quite ubiquitous and clearly computer-efficient in the terms outlined above. It is human-efficient in terms of the number of keystrokes required for data entry and query submission once the desired value is known, but this character level efficiency may be gained at the expense of significant table lookup and value verification costs incurred by original informants, data entry operators, managers submitting queries, etc.

A computer centered approach such as this was very clearly justified in earlier days when equipment costs dominated costs of operator and user time, but with diminished hardware and increased labor costs I suggest that it should no longer be automatically accepted.

Fully mnemonic abbreviation identifiers

As illustrated by the library example above, many entity names lead themselves to abbreviation in such a way that knowledgeable users can confidently reconstruct the identifier from the full name and vice versa, or else, which may be more human-efficient, directly recall an identifier based on (psychological) association to the recognized entity. I shall call this approach, where all of the characters in the identifier are also present in the full name, "fully mnemonic abbreviation". Its feasibility and effectiveness depend on various features of the full names themselves, as well as on the relationships between the names of the different entities within the set being identified.

Partially mnemonic abbreviation identifiers

As illustrated in the examples below full names and hence fully mnemonic abbreviations, are often found to differ by only a few characters. If these differences occur at irregular locations, little and/or arbitrary abbreviation may be all that is compatible with uniqueness. In such cases it seems appropriate to create a hybrid code combining features of both arbitrary numeric and fully mnemonic abbreviation identifiers. To do so we can use substrings selected from the full name and break ties (resolve conflicts) by appending short arbitrary numeric codes as needed.

Because even the knowledgeable user cannot confidently construct identifier values solely from the full names of given entities, or vice versa, constructed in this way, I shall call them "semimnemonic abbreviation" identifiers. In my view this class represents the most

generally applicable approach to construction of mnemonic identifiers. The
next section outlines a procedure I have developed for constructing
identification codes of this type.

A PROCEDURE FOR CONSTRUCTING SEMIMNEMONIC IDENTIFIERS Outline and discussion

We start with a list of the "official" full names of the entire set of
entities to be identified. We express them in uppercase, and sort into
lexical order to facilitate finding conflicts. Then we abbreviate the full
name as far as possible consistent with minimal identifier requirements, and
with ability of test-users to recognize the corresponding full names and/or
correctly reconstruct identifiers given full names. This will most likely
create conflicts and we proceed to restore uniqueness by appending otherwise
meaningless digits, which I shall call "discrimination-digits", as needed.

Rules are needed to determine how to abbreviate, for instance by simple
truncation, or by selecting initial letters, etc. While neither linguistic
nor cognitive psychology literatures appear to have established any general
principles to guide us here, the primacy and recency effects found to occur
in free recall (Murdock, 1962) suggest that we should selectively preserve
initial and/or terminal character strings of single-word names. But how
should this rule be applied to multiword and hyphenated names?   Experiments
so far suggest that initials of multiword names (i.e. acronyms) are better
recognized and constructed than the same number of characters taken from the
first name only.   But because codes are constructed for specific sets of
entities, generalized properties seem less important than intra-set
resolution of conflicts arising in recognition, etc.

However a principle that does seem clearly required is that of
regularity, for user's identifier-reconstruction efforts will be much
facilitated by predictability in the application of abbreviation rules.   We
should therefore value uniformity above association-value in creating
abbreviation rules for any given case, and we · should as far as possible
avoid totally arbitrary abbreviations.   For much the same reason
discrimination-digits should be assigned in lexical sequence of abbreviated
strings, so that users can determine their values with reasonable assurance
based on conventional lists of names.

Summary of proposed procedure

In summary we proceed as follows:- 1) List definitive and correctly
spelled versions of the full names of each entity in the set being
considered. 2) Transform into uppercase and sort into lexical sequence. 3)
Abbreviate (i.e. delete characters from) all of the listed names according
to regular rules until too many subsets of successive strings become

identical.   4) Designate those strings that are still unique as identifiers for the entities associated with the corresponding full names.   5) Append discrimination-digits 1,2,... etc. to the second, third, etc. members of subsets found to have identical abbreviations, and designate the resulting alphanumeric strings as identifiers.

   The exact meaning of "too many" in step 3 remains to be defined, and so far as I can see at the moment we have no prospects of arriving at a sound definition until the operational consequences of assigning various numbers of discrimination-digits have been explored experimentally. Meanwhile it must remain a judgement call for the designer. Naturally if the full names can be abbreviated adequately `before any subsets become identical, we terminate at step (4), assign no discrimination-digits, and simply designate the resulting fully mnemonic abbreviations as identifiers.

ILLUSTRATIVE EXAMPLES Employee identification within a city department
   The list of employees used in an absence and leave tracking database application contained 129 uppercase first name/last name pairs.   An arbitrary numeric identification code for entity EMPLOYEE in this case would of course require 3 digits.   Because some last names were duplicated (several members of the same family were employed by the department), a fully mnemonic abbreviation code was found to require two first name plus three last name characters, e.g. JANEW and JONEW respectively for James and John Newman (the worst conflict). This would be acceptable, possibly better than the semimnemonic solution considered later and finally adopted.

   Using conventional initials there were 100 unique diagrams and 29   2- or 3-way conflicts.   This would have required assignment of discrimination digits in 25 cases and was judged marginally unacceptable. Using the first name initial with the first two letters of the last name yielded 123 unique abbreviations and required assignment of discrimination-digits in only 3 cases.   This semimnemonic abbreviation code was judged preferable to either of the others just considered, and was put into service.   The resulting 4-character identifiers require an average 3.2 keystrokes per update or per query submission as against 3.0 in the arbitrary numeric case. We note in passing that the former three are alphabetic characters, unusable on a key-pad, so this solution could prove mechanically unacceptable in other circumstances, however in our case data entry is performed by touch-typing on a typewriter style keyboard so numerical characters are not distinguished from alphabetic ones.

Identification of city streets

A city's gazetteer listed 2,032 name/type pairs (10.99 bits), of which 1950 were alphabetic names with lengths ranging from short (A Street) to long (Grizzly Peak Boulevard), and 150 were numeric (108th Avenue). Types were the usual Street, Close, Court, etc. An arbitrary numeric code would require 4 digits (13.3 bits) and would clearly have been computer-efficient (U=83.5%), but operators would require considerable time to memorize such a long list, and meanwhile human-efficiency would suffer, therefore we explored mnemonic possibilities. Because the same name recurred with different types and vice-versa, and there were many compound names, a fully mnemonic abbreviation scheme was judged excessively complex, and seemed only slightly better than using the full name (i.e. name/type pair) directly.

To construct semimnemonic abbreviations the alphabetic name/type strings were separated out, compressed and truncated to length 3, yielding for example ABB for Abbey Street; this gave around 1000 unique 3-character abbreviations and called for assignment of 1200-odd discrimination digits and digit pairs ranging up to 19. The numerically named streets were already unique, and were truncated to length 3 through 5, with two or three somewhat arbitrary abbreviations of the "type". As finally assigned all identifiers had lengths 3 through 5, excluding implicit terminal zeros which was turned into spaces.

The average number of nonblank characters assigned was 4.8 (24.82 bits), for 43.8% utilization. A small sample of the final listing is given below to illustrate the result, which was put into service about 9 months ago. It was now being borrowed by other departments which had apparently long needed a compact coding scheme for street identification.

Abbey Street	ABB	Ziegler Avenue	ZIe	Second Avenue	2AV
Abbott Drive	ABB1	Zinn Drive	ZIN	Second Street	2ST
Aberfoil Avenue	ABE	Zorah Street	ZOR	Third Avenue	3AV
Acacia Avenue	ACA	First Avenue	1AV	Third Street	3ST
Acalanes Drive	ACA1	First Avenue Place	1AVP		

CONCLUSION

It seems apparent from the foregoing analysis and discussion that the problem of constructing globally efficient identification codes is not as simple as the textbooks suggest when one attempts to improve human as well as computer efficiencies. I have only been able to scratch the surface of the subject here, and I anticipate a very interesting period ahead as the various relevant skills and varieties of experience are brought to bear on this significant problem area in Human/Computer Interaction.

176

REFERENCES
Aume, N.M., and Topmiller, D.A., 1970. An evaluation of experimental how-malfunctioned codes. Human Factors 12, 261-269.
Chen, P.P., 1976. The entity-relationship model - toward a unified view of data. ACM Trans. on Database Systems 1 9-36.
Martin, J., 1982. Strategic Data-planning Methodologies Englewood Cliffs: Prentice Hall.
Miller, I., 1977. Computer entry of product information by housewives. Human Factors 19 201-203.
Murdock, B.B., 1962. The serial effect of free recall. J. Exper. Psychol. 64 482-488.
Pasel, D.P., Malhotra, A., and Markowitz, H.M., 1983. The system architecture of EAS-E: An integrated programming and database language. IBM Systems J. 22 188-198
Shannon, C.E., and Weaver, W., 1949. The Mathematical Theory of Communication Urbana: U. of Illinois Press.
Teorey, T.J., and Fry, J.P., 1982. Design of Database Structures Englewood Cliffs: Prentice Hall
Wright, P., Aldrich, A., and Wilcox, P., 1977. Some effects of coding answers for optical mark reading on the accuracy of answering multiple-choice questions Human Factors 19 83-87

Human—Computer Interaction, edited by G. Salvendy
Elsevier Science Publishers B.V., Amsterdam, 1984 — Printed in The Netherlands

EFFECTS OF COMMAND LANGUAGE PUNCTUATION ON HUMAN PERFORMANCE

Dean I. Radin

AT&T Bell Laboratories, 6200 E. Broad St., Columbus, Ohio 43213 USA

INTRODUCTION

Untold millions of computer commands are typed daily. The great majority of these commands use some form of punctuation to delimit elements of the command language. Considering the cumulative effort expended in typing these commands, it behooves us to ask whether certain punctuation delimiters are more efficient than others.

Only a few pertinant guidelines can be found in the literature. For example, in Smith and Aucella's (1983) extensive compilation of design guidelines, only two of over 500 recommendations referred to punctuation in command languages.

Likewise, few empirical studies have addressed performance effects of command syntax (cf Cooper, 1983). One exception is an experiment by Ledgard et al (1980). They investigated performance effects of two semantically identical text editors. One editor used colons and semicolons as command delimiters and the other used spaces as the primary delimiter. They found that both experienced and naive users were faster and more accurate with the space-based editor than the punctuated editor. Nearly twice as many errors were made with the punctuated editor.

The present experiments were designed to directly address performance effects of punctuation in command languages and to empirically test the guidelines offered in the literature.

EXPERIMENT 1: SPEED AND ACCURACY

Subjects were eighteen adults familiar with a variety of command languages their average typing rate was 60 wpm. Each subject was asked to type a command

in one of eight possible syntax styles displayed at the bottom of a video
display terminal (VDT) screen. The typed characters were echoed below the
original command. When the subject finished typing, she pressed a carriage
return key, the screen erased and two seconds later the next command appeared.
The computer timed each trial with 16 msec resolution from the initial display
of a command to hitting the carriage return key. Subjects were instructed to
type as quickly and as accurately as possible.

Examples of the eight syntax styles and results of the experiment are shown
in Table 1. Dependent measures were characters per second (cps) typing rate and
count of syntax errors in each condition. Ten commands were presented in each
of eight syntaxes for a total of 80 commands per subject. Presentation of
commands were counterbalanced between subjects and the 80 commands were
randomized within subjects. Data were analyzed by analysis of variance.

TABLE 1
Command formats and results of speed and accuracy experiment.

Syntax Name	Syntax Style	Example Command	Typing Rate*	Detected Errors+	Undetected Errors+
P3	:=,	ENT:MA=1PN,OR=3	2.68	123	10
P2	:= _	ENT:MA=1PN OR=3	2.78	122	14
P2	:_,	ENT:MA 1PN,OR 3	2.89	114	5
P2	_=,	ENT MA=1PN,OR=3	2.98	102	8
P1	:_ _	ENT:MA 1PN OR 3	3.12	125	9
P1	_=_	ENT MA=1PN OR=3	3.43	101	5
P1	_ _,	ENT MA 1PN,OR 3	3.48	73	8
P0	_ _ _	ENT MA 1PN OR 3	3.87	64	1

* Average characters per second
+ Total errors, summed across subjects

Results

In summary, 1) syntax styles resulted in different command entry rates
($p < 0.001$); 2) P0 syntax was faster than any other syntax ($p < 0.01$) and P3 syntax
was slower than all but the ":=_" syntax ($p < 0.01$); 3) adding from 0 (P0) to 3
(P3) punctuation marks decreased the entry rate ($p < 0.001$) and increased detected
syntax errors ($p < 0.001$); and 4) as detected errors increased, undetected errors
also increased ($r = 0.67$).

EXPERIMENT 2: READABILITY

Thirteen subjects were asked to find mismatches between pairs of commands displayed in either P3 or P0 syntax. Commands were presented on a VDT with the correct command near the top of the screen and the incorrect command near the bottom. The mismatch occurred in one of two ways: Two characters of the correct command were transposed or one character was changed (see Table 2).

TABLE 2
Readability experiment commands and results.

Name	Style	Example	RT*	Errors+
	Correct	ENT MA 1PN		
P0	Transpose	EN TMA 1PN	3.02	11
	Character	ENT MB 1PN	3.42	5
	Correct	ENT:MA=1PN		
P3	Transpose	EN:TMA=1PN	4.04	18
	Character	ENT:MB=1PN	3.90	9

  * Average characters per second
 + Total errors, summed across subjects

Subjects scanned for the first mismatched character in the bottom command. When found, they pressed the carriage return key to stop a clock and erase the screen, then they typed in the mismatched character. Each subject received 40 randomized trials containing 20 pairs each of P3 and P0 commands. Dependent measure was time to find a mismatch (in 16 msec intervals).

Results

P3 commands took longer to scan for mismatches than P0 commands ($p < 0.001$). Of 43 total errors, 27 occurred in the P3 condition, 16 in the P0 condition. A mismatch-type by syntax interaction revealed that subjects found character mismatches faster than transpose mismatches in the P3 condition and vice versa in the P0 condition ($p < 0.002$).

CONCLUSION

Punctuated commands result in lower entry speed, accuracy, and readability than semantically identical, space-based commands. Punctuated commands are probably more difficult to read since punctuation obscures word boundaries which are important redundant features of written language (Fisher, 1976).

Would practice overcome the effects of punctuation? Clearly people can and do adapt to heavily punctuated command languages, but people can also learn to transmit Morse code at rates comparable to typing speeds. Surely no one would then argue that keyboards should be replaced with telegraph keys. People can adapt, but at what cost in job performance and satisfaction? Therefore, when command language typing efficiency is important, the space should be used as the primary command delimiter.

REFERENCES

Cooper, William E. (Editor), 1983. Cognitive aspects of skilled typewriting. Springer-Verlag, New York.

Fisher, D. F., 1976. Spatial factors in reading and search: The case for space. In: R. A. Monty & J. W. Senders (Editors), Eye Movements and Psychological Processes. Erlbaum, Hillsdale, N.J.

Ledgard, H. Whiteside, J.A., Singer, A. & Seymour, W., 1980. The natural language of interactive systems. Communications of the ACM, 23, 10, 556-563.

Smith, S. L. & Aucella, A. F., 1983. Design guidelines for the user interface to computer-based information systems. MITRE Corporation Report MTR-8857.

Human—Computer Interaction, edited by G. Salvendy
Elsevier Science Publishers B.V., Amsterdam, 1984 — Printed in The Netherlands

METHODOLOGY REVISITED:
THE COGNITIVE UNDERPINNINGS OF PROGRAMMERS' BEHAVIOR[1]

Beth Adelson and Elliot Soloway

Cognition and Programming Project, Department of Computer Science
Yale University, New Haven, Connecticut 06520

ABSTRACT

In this paper we argue that there is significant utility in applying cognitive theory to human-computer interaction research. As an example, we use cognitive principles to (1) *explain* programmers' poor performance in the use of Pascal's WHILE loop, (2) *design* an alternative construct that does facilitate programmers' performance. Experimental results support our theoretical claims. Key to our practical success was our theoretical analysis.

GOALS AND MOTIVATION

The field of human-computer interaction research is gaining respectability because there is growing recognition that, afterall, people are the ones using computer systems. In this paper we argue that a methodology for research in this area that is rooted in cognitive theory is one that will result in both theoretical and practical payoffs. Why *should* this approach be useful? Because it provides *explanations* in terms of the mental mechanisms that are the driving force behind the observed behavior. Armed with such an understanding, we can *design* systems and languages with some hope of success; we won't be groping in the dark. Herein, we present an example of the use of this methodology which has resulted in just such a theoretical and practical payoff.

First we describe the surprisingly poor performance we observed of programmers using Pascal's WHILE loop. We go on to provide a cognitive explanation of that behavior. Next, we describe an alternative language construct designed on the basis of the cognitive explanation. Finally, we describe the successful testing of that construct with programmers. The theoretical analysis presented here significantly expands upon the empirical results published previously in Soloway, Bonar and Ehrlich, 1983.

THE BEHAVIOR: POOR PROGRAMMERS' PERFORMANCE

Consider the following programming problem:

[1]This work was sponsored by the National Science Foundation, under NSF Grants MCS-8302382 and IST-8310659.

> PROBLEM: Write a Pascal program which reads in a series of integers, and which computes the average of these numbers. The program should stop reading integers when it has read the number 99999. NOTE: the final 99999 should NOT be reflected in the average you calculate.

As reported in Soloway et. al 1984, we observed that that 86% of the novices, 64% of the intermediates and 31% of the advanced student programmers were *not* able to write a correct program for this problem. Correct performance involved generating a Pascal program like the one generated by one of our subjects and shown below.

```
PROGRAM Student6 (input, output);
VAR Count, Sum, Number : INTEGER; Average : REAL;
BEGIN
  Count := 0;
  Sum := 0;
  Read (Number);
  WHILE Number <> 99999 DO
      BEGIN
        Sum := Sum + Number;
        Count := Count + 1;
        Read (Number)
      END;
  IF Count > 0
      THEN
        BEGIN
          Average := Sum / Count;
          Writeln (Average);
        END
      ELSE
        Writeln ('No numbers input: average undefined');
END.
```

Knuth (1974) and Wegner (1979) have both described the WHILE loop as the "one and half loop." However, given that the WHILE construct is central to most Algol-like languages, and given that WHILE loops appear in a substantial number of programs, this behavior demands some deeper explanation.

THE COGNITIVE EXPLANATION

The strategy that the program shown above embodies can be characterized as:

```
Read (first value)
WHILE Test (i'th value)
    DO BEGIN
          Process (i'th value)
          Read (i+1st value)
    END
```

This means that on each iteration, in the body of the loop the *ith* value is processed and the *ith + 1* value is read in. We call this strategy "process i/read next-i" (henceforth referred to as process/read).

If we think about the cognitive processes involved in learning the process/read strategy we will see why it is a difficult one: The natural way to transform a set of elements in the physical world is to "get the first and process it", get the second and process it and so on, i.e., "read i/process i." Very early on we learn that a necessary precondition for transforming an element is having the element, which very likely entails getting it. Therefore we represent the sequence of getting an element and then processing it as a single chunk in short term memory. We also store this chunk in long term memory and retrieve it again, as a single entity, when we think about serial transformations. The read/process strategy is an effective one and thus is carried out repeatedly, which in turn, results in it becoming a strong representation in our minds. By contrast, the strategy of transforming "the first element and getting the next" is not likely to be built up as a single chunk in memory since the former is not a necessary precondition of the latter.

Suddenly, when learning to work in Pascal, the programmer finds that he cannot represent transforming a set of elements as the "read/process chunk" which he knows. Instead he finds that he must *rechunk* his knowledge so that he now represents serial processing as the second half of his read/process chunk followed by the first half of his read/process chunk. Rechunking a concept is a process which is error prone since it places a substantial strain on both short term memory's storage space and processing capacity. When the structure of the new, to-be-learned, chunk is not coherent the task becomes more difficult. Learning a incoherent chunk is made even more difficult when a meaningful chunk already exists as a representation.

Given the above cognitive explanation of why a read/process strategy is more likely to be developed, and why a process/read strategy would be harder to learn, we are in a position of explaining why our subjects had so much difficulty using Pascal's WHILE construct: the strategy underlying the effective use of the WHILE loop is process/read -- a cognitive strategy that runs counter to the strategy we hypothesize as the preferred one. Moreover, this explanation leads us directly to the design of a looping construct that would be easier to learn: one that enables subjects to use their preferred read/process strategy. In the next section, we report on an experiment in which we designed a construct that met this condition, and then tested to see if indeed it resulted in improved performance.

A COGNITIVELY MOTIVATED ITERATION CONSTRUCT

In the second part of the experiment reported in Soloway et. al 1984, new groups of novice, intermediate and advanced student programmers were asked to write a program to solve the same problem given above using a new construct:

PROBLEM: We have just designed a new language called Pascal-L. It is just like standard Pascal except that it does NOT have the WHILE, REPEAT, and FOR looping statements. Rather, Pascal-L has a new kind of statement: LOOP..LEAVE..AGAIN. The following describes how this new looping statement works:

```
LOOP
    statements-alpha
    IF expression LEAVE
    statements-beta
AGAIN
```

In this task, using the new looping construct provided by Pascal-L, subjects are given the opportunity to solve the averaging problem by using a read/process strategy. Based on our cognitive analysis, we predicted that performance would be improved using this construct since it facilitated subjects' preferred looping strategy.

In fact, we did find that novice, intermediate and expert subjects all made fewer errors when they used Pascal-L as compared to standard Pascal. (The percent incorrect for each group was 76%, 39% and 4% respectively.) The increase in performance is even more striking when we consider that whereas the subjects knew the standard Pascal WHILE construct they had never seen the Pascal-L LOOP[2] construct before the experiment.

CONCLUDING REMARKS

The significant increase in performance we observed in programmers using a looping construct whose design was cognitively motivated, lends support to two claims: (1) we were able to develop an accurate theoretical cognitive model that explains, in terms of the underlying mental mechanisms, why there was such poor performance for programmers when using Pascal's WHILE construct, and (2) we were able to achieve a practical benefit in the way of improved performance (an overall increase of 21%) by designing a construct that directly reflects our cognitive theory.

In closing, then, we have presented an argument for the use of cognitive theory in human-computer interaction research. In support of this claim we have presented on example in which a cognitive approach can in fact have theoretical and practical payoffs. In Soloway and Ehrlich 1984, and Adelson et al. 1984 we present other examples of this approach. While carrying through with such an approach is not without its problems, we feel that it can provide the basis upon which valuable, principled human-computer interaction research can be conducted.

REFERENCES

Adelson, B., Littman, D., Ehrlich, K., Black, J. and Soloway, E. (1984) Novice-Expert Differences In Software Design, First Conference on Human-Computer Interaction, London, in press.

Knuth, D. (1974) Structured Programming with GO TO Statements, *ACM Computing Surveys*, Vol. 6, No., 4.

Soloway, E., Bonar, J. and Ehrlich, K. Cognitive strategies and looping constructs: An empirical study. *CACM*, 1983, *26* (11), 1983.

Soloway, E., Ehrlich, K. (1984) Empirical Studies of Programming Knowledge, *IEEE Transactions on Software Engineering*, to appear.

Wegner, P. (1979) Programming Languages - Concepts and Research Directions, in *Research Directions in Software Technology*, MIT Press.

Human—Computer Interaction, edited by G. Salvendy
Elsevier Science Publishers B.V., Amsterdam, 1984 — Printed in The Netherlands

PRODUCTIVITY ANALYSIS IN SOFTWARE DEVELOPMENT
--- SOME EXPERIENCES ON INTERACTIVE SOFTWARE DEVELOPMENT ENVIRONMENT

K. Fujino

Software Product Engineering Laboratory, NEC Corporation, 5-7-15, Minato-ku, Tokyo 108, Japan

ABSTRACT
Whether man-machine interface of an interactive software tool is good or not is one of the most important issue to enhance the software development productivity. However, a good man-machine interface to a man in a certain phase is not always good to another man in another phase. In this paper, design strategies of software tools we developed and lessons to attain good man-machine interface learned by developing and using them are introduced. Examples shown in this paper cover whole software life cycle, that is, SPECDOQ for requirement, SDMS for design, editors for implementation, and FMT/TOMATO for management.

INTRODUCTION

Various types of software have to be produced, because of wide variety of C&C products, ranging from micro computer based key telephone, mini computer based control system, to very large mainframe computer. In this circumstance, in order to educate software personnel and keep them rotatable so as to utilize software personnel resource maximum, improving and unifying software technologies is one of the most important issues. Among them, improving and unifying man-machine interface of interactive software environment is essential.

Since utilizing software tool requires training and lots of practices, ill designed, ununifyed man-machine interface may causes error, law productivity and user exhausted.

Software Product Engineering Laboratory was established in 1980, with a mission of improving corporate wide software productivity. Since then much effort have been made to develop, evaluate and prevail software engineering tools and methodologies.

In this paper several lessons we have obtained through our activities are discussed, especially from the view of man-machine interface productivity impact.

SPECDOQ

SPECDOQ (Kitagawa, 1984) is a form based specification management system, which has such function as form editor, specification database, specification analyzer and open ended application interfaces.

Design strategies and characteristics of SPECDOQ man-machine interface are as follows.

* Use of forms with user-determined formats for creation and manipulation of requirements specifications.

* Multiple window environments for efficient utilization of several resources in the system.

* Combination of graphics icons and thumbwheels for direct manipulation of abstract objects.

* Japanese Kanji/Kana character handling to enable Japanese people to capture semantics of specifications easily.

Following comments are obtained from the result of trial use and evaluation of the prototype version.

* Forms are very general and helpful tools for entry and editing of data including diagrams, text, and alphanumeric data. In addition, such form-based documents are appropriate units for people to manipulate and understand specifications.

* Graphics man-machine interface consisting of multiple windows, graphics icons, and thumbwheels is friendly and attractive for users. Efficient access to system function and resources is realized.

* The thumbwheels are useful for designing forms which usually consist of vertical and horizontal lines, while the mouse is efficient for selecting icon.

* Use of Natural Language (for us Japanese, Kanji/Kana characters) is vitally important for understanding the contents of documents, especially requirement specification, and system messages at a glance.

SDMS (Software Development and Maintenance System)

SDMS (Iwamoto, 1981, 1983) is an integrated tool which support software development and maintenance throughout software life cycle.

Design strategies and characteristics of SDMS design support function are as follows.

* To provide System Description Language which define software system structure by functional hierarchy and relation among units of target system.

* To provide automatic specification analysis function which can detect inconsistency.

* To support documentation.

Lessons learned from the experience of the project are as follows.

* Originally the system generated a chart from SDL. But afterwards, the system was enhanced, by taking into consideration user's requirement, to have new function which translate pictorial language into SDL. A designer can input a system description by pictorial language using graphic editor. The effect to reduce a syntax error and support design process is great.

* As a sub-effect, user can define customized pictorial language. For example, special state transition diagram is defined for electronic switching system

software.

EDITORS AS IMPLEMENTAION TOOLS

There are several well known editors implemented on UNIX environment (Joy, 1980a, b, Kernighan, 1978a, b, Rand Corp., 1980). Comparison among them are shown in TABLE 1.

From the man-machine interface viewpoint, followings can be claimed.

* An experienced programmer tends to use "vi" while a novice or a person who uses an editor just for making text intends to use "e".

* "Emacs" is convenient for a user who wants to customize an editor for himself.

* Various levels of editors are required for better man-machine interface, provided various kind of persons, e.g. experienced, beginner, professional, part-timer, are working.

FMT/TOMATO (Friendly Management Tool/ Table Oriented Manager's Tool)

TOMATO (Azuma, 1982) is a tool which integrate relational database, spread sheet and business graphics functions.

Design strategy and characteristics of TOMATO are as follows.

* To develop a tool for software manager who has enough computer hardware and software knowledge to use but has no time to make a program for his own use.

* To facilitate catalogued procedure so that not only it can be used as independent tool but also as management system base.

Following lessons are learned through this project.

* Command is not easy to study even for experienced software manager. But when mastered, the speedyness and merit of catalogued procedure covers the demerit.

* An integrated tool is very effective compared with a set of independent tools.

* The early version of the system responded very slow because it was implemented by BASIC on 8 bits personal computer environment. Not a few users complained of it and quitted to use it no matter how they liked the function. After it was modified and transferred to more powerful 16 bits personal computer, the response became quick enough, and, as a result, it acquired many users. Users are very sensitive to response time of a system, even it is implemented on a personal computer.

CONCLUSION

Applying interactive software tools is one of the best solution to enhance productivity and quality of software. However, in order to make the tool really effective, to improve man-machine interface is vitaly important.

In this article, several experiences which may help to improve man-machine interface are described. It shows that evaluation criteria varies depending on user's properties, e.g. experience, profession, type of work, and so on. Therefore, more experiences should be accumulated, and analyzed deliberately. Especially for non alphabetic character language people, like Japanese, to attain good man-machine interface is a long way, because to input thousands of Kanji/ Kana character is still a big problem to be solved.

REFERENCE

Azuma, M., 1982. Table and Graphics Tools Integration for Improving Office Productivity. Proceedings of COMPSAC 82. IEEE, Chicago, 87 pp.
Iwamoto, K. and Shigo, O., 1981. Unifying Data Flow and Control Flow Based Modularization Techniques. Proceedings of COMPCON Fall 81. IEEE, Washington D.C., 271 pp.
Iwamoto, K., Yoneda, K., and Nakano, e., 1983. Humanized Output of System Structure Graphics From System Design Description. Proceeding of COMPCON Spring 83. IEEE, San Francisco, 236 pp.
Gosling, J., 1982. Unix Emacs. Carnegie-Mellon Univ.
Kitagawa, H., Gotoh, M., Misaki, S., and Azuma, M., 1984. From Document Management System SPECDOQ - Its Architecture and Implementation -. Proceedings of the 2nd ACM Conference on Office Information Systems. ACM, Toronto.
Joy, W., 1980a. An Introduction to Display Editing with Vi. UNIX Programmer's Manual 2C. Univ. of California, Berkeley.
Joy, W., 1980b. Ex Reference Manual Version 3.5/2.13. UNIX Programmer's Manual 2C. Univ. of California, Berkeley.
Kernighan, B. W., 1978a. A Tutorial Introduction to the UNIX Text Editor. UNIX Programmer's Manual (Seventh Edition). Bell Laboratories.
Kernighan, B. W., 1978b. A Advanced Editing on UNIX. UNIX Programmer's Manual (Seventh Edition). Bell Laboratories.
Rand Corp., 1980. The Rand Editor, E. Rand Corp.

TABLE 1

Editor comparison on UNIX

Editor	Function	Command Features	Command Customization	User's level	Other
ed	Line editor for low speed or hardcopy terminal	-Simple but needs knowledge of RE(Regular Expression) for free format correction	Non	all	Helpful if RE is applicable
e	Multi-window full-screen editor for text editing	-Easy to remember -Some text formatting commands.	Function key mappable	Novice to middle	Suitable for documentation
vi	Fullscreen editor for programming	-Many escape and control-keys should be remembered -Abbreviation for long word	Function key mappable	Middle to high	Efficient if practiced
emacs	Multi-window. full-screen editor aiming good software development environment	-So many to remember -Job executable on same screen	Can bind any key action to original command	Hacker	Very efficient if fully practiced

Human—Computer Interaction, edited by G. Salvendy
Elsevier Science Publishers B.V., Amsterdam, 1984 — Printed in The Netherlands

STATISTICAL METHODOLOGY IN THE LITERATURE ON HUMAN FACTORS IN COMPUTER PROGRAMMING

JOHN M. HAMMER

Center for Man-Machine Systems Research, Georgia Institute of Technology, Atlanta, Georgia 30332 (USA)

INTRODUCTION
    This article examines some actual and recommended practices for design of experiments in human factors of computer programming. The first practice examined is the actual level of power in the statistical tests conducted on controlled experiments. Power is defined as the probability of accepting the alternative hypothesis (that a difference exists) when it is true. Power depends on the number of subjects, the squared difference in means relative to subject variance (termed effect size), and the commonly reported significance level, usually p=.05. Because programmer variance is usually considered to be relatively high, statistical power was hypothesized to be relatively low in this literature. This hypothesis was tested by calculating the power of tests in the published literature and comparing the average power to recommended levels and to other similar studies.
    The second experimental practice examined was methods for controlling programmer variance. Basically, this was an examination of the literature for tests (e.g., grade point average, months of experience) that correlated with programmer performance. If good tests can be found, they can be used to make experiments more sensitive by accounting for the predicted performance in the experimental design.

POWER OF STATISTICAL TESTS IN THE LITERATURE
    Power has been defined as the probability of accepting the alternative hypothesis of a difference due to treatments, given that this hypothesis is true. In general, statistical testing involves establishing two mutually exclusive hypotheses. The first is the null hypothesis (H0) of no difference due to changes in the independent variable. The second is the alternative hypothesis (H1) that this difference does exist. There are Type I and Type II errors which correspond to H0 and H1, respectively. The probability of a Type I error (Type II error) is that of accepting H0 (H1) when it is false. Reported for virtually every statistical test is the probability of Type I error, or significance level (e.g., "p<.05"). Power, which is virtually always omitted, is 1 minus the probability of Type II error.
    Power is important both before and after an experiment. Before an experiment, power can be used to plan rationally the number of subjects to be used. The experimenter must select a significance level (usually, p=.05), a minimal power level (power=.80 is recommended (Cohen, 1977)), and an effect size. From power tables, the appropriate number of subjects can be determined. The most difficult selection is effect size, since it requires the experimenter to predict the cell means and the variance before the experiment is run. In this study, observed effect sizes are calculated and tabulated along with power. Knowledge of these observed values should be an aid to future experimental planning. Prediction can be based, at least partially, on past observation.
    Power is also important after an experiment, especially for interpreting effects that lack significance. Many researchers are reluctant to accept the

null hypothesis in this situation. In fact, a calculation of power reveals what should be done. If, for effects of interest, power is high, the null hypothesis might well be accepted. High power simply indicates that the posited effect size of interest would have been detected if it existed. If, on the other hand, power is low, judgment should be suspended until an experiment is run (or the existing one replicated) with more subjects or other precision-increasing refinements.

Literature Reviewed

Articles from journal articles and conference proceedings on human factors in computer programming were selected for power analysis. Technical reports and theses were not examined. This admittedly biases the results somewhat, since unpublished experimentation, especially that never committed to paper, is often suspected to have low power.

The literature of controlled experiments on software complexity was, notwithstanding the above, also omitted from the study. The reason is the fundamental difference in the goal of this area for explaining variance in human performance. Human factors experiments attempt to show that an experimental factor has a significant effect on human performance. As will be shown later, such a factor might typically account for 10 to 40% of the variance. Software complexity, on the other hand, tries to predict human performance as completely as possible. It typically can account for 60 to 80% of the variance.

Rules for Power Analysis

The rules for power analysis were as follows:
1. Only tests significant at $p \leq .05$ were examined even though other marginally significant results were reported. This practice further biases the observed power in an upward direction. Further, power was computed using $p=.05$ even if a lower p was stated. Only two-sided testing was used, even if the author(s) used one-sided tests.
2. Only ANOVA F-ratios, t tests, and correlation coefficients (r) were examined. Chi-square, binomial, and nonparametric tests were ignored. No tests on differences in means (Duncan, Newman-Keuls) were examined.
3. In ANOVAs, the significance of the overall mean and all interactions were ignored. The latter were ignored because interactions are not typically sought in most designs, are difficult to interpret in the framework of this study, and often could not be studied due to lack of information.
4. A maximum of 10 tests per experiment were analyzed for power. If an article reported more than one experiment, it could have up to 10 tests included for each experiment. This was done to avoid a bias in favor of experiments with many tests. The first ten tests presented were analyzed.
5. Sufficient information had to be present to do the power calculations (F-test: cell size, means; t-test: cell size; r: cell size). For F tests, the mean square error often had to be estimated from the expected value formula for F.
6. The test must have been on some aspect of human performance that was measured under controlled experimental conditions. Regressions between two variables, neither of which represented human performance, were ignored.

All F and t test measures of effect size were converted to the square root of percent variance explained to allow comparison with r (Cohen, 1977).

Results

The total number of tests that were power analyzed was 122. The power averaged .83; its standard deviation was .19. Only 36% of the tests had power less than the recommended value of .80. The effect size, expressed in terms of the square root of the percentage of variance explained, averaged .44; its number of computer science courses and program writing time. Their high correlations must not be viewed too enthusiastically, for they purposefully sought out very diverse groups of subjects. Higher correlations are expected under such situations (Montgomery and Peck, 1982).

For professional programmers, there does not appear to be any good predictor for debugging tasks. No significant correlations were found between experience and debugging time in (Grant and Sackman, 1967). Experience was not found significant on tasks of program comprehension, modification, or debugging in (Sheppard et al., 1979). This result is counter to the above findings of Chrysler and Moher and Schneider. They did find the number of known programming languages and the number of familiar FORTRAN concepts to be correlated with debugging performance for professionals with less than 3 years experience. This result did not hold for more experienced professionals.

For advanced computer science students, a number of highly predictive measures appear to be available. In (Moher and Schneider, 1981), multiple correlations of .66 to .74 were found between program comprehension and writing tasks and the regressors: number of computer science courses, computer science grade point, and years of programming. The advantage of these three regressors is that they are relatively independent.

For beginning programmers, many regressors were tried in (Barfield et al., 1983), (Lucas and Kaplan, 1974), (Mayer, 1975), and (Shneiderman, 1977). From the standpoint of having large correlation coefficients and appearing in more than one study, the best regressors would appear to be SAT-Math scores, college course grade(s) either in the introductory programming course or in calculus or chemistry, and years of experience programming. Given that many beginning students today will have personal computer experience, it should be included in any attempt to predict performance.

For both professional and student programmers, a pretest is a possible choice for a concomitant variable. If the experimental task is program comprehension, one or more initial program comprehension pretests (the same test(s) for all subjects) could be used as a concomitant variable. Correlations between 3 modification task scores ranged from .31 to .60 and between 3 modification scores and recall scores ranged from .39 to .49 (Shneiderman, 1977). Correlations between scores on reading and writing tasks varied from .63 to .69. One disadvantage of pretesting is additional resources invested in it. This may be especially so if multiple pretests must be given to determine a stable level of performance.

An alternative to any use of concomitant variables is repeated measures, in which a subject is run under every experimental condition in the experiment. The subject serves in effect as his or her own control. While this approach may at first seem to be ideal, problems can and do arise. Consult (Poulton, 1982) and (Greenwald, 1976) for details.

Conclusion

Methods have been discussed for reducing programmer variance through the use of a concomitant variable for randomized blocking. Using these results, it should be possible to increase substantially the precision of experiments on computer programming. Very little effort is required to sort subjects into relatively homogeneous blocks prior to random assignment to experimental conditions. Given the wide range of research from which these conclusions have been drawn, they should be regarded cautiously. The potentially large returns certainly merit investigation.

SUMMARY

This study has examined the literature on human factors in computer programming to study two aspects of programmer variance. The first was to determine if the reportedly large differences in programmers caused statistical tests to be of low power and effects small relative to noise. This appears to be untrue. The second aspect studied was methods for controlling for large programmer variance in experimental designs. A number of promising concomitant standard deviation was .14. The effect size data were roughly normally distributed, though skewed slightly to the right. Using Cohen's terminology of small (r=.10), medium (r=.25), and large (r=.50) effects, 67% of the effects are medium up to large, and 28% are large (Cohen, 1977). Using recommended medium effect size in pre-experimental power analysis would appear to be quite conservative, since less than 5% of the effects are less than medium.

Similar power analyses of other published literature have been done. Comparison of this study with others is difficult because we calculated effect sizes whereas others assumed various sizes and then determined the power. When an effect size of r=.50 was assumed (the closest value to our observed r=.44), the following were observed:

Study	Average Power	Tests with power<.80
Chase and Chase, 1976	.86	28%
Brewer, 1972	.78	29%
Katzer and Sodt, 1973	.79	46%

It should not be assumed that actual effect sizes in these other areas are as large as r=.50.

Conclusion

The power of tests in human factors literature on computer programming is as high as that in other areas where power analytic studies have been done. The original hypothesis of low power is incorrect. Ideally, experimenters would begin to incorporate a power analysis into their research planning. The distribution of (significant) observed effect sizes, as given above, should assist this planning.

VARIANCE CONTROL

Individual differences in programmer performance are a major problem in designing experiments. The ratio of best to worst performance for a group of programmers is often claimed to be 10:1 or 20:1 (Grant and Sackman, 1967) (Curtis, 1980) (Dickey, 1981) (Curtis, 1981). This difference is much larger than the 1.5:1 and 4:1 found for experts and intermediate level users, respectively, in a text editing task (Card et al., 1983). It should be noted that these large differences have been observed primarily on debugging times.

If tests were available to predict these differences to some degree, the predictions could be accounted for in the experimental design. The experiment would then become more sensitive, i.e., better able to detect true effect differences or to use fewer subjects. The appropriate designs which account for tests (termed concomitant variables) are randomized block designs and analysis of covariance (ANOCVA). The former uses the concomitant variable to group subjects into relatively homogeneous blocks. Each subject in the block is then randomly assigned to a treatment. ANOCVA performs a regression on concomitant variable simultaneously with an analysis of variance on the independent and dependent variables. ANOCVA is, however, not likely to be useful for two reasons (Keppel, 1973). First, ANOCVA requires many assumptions be true for it to be valid. Second, it is superior to randomized blocks designs only when the concomitant variable is correlated r>.60 with programmer performance. Since this is unlikely, randomized block designs would be preferred.

The results reported here are based on an examination of the same literature used in the power study. Basically, I looked at regression studies and experiments which had already attempted to account for programmer differences. Space limitations preclude the inclusion of a table which would allow direction examination of the correlations.

For professional programmers, months of programming experience has been found to be a fair predictor for program reading and writing performance. Correlations of .50 were found between the logs of experience and program writing plus debugging time (Chrysler, 1978). Correlations of .45 and .78 were found between experience and program comprehension scores (Moher and Schneider, 1981). They also found a multiple correlation of .62 between experience plus variables were identified for randomized blocking, which should be able to increase the precision of experiments in this area.

ACKNOWLEDGMENT

This research was supported under NSF Grant IST 82-17440.

REFERENCES

Barfield, W., LeBold, W.K., Salvendy, G., and Shodja, S., 1983. Cognitive factors related to computer programming and software productivity. Proc. Human Factors Society - 27th Annual Meeting, 647-651.

Card, S.K., Moran, T.P., and Newell, A., 1983. The Psychology of Human-Computer Interaction. Erlbaum, Hillsdale, NJ, 469 pp.

Brewer, J.K., 1972. On the power of statistical tests in the American Educational Research Journal. Amer. Educ. Res. J., 9: 391-401.

Chase, L.J. and Chase, R.B., 1976. A statistical power analysis of applied psychological research. J. Applied Psychol., 61: 234-237.

Chrysler, E., 1978. Some basic determinants of computer programming productivity. Comm. ACM, 21: 472-483.

Cohen, J., 1977. Statistical Power Analysis for the Behavioral Sciences. Academic, New York, 474 pp.

Curtis, B., 1980. Measurement and experimentation in software engineering. Proc. IEEE., 68: 1144-1157.

Curtis, B., 1981. Substantiating programmer variability. Proc. IEEE., 69: 846.

Dickey, T.E., 1981. Programmer variability. Proc. IEEE., 69: 844-845.

Grant, E.E. and Sackman, H., 1967. An exploratory investigation of programmer performance under on-line and off-line conditions. IEEE Trans. Human Factors Elec., 8: 33-48.

Greenwald, A.G., 1976. Within-subjects designs: To use or not to use? Psychol. Bull., 83: 314-320.

Katzer, J. and Sodt, J., 1973. An analysis of the use of statistical testing in communication research. J. of Communication, 23: 251-265.

Keppel, G., 1973. Design and Analysis: A Researcher's Handbook. Prentice-Hall, Englewood Cliffs, NJ, 658 pp.

Mayer, R.E., 1975. Different problem-solving competencies established in learning computer programming with and without meaningful models. J. Educ. Psychol., 67: 725-734.

Moher, T. and Schneider, G.M., 1981. Methods for improving controlled experimentation in software engineering. Proc. Fifth Int. Conf. Soft. Eng., 224-233.

Montgomery, D.C. and Peck, E.A., 1982. Introduction to Linear Regression Analysis. Wiley, New York, 504 pp.

Poulton, E.C., 1982. Influential companions: Effects of one strategy on another in the within-subjects designs of cognitive psychology. Psychol. Bull., 91: 673-690.

Sheppard, S.B., Curtis, B., Milliman, P., and Love, T., 1979. Modern coding practices and programmer performance. Computer, 12: 12, 138-146.

Shneiderman, B., 1977. Measuring computer program quality and comprehension. Int. J. Man-Machine Studies, 9: 465-478.

Human—Computer Interaction, edited by G. Salvendy
Elsevier Science Publishers B.V., Amsterdam, 1984 — Printed in The Netherlands

METRICS AND METHODOLOGIES FOR ASSESSMENT OF COMPUTER PROGRAMMER PERFORMANCE

J.J. O'HARE

Office of Naval Research, Arlington, VA 22217 (USA)

INTRODUCTION

Metrics or quantitative indices of merit have been diligently pursued for the several stages of the life cycle of software development with no consensus that the search has been successful (Perlis et al., 1981). However, a generally-accepted measure of the quality of the software product should precede system-atic measurement of computer-programmer performance. After a review of the candidate metrics and their application to programmer performance, the most promising option is identified. Numerous methodologies that analyze, express, or test the properties of software systems at the various stages of the software life cycle have been designed (Curtis, 1981). The techniques for the assessment of programmer performance have been as diverse as the behaviors that are generated during those activities (Shneiderman, 1930). A review of those methodologies leads to a conclusion on the most suitable technique for the measurement of programmer performance.

METRICS

Correct and efficient execution of the software system are primary measures; however, assessment of the development stages and processes prior to that point are troublesome with extensive effort placed on the determinants of production costs. Calculations of productivity, so important to the management and acquisition of software systems, is estimated in terms of the ratio of delivered source lines of code to the man-months of effort required (Basili, 1980). A nearly linear relationship has been reported (Basili, 1980) between each thousand lines of code (L) and man-months of effort (E): $E = 5.2 L^{.91}$; thus, productivity for 1 man-month is estimated to be 200 lines of delivered code. Sources of the variation observed for that equation were sought in 29 variables and their weightings permitted the development of a sensitive index of productivity. Such an index provides norms for various stages of program development and reference levels against which to evaluate new programming tasks, techniques, and procedures.

There also remains a requirement that the quality of the software system be high. A quality software system is characterized as easily understandable, modifiable, usable, and which offers other desired operational features (Basili,

1980). Metrics have been sought for each feature rather than a general index of quality since it is expected that the various features will be measured with scales of different power. Regrettably, the metrics that have been proposed for those features have not as yet been validated.

The feature of complexity which is an important element of quality has been defined by the software-code structure (Halstead, 1977) and by program-control flow (Basili, 1980), and those two quantitative metrics have been frequently tested. The latter metric that is based on counts of the number of linearly independent control-paths in a program remains at the level of a mathematical technique and addresses the computational complexity of a program. The former metric is of greater interest since it is concerned with psychological complexity and other features intuitively relevant to the programmer's understanding of a program. Its starting point is a simple count of the number of different operators (n_1) and operands (n_2) in a program, and their total number of occurrences (N_1, N_2). Operands include all variable names and constants. Operators consist of arithmetic symbols, delimiters, logical and arithmetic statements, names of functions, subroutines and entry points. From those elements a coherent theoretical schema has been constructed that includes the definition of the psychological effort (E) required at all stages of development: $E = n_1 N_2 (N_1 + N_2) \log_2 (n_1 + n_2) / 2 n_2$.

At the summary level when the computer program is in final form, E has provided good predictions of time to write a program, succeed in debugging, and other operations (Basili, 1980; Halstead, 1977); however, later studies show weaker predictive success for the E metric (Basili et al., 1983). On the other hand, when measurements are made at the level of the individual programmer, performance in terms of correctness and speed of understanding, debugging, and modifying code, the relationship to E is modest (Basili, 1980). Wide individual differences in programmer performance which have been estimated to range as high as a factor of 100 (Curtis, 1981) tend to obscure relationships. Nonetheless, in those studies the E metric was more predictive of the performance of the novice that the less-experienced programmers. Recent assessments of the theory have pointed out some of its incorrect assumptions about cognitive science (Coulter, 1983) while others (Shen et al., 1983) assert that the E metric is as good as others now in use.

Past measurements of programmer performance have been criticized on methodological (Brooks, 1980) and conceptual (Sheil, 1981) grounds, and there is some uncertainty on the choice of the proper metric. Correctness, speed, frequency of usage, and computer-resource demands have been measured in the course of programming studies but their suitability was weakened by the great variation between individual performers, persistent change with practice, low reliability, and the modest magnitude of the observed effects. The choice of metric is also strongly influenced by whether the objectives of the research are to reduce the cost of program development, to introduce an aiding procedure or different interface with the program, or to determine the elements underlying expert skill. The principal step toward that goal has come from research programs that attempt to discover the cognitive processes and knowledge elements that underlie programming procedures (Curtis, 1981), their frequency of usage, and the identification of their structure, abstractions, and organization. It is for those fundamental entities that metrics need to be devised since they offer the most promise for measuring programmer performance.

METHODOLOGIES

Tools and techniques are introduced to assure the integrity of the software development process from the statement of requirements to specifications, design, implementation, testing, and its modification. Many reporting systems have been designed to record errors, costs, the achievement of schedule milestones, time spent on each module during design, code and test, and related efforts such as the preparation of documentation. Management techniques have been introduced to enhance programming efficiency, such as chief programmer teams, structural programming, design and code inspections, and top-down development. Most of these methodologies analyze aggregated events in the developmental process and the results of Basili and Reiter (Basili, 1980) illustrate how difficult it is for such techniques to provide clear understanding of the impact of system procedures. In that study approximately 350 statistical analyses were presented and almost 80 of them showed a significant difference at the weak confidence level ($p = .20$) selected by the authors; it is not possible to distinguish the chance from the real effects in those circumstances.

Verbalization of cognitive processes and knowledge events in response to an instruction or a probe question is a methodology that attempts to trace the course of cognitive processes (Newell and Simon, 1972) and its procedures have been questioned. However, Ericsson and Simon (1980) effectively rebutted criticisms of that technique by demonstrating that where inconsistent verbalizations are alleged. the conditions often included (a) probe questions that contained biasing information so that the respondents did not search for their cognitive procedures; (b) the excessive length of the time between the task and probe rendered it unlikely that the information remained in the observer's short-term memory; (c) the probe was not appropriate for the relevant information; (d) the probe asked for responses to hypothetical conditions; or (e) the probe asked for a summarization or a generalization of the processes that were used. These authors affirm that veridical reports can be obtained when the observer addresses events in short-term memory; and they advise that retrospective events which are represented in long-term memory are prone to incompleteness and confusion

198

with current processes so that they are best probed with experimental tasks of
short duration. The technique of verbalization has been applied successfully to
the identification of procedures adopted by programmers during coding (Curtis,
1981). Verbal reports during a study of FORTRAN-based problems led to the generation of production rules which could be categorized into three functional
groups: (a) overall control and goal management; (b) updating the contents of
the written, external code; and (c) generation of the code. A model of coding
behavior was constructed from those rules that generated programming-language
statements correctly. In a review of programming as a cognitive activity (Smith
and Green, 1980) Green is skeptical about the verbal methodology but offers no
reasoned dissent. Nonetheless, this methodology is the best technique that we
have at hand to probe the complex skills of the computer programmer. A research
program to extend the E metric by counts of cognitive processes and knowledge
events to provide a measure of the software product, and the utilization of the
verbal-report methodology for the elicitation of those processes and events, is
under consideration for the programming task of software modification.

REFERENCES

Basili, V.R. (Ed.), 1980. Tutorial on Models and Metrics for Software Management
    and Engineering. Los Angeles, CA: IEEE Computer Society, 343 pp.
Basili, V.R., Selby, R.W., Jr., and Phillips, T-Y., 1983. Metric analysis and
    data validation across FORTRAN projects. IEEE Trans. on Software Engineering,
    SE-9(6): 652-663.
Brooks, R.E., 1980. Studying programmer behavior experimentally: The problems of
    proper methodology. Communications of the ACM, 23(4): 207-213.
Coulter, N.S., 1983. Software science and cognitive psychology. IEEE Trans. on
    Software Engineering, SE-9(2): 166-171.
Curtis, B. (Ed.), 1981. Tutorial: Human Factors in Software Development. Los
    Angeles, CA: IEEE Computer Society, 641 pp.
Ericsson, K.A. and Simon, H.A., 1980. Voice reports as data. Psychological
    Review, 87: 215-251.
Halstead, M.H., 1977. Elements of Software Science. New York: Elsevier North-
    Holland, 127 pp.
Newell, A. and Simon, H.A., 1972. Human Problem Solving. Englewood Cliffs, NJ:
    Prentice-Hall, 920 pp.
Perlis, A.J., Sayward, F.G., and Shaw, M., 1981. Software Metrics. Cambridge,
    MA: MIT Press, 404 pp.
Sheil, B.A., 1981. The psychological study of programming. Computing Surveys,
    13(1): 101-120.
Shen, V.Y., Conte, S.D., and Dunsmore, H.E., 1983. Software science revisited: A
    critical analysis of the theory and its empirical support. IEEE Trans. on
    Software Engineering, SE-9(2): 155-165.
Shneiderman, B., 1980. Software Psychology: Human Factors in Computer and
    Information Systems. Cambridge, MA: Winthrop Publishers, 320 pp.
Smith, H.T. and Green, T.R.G. (Eds.), 1980. Human Interaction with Computers.
    New York: Academic Press, 369 pp.

Human—Computer Interaction, edited by G. Salvendy
Elsevier Science Publishers B.V., Amsterdam, 1984 — Printed in The Netherlands

APPLICATION OF MAGNITUDE ESTIMATION FOR EVALUATING SOFTWARE EASE-OF-USE

R. E. Cordes[1]
[1] IBM Corporation, General Products Division, Tucson, Arizona (U.S.A.)

INTRODUCTION

It is generally assumed that by examining user-performance measures (such as task-completion time, number of errors, error-recovery time, number of requests for assistance, number of attempts, and number of tasks successfully completed), a product's ease-of-use can be measured (Bennett, 1979; Miller, 1971; Neal and Simons, 1983). However, mental workload, effort, vigilance, and other subjective variables may be more of a determining factor in the perception of ease-of-use than user-performance measures. The purpose of this paper is to examine magnitude estimation (line production) as a supplement to performance measures, for evaluating the ease-of-use of a software product.

The product evaluated was the Hierarchical Storage Manager (HSM), Release 3.2. HSM is an IBM program product that provides space management (such as backup, recovery, and migration) of user data sets. While HSM usually provides these functions automatically, they are also under user control using the HSM command language. In addition, HSM Release 3.2 provides a panel-entry user interface (called space maintenance). The space maintenance panels were developed on ISPF (Interactive Systems Productivity Facility; see Joslin, 1981, or Maurer, 1983, for a review) to enhance the features and usability of HSM Release 3.2. The space maintenance panels consist of page-oriented screens containing fill-in-the-blank and/or selection entry fields. It also provides numerous prompts and tutorials (help panels) that are designed to be of assistance, particularly for first-time users.

Two studies are reported in this paper. The first one examines the ease-of-learning of prototype HSM panels, commands, and the supporting user documentation (on-line and hard copy). Based on the results of this study, numerous suggestions were made for improving the panels and tutorials of the space maintenance interface. These recommendations were incorporated into HSM Release 3.2. The second experiment is a follow-up study, designed to determine whether the usability changes did indeed improve the ease-of-learning of the space maintenance panels.

A major obstacle in studies of this type is obtaining subjective measures. A within-subjects design is usually conducted so that subjects can make comparative judgments (direct-comparison approach). However, once subjects learn how to use the product they will also know how to use (to a large extent) the redesign. This large, positive, transfer effect in learning, dictates the use of a between-subjects design. In this design, direct comparisons between products is not possible because the subjects are exposed to only one product. A solution to this problem is to have each group rate its respective product against a common-reference task (Cordes, 1983). Having at least one reference task for each group allows indirect comparisons to be made between the subjective estimates of each group. The HSM studies used both the direct- and indirect-comparison approaches in obtaining magnitude estimates of task difficulty.

EXPERIMENT 1

METHOD

Subjects

The sixteen people used in this study had some experience with TSO/ISPF but had never used HSM or performed magnitude estimation before.

Procedure

The participants were divided into two groups of eight people each. One group used available on-line support only (space maintenance tutorials for the panels and TSO help for the commands). The other group, in addition, was given the OS/VS2 MVS HSM: User's Guide (SH35-0024) and HSM User·Commands Reference Summary (GX20-2024). Half of the participants in each group used the prototype panels first and the other half used the HSM commands first to accomplish eight comparison tasks (invoking the HLIST, HALTERDS, HBACKDS, HDELETE, HRECOVER, HBDELETE, HMIGRATE, and HRECALL functions). The order of task presentation was also counterbalanced across subjects.

Immediately after accomplishing a task the subjects were instructed to rate its difficulty. A measure of task difficulty was obtained after each task by having subjects draw a horizontal line on sheet(s) of graph paper matching in length with their perceived difficulty. A short line (two blocks in length), representing the difficulty of simply logging on to TSO, served as the reference task for making comparisons.

RESULTS

The ease-of-learning of the HSM tasks was evaluated by comparing the results using the HSM commands with those using the prototype panels. A 2 (support) x 2 (interface) x 8 (task) multivariate analysis of variance (MANOVA) was conducted on the comparison data. The results showed that the HSM commands were significantly superior to the prototype panels ($p < 0.002$). There were also significant differences among the tasks ($p < 0.0001$). There was no significant benefit in having hard-copy documentation available (subjects tended to rely on the on-line help) and no interactive terms were significant. Separate analysis of variances (ANOVAs) for each dependent measure supported these results.

DISCUSSION

The poor performance of the prototype panels was unexpected. Further analysis revealed that the primary source of user difficulty was associated with only two of the prototype panels. As a result of this study, a number of the panels (including the two mentioned above) were redesigned to improve their ease-of-learning. The re-designed panels were incorporated into Release 3.2 of HSM and a follow-up study was conducted.

EXPERIMENT 2
METHOD
Subjects

The eight participants used in this study had the same background and followed the same procedures as reported in Experiment 1 ("with hard copy documentation" group only).

RESULTS

The ease-of-learning improvement was evaluated by comparing the results of this study with the results of Experiment 1 ("with hard copy documentation" group only). A 2 (design) x 2 (interface) x 8 (task) MANOVA was conducted on the results of these studies. The results showed that the interface, task, and design x interface effects were statistically significant ($p < 0.05$). Separate ANOVAs performed for each dependent measure supported these results. The interaction between design and interface indicates that the significant difference between the interfaces (panels and commands) depends on which design or study you examine. A Duncan's multiple-range test revealed that for all of the dependent variables, the original space maintenance panels were significantly poorer ($p < 0.05$) than the improved panels and the HSM commands. Table 1 shows the results of the means of this interaction and the percentage of improvement for the space maintenance panels.

CONCLUSIONS AND DISCUSSION

It was concluded that the usability changes made to the panels significantly improved the space maintenance interface. Since subjective ratio scales of difficulty were developed, it can be stated that the improved space maintenance panels were about half as difficult (twice as easy) as the original panels. The performance measures (task-completion time and number of errors) supported this result.

Table 1. A Comparison of Before and After Usability Improvements

Measures	Original Panels	Improved Panels	Percent Improvement
Time (seconds per task)	443.64	274.17	38.2%
Errors (number per task)	1.5	0.703	53.1%
Perceived Difficulty (ratings)	36.09	16.83	53.4%

Magnitude estimation appears to be quite successful when applied in the evaluation of real-world products. Both experiments showed that the direct- and indirect-comparison approaches have practical application in the evaluation of a software product. The common reference task appeared to work well as a method for calibrating the subjective estimates in a between-subjects design. Of course, more studies are needed to firmly establish the validity of this approach. However, based on the results of these studies, the indirect-comparison approach looks quite promising.

Also, the use of magnitude estimation permitted ratio comparisons of task difficulty to be made. For example, in Experiment 1, the HSM panels were judged to be 1.6 times more difficult than the HSM commands. In Experiment 2, the original HSM panels were judged to be twice as difficult as the improved HSM panels. This may be the first time that these comparative statements, related to the ease-of-use of a software product, can legitimately be made. Hopefully, this success in applying magnitude estimation in the evaluation of a real product will encourage others to also try these techniques.

REFERENCES

Bennett, J. L., Incorporating usability into system design. Paper presented at Design '79 Symposium, Monterey, California, April 1979.
Cordes, R. E., Use of magnitude estimation for evaluating product ease-of-use. Paper to appear in the proceedings of the International Scientific Conference on Ergonomic and Health Aspects of Modern Offices, Turino, November 7-9, 1983.
Joslin, P. H., Systems productivity facility, IBM Systems Journal, 1981, 20, pp. 388-406.
Maurer, M. E., Full-screen testing of interactive applications. IBM Systems Journal, 1983, 22, pp. 246-261.
Miller, L. A., Human ease-of-use criteria and their trade-offs. IBM Technical Report TR00.2185, Poughkeepsie, New York, April 1971.
Neal, A. S. and Simons, R. M., Playback: A method for evaluating the usability of software and its documentation. IBM Human Factors Center Technical Report HFC-48, San Jose, California, September 1983.

Human—Computer Interaction, edited by G. Salvendy   203
Elsevier Science Publishers B.V., Amsterdam, 1984 — Printed in The Netherlands

The Role of Documentation in Human-Computer Interaction

Darlene Clement
Institute of Human Learning, University of California, Berkeley, CA 94720, U.S.A.

Introduction

An important component of human-computer interaction is the role played by documentation in learning to use a system. This paper analyzes this role from two perspectives. First, documentation is globally viewed as an extension of the system interface. Manual content is determined to a large extent by the naturalness or unnaturalness of the interface it describes. Second, documentation is viewed as a specific kind of text, the analysis of which should yield suggestions for improving document design. Certainly, the problems new users experience could be greatly reduced if manuals were designed to meet their needs, yet few studies have investigated novices' comprehension difficulties, or suggested ways to optimize manual design. To this end, this paper presents both an empirical study of novices' problems in understanding computer documentation, and a model derived from it which suggests heuristics for writing more effective documentation. The emphasis is on the fundamental conceptual issues involved in the comprehension problem, rather than on superficial issues of sentence structure, or writing style. Since conceptual problems ultimately derive from the complexity of the particular computer system, the analysis also has ramifications for system design.

Documentation as an extension of the interface

The difficulty of learning to use a computer system is a function of three factors: the user's prior knowledge of computers, the quality of the documentation, and the complexity of the system's interface. A central feature of the learning process is **translating** familiar procedures such as sorting, editing, and copying into terms the system understands (described in detail in Moran, 1983). Some interfaces, especially those designed for non-technical users, make the task-translation process relatively simple. For example, the Xerox Star system is organized around familiar entities such as pictures of file-folders, in-baskets, and so on. It allows users to perform office tasks with minimal knowledge of computing concepts. If interfaces were placed on a continuum with "unnatural" at one end and "very natural" at the other, the Star interface would be closer to the natural end—the most natural interface being one in which users specify in ordinary natural language what they want done.

An interface that is closer to the opposite end of the continuum is that of the UNIX[1] operating system. A powerful system designed for technical users, UNIX functions are specified abstractly, or in terms that are closer to the actual implementation (relative to Star). Beyond a small subset of commands, it is generally difficult for non-

---

[1] UNIX is a trademark of Bell Laboratories.

programmers to induce from one task how a slightly different one is performed. For example, a user might know how to move a file from the login or home directory to a subdirectory, but be unable to figure out how to move the file back.

There are two important tradeoffs to consider here. First, natural interfaces do most of the task translation which makes them easy to learn; however, their concreteness limits their flexibility. Unnatural interfaces, on the other hand, have greater flexibility owing to their abstractness, but are harder to learn since their interface contributes little to the translation process. The interface begins the translation, and the documentation makes up for where the interface leaves off which leads to the second tradeoff. The role of documentation varies depending on the interface that it describes. If effort is put into making the interface natural, then less effort needs to go into the documentation. Conversely, if minimal effort is put into making the interface natural, then maximal effort must be put into the documentation. In this second case, the documentation plays a major role in translating the system into terms the user understands. Since the interface and the documentation are so closely bound, analysis of one has ramifications for the other. Moreover, given its role in system learning, it is important to investigate what the comprehension of documentation entails in order to optimize manual design. Thus the study which follows is a first step toward providing a framework for discussing the comprehension problems that arise in this domain. The manual used in the study describes a complex interface which taxes both the reader's comprehension mechanisms, as well as the writer's ability to present the information.

Documentation as a kind of text

The study

To investigate computer-manual comprehension problems an in-depth qualitative study was carried out in which 5 non-programmers attempted to learn UNIX with only a manual to guide them. The subjects were asked to read a section of two locally produced tutorials before meeting with the researcher. The tutorials covered file manipulation and text editing with a line-oriented editor called "Edit." During the meetings the subjects used the computer to follow the instructions in the tutorial. The 5 sessions lasted two hours on average and were tape recorded, yielding about 10 hours of tape from each subject.[2]

The model

The model derived from these data partitions the information contained in computer manuals into four classes, each with a corresponding comprehension task. **Functional** information describes the purpose of each command and triggers a **task-mapping** comprehension process. In this process, users map the new functional information given in the manual onto their tacit models of regular text-editing and general office procedures. Examples of such pre-existing models are the familiar procedures of cutting and pasting text in documents, creating new files, and typewriter editing. **Structural** information describes the underlying structures and processes of the

---

[2] Details of the study are described in Clement, unpublished.

computer system itself. A description of a device triggers a **model-building** process in which the reader attempts to construct a mental model of how the device functions, for example, how the editor buffer and disk (important entities which the user never sees) are related. **Command** information describes the way in which commands are issued. It triggers the **command learning** process in which users attempt to learn the syntax and semantics of the command language. **Procedural** information provides directions for navigating through the system, i.e., knowing which command to issue in which context. The corresponding **procedure learning** process entails recognizing these different program contexts, and learning the order in which commands must be issued.

Examples

a) Task mapping. Subjects had difficulty understanding the relationship between the computer and non-computer ways of performing tasks. For example, one problem concerned subjects' expectations about the **mail** program. Initially, they expected to have to type in a home address—an indication that their implicit mail schema had been triggered. This implicit knowledge does not map onto the electronic mail since the computer destination for a message is another computer account, not a home. Knowing that this mapping process will occur, writers could explicitly map each aspect of the known task structure onto the computer task structure.[3] Note that task-analysis is the first step a system designer performs, and it should also be an integral part of the document development process (cf. Sullivan and Chapanis, 1983). Therefore, one task-mapping heuristic is the following:[4]

> *Compare steps and outcomes of regular procedures with computer procedures in order to anticipate the reader's expectations and questions.*

b) Model-building. In general, the subjects had sketchy and erroneous ideas of what the computer was like and how it worked. The manual attempted to describe the basic components (the executive program, the editor buffer, the disk, etc.) by defining each in a glossary. Subjects' inability to construct a coherent model of the system may stem from a need to read an overview of the system components and their interrelationships. This leads, then, to a third heuristic.

> *Provide an overview at the beginning of the manual that describes the major components of the particular computer system and their interrelationships.*

c) Command learning. The data revealed that novices do not easily learn the grammar of the command language from the examples in the manual. The UNIX command language is a typing-oriented prefix language (verb then object) which is very complex. Nevertheless, it is striking that even after many hours using the system, some novices still fail to understand that the program name is always typed first on the command line. This, together with the other command language errors they made, gave rise to the following heuristic:

---

[3] Plans for a knowledge representation system which attempts to do just this are described in Sidner and Vital, 1983.

[4] Specific recommendations derived from these heuristics are detailed in a paper presented at the ACM-SIGDOC conference, Mexico City, May, 1984.

Make the structure of the command language explicit.

d) Procedure learning. Subjects had difficulty recognizing the different program contexts, sometimes issuing editor commands to the executive program, and vice versa. They also had trouble understanding which commands had to be issued in a fixed sequence, and which could be issued at any point. Thus, the last heuristic focuses on the relationship between different program contexts, stressing that writers need to

Make the relationship between different program contexts clear.

Conclusions

In both interface design and documentation design, tasks are central. They are what the system is configured around and what the novice expects to learn. Making it possible for novices to "reformulate" tasks into computer terms (Moran, 1983) requires that the system's entities and operations be described. In addition, since tasks are carried out through a command language it too must be described, together with the computer procedures which lead to the particular task context. This paper emphasizes the different presentation requirements of each of these kinds of information. It is hoped that this analysis will both benefit future investigations into the best way to present this complex information, and generate greater interest in document development because of the important role that documentation plays in human-computer interaction.

References

Clement, D. Comprehending Computer Documentation, Unpublished manuscript. (March, 1983).

Moran, T. P. Getting into a System: External-Internal Task Mapping Analysis, *Proceedings of the Conference on Human-Computer Interaction* (Boston, MA. 1983).

Sidner, C. L., & Vittal, J. J. Knowledge representation tools for the design, training, and use of information systems. *Integrated Interactive Computer Systems,* P. Degano and E. Sandewall, (Eds.), North-Holland, 1983.

Sullivan, M. A. & Chapanis, A. Human factoring a text editor manual. *Behaviour and Information Technology,* 2(2), 113-125, 1983.

Human—Computer Interaction, edited by G. Salvendy
Elsevier Science Publishers B.V., Amsterdam, 1984 — Printed in The Netherlands

HUMAN-COMPUTER INTERACTION AND INDIVIDUAL DIFFERENCES

Anita Kak Ambardar

Northeastern Illinois University

Perhaps the most widely accepted axiom among those concerned with the design of human/computer interfaces is that characteristics of the interface must be matched to those of the user (e.g., Martin, 1973). However, closer examination of the data bearing on the validity of this fundamental axiom reveals an interesting fact: almost without exception, the only user characteristic that has been systematically co-varied with interface design is what might generally be termed "training." This work has led, for example, to the well known recommendations that "novices" generally required "constrained" designs such as menu-based interfaces while "expert" users (i.e., trained) users require more flexible approaches such as keyword-based commands.

More recently, increasing interest has focused on more general aspects of user experience and training. For example, Barnard et. al, (1981) have considered how the syntax of a user's natural language might interact with features of the command structure in a human/computer interface. While this study provided only relatively weak support for the axiom that an interface design is improved by matching to user cognitive characteristics, they do point out the direction toward a potentially significant area of concern in the design of human/computer interfaces.

Barnard, et. al's study is essentially concerned with the manner in which general, cognitive, rather than computer-specific, characteristics of people might interact with computer interface features.

Although the cited study was basically concerned with the impact of training - albeit training not specifically related to computers - it leads to the extended hypothesis that basic, global, cognitive individual differences among people may significantly interact with computer interface design features.

In this paper, I will describe a research project which is currently underway, aimed specifically at the questions: (1) Do basic cognitive individual differences among users interact with specific human/computer interface features, and (2) if so, what cognitive individual difference features and user computer interface features are important in designing human/computer systems?

This project is based upon the following line of reasoning. First, cognitive individual differences are known to profoundly affect many aspects of traditional problem-solving performance. Effects of individual cognitive differences have been found in studies of many forms of problem solving including anagrams, twenty-questions, insight-problems, and spatial-perceptual problem tasks.

In this context, individual cognitive differences of interest are often referred to as "cognitive styles." Over 23 dimensions of cognitive style have been hypothesized although the most well-known and heavily researched is the dimension termed "field dependence/independence." The concept of field dependence/independence refers to the general processing strategy used to separate information from the context in which it occurs.

This dimension of cognitive style, as well as most others, has been carefully distinguished from "ability" or "training" differences. For one thing, cognitive style seems to cut across many task situations whereas ability factors are often task specific (i.e., a person may be good at mathematical problems but poor at verbal problems). Also in contrast, cognitive styles reveal their presence in many tasks, being a general "approach" or "strategy" habitually preferred for solving a problem. Furthermore, cognitive styles are relatively stable and enduring, unlike training factors, for example.

It may be hypothesized that much activity involving computers can be viewed as problem solving. This occurs at two levels: First, the user generally is employing the computer to solve some sort of problem which would otherwise be more difficult. This is the extrinsic problem-solving level. Secondly, the user must solve the problem (actually a continuing series of problems) of getting the computer to carry out the actions which the user intends. In other words, the user must solve the problem of communicating effectively with the computer. This is the intrinsic problem-solving level. While both levels are involved in the current project, most attention is directed toward the intrinsic level.

Now, if basic cognitive style individual differences affect problem solving in traditional domains, and if it is valid to view human/computer interactions as largely problem-solving activities, then a reasonable assumption is that these basic cognitive differences will influence human/computer interactions.

It is important to note again that cognitive styles are not thought of as ability factors. Thus, people possessing different cognitive styles may both be able to solve a particular problem. However, the efficiency of solving a problem will be best when the problem elements are presented in a way best suited for each particular cognitive style. Thus, the fundamental hypothesis of this research is that human/computer interaction will be most efficient when the features of a computer interface are matched to the requirements of an individual user's cognitive style.

EXPERIMENT I: The first experiment was designed to search for any evidence that performance is influenced by interaction between user's cognitive style and interface design. The cognitive style dimension of Field Dependence/Independence was selected for several reasons. First, this dimension is the most thoroughly researched concerning its effects on traditional problem-solving tasks. The theoretical foundations for this dimension are the best defined, as well. In addition, fairly strong and consistent effects of FD/FI differences have been found. Therefore, I felt that if interactions between cognitive style characteristics and interface features do exist, they should arise via FD/FI differences.

The objective of this study was to determine if, under the most sensitive conditions, some characteristically different interaction patterns distinguished FI and FD computer users. Therefore, all subjects used the same complex, realistic computer interface system. This system was based on actual, commercially available software, modified for experimental purposes. The basic task addressed by this software was management of personal financial records - primarily maintaining a checkbook. This system provided a realistic task with enough complexity and depth so that the experiment had reasonable external validity. It was hypothesized that users of differing cognitive styles would use different features of the interface or use the interface features in distinctive sequences in solving the personal finance management tasks presented during the experiment.

The computer system was modified so that a complete record of all user responses above the individual keystroke level (i.e., "backspaces" are not recorded) as well as all displays presented to the subject were recorded. Timing accuracy was to the nearest second. The experiment hardware consisted of two Apple II computers operating in tandem along with necessary peripherals.

EXPERIMENTAL PROCEDURES AND TASKS: The experiment involved three phases. The first phase was training. During the second phase subjects were required to enter a list of items in the database. In the third phase, subjects were given a simulated bank statement and were required to reconcile the statement with the balance showing on their computerized database. Subjects were told that the bank statement was completely accurate. They had to find and correct all errors in their computerized database. Subjects were tested individually. This task was designed to be realistic, complex and difficult.

RESULTS: Although this experiment generated a large and complex body of data, three results are most important. First and most important, there was a strong differential preference for search mode type between field independent and field dependent subjects. Overall, field dependent subjects strongly preferred the strictly organized, sequential item number search mode. This was significant at p.005 level. Overall, field independent subjects preferred the less organized key-word search mode and this was significant at p.02 level. These preference differences were based on the number of times a subject used a particular search mode. For field dependent subjects (who preferred item number search)it took 15.1 seconds to retrieve a target record in item number mode, but 27.6 seconds, nearly twice as long, with the non preferred mode. For field independent subjects, the reverse was found. Using the preferred key-word mode, only 5.8 seconds were needed to retrieve a target while 7.8 seconds were needed when item number mode was used--a 25% efficiency difference. Third and finally, the preceeding two results can be further clarified by another difference between the ways the field dependent and field independent subjects used the system. Two functions for retrieving records were provided; these were called "view" and "change." With the view function items could only be retrieved and displayed, while with the change function it could be retrieved and displayed as well as altered and replaced. Change could be used both to view and change records, but each function was most efficient when used for its primary purpose. A comparison showed that field independent subjects separated the functional command usage while field dependent subjects did not. Field independent subjects used view for examining and change for altering, while field dependent subjects used change for viewing and changing. Differences in use of view function were significant at p.002 level and amounted to 62%.

CONCLUSIONS: The first experiment has provided some important support for the basic hypothesis that interactions affecting the efficiency with which people use computer systems arise between fundamental user cognitive characteristics and design features of a human/computer interface. The first experiment appears to show that the cognitive style dimension of FI/FD is a good experimental model for investigating these effect interactions since it appears to produce measurable effects. There are a number of important questions that arise from the results of the first experiment. The first, and perhaps most important, concerns the underlying mechanisms for the effects noted in this study. Why did FI users prefer to use the interface features differently than FD users? Several hypotheses may be raised concerning the difference in search mode usage (keyword vs. item number). The following proposal might be made: in the keyword mode, subjects are presented with a relatively unstructured database view. The structure or organization which users see may be that which they themselves impose. This structure, in turn, gives rise to their choices of specific keywords used while searching for items in the database. What this structure might be is unclear, but the important point is that it is generated by the user an may be quite complex (i.e., semantic networks, complex hierachies or pseudo-hierachies). This complex database structure might be comfortable for FI subject users who are able to identify search paths to information items embedded in a complex structure.

In contrast, the item number search mode, preferred by FD subjects, presents a highly structured, straightforward database view - i.e., a simple linear order-ing. Perhaps the preference exhibited by FD users reflects their preference for less complex database views.

Another possibility concerns the difference between FD and FI users in their use of the "search view" and "change" commands. One interpretation and pos-sible hypothesis concerning this result is that perhaps the preference among FD subjects to use the "change " command for both finding and altering items reflects a general preference for interface command systems based on a small number of general-purpose commands. In contrast, FI subjects generally used "view" for finding items and "change" for altering items. Thus, we might con-jecture that FI users prefer command systems containing a larger number of more specialized commands. These and several other hypotheses are being tested in the experiment II. Experiment II is currently in progress and results are not yet available. However, the methodology and procedures are briefly outlined below:

EXPERIMENT II. Experiment II was designed to test some of the hypotheses out-lined above as well as several others. However, the main purpose of experiment II was to more directly test and validate the major implication of experiment I - i.e., that the cognitive characteristics distinguishing FD and FI users signi-ficantly interact with interface design features. To provide some convergent validity, an entirely different experimental design is used. In experiment II, 12 different interfaces are directly crossed with two user-groups representing FD and FI individuals cognitive styles. Thus, experiment II is more directly experimental, rather than correlational, in approach.

The basic task used in experiment II is retrieving information from a large (1500 items) database of food recipes. The details of this experiment will be presented elsewhere as results become available.

I think that the issue of the relationship between user individual cognitive differences and interface design features is an important one and represents an area in which some very specific principles for improving the "friendliness" of human/computer interfaces, will emerge.

References:

Barnard, P. J., Hammond, N.Y., Morton, J., Long, J.B. & Clark, I.A.
    Consistency and compatibility in human-computer dialogue. International
    Journal of Man-Machine Studies, 14. (1981) in press.

Martin, J. The design on man-computer dialogues. Englewood Cliffs, N.J.:
    Prentice Hall. (1973).

Human—Computer Interaction, edited by G. Salvendy
Elsevier Science Publishers B.V., Amsterdam, 1984 — Printed in The Netherlands

DYNAMIC PROCESS CONTROL: COGNITIVE REQUIREMENTS AND EXPERT SYSTEMS

Ray E. Eberts, Shimon Y. Nof, Bernhard Zimolong,[1] and Gavriel Salvendy

Industrial Engineering, Purdue University, West Lafayette, IN 47907

ABSTRACT

Dynamic process control, because of the wide range of human abilities
needed to perform the tasks, is an excellent candidate for expert system
support. To design an expert system for process control, knowledge about
how the experts perform the tasks must by quantified and applied. This
paper summarizes research on the expert operator by examining extant expert
systems, computational   models, and cognitive descriptions of expert
behavior. In so doing, a foundation for the design of an expert system is
built.

OVERVIEW

Expert systems, although receiving much attention recently, have yet to
realize their potential. One recent evaluation by a well-known researcher
in artificial intelligence (AI) states that only one expert system, a
program for installing computer systems, has been economically successful to
date. This lack of success is not surprising. Much of the work on expert
systems has only occurred in recent years and systems that are currently in
the laboratory may find more economic success in the next few years.   The
lack of success is not necessarily surprising to cognitive psychologists;
modeling expert behavior has traditionally been a very difficult job. Also,
the lack of success is not very surprising to engineers; systems, such as
the dynamic process control system we are interested in, are highly complex
and difficult to understand.   If an expert system is to be effective, it
must be carefully designed. This paper presents background material which
can be useful in the design of an expert system for dynamic process control.

---

[1]At the time of writing this paper the author was a Heisenberg Fund re-
cipient and a visiting scholar; he is now professor of psychology at the
University of Bochum, West Germany.

Three main steps are required in the design of an expert system. First, a task analysis of the process control operation must be performed so that tasks can be broken down into defined subareas. Next, knowledge must be extracted from experts in each of the subareas. This can be done in three ways: 1) examine the programs from extant expert systems; 2) apply computational and descriptive models of expert behavior; and 3) quantify and apply cognitive psychology descriptions of expert behavior. In the following, each of these three information sources will be reviewed. After identifying the tasks and extracting the expert knowledge, the final step in the design process is to incorporate this information in an expert system.

The authors are currently in the process of conceptually laying the foundation for designing an expert system for dynamic process control tasks. In the first section of this paper, the current state of expert systems is reviewed. In the next sections of this paper, the conceptual bases for the design of an expert system for dynamic process control is presented.

REVIEW OF EXPERT SYSTEMS

An expert system is defined as an intelligent problem solving computer program that uses knowledge and inference procedures to achieve a high level of performance in some specialized problem domain. This domain is considered to be difficult and requiring specialized knowledge and skill. An expert system is characterized by being:

- heuristic -- it employs judgmental as well as formal reasoning in solving problems;
- transparent -- it has the ability to explain and justify its line of reasoning to its users;
- flexible -- domain-specific knowledge is generally separate from domain-independent inference procedures, thus, knowledge updating is made considerably easier than in conventional programs.

Specific expert systems have been developed for a number of domains, including medical diagnosis, organic chemistry analysis, and mineral exploration. Of particular interest to the domain of process control are systems for electrical circuit analysis and design (Stellman and Sussman, 1977), computer configuration (McDermott, 1982), computer fault diagnosis (Bennett and Hollander, 1981), structural analysis (Bennett and Engelmore, 1979), computer aided design (Krueger et al., 1981), process controller design (Mamdani, 1982), and robot control (Michie, in press, Rembold, et al., in press).

As with other AI approaches, the emphasis in an expert system is on symbolic knowledge representation and inference, rather than the numerical computation characteristic of traditional programming languages. Expert systems differ from other AI programs in their focus on narrow, domain-specific knowledge and reasoning methods. This is in contrast to some AI problem solvers which have employed a more general, "weak" line of reasoning. By concentrating on domain-specific knowledge, expert systems have been somewhat successful, at least in the laboratory, in solving difficult and interesting problems within their intended domain. Moreover, the ability of an expert system to use plausible reasoning (essentially, efficient guessing) within its domain, allows solution of problems which are otherwise intractable when conventional techniques are applied. For further reading on expert systems, see Michie (1979), Hayes-Roth et al. (1983), and Nau (1983).

Architecture of Expert Systems

An expert system architecture requires at a minimum the following components:

- Knowledge base -- the collection of domain-specific problem solving axioms, heuristics, "rules-of thumb."
- Task-specific data -- current facts and hypotheses concerning the problem solving task being performed.
- Inference engine -- this controls the problem solving interaction. It infers new beliefs by applying axiomatic knowledge in the knowledge base to current beliefs in the task specific data. This process continues in an attempt to satisfy either an explicitly or implicitly stated goal.

In addition to these three components, an ideal architecture of an expert system would include an interface program which aids input/output understandability by the user; an explanation system which accepts and replies to natural language queries from the user about the dynamic line of reasoning, or about the static knowledge base; a knowledge base editor to aid in constructing, debugging, and updating knowledge bases; a blackboard which allows for intermediate analysis of alternatives; and a scheduler for controlling which relevant set of knowledge is to be applied at any particular time.

Inferences and Knowledge Representation

A powerful inference capability in expert systems is the use of pattern-invoked programs. These are inference programs that are activated by the system controller when certain condition patterns emerge in the problem. The two common forms of pattern-invoked programs are production rules and logic procedures. Production rules are of the form:

IF (premise) THEN (action

The premise is a combination of predicates, which when evaluated by the program as true lead to the specified action. AI systems in which knowledge is represented by production rules are called Production Systems (for example, OPS5, Forgy and McDermott, 1977).

Production rules tend to better handle plausible reasoning, while logic procedures are very useful with logical, deductive inference. In logic procedures, knowledge is typically given in first order predicate logic, and inference is carried out by inference rules, such as modus ponens and modus tollens (Chang and Lee, 1973). PROLOG is an example of an AI language that relies on logic procedures (Clocksin and Mellish, 1981).

Knowledge representation depends on the inference approach, and is critical to the effectiveness of an expert system. It can be tailored to the specific needs of the expertise domain. While the subject of knowledge representation is still developing, the three most typical schemes are:

- Rule based -- knowledge as production rules;
- Logic based -- knowledge as logic procedures
- Frame based -- semantic nets are employed to organize and associate knowledge about each object in terms of various slots and slot-values within logical frames.

One or more representation schemes can be selected for a particular expert system. Nau (1983) describes various representation implementations in expert systems.

DYNAMIC PROCESS CONTROL

Dynamic process control is an excellent candidate for an expert system because the operator abilities needed for controlling such a system encompass the whole range of human abilities from predominantly perceptual motor tasks, such as tracking and manual control, to predominantly cognitive tasks, such as decision making and problem solving. Lees (1974) provides an excellent review of the research on process control operators. Several subtasks for process control have been extracted from the Lees (1974) article, categorized under headings, and presented in Table 1 along with a description of the subtasks and relevant articles pertaining to them. This list of subtasks will be used throughout the rest of the paper to guide the search for relevant models of the subtasks which can be incorporated in an expert system.

EXTANT EXPERT SYSTEMS FOR THE SUBTASKS

A sample list of extant expert systems which cover the subtasks listed in

Table 1 is given in Table 2. Expert systems were identified for all the subtasks from monitoring to diagnosing. KARL, reported by Knaeupper and Rouse (1983), is a production rule based system for process control and covers many of the subtasks which were listed in Table 1. A fifth category heading, design, was included in Table 2 because it is important in process control, especially control of flexible manufacturing systems. However, design is not necessarily part of the actual control process.

COMPUTATIONAL AND DESCRIPTIVE MODELS

Computational and descriptive models of the subtasks listed in Table 1 can be defined as mathematical descriptions of how the various subtasks are performed by humans. In most cases, however, the human model of performance is for an ideal observer or performer. The models of this type can be differentiated from the models which were earlier listed in the expert system section on two criteria: computational models are algorithmic, instead of the heuristics which characterize expert systems; those models, to our knowledge, have not yet been implemented in a computer program to observe or control physical processes. Table 3 presents a list of computational models for the subtasks which were earlier listed in Table 1. As the subtasks become more cognitive in nature and, thus, less algorithmic

TABLE 1 -- PROCESS CONTROL SUBTASKS

Subtask	Description	References

Monitor
  vigilance
  signal detection
	monitor for seldom occur-
	ring event; separate signal
	from noise
		Mackworth (1948);
		Swets (1964);
		Mackie (1977)

Control Tracking	keep system on optimal course	Poulton (1974)

Interpret
  categorization
  quantization
  estimating averages
  filtering
	separate random fluctua-
	tions of system from actual
	course; filter out noise
		Rouse (1973, 1976)

Plan (Decisions)
  resource alloca-
    tion
  resource sharing
  heuristics
  strategy
    development
	setting goals and strate-
	gies; efficient use of
	resources; sequencing
	of tasks
		Bainbridge (1974)
		Beishon (1969)
		Peterson and Beach
		  (1967)

Diagnose fault diagnosis	identifying the problem when a fault occurs	Rasmussen (1981)

TABLE 2 -- EXPERT SYSTEMS

Subtask	Expert System
Monitor	VM (Fagan et al., 1979)
Interpret	DENDRAL (Buchanan & Feigenbaum, 1978)
Plan	Sacerdoti (1977) GARI (Descotte & Latombe, 1981) Molgen (Stefic, 1981) ISIS (Fox et al., 1982)
Diagnose	MYCIN (Shortliffe, 1976) EL (Stellman & Sussman, 1977) Drilling Advisor (Hollander & Iwasaki, 1983) KARL (Knaeupper & Rouse, 1983)
Design	Fades (Fisher & Nof, 1984)

TABLE 3 -- COMPUTATION MODELS

Subtask	Model	References
Monitor	Queueing theory	Carbonell (1969); Carbonell et al. (1969); Rouse (1981)
	Optimal observer	Gai & Curry (1976); Sheridan & Ferrell (1974); Rouse (1980)
	Signal detection theory	Sheridan & Ferrell (1974)
	Luce choice axiom	Pattipatti et al. (1983)
Control	Manual control theory	Kleinman & Curry (1977); Baron & Levinson (1980)
Interpret	Sequential decision theory	Gai & Curry (1976); Curry (1981)
	Discriminant analysis	Greenstein & Rouse (1982)
Diagnose	(see expert systems)	

in nature (such as for the diagnosis tasks), computational models could not be found for these subtasks. For this class of subtask, expert systems are needed.

COGNITIVE PSYCHOLOGY AND EXPERT BEHAVIOR

Research in cognitive psychology is important for expert systems in two ways. First, expert systems must try to perform similar to an expert who is, in this case, controlling a process plant. Cognitive psychologists study experts as part of the overall investigation of human cognitive behavior, and the results of these investigations can be used to guide the kinds of strategies and procedures which are incorporated into an expert system. For the purposes of this paper, cognitive abilities in problem solving and process control will be reviewed to ensure that the important characteristics of the expert are being incorporated into current expert systems. Another important role of cognitive psychology is in trying to improve the interaction between the expert system and human operators. To this end, we must know about the cognitive abilities of the operator; the expert system must be able to present information to operators which will fit in their cognitive structures and at their appropriate skill level. Both these issues of strategies and interaction are considered next.

Problem solving is an important task in process control. Learning how to use a system, diagnosing faults, and troubleshooting are all tasks which could fall under the general category of problem solving. Many of the problem solving strategies which have been identified by researchers are listed in Table 4. Of major interest to this paper are the areas of

TABLE 4 -- HUMAN PROBLEM SOLVING STRATEGIES

Strategy	Implemented in Expert Systems?	Reference
Backward search	Yes	Simon & Simon (1978)
Means-end analysis	Yes	Newell, Shaw, and Simon (1960)
Hill climbing	Yes	Newell, Shaw, and Simon (1960)
Scan-and-search	Yes	Simon & Newell (1971)
Progressive deepening	Yes	DeGroot (1965)
Symptomatic search	Yes	Rasmussen (1981); Wortman (1971)
Applying examples	No	Anderson et al (1981)
Analogies	No	Mayer (1981); Rumelhart & Norman (1981); Gentner & Gentner (1983); Carroll et al (1981)
Mental simulation	No	Hollan et al. (1980)
Topographic search	No	Rasmussen (1981)
Differing ability level	No	Rasmussen (1981)

nonoverlap between what we know about the cognitive abilities of human problem solvers and what has been incorporated into expert or AI systems. By looking at this nonoverlap region, we can start to define the areas in which advances in expert systems are needed. In the table, these areas of nonoverlap are indicated in the second column. The problem solving strategies which have not yet been implemented in expert systems are discussed in more detail.

Application of Examples

Often, when solving a new problem, we tend to use an example of an already solved problem to determine how to solve the new one, or, we recognize a new problem to be similar to a problem which has been recently solved. Anderson et al. (1981) found that application of examples is the procedure most often used in mathematics texts to teach students how to solve math problems. In particular, it was found that application of examples is the dominant strategy used by novices in developing geometry proofs. As a result, Anderson et al. (1981) have incorporated the application of examples into ACT, a production rule based simulation of human cognitive abilities, to solve geometry problems. A similar capability is needed for an expert system in process control.

Analogies

Solving problems by analogy is very similar to solving problems by example; the only difference is the degree of similarity between the new problem and the old problem. In using analogies, a problem solver may use a familiar domain to solve a problem in an unfamiliar domain. For instance, a human may use the hydraulic model (e.g., "electricity is like a hydraulic system") to solve an electricity problem. In fact, Gentner and Gentner (1983) have shown that the kinds of misconceptions humans have in solving electricity problems could be attributed to the kinds of analogies that they apply. Research has shown that analogies are a useful strategy for learning computer systems (Rumelhart and Norman, 1981); for learning computer programs (Mayer, 1981); for solving problems on calculators (Halasz and Moran, 1983); and for solving office design problems (Carroll, Thomas, and Malhotra, 1980). Although they constitute an important problem solving technique, expert systems do not yet have the capability to solve problems using this strategy.

Mental Simulations

For many kinds of problems that need to be solved, humans do not store the particular fact which is needed for the solution. Rather, we prefer to store the procedure which can be used to reconstruct the fact. As an example used by Shepard (1966), try to recall how many windows are in your house. We do not store the actual number but reconstruct it by "running" a mental simulation of envisioning ourselves walking through the house and counting the windows as we go. Mental simulations seem to be important for a variety of other kinds of problem solutions. Hollan et al. (1980), in the design of the STEAMER project, asked expert steam plant operators how they diagnosed faults in the system. Many of the experts indicated that, instead of retrieving specific facts, they "ran" simulations in their mind to find the source of the problem. Thus, a rising water level could be diagnosed as a stuck valve if a mental simulation produced a potential symptom similar to the one seen in the actual system. The ability to run such simulations have not yet been incorporated in expert systems.

Topographic Search

Rasmussen (1981) observed that experts diagnose faults by incorporating what he called a "topographic search." For a topographic search, a mental representation of how the system normally functions is built up by observing normal operations (this is sometimes called the internal model of the system, Kessel and Wickens, 1982; Young, 1969). If a problem occurs in the system, a path is searched to determine if the path is good or bad, i.e, if a problem could occur on the path or not. This search can take place mentally by comparing what is known about how the system failed to do what should normally take place. Alternatively, it can be carried out externally, e.g., by using troubleshooting equipment such as logic analyzers or oscilloscopes to physically find the problem. Also, it can be done by a combination of the both mental and external search.

Differing Ability Levels

Every task requires a certain ability level. The particular level that is required is a function of the situational demands and the experience of the operator. Rasmussen (1983) distinguishes between three levels of cognitive ability: skill (routine), rule, and knowledge-based performance. The skill level is highly automated and is characterized by pattern-evoked behavior; the operator would respond to a particular pattern of stimuli or situations with little conscious effort. The rule based level is based on a hierarchy of rules; to implement the appropriate response, the operator must mentally scan the rules until the correct one is found. The knowledge-based level is evoked when entirely new, unstructured, or complex problems are encountered; the operator will employ various kinds of strategies to perform the task. In a particular situation, the level of the cognitive task is dependent on the task demands which are, in turn, dependent on the experience of the operator (see Figure 1). A skill-based behavior for an expert (e.g., diagnosis of a fault by recognizing a pattern of events) may be knowledge-based for a novice (e.g., several strategies may be evoked to try to diagnose a problem).

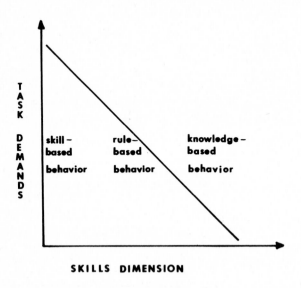

Fig 1. The relationship between the
task demands and the ability level
(from skill-based to knowledge
based) needed to perform the task.

Following the above argument, the categories and subtasks identified in the previous tables may not have absolute boundaries between classifications but will probably be dependent on the cognitive level of the operator. This has important implications when the expert system interacts with the user. The expert system must be "aware" of the cognitive level of the user to communicate useful results; the information given to the user must be at the proper level. As an example, an expert system would present the rule used for diagnosing a fault to an operator at the skill level. A novice would require, first of all, the kind of strategy that was used to diagnose the problem. Goodstein (1981) provides an excellent analysis of the methods available to present information to operators depending on the operator's particular level of ability.

CONCLUSIONS AND IMPLICATIONS

Because of the wide range of human abilities needed to perform the tasks, dynamic process control is an excellent candidate for expert system support. Process control requires an extensive data base, it requires that inferences be made from the data base, and it requires transparency so that an operator can easily, yet precisely, monitor system performance in complex environments. All of these are also characteristics of the domains for which expert systems are developed. To design a successful expert system for process control, we must be aware of the computational models, the current capabilities of expert systems, and the cognitive abilities which are required to accomplish the various tasks. This paper has examined these areas in order to build the foundation for the design of an expert system for dynamic process control.

REFERENCES

Anderson, J. R., Greeno, J. G., and Neves, D. M., 1981. Acquisition of problem-solving skill. In: J. R. Anderson (Editor), Cognitive Skills and their Acquisition. Erlbaum, Hillsdale, NJ, pp. 57-84.

Bainbridge, L., 1974. Analysis of verbal protocols from a process control task. In: E. Edwards and F. P. Lees (Editors), The Human Operator in Process Control. Halsted Press, New York, pp. 146-158.

Baron, S., and Levison, W. H., 1977. Display analysis using the optimal control model of the human operator. Human Factors, 19: 437 457.

Beishon, R. J., 1969. An analysis and simulation of an operator's behavior in controlling continuous baking ovens. In: F. Bressen and M. deMontmollen (Editors), The Simulation of Human Behavior. Durod, Paris.

Bennett, J. S., and Engelmore, R., 1979. A knowledge-based consultant for structural analysis. Proc. IJCAI-1979, pp. 47-49.

Bennett, J. S., and Hollander, C. R., 1981. DART: An expert system for computer fault diagnosis. Proc. IJCAI-1981, pp. 843-845.

Buchanan, E. G., and Feigenbaum, E. A., 1978. DENDRAL and Meta DENDRAL: Their applications dimension. Artificial Intelligence, 11: 5-24.

Carbonell, J. R., 1966. A queueing model of many instrument visual sampling. IEEE Trans. Human Factors in Electronics, HFE-4: 157-164.

Carbonell, J. R., Ward, J. L., and Senders, J. W., 1968. A queueing model of visual sampling: Experimental validation. IEEE Trans Man Machine Systems, MMS-9: 82-87.

Carroll, J. M., Thomas, J. C. and Malhotra, A., 1980. Presentation and representation in design problem-solving. Br. J. of Psych., 71: 143 153.

Chang, C., and Lee, R. C., 1974. Symbolic Logic and Mechanical Theorem Proving. Academic Press, New York.

Clocksin, W. F., and Mellish, C. S., 1981. Programming in PROLOG. Springer-Verlag, Berlin.

Curry, R. E., 1981. A model of human fault detection for complex dynamic processes. In: J. Rasmussen and W. B. Rouse (Editors), Human Detection and Diagnosis of System Failures. Plenum, New York, pp. 171 183.

DeGroot, A. D., 1965. Thought and Choice in Chess. Mouton, The Hague.

Descotte, Y. and Latombe, J., 1981. GARI: A problem solver that plans how to machine mechanical parts. Proc. IJCAI-81, pp. 766-772.

Fagan, L. M., Kunz, J. C., Feigenbaum, E. A., and Osborn, J., 1979. Representation of dynamic clinical knowledge: Measurement interpretation in the intensive care unit. Proc. IJCAI-79, pp. 260 262.

Fisher, E. L., and Nof, S. Y., 1984. FADES: Knowledge based facility design. Proc. IIE Conference, Chicago, May 1984.

Forgy, C., and McDermott, J., 1977. OPS, a domain independent production system language. Proc IJCAI-77, pp. 933-939.

Fox, M. S., Allen, B., and Strohm, G., 1982. Job shop scheduling: An investigation in constraint directed reasoning. Proc. NCAI, pp. 155 158.

Gai, E. G., and Curry, R. E., 1976. A model of the human observer in failure detection tasks. IEEE Trans. on Systems, Man, and Cybernetics, SMC-6: 85-94.

Gentner, D., and Gentner, D. R., 1983. Flowing water or teeming crowds: Mental models of electricity. In: D. Gentner and A. L. Stevens (Editors), Mental Models. Erlbaum, Hillsdale, NJ, pp. 99-130.

Goodstein, L. P., 1981. Discriminative display support for process operators. In: J. Rasmussen and W. B. Rouse (Editors), Human Detection and Diagnosis of Systems Failures. Plenum Press, New York, pp. 433 449.

Greenstein, J. S., and Rouse, W. B., 1982. A model of human decisionmaking in multiple process monitoring situations. IEEE Trans. on Systems, Man, and Cybernetics. SMC-12: 182-193.

Halasz, F. G., and Moran, T. P., 1983. Mental models and problem solving in using a calculator. Proc. CHI '83 Human Factors in Computing Systems, pp. 212-217.

Hayes-Roth, F., Waterman, D. A., and Lenat, D. B. (Editors), 1983. Building Expert Systems. Addison-Wesley, Reading, MA.

Hollan, J., Stevens, A., and Williams, N., 1980. STEAMER: An advanced computer-assisted instruction system for propulsion engineering. Paper presented at the Summer Simulation Conference, Seattle, 1980.

Hollander, C., and Iwasaki, Y., 1983. The drilling advisor. Proc. COMPCON.

Kessel, C. J., and Wickens, C. D., 1982. The transfer of failure detection skills between monitoring and controlling dynamic systems. Human Factors, 24: 49-60.

Kleinman, D. L., and Curry, R. E., 1977. Some new control theoretic models for human operator display monitoring. IEEE Trans. on Systems, Man, and Cybernetics, SMC-7: 778-784.

Knaeupper, A., and Rouse, W. B., 1983. A model of human problem solving in dynamic environments. Proc. Human Factors Society, pp. 695 699.

Krueger, M. W., Cullingford, R. E., and Bellavance, D. A., 1981. Control issues in a multiprocess computer aided design system containing expert knowledge. Proc. ICCS-81, pp. 139-143.

Lees, F. P., 1974. Research on the process operator. In: E. Edwards and F. P. Lees (Editors), The Human Operator in Process Control. Halsted Press, New York, pp. 386-425.

Mackie, R. R., 1977. Vigilance: Relationships among Theories, Physiological Correlates, and Operational Performance. Plenum Press, New York.

Mackworth, N. H., 1948. The breakdown of vigilance during prolonged visual search. Quarterly J. of Exp. Psych., 1: 5-61.

Mamdani, E. H., 1982. Rule based methods for designing industrial process controllers. Proc. Col. on Application of Knowledge Based Systems.

Mayer, R. E., 1981. The psychology of how novices learn computer programming. Computing Surveys, 13: 121-141.

McDermott, J., 1982. R1: A rule based configurer of computer systems. Artificial Intelligence, 18: 39-88.

Michie, D. (Editor), 1979. Expert Systems in the Microelectronic Age. Edinburgh University Press, Edinburgh.

Michie, D., (in press). Expert systems and robotics. In: S. Y. Nof (Editor), Handbook of Industrial Robotics. Wiley, New York.

Nau, D. S., 1983. Expert computer systems. IEEE Computer, February 1983: 63-85.

Newell, A., Shaw, J. C., and Simon, H. A., 1960. A variety of intelligent learning in a general problem solver. In: M. C. Yovits and S. Cameron (Editors), Self-Organizing Systems: Proceedings of an Interdisciplinary Conference. Pergamon Press, New York, pp. 153-189.

Pattipatti, K. R., Kleinman, D. L., and Ephrath, A. R., 1983. A dynamic decision model of human task selection performance. IEEE Trans. on Systems, Science, and Cybernetics, SSC-5: 333-351.

Peterson, C. R., and Beach, L. R., 1967. Man as an intuitive statistician. Psych. Bulletin, 68: 29-46.

Poulton, E. C., 1974. Tracking Skill and Manual Control. Academic Press, New York.

Rasmussen, J., 1981. Models of mental strategies in process plant diagnosis. In: J. Rasmussen and W. B. Rouse (Editors), Human Detection and Diagnosis of System Failures. Plenum Press, New York.

Rasmussen, J., 1983. Skills, rules, and knowledge; signals, signs and symbols, and other distinctions in human performance models. IEEE Trans. on Systems, Man, and Cybernetics, SMC-13:257-266.

Rembold, U., Dillman, R., and Levi, P., (in press). The role of the computer in robot intelligence. In: S. Y. Nof (Editor), Handbook of Industrial Robotics. Wiley, New York.

Rouse, W. B., 1973. A model of the human in a cognitive prediction task. IEEE Trans. on Systems, Man, and Cybernetics, SMC-3: 473-477.

Rouse, W. B., 1976. Human perception of the statistical properties of discrete time series: Effects of interpolation methods. IEEE Trans. on Systems, Man, and Cybernetics, SMC-6: 466-472.

Rouse, W. B., 1980. Systems Engineering Models of Human-Machine Interaction. North-Holland, Amsterdam.

Rumelhart, D. E., and Norman, D. A., 1981. Analogical processes in learning. In: J. R. Anderson (Editor), Cognitive Skills and their Acquisition. Erlbaum, Hillsdale, NJ, pp. 335-359.

Sacerdoti, E. D., 1977. A Structure for Plans and Behavior. Elsevier, Amsterdam.

Shepard, R. N., 1966. Learning and recall as organization and search. J. of Verbal Learning and Verbal Behavior, 5: 201-204.

Sheridan, T. B., and Ferrell, W. R., 1974. Man-Machine Systems: Information, Control and Decision Models of Human Performance. MIT Press, Cambridge, MA.

Shortliffe, E. H., 1976. Computer Based Medical Consultations: MYCIN. Elsevier, Amsterdam.

Simon, H. A., and Newell, A., 1971. Human problem solving: The state of the theory in 1970. American Psychologist, 26: 145-159.

Simon, D. P., and Simon, H. A., 1978. Individual differences in solving physics problems. In: R. Siegler (Editor), Children's Thinking: What Develops? Erlbaum, Hillsdale, NJ.

Stefic, M. J., 1981. Planning with constraints. Artificial Intelligence, 16: 111-140.

Stellman, R. M., and Sussman, G. J., 1977. Forward reasoning in a system for computer aided circuit analysis. Artificial Intelligence, 9: 135-196.

Swets, J. A., (Editor), 1964. Signal Detection and Recognition by Human Observers: Contemporary Readings. Wiley, New York.

Wortman, P. M., 1971. Medical diagnosis: An information-processing approach. Computer and Biomedical Research, 5: 315-328.

Young, L. R., 1969. On adaptive manual control. IEEE Trans. on Man Machine Systems, MMS-10: 292-331.

Human—Computer Interaction, edited by G. Salvendy
Elsevier Science Publishers B.V., Amsterdam, 1984 — Printed in The Netherlands

DESIGN AND EVALUATION OF COMPUTER-BASED DECISION SUPPORT SYSTEMS

William B. Rouse

Search Technology, Inc., 25B Technology Park, Norcross, Georgia 30092 (USA)

Georgia Institute of Technology, Atlanta, Georgia 300332 (USA)

ABSTRACT

An integrated methodology is presented for design and evaluation of computer-based decision support systems. The design process explicitly considers types of decision making task, situation, and strategy as well as forms of information, prototypical messages, and adaptive aids. A multi-level approach to evaluation is discussed, with the nature of the approach varying depending on whether analytical or empirical evaluation is pursued. In general, it is argued that the systematic integration of design and evaluation can lead to substantial improvements in the efficiency and effectiveness of the overall process.

INTRODUCTION

Advances in computer and communications technology, as well as population growth and evolving organizational forms, are resulting in increasingly complex systems. Because of the many elements and relationships among elements in these systems, very information-rich situations tend to arise. In addition, the large-scale nature of these systems can present the possibility of large losses of money, and perhaps lives, if these systems are not operated, maintained, and managed approriately. This trend toward very complex and often high-risk systems has substantially increased the need for and interest in decision support systems for aiding humans in decision making and problem solving.

It is quite natural to suggest that the computer technology that prompted this trend can also provide the means for assisting human operators, maintainers, and managers in coping with it. To a great extent, computer-based decision support systems represent the only viable approach. However, the computer is not quite the panacea that everyone would like.

For quite some time, there has been an implicitly shared assumption in the technological community that the introduction of computer-based systems is inherently a good idea. In recent years, this assumption has been shown to have a limited range of validity. For example, it has been found that shifting procedural information from hardcopy to computer-generated displays can degrade performance unless appropriate aids are provided (Rouse and Rouse, 1980; Rouse, et al., 1982). Similarly, it has been found that additional information on bibliographic data base structure (made feasible by computer technology) can degrade performance without additional aiding (Morehead and Rouse, 1983). Therefore, computer-based approaches are not always inherently better.

The implication of this conclusion is <u>not</u> that alternatives to computer-based approaches should be sought. Instead, the implication is that computer-based decision support systems must be carefully designed and evaluated if the anticipated benefits are to be realized. The purpose of this paper is to propose an overall approach to design and evaluation.

An overall methodology is needed for two reasons. First, design has to be systematic if one is to avoid producing ad hoc aids, with the concomitant potential for repeating previous mistakes. Second, a methodology is needed whereby design and evaluation are pursued, to the extent possible, in parallel. Such a parallel approach will allow necessary modifications to be identified while it is still possible to implement them. This will make the design and evaluation process more efficient as well as more effective.

This paper presents an integrated design and evaluation methodology based on a top-down view of human decision making and decision aiding. The discussion begins with an outline of a design process that explicitly considers types of decision making task, situation, and strategy as well as forms of information, prototypical messages, and adaptive aids. The discussion then proceeds to outline a multi-level approach to evaluation. Finally, the paper concludes with a brief summary of applications and implications.

DESIGN METHODOLOGY

While decision support systems can be designed to aid humans in a variety of tasks and situations, this variety is not as great as one might imagine. It can easily be argued that there are a limited set of general tasks and situations that is sufficiently robust to describe the domain of virtually any decision support system. Such a "standard" description allows one to prescribe analytically the types of strategy, forms of information, and prototypical messages associated with an aid. This results in the normative view of design advocated in this paper. The presentation in this section draws heavily from Rouse and Rouse (1983) and Rouse, et al. (1984).

Decision Making Tasks

A recent review of the literature on decision support systems (Rouse and Rouse, 1983) led to the conclusion that virtually every aid discussed is aimed at supporting one or more of three general decision making tasks: 1) situation assessment, 2) planning and commitment, and 3) execution and monitoring.

Situation assessment is required when the information received by humans differs from their expectations in other than an acceptable manner. The unexpected deviations prompt humans to question the validity of their a priori assumptions regarding the status quo. This questioning leads to information seeking in search of an explanation of what has happened, is happening, or may happen. As the phrase implies, the goal is to assess the underlying situation that produced the unexpected information.

Given an explanation of the new situation, the next general task is planning and commitment which involves generating, evaluating, and selecting among alternative courses of action relative to criteria which reflect tradeoffs between possibly competing objectives (e.g., maintaining normal operations vs. ceasing operation to isolate a problem). In many systems, alternative plans are readily available in terms of formal procedures for dealing with particular situations. Further, humans' training may, in effect, prescribe the course of action they will take and, therefore, alternatives need not be actively considered. However, when situations arise that were not anticipated in the design of the procedures, or situations arise that are unfamiliar because they were not considered in the design of the training, humans can be required to pursue planning and commitment. In such situations, humans' decision making and problem solving abilities, as well as their breadth of experience, are likely to be crucial.

The third general decision making task, execution and monitoring, involves implementing the plan selected, observing its consequences, and evaluating deviations of observed consequences from expectations. Most of humans' activities are dominated by execution and monitoring. The vast majority of the time, differences between observations and expectations are minor and, consequently, situation assessment or planning and commitment are not required. However, when they are required (i.e., deviations are unacceptable), the role of humans becomes central to resolving any potential problems.

While situation assessment, planning and commitment, and execution and monitoring are the general decision making tasks of interest, they are somewhat too broad in scope to provide an operationally useful categorization of functions of decision support systems. Therefore, these three general tasks were further subdivided to yield thirteen tasks.

Situation assessment was divided into information seeking and explanation. Within information seeking, the three tasks are generation/identification, evaluation, and selection among alternative information sources. Similarly, explanation includes the three tasks of generation, evaluation, and selection among alternative explanations. Planning and commitment includes the three tasks of generation, evaluation and selection among alternative courses of action. Execution and monitoring does not completely follow the above pattern. The four tasks here include implementation of plan, observation of consequences, evaluation of deviations from expectations, and selection between acceptance and rejection of the deviations as significant. In summary, eleven of the thirteen tasks involve generation, evaluation, and selection, and the remaining two tasks involve implementation and observation.

Definitions and detailed examples of each of these thirteen tasks are presented by Rouse and Rouse (1983) for command and control situations, and by Rouse, et al. (1984) for process control situations. Thus, this taxonomy of decision making tasks has a wide range of applicability, in part because the synthesis of this taxonomy benefitted greatly from previous efforts in this area (Rasmussen, 1976; Wohl, 1981; Rouse, 1983).

Decision Making Situations

The choosing of decision making tasks to be supported, as well as identification of the information requirements which must be met to support these tasks, depends on the types of decision making situation in which the aid will be employed. There are three general classes of situation of interest. These classes can be described in terms of familiarity and frequency.

Most situations are familiar and frequent. They are familiar in that the possibility of their occurrence has been anticipated. They are frequent in the sense that considerable experience has been gained in dealing with them. For such situations, decision makers usually "know" what to do; upon observing the situation, the course of action is apparent.

Familiar and infrequent situations usually do not allow for such immediate action because the humans involved do not have much experience with these types of situation, although the possibility of their occurrence was anticipated. As a result, a course of action may be hypothesized immediately, but a variety of information is collected before this course of action is implemented.

Unfamiliar and infrequent situations are such that they are not anticipated by the decision maker and, by definition, seldom if ever previously experienced. As a result, the appropriate course of action is not at all obvious. Further, available procedures may be inadequate or even inappropriate for coping with the situation. Therefore, decision makers have to rely on knowledge that goes beyond situation-specific experiences and job aids.

Not all of the thirteen decision making tasks are relevant to the three types of situation. Since familiar and frequent situations are such that the decision maker "knows what to do," alternative information sources, explanations, and courses of action need not be considered. Thus, the four execution and monitoring tasks are usually the only applicable tasks.

Familiar and infrequent situations require that the situation be verified prior to action. The verification process is likely to require consideration of sources of verifying information. However, once the situation is verified, alternative courses of action need not be considered. Therefore, decision making proceeds immediately to execution and monitoring.

Unfamiliar, and by definition infrequent, situations are likely to require the full range of decision making tasks. In the process of synthesizing a course of action, the decision maker will usually have to consider a variety of hypotheses and options. This process tends to be far removed from "knowing what to do."

Decision Making Strategies

As might be expected, decision makers approach the three types of situation quite differently (Rasmussen, 1983; Rouse, 1983). Familiar situations call upon humans' pattern recognition abilities, and decision making strategies tend to be symptomatic in the sense that observed patterns of information are mapped directly to appropriate courses of action. Therefore, information to support this type of strategy should be pattern oriented and, in particular, utilize patterns that are stereotypical for the population of decision makers of interest.

At the other extreme, unfamiliar situations call upon humans' analytical reasoning abilities, with the result that decision making strategies tend to be topographic in the sense that structural relationships among elements of information are explicitly considered. Information to support topographic strategies should be structure oriented and emphasize causal or functional relationships. This will allow the tracing of unfamiliar patterns that is typical for topographic strategies, rather than the mapping from patterns to courses of action that is usual for symptomatic strategies.

Familiar and infrequent situations are likely to result in mixed strategies. Execution and monitoring will primarily be approached symptomatically while some aspects of situation assessment may require a topographic approach. This does not necessarily imply that topographic or structural information be explicitly displayed. In familiar situations it is quite likely that decision makers will have complete knowledge of the relevant structural information (i.e., will have a good "mental model"). However, in order to use this structural information to assess the situation, the information that is displayed must be consistent with a topographic approach. Therefore, aggregated patterns would be inappropriate. Instead, displays should show disaggregated elements of information that allow decision makers to trace patterns through their mental models of causal or functional relationships among these elements of information.

Forms of Information

The distinction between aggregated patterns and disaggregated elements is important for determining how the state of the system should be displayed. The term "state" is used here to denote the set of physical, economic, organizational, and environmental variables that is sufficient to describe the current status of the system, as well as serve as input for any projections of the future status of the system.

For symptomatic strategies, system state should be displayed as an aggregated pattern. Some types of display are excellent for emphasizing patterns. For example, colorgraphic pie–charts of economic information for a business, or circular profiles of physical variables for an engineering system, are oriented toward pattern recognition. In general, displays intended to present an "overall impression" are pattern oriented.

In contrast, topographic strategies require that the system state be displayed as disaggregated elements. This is due to the fact that particular variables (i.e., temperatures, inflation rates, employee turnover rates, etc.) are usually needed to trace through causal or functional relationships. This allows the decision maker in an unfamiliar situation to determine "why" the current system state has emerged; for familiar situations, this question is unnecessary.

Displays that explicitly depict both structural relationships and the variables associated with each element of the structure are good choices when disaggregated elements are needed. For example, a display indicating resource flows (e.g., raw materials, finished products, and capital) in a production and distribution system, or mass and energy flows in an engineering system, provide support for topographic strategies. Of course, as noted earlier, the structure of the system need not be shown explicitly if it is reasonable to assume that decision makers' mental models of this structure are sufficiently accurate and accessible for this purpose.

Another consideration relative to the form of information is the extent to which information about future system states is needed. Current information (which may include information related to past system states) is sufficient for familiar and frequent situations because the decision maker "knows" what will happen. In contrast, unfamiliar and infrequent situations often require projected information, particularly for those tasks in the planning and commitment category. The intermediate type of situation (i.e., familiar and infrequent) may also be benefited by projected information for the purpose of verifying that the situation is likely to evolve as hypothesized.

Thus, forms of information can be described in terms of two dichotomies: 1) patterns vs. elements, and 2) current vs. projected. The most appropriate forms depend on the combination of task and situation. For execution and monitoring, current patterns are appropriate for all types of situation, with possibly the addition of current elements for unfamiliar and infrequent situations. For situation assessment, which usually only applies to infrequent situations, current patterns are appropriate for familiar situations and current elements for unfamiliar situations, with projected elements appropriate for both types of situation. For planning and commitment, which is usually only necessary for unfamiliar and infrequent situations, current and projected elements are appropriate. Therefore, one can see that the choice of task and type of situation dictates the strategy which, in turn, dictates the form of information and, hence, the choice of how information should be displayed.

Of course, the extent to which the resulting choices are appropriate depends on having correctly specified tasks and situations. With regard to situations, this can be somewhat difficult because familiarity and frequency are, at least partially, defined relative to particular individuals. Therefore, it is quite possible that a given situation will be viewed as familiar by one individual and unfamiliar by another.

This possibility usually results in designers hedging by providing more information than strictly required, "just in case" particular individuals need it. This hedging also tends to occur when decision makers are asked about what information they need. Numerous studies (see Rouse and Rouse (1984) and Morehead (1984) for reviews) have shown that operators, managers, commanders, researchers, etc. tend to over-specify their information requirements. Decision makers apparently find some "comfort" in additional and perhaps redundant information. Unfortunately, this can become a problem when display space is limited.

There appear to be two viable ways of dealing with this problem. One is to view the information requirements that emerge from the top-down analysis espoused in this paper as minimum requirements. Additional information is acceptable to the extent that clutter, confusion, and other human factors incompatibilities are not likely to result. An alternative approach to dealing with over-specification of information requirements is to adapt the decision support system to particular decision makers. This approach is discussed in some detail in a later section of this paper.

Prototypical Messages

Form is only one attribute of the information provided by decision support systems. Of greater importance is content (i.e., the "what" as opposed to the "how"). Specifying the content of a decision support system's displays (i.e., the variables to appear) independent of any particular application is virtually impossible. However, it is possible to specify the nature of the messages that must be transmitted to support each task and situation.

This approach requires that one define a set of "prototypical" messages that are relevant to a range of applications. Considering the thirteen decision making tasks discussed earlier, it was noted then that eleven of these tasks can be classified by one of three terms: 1) generation/identification, 2) evaluation, and 3) selection. For each of these terms, a fairly general set of prototypical messages can be formulated. This set of prototypical messages is elaborated on in (Rouse, et al., 1984); unfortunately, space limitations do not allow presentation of this material here.

However, the genesis of this set of messages was fairly straightforward. Messages for generation/identification are simply expressed in terms of alternative information sources, explanations, and courses of action. Messages for selection are also quite easy to envision, simply specifying the alternative that should be selected. Evaluation is much more complicated because evaluation can be with respect to deviations, confidence, consequences, resource requirements, or comparisons of alternatives.

Given this set of prototypical messages, one is in a position to be much more specific about how an aid might support each of the thirteen decision making tasks. Succinctly, in order for an aid to support a particular task, it must provide at least one of the prototypical messages associated with the task. Of course, while this set provides the alternative messages, the choice of which alternatives are most appropriate depends on the particular application.

The top-down approach presented here for specifying a set of messages provides an alternative means for dealing with the traditional problem of defining information requirements, which is typically pursued in a bottom-up manner (i.e., "up" from activity primitives rather than "down" from overall objectives). Once the messages/information requirements have been defined, one is in a position to determine display elements and formats, dialogue structures, etc. Considerations of these issues is beyond the scope of this paper. The interested reader is referred to Frey, et al. (1984), which basically picks up where this paper leaves off.

Adaptive Aids

It was noted earlier that the familiarity characteristics of situations are likely to be dependent on the particular individual who is to be supported by the aid. As a result, strategies, and hence appropriate forms of information, are likely to vary with individuals. Ideally, therefore, the nature of the aiding as well as the human-computer interface should be adapted to individual users.

A recent report presents a framework for characterizing adaptive decision aids (Rouse and Rouse, 1983). Beyond the typical characteristics of type of decision task (i.e., the thirteen discussed earlier) and level of decision aiding (i.e., ranging from cautions and warnings to expert advice), the framework involves four key attributes: 1) form, 2) mode, 3) method, and 4) means.

The form of adaptation relates to the question: what is adapted to? This question can be answered at several levels. At the highest level, adaptation can be relative to the task or user. At lower levels of detail, adaptation can involve a class of tasks or users, a particular member of a class, or the state of a particular member. Virtually any aid is adapted (albeit offline by the designer) to a class of tasks or users. Thus, the key distinction here is between adapting to members (e.g., particular users) versus states (e.g., specific situations at particular points in time).

The mode of adaptation concerns the question: who does the adapting? There are three possible answers to this question: 1) designer, 2) user, and 3) aid. A further aspect of the mode of adaptation is whether it is done offline or online. Any adaptation by the designer is, by definition, performed offline while users and aids usually adapt online. Designer-offline adaption typically involves classes of tasks and users, and can be viewed as the special case of non-adaptive aiding.

The method of adaption relates to the question: how is the adaption done? In general, adaptation involves measurements which are manipulated using models such that modifications of various types may result. A continuum of modifications is possible. The highest level modification is the allocation of tasks (e.g., does human or computer select among courses of action?). A lower level modification involves partitioning of a task (e.g., human chooses goal and computer controls system to achieve this goal). The lowest level modification involves transformation of a task (e.g., abstracting of a display from a physical to a functional representation).

The means of communication concerns the question: how is information transmitted? This refers to the manner in which measurements are made and the ways in which users and aids inform each other of the status of the decision making process. Communication can be either explicit or implicit. Explicit communication may involve specific displays and controls, standard dialogues via keyboard or voice, or natural language via keyboards or voice. Implicit communication can be accomplished using unobtrusive but direct observations, indirect measurements, or inference via models.

The previously noted report on adaptive aids (Rouse and Rouse, 1983) discusses the above attributes in great detail with a variety of examples. In addition, command and control decision making is described in terms of the thirteen decision making tasks discussed earlier. This description is used, in conjunction with the framework for adaptive aiding outlined in this section, to identify opportunities for aiding in general, and possibilities of adaptive aiding in particular.

Summary

The approach to design presented in this section espouses a top-down view of decision support systems. By specifying the types of situation of interest, one defines the possible tasks of interest as well as the expected strategies. The situations, tasks, and strategies dictate the appropriate forms of information. Tasks also define the alternative prototypical messages that might be provided. Given the types of message and the general forms they should take, one is in a position to proceed with detailed design such as prescribed by Frey, et al. (1984). Finally, since the perceived characteristics of situations and the resulting decision making strategies are often very sensitive to differences among individuals, it may be appropriate to consider adaptive aids in terms of the attributes that were briefly outlined above.

EVALUATION METHODOLOGY

The use of the word "evaluation" is somewhat problematic because its colloquial usage allows a very broad range of interpretations. One common use of the word evaluation is as a synonym of "demonstration." From this perspective, evaluation simply involves turning the system on and seeing if, for example, the display appears and basically looks something like what the designer intended. This type of evaluation gives one an overall impression of a system, but provides no definitive information on performance. For this reason, within this paper, evaluation and demonstration are by no means synonymous.

Industry tends to dichotomize evaluation into verification and validation. Verification is the process of demonstrating that hardware has been fabricated and software programmed as designed. In other words, verification involves determining that design drawings and other documentation have been accurately translated into an end product.

In contrast, validation is the process of assessing the degree to which a design achieves the objectives of interest. Thus, validation goes beyond asking whether or not the system was built according to plans; validation asks whether or not the plan was a suitable means for achieving the end specified by the design objectives. This type of evaluation can be difficult because it involves assessing the products of synthesis (i.e., design) rather than the products of translation (i.e., fabrication and programming). Nevertheless, validation is the type of evaluation emphasized in this paper.

Levels of Evaluation

It is quite useful to approach evaluation of decision support systems in terms of three types of issue (Rouse, 1984). The first type of issue is compatibility. The nature of physical presentations to the user and the responses expected from the user must be compatible with human input-output abilitites and limitations. Succinctly, regardless of the overall design objectives, users have to be able to read the displays, reach the keyboard, etc. Otherwise, there is a great risk that the value of higher-level design features (i.e., the decision aiding) will be hidden amidst compatibility deficiencies.

However, a system that is compatible with human abilities and limitations is not necessarily understandable. Thus, the second type of issue is understandability in the sense that the structure, format, and content of the user-system dialogue must result in meaningful communication. In other words, the "messages" displayed by the system must be interpretable by the user, and the "messages" which the user wants to transmit to the system have to be expressible. If a user can read the menu of options and reach the touch panel to select an option, but the options available are meaningless, then the effort invested in assuring compatibility will have been wasted to the extent that there is a lack of understandability.

Therefore, the designer of a decision support system must assure that it is compatible and understandable. However, while compatibility and understandability are necessary, they are not sufficient; the designer must also assure effectiveness. A decision support system is effective to the extent that it supports a decision maker in a manner that leads to improved performance, results in a difficult task being less difficult, or enables accomplishing a task that could not otherwise be accomplished. Assessing effectiveness obviously depends on defining appropriate measures of performance, difficulty, etc.

In summary, evaluation of a decision support system involves assuring that the system is compatible with human input-output abilities and limitations, understandable in terms of the messages transmitted, and effective in the sense that design objectives are achieved. In general, these three levels of evaluation cannot all be performed simultaneously. Instead, a multi-phase evaluation is needed, the nature of which depends on the approach employed.

Aproaches to Evaluation

There are two fundamentally different approaches to evaluation. If a prototype system and population of potential users are available, and if time and resources allow, an empirical evaluation can be performed. In contrast, if the system only exists in terms of design documentation, or the population of potential users is not yet available, or time and resources are constrained, then an analytical evaluation will have to suffice.

The implication of this contrast is, of course, that empirical evaluation is preferred to analytical evaluation. This is due to the fact that analytical evaluation is inherently limited in that design objectives, concepts, and details may be carefully and systematically reviewed, but they are not tested. In a sense, an analytical evaluation can verify the tenability of a design, but cannot validate the design in terms of having achieved the design objectives. Nevertheless, analytical evaluation can be a very efficient means for providing an assessment of a decision support system's potential for effectiveness.

Analytical Evaluation

It is possible for an analytical evaluation to be very straightforward. If an analytical process, such as outlined earlier in this paper, has been used to design the decision support system, and the use and results of that process are well documented, then one need only audit the lines of reasoning and resulting design decisions from which the system emerged. Unfortunately, such information is seldom available. The evaluation problem, therefore, becomes one of attempting to verify that a design is consistent with objectives that are usually only vaguely defined.

Clearly, this is almost an impossible task. However, it is feasible if a design framework can be developed such that any decision support system can be viewed as if it was designed using this framework. The design process outlined earlier can serve this function (Rouse, et al., 1984). This process enables one to proceed from design objectives (i.e., situations and tasks) to information requirements (i.e., types and forms of message) to detailed design (i.e., particular displays). The detailed review of displays can be performed using a guide such as developed by Frey and his colleagues (Frey, et al., 1984).

The analytical evaluation process proposed in this paper proceeds in a top-down manner from effectiveness, to understandability, to compatibility. As noted earlier, effectiveness is the degree to which a decision support system enables achievement of design objectives. To the extent that effectiveness can be assessed analytically, the design process espoused in this paper assures effectiveness. Further evaluation requires empirical testing.

A decision support system is understandable if information communicated to decision makers is meaningful to these individuals. To assess understandability, one must first determine the knowledge required of decision makers in order for them to understand the messages displayed. Once these knowledge requirements are identified, one then must assess the extent to which decision makers can be expected to have this knowledge. Any knowledge that is lacking can be designated as presenting a potential limit to understandability.

The author and his colleagues (Rouse, et al., 1984) have developed a method for performing this type of analysis. Using a taxonomy of knowledge requirements, each type of message is considered as it is manifested by the decision support system. Knowledge requirements in the categories of display (e.g., coding), command (e.g., dialogue), and system (e.g., functions) are then identified. The extent to which decision makers have this knowledge is then determined on the basis of their overall training, likely experience, training specific to the decision support system, and access to sources of information other than supplied by the decision support system. One particularily useful output of this process is identification of aspects of training for use of the system that should be augmented.

Analytical evaluation of compatibility is reasonably straightforward. A variety of checklists are available, some of which are fairly general while others are targeted at particular application domains. A variety of these checklists are reviewed by Frey and coworkers (Frey, et al., 1984). The design methodology proposed in their volume is such that compatibility is assured if the method is followed.

Empirical Evaluation

While analytical evaluation is necessarily top-down because it proceeds from design objectives to the resulting product, empirical evaluation must be bottom-up because it requires decision makers to interact with the product rather than the objectives. Therefore, compatibility must be considered first; otherwise understandability and effectiveness may be moot points. For example, it is unreasonable to attempt an assessment of the understandability of messages if the level of incompatibility is such that the messages are too small to read. Similarly understandability must be assessed prior to effectiveness because it is unreasonable to try to determine if a less than fully meaningful message is useful.

Empirical evaluations are also more efficient if compatibility is pursued first, followed by understandability, and finally effectiveness (Rouse, 1984). This is due to the efficiency of the evaluation methods which are best employed for each of the three levels of evaluation. In general, the cost and sophistication of appropriate evaluation methods increase as one proceeds from compatibility to understandability, etc. Therefore, one should try to address and resolve compatibility issues early with the faster, less expensive methods; one can then deal with the understandability and effectiveness issues, which require slower, more expensive methods, unhampered by compatibility problems.

The author has proposed a multi-method approach to dealing successively with compatibility, understandability, and effectiveness (Rouse, 1984). Paper evaluations (e.g., checklists) are recommended for compatibility. Both static and dynamic features of a decision support system can be evaluated in this manner. This type of evaluation is equivalent to the analytical assessment of compatibility noted early, with the one exception that it usually involves the actual system rather than design documentation for an eventual system.

Part-task simulator evaluations are suggested for assessing understandability. A part-task simulator is a device that roughly approximates the real system of interest in terms of appearance, static and dynamic characteristics, and range of decision maker activities required. A wide range of part-task simulators are possible, delimited on the low end by static mockups and, on the high end, by full-scope simulators (see below).

The primary objective of part-task simulator evaluation is to assess understandability by determining if decision makers can comprehend the messages transmitted to them by the decision support system and, if decision makers can communicate their desires and perhaps intentions to the system. This message orientation is based on the approach to design discussed earlier and, to an extent, the analytical approach outlined above for evaluating understandability; the key difference is that empirical evaluation involves assessing the meaningfullness of messages for particular decision makers during actual use of the part-task simulator. Hunt (1984) discusses two case studies where this approach was utilized.

Full-scope simulator and/or real system evaluations are recommended for effectiveness. A full-scope simulator is a high-fidelity replica of a real system that allows decision makers to experience virtually the full range of system behaviors, without waiting for all these behaviors to occur in the normal course of events or endangering anyone by initiating the situations of interest in the real system. In general, full-scope simulators are the preferred way to assess effectiveness whenever the potential cost or danger or using the real system for evaluation is unacceptable. (Interestingly, as more and more real systems become computer-based, the difference between full-scope simulator and real system may simply be one of the position of a mode switch.)

As noted earlier, effectiveness can be defined as the degree to which design objectives are achieved. This determination requires that one define measures of effectiveness, as well as criteria whereby one can decide about the acceptability of any particular set of measurements. This is a complex issue that cannot be treated adequately in the space allowed here. The reader is referred to Rouse (1984) for a thorough discussion related to decision support systems, as well as Henneman and Rouse (1984) for measurement issues in the area of decision making and problem solving.

Summary

There are three primary evaluation concerns: compatibility, understandability, and effectiveness. There are two fairly different, yet complementary, ways of approaching these concerns. One way is top-down analytical evaluation which involves viewing a decision support system as if it was designed using the design process proposed earlier in this paper; if the system actually was designed using this process, then analytical evaluation is quite straightforward. The second way is bottom-up empirical evaluation which involves first assuring compatibility (via paper evaluation) and then assessing understandability and effectiveness (via part-task and full-scope simulator evaluations, respectively). For more information and guidance on evaluation of decision support systems, see (Rouse, et al., 1984) for analytical evaluation and Rouse (1984) for empirical evaluation.

CONCLUSIONS

The paper has outlined an integrated methodology for design and evaluation of computer-based decision support systems. Most of the design-oriented aspects of the methodology were drawn from Rouse and Rouse (1983) and Rouse, et al. (1984); most of the evaluation-oriented aspects were drawn from Rouse (1984) and Rouse, et al. (1984). Obviously, an individual paper can only provide, at best, an overview of three comprehensive reports totalling 350 pages. Thus, emphasis was placed on the overall structure of the methodology, as well as the key concepts that provide the basis of the approach.

Various aspects of the methodology have been applied, or are being applied, in several different domains. Design of decision support systems in the area of command and control systems, and in the area of process control (i.e., nuclear power plants) are two examples. Evaluations of several process control aids have also been pursued. An evaluation of a computer-based training system is a current application of the methodology.

All of these applications have led, or are leading, to new insights into how the design and evaluation methodology should be modified and extended. Thus, the presentation in this paper is, in many ways, a status report on an evolving technology. Much research and experience is needed if the methodology is to mature and be widely used. Such efforts are absolutely necessary if the design of decision support systems is to move beyond the "gadgetry" phase that so often predominates in domains where rapidly-evolving technologies are applicable.

ACKNOWLEDGEMENTS

The perspective espoused in this paper emerged from the author's involvement with a variety of people and projects. Several of the author's colleagues at Search Technology Inc. contributed to these efforts, including R.M. Hunt, S.H. Rouse, P.R. Frey, and M.E. Maddox. J. Rasmussen of Riso National Laboratory in Denmark provided many keen insights. S. Ward of the Aerospace Medical Research Laboratory, J.F. O'Brien of the Electric Power Research Institute, and J. Jenkins of the Nuclear Regulatory Commission provided research support as well as valuable comments and suggestions. W.H. Sides, R.A. Kisner, and P. Haas of Oak Ridge National Laboratory and J.G. Wohl of ALPHATECH, Inc. also contributed timely and useful reviews of various aspect of this work.

246

REFERENCES

Frey, P.R., Sides, W.H., Hunt, R.M. and Rouse, W.B. 1984. Computer-Generated Display System Guidelines: Volume 1, Display Design. Electric Power Research Institute, Palo Alto, California.

Henneman, R.L. and Rouse, W.B. 1984. Measures of human problem solving performance in fault diagnosis tasks. IEEE Trans. Systems, Man, and Cybernetics, SMC-14 (1).

Hunt, R.M. 1984. Computer-Generated Display System Guidelines: Volume 3, Applications of Volumes 1 and 2. Electric Power Research Institute, Palo Alto, California.

Morehead, D.R. 1984. The Value of Information in Simulated and Real Search Environments. Ph.D. dissertation, Georgia Institute of Technology, Atlanta, Georgia.

Morehead, D.R. and Rouse, W.B. 1983. Human-computer interaction in information seeking tasks. Info. Proc. and Mgt. 19(4): 243-253.

Rasmussen, J. 1976. Outline of a hybrid model of the process plant operator. In: T. Sheridan and G. Johannsen (Editors), Monitoring Behavior and Supervisory Control. Plenum Press, New York, 371-383.

Rasmussen, J. 1983. Skills, rules, and knowledge; signals, signs, and symbols and other distinctions in human performance models. IEEE Trans. Systems, Man, and Cybernetics. SMC-13(3): 257-266.

Rouse, S.H. and Rouse, W.B. 1980. Computer-based manuals for procedural information. IEEE Trans. Systems, Man, and Cybernetics. SMC-10(8): 506-510.

Rouse, S.H., Rouse, W.B. and Hammer, J.M. 1982. Design and evaluation of an onboard computer-based information system for aircraft. IEEE Trans. Systems, Man, and Cybernetics. SMC-12(4): 451-463.

Rouse, W.B. 1983. Models of human problem solving: detection, diagnosis, and compensation for system failures. Automatica. 19(6): 613-625.

Rouse, W.B. 1984. Computer-Generated Display System Guidelines: Volume 2, Developing an Evaluation Plan. Electric Power Research Institute, Palo Alto, California.

Rouse, W.B. and Rouse, S.H. 1983. A Framework for Research on Adaptive Decision Aids. Aerospace Medical Research Laboratory, Wright-Patterson Air Force Base, Ohio, Report No. AFAMRL-TR-83-082.

Rouse, W.B. and Rouse, S.H. 1984. Human information seeking and design of information systems. Info. Proc. and Mgt. 20(1): 129-138.

Rouse, W.B., Frey, P.R. and Rouse, S.H. 1984. Classification and Evaluation of Decision Aids for Nuclear Power Plant Operators. Search Technology, Inc., Norcross, Georgia, Report No. 8303-1.

Wohl, J.G. 1981. Force management decision requirements for Air Force tactical command and control. IEEE Trans. Systems, Man, and Cybernetics. SMC-11(9): 618-639.

Human—Computer Interaction, edited by G. Salvendy
Elsevier Science Publishers B.V., Amsterdam, 1984 — Printed in The Netherlands

A FRAMEWORK FOR TRANSFERRING HUMAN EXPERTISE

John Boose
Artificial Intelligence Center, Boeing Computer Services
M/S 7A-03, P.O. Box 24346, Seattle, Washington, 98124, USA

ABSTRACT

The bottleneck in the process of building expert systems is retrieving the appropriate problem-solving knowledge from information sources, especially a human expert. A framework for knowledge·elicitation, analysis, and testing is shown. Methods from psychotherapy based on enhancements to George Kelly's Personal Construct Theory are applied to this problem. The Expertise Transfer System is described which interviews a human expert and constructs and analyzes the knowledge that the expert uses to solve his particular problem. The first version of the system elicits the initial knowledge needed to solve analysis problems. Fast (two hour) initial prototyping of expert systems which run on KS-300$_{tm}$* (an extended version of EMYCIN) and OPS5 is also performed. Conflicts in the problem-solving methods of the expert may also be enumerated and explored.

*KS-300$_{tm}$ is a trademark of Teknowledge, Inc., of Palo Alto, California.

INTRODUCTION

An *expert system* is a computer system that uses the experience of one or more experts in some problem domain and applies their problem-solving expertise to make useful inferences for the user of the system (Waterman and Hayes-Roth, 1982). This knowledge consists largely of rules of thumb, or *heuristics*. Heuristics enable a human expert to make educated guesses when necessary, to recognize promising approaches to problems, and to deal effectively with incomplete or inconsistent data.

Eliciting problem-solving knowledge from an expert is a critical problem in building expert systems. A long series of interview, build, and test cycles are necessary before a system achieves expert performance. The time required to build an expert-level prototype is typically six to twenty-four months. *Knowledge engineering* is the process of acquiring knowledge and building an expert system (Feigenbaum, 1977).

Figure 1 shows a system for knowledge elicitation, analysis, testing, combination, and expert system delivery. The system provides a framework for interconnecting many acquisition methods. Development of this system is underway at the Artificial Intelligence Center of Boeing Computer Services.

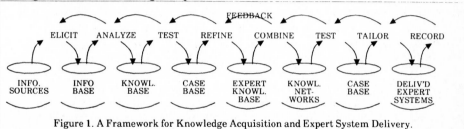

Figure 1. A Framework for Knowledge Acquisition and Expert System Delivery.

Knowledge is elicited from *information sources*, and placed into an *information base*. From there, it is *analyzed* and organized into *knowledge bases*, which may be directly read with expert system building tools such as KS-300$_{tm}$ or OPS5. Such tools are used to test the knowledge for *sufficiency* and *necessity*, and *test-case histories* are built up as the knowledge base is incrementally *refined*. Individual knowledge bases are then combined into *knowledge networks*, where further testing occurs. Finally, efficient delivery systems are tailored from the validated networks, and case histories are recorded from the working expert system in order to further imporve it. The Expertise Transfer System described in this paper combines several elicitation, analysis, and testing tools from this overall framework.

The goal in building the Expertise Transfer System (ETS) is to provide a tool set to significantly shorten the knowledge acquisition process, and help improve the quality of the elicited problem-solving knowledge. To do this, ETS automatically interviews the expert, and helps construct and analyze an initial set of heuristics and parameters for the problem. Experts need no special training to use ETS; an initial fifteen minute explanation is usually all that is necessary.

Using ETS, the quality of the first problem-solving information elicited from the expert is improved over manual methods. ETS provides the expert with knowledge analysis methods and a mechanism for exploring conflicts in the way that different problem cases are handled. *Consistency* is used conceptually to elaborate important problem aspects. With results from ETS, the knowledge engineering team does not need to begin from scratch when interviewing the expert. They have basic problem vocabulary, important problem traits, an implication hierarchy of these traits, and conflict areas where discussions may begin.

In addition to eliciting the initial knowledge and producing knowledge base reports and listings, ETS automatically produces KS-300$_{tm}$ and OPS5 (Forgy, 1981) knowledge bases. KS-300$_{tm}$ is an extended version of EMYCIN developed by Teknowledge, Incorporated, of Palo Alto, California. EMYCIN, an expert system building tool, was extracted from MYCIN, developed at Stanford University (Shortliffe, 1976; van Melle et al., 1981).

In-depth analyses of ETS's knowledge base listings and reports by both the expert and knowledge engineers provide a wealth of problem-solving information prior to any human interviewing. Most of the initial interviewing process is eliminated, which is typically the most painful, time-consuming part of the knowledge acquisition process.

First, in this paper, aspects of Personal Construct Theory methodology will be discussed which are relevant to the Expertise Transfer System. Next, the system itself is described, along with its relation to the knowledge engineering process. Finally, results and limitations of the methodology are discussed.

PERSONAL CONSTRUCT THEORY

ETS employs clinical psychotherapeutic interviewing methods originally developed by George Kelly, who was interested in aiding people categorize experiences and classifiy their environment. A person can use this organization to predict events more accurately and act more effectively, and also can change the organization to fit specific perceived needs (Shaw, 1981). George Kelly's (Kelly, 1955) theory of a *personal scientist* was that each individual seeks to predict and control events by forming theories, testing hypotheses, and weighing experimental evidence.

Certain techniques for use in psychotherapy were developed by Kelly based on this philosophy. In a Repertory Grid Test for eliciting role models, Kelly asked his clients to list, compare, and rate role models to derive and analyze character traits. Roles were listed along the top of a grid; Kelly referred to these items as *elements*. Clients were then asked to compare successive sets of three elements, listing distinguishing characteristics and their opposites down the right hand side of the grid: "What trait distinguishes two of the elements from the other one?" A trait and its opposite represented an internal bipolar scaled dimension or *construct*, and were respectively called the left and right hand *poles* of the construct. This construct was the internal concept represented by the verbal label.

As each construct was elicited, all the elements were rated against it along its bipolar scale. A collection of elements, constructs, and ratings was called a *rating grid*. A non-parametric factor analysis method was used to analyze the grid (Kelly, 1963). The results helped Kelly and his client understand the degree of similarity between the constructs.

Following construction and analysis of the grid, the clinician entered an interviewing phase. Typically, in this phase, the interviewer would attempt to help the subject expand on and verify the relationships between constructs pointed out by the grid analysis.

One interviewing technique was known as *laddering*. This was a method which helped connect the elicited constructs in their *superordinate* and *subordinate* relationships. The clinician might start with the elicited construct "works hard - lazy," and ask the client, "Why does someone work hard?" The client might respond, "To perform their job well." Next, he might ask, "Why does someone want to perform their job well?" and get the response, "To be sucessful," and so on. Each answer to "why" develops another superordinate connection in the hierarchy of constructs. To move in the subordinate direction in the grid, "how" questions are asked, such as "How do you know that?" or "What is your evidence for that?" Other techniques are useful in verifying the relationships pointed out by the grid analysis, and construct "meaningfulness." Less meaningful constructs, such as, "they both have red shirts," may be identified and used to try and find more meaningful ones in the hierarchy.

Hinkle (Hinkle, 1965) further developed the idea that constructs have locations in a hierarchy of implications. He developed a taxonomy of implication types for two construct pairs. Hinkle suggests *ambiguity* may arise when a subject has an incomplete abstraction of the differences between the contexts in which the construct was used, or a subject uses one construct label for two independent constructs. He also felt that the processes of psychological movement, conflict resolution, and insight depend on locating and resolving such points of ambiguous implication into *parallel* or *orthogonal* forms, using techniques similar to laddering.

Researchers have extended Kelly's original binary rating method ("X" or blank) to include rating scales. Instead of simply deciding whether or not some left hand part of a construct pair applies to an element, the subject rates the construct's applicability on a scale, thereby allowing the subject to express finer shades of distinction. Another rating technique (Landfield, 1976) goes beyond this, and allows subjects to use "N" - neither pole applies - and "?" - both poles apply - in addition to a rating scale.

More recently, elicitation and analysis of repertory grids has been made available through interactive computer programs (Shaw, 1979). A variety of grid analysis techniques using distance-based measures between vectors - either rows or columns of the grid - have been used, where both elements and constructs may be graphically compared by the subject to find similarities and differences. Some of these techniques include principal components analysis (INGRID, Slater, 1977), a Q-Analysis of the grid in a cluster-analyzed hierarchical format (QARMS, Atkin, 1974), and a linear cluster analysis (FOCUS, Shaw, 1980).

Most of these interactive computer systems use a simple interview technique in which the subject lists elements, produces constructs, and the results are analyzed. Keen, however (Keen, 1981), developed a unique incremental interviewing technique in his program DYAD.

A more formal description of implication relationships is presented by Gaines which is based on logic (Gaines and Shaw, 1981). Instead of looking at grid rows and columns as vectors in space, Gaines looks at them as assignments of truth-values to logical predicates. In binary rating systems, such as those used in Kelly's original grid methodology, an "X" would simply mean true, and a blank would mean false. A grid, then, can be seen as a matrix of truth values. Gaines goes on to show a method of deriving implications from grids which use rating scales rather than binary scales. The method is based on multi-valued logics (Rescher, 1969) using fuzzy set theory (Zadeh, 1965). Using this method, the implication relation can be extended to include *implication strength*. The program ENTAIL does this, producing graphs which show entailment relations among constructs and elements (Gaines, 1981).

EXPERTISE TRANSFER SYSTEM

In an effort to apply grid methodology techniques to knowledge acquisition, the Expertise Transfer System (ETS) has been developed. ETS runs in Interlisp-D on a Xerox 1100 Dolphin Lisp Machine, using the high-resolution bitmap windows, pop-up menus, and mouse interaction capabilities provided.

In the following example, an expert will attempt to build a knowledge base for a Database Management System Advisor. The completed expert system would be able to advise a software engineer as to which database management system to use for an application problem.

First, the Expertise Transfer System elicits conclusion items (elements) from the expert. An expert system would be expected to recommend some subset of these items based on a given set of problem characteristics. In this case, they consist of all the databases which the expert believes the expert system should be knowledgeable about.

After the system has elicited the database management systems which the expert wishes to consider, ETS asks him to compare successive groups of three databases, and name an important attribute or trait which distinguishes two members of this triad from the third one. The result of this first phase of the interview process is a list of elements to be classified, and a list of classification parameters, all of which were derived from the expert.

As Kelly points out, an initial set of constructs will probably not be a sufficient window into an individual's construct system. Later in the interviewing process, ETS uses Kelly's technique of laddering as well as construct volunteering and further triad formation to expand the construct network. So far, these techniques have been sufficient for building rapid prototype systems with reasonable behavior. Laddering may also be continued later on in the manual interviewing process, as the expert and knowledge engineers work together to refine the knowledge base.

Next, the system asks the expert to rate each element against each construct, thereby forming a rating grid (see Figure 2). In addition to allowing numerically scaled ratings, ETS accepts the ratings "N" and "?."

Once this grid is established, ETS invokes several analysis methods to structure the knowledge. Currently, the system performs a non-parametric factor analysis to cluster into constellations construct pairs which are used in a similar manner (Kelly, 1963), and then builds an entailment graph of implication relationships using the methodology of ENTAIL (see Figure 2). The constellation analysis shows construct pairs which are nearly functionally equivalent, given the elements chosen by the expert.

Figure 2. Screen Snapshot of ETS Showing Rating Grid and Entailment Graph.

ETS AND CONFLICT ANALYSIS

The entailment graph shows implication relationships between various poles of the constructs. For instance, "RUN ON VAX," implies both "NOT TEXT RETRIEVAL" and "NOT INVERTED." These graph arcs should correspond with paths in the expert's construct system. However, as Kelly points out, logical representations do not necessarily correspond to a person's internal construct hierarchy. Typically, the expert is surprised at many of the relationships which are revealed by the graph.

Relations with which the expert disagrees can point to conflict points in the expert's problem-solving methods. These may be resolved with tools in ETS or in discussions between the knowledge engineers and the expert. The process of resolving them involves "psychological movement, conflict resolution, and insight" (Hinkle, 1965). These are points of interest where further exploration is necessary both in producing the expert system, and in refining the expert's own problem-solving processes. Conflict points are generated as part of the knowledge base report listings.

RULE GENERATION

After the entailment graph has been constructed, ETS generates two types of heuristic production rules: *conclusion rules*, and *intermediate rules*. Each production rule is generated with a belief strength, or *certainty factor*.

Conclusion rules are created from individual ratings in the grid. Each rating has the potential for generating a rule. The expert is first asked to rate the relative importance of each construct in terms of its potential importance in solving the problem. Then, ETS employs an empirical algorithm to generate certainty factors for each rule. The algorithm takes into account grid ratings, relative construct importance, and the certainty factor combination algorithm in the target expert system building tool.

Intermediate rules are based on relations in the entailment graph. For each entailment, one rule is generated. The strength of the rule's certainty factor is based on the relative strength of the entailment. These rules generate intermediate pieces of evidence at a higher conceptual level than those of conclusion rules.

TESTING - RAPID PROTOTYPING OF AN EXPERT SYSTEM

Once the rules have been generated, ETS has enough information to generate a knowledge base for an expert system building tool based on production rules. Currently, ETS can generate a knowledge base for $KS-300_{tm}$ and OPS5. These prototypes are then run to test the knowledge for necessity and sufficiency.

Manual interviewing and incremental knowledge refinement are still necessary to produce a system that performs at an expert level. It is not suggested that the initially generated knowledge base will necessarily be similar in structure to later ones. However, fast prototyping can be used to help analyze the sufficiency of the initial knowledge base.

OTHER EFFORTS IN DEVELOPING KNOWLEDGE ACQUISITION SYSTEMS

ETS could be used in combination with any of the knowledge acquisition tool families described below as a front-end processor to elicit initial traits and heuristics.

TEIRESIAS (Davis and Lenat, 1982) is a subsystem of EMYCIN, which aids the expert and knowledge engineers when they attempt to refine an existing knowledge base. ETS can be used to supply the initial knowledge base, since TEIRESIAS is not capable of eliciting such information on its own.

META-DENDRAL (Buchanan and Feigenbaum, 1978) and AQ11 (Michalski, 1980) both perform classification analyses of training examples from their respective knowledge bases in order to produce generalized rules using inductive inference strategies. META-DENDRAL learns rules that predict how classes of compounds fragment in a mass spectrometer, and AQ11 formulates rules from traits and test cases. Both of these systems need an initial set of problem traits before classification can begin; it is up to the expert and knowledge engineer to produce the initial list of applicable traits and relevant training examples. Again, ETS could be used as a front-end for these systems to elicit the problem characteristics.

NANOKLAUS (Hass and Hendrix, 1981) attempts to elicit a classification hierarchy from an expert through a natural language dialog. The information is then used for certain classes of deductive data retrieval. The expert uses NANOKLAUS to enter *IS-A* hierarchy relations and object descriptions. The expert needs to have such a hierarchy developed in mind before using NANOKLAUS. ETS could be combined with this system to elicit initial relevant concepts in terms of constructs derived from objects, and to produce heuristic rules.

DISCUSSION

ETS is best suited for analysis class problems (debugging, diagnosis, interpretation, classification), whose solutions could be based on production systems. The system can not readily handle synthesis class problems (design and planning), or problems which require a combination of analysis and synthesis (control, monitoring, prediction, repair). However, ETS can handle the analysis portions of these problems, and it should be noted that many planning and design problems involve synthesizing the results of several analysis components (eg., R1, in McDermott, 1980a and 1980b). These components may be investigated with ETS.

One assumption of grid methodology (Kelly, 1955) is that the elicited set of elements will be a sufficient representation of the problem conclusion set. It must be assumed that the expert knows what these conclusions are, or that the relevant set will be built with ETS knowledge expansion methods or subsequent manual interviewing.

It is difficult to verify that a sufficient set of constructs have been elicited. Inappropriate constructs are relatively easy to weed out of the system, but errors of omission are harder to detect. Some important constructs which are missing may be elicited using ETS's knowledge base expansion techniques, but there is no guarantee that a sufficient set will be found. This is a problem with knowledge acquisition in general. Expert-level performance of the final expert system is critically dependent on obtaining and effectively using a sufficient set of problem-solving knowledge.

Many enhancements are being considered to improve ETS's utility. These include expansion of the interview methods, inclusion of more analysis tools to identify the relative importance and validity of elicited constructs and elements (such as in Hinkle, 1965, and principle components analysis), and development of feedback paths between ETS and the target expert system building tool. Other psychological techniques such as multi-dimensional scaling are being analyzed. A knowledge engineering guide, illustrating the use of ETS and its associated manual interviewing methods, is also being prepared.

In conclusion, ETS and its related techniques have been invaluable aids during knowledge engineering, dramatically streamlining the knowledge acquisition process.

ACKNOWLEDGEMENTS.

Thanks to Roger Beeman, Keith Butler, Alistair Holden, Earl Hunt, Art Nagai, Steve Tanimoto, Lisle Tinglof, Rand Waltzman, and Bruce Wilson for their contributions and support. This work was performed at the Artificial Intelligence Center of Boeing Computer Services in Seattle, Washington.

REFERENCES

Atkin, R. H., Mathematical Structure in Human Affairs, London: Heinemann, 1974.
Bannister, D., and Mair, J. M. M., The Evaluation of Personal Constructs, Academic Press, 1968.
Barstow, D. R., Aiello, N., Duda, R., Erman, L., Forgy, C., Greiner, R.,Lenat, D. B., London, P., McDermott, J., Nii, H. P., and Weiss, S., "Languages and Tools for Building Expert Systems," in F. Hayes-Roth, D. A. Waterman, and D. B. Lenat (eds.), Building Expert Systems, Addison-Wesley, 1983.
Buchanan, B. G., and Feigenbaum, E. A., "DENDRAL and META-DENDRAL: Their Applications Dimension," Artificial Intelligence, 11, 1978.

Buchanan, B. G., Barstow, D., Bechtal, R., Bennet, J., Clancey, W., Kulikowski, C., Mitchell, T. M., and Waterman, D. A., "Constructing an Expert System," in F. Hayes-Roth, D. A. Waterman, and D. B. Lenat (eds.), Building Expert Systems, Addison-Wesley, 1983.

Davis, R., and Lenat, D. B., Knowledge-Based Systems in Artificial Intelligence, New York: McGraw-Hill, 1982.

Feigenbaum, E. A., "The Art of Artificial Intelligence: I. Themes and Case studies of Knowledge Engineering," Proceedings, Fifth International Joint Conference on Artificial Intelligence, Massachusetts Institute of Technology, 1977.

Forgy, C. L., OPS5 User's Manual, Department of Computer Science, Carnegie-Mellon University, 1981.

Gaines, B. R., and Shaw, M. L. G., "New Directions in the Analysis and Interactive Elicitation of Personal Construct Systems," in M. Shaw (ed.), Recent Advances in Personal Construct Technology , New York: Academic Press, 1981.

Hass, N., and Hendrix, G., "Learning by Being Told: Acquiring Knowledge for Information Management," in R. S. Michalski, J. Carbonell, and T. M.Mitchell (eds.), Machine Learning: An Artificial Intelligence Approach, Palo Alto, Calif: Tioga Press, 1983.

Hinkle, D. N., The Change of Personal Constructs from the Viewpoint of a Theory of Implications, Ph.D. Dissertation, Ohio State University, 1965.

Keen, T. R., and Bell, R. C., "One Thing Leads to Another: A New Approach to Elicitation in the Repertory Grid Technique," in M. Shaw (ed.), Recent Advances in Personal Construct Technology , New York: Academic Press, 1981.

Kelly, G. A., The Psychology of Personal Constructs, New York: Norton, 1955.

Kelly, G. A., "Non-parametric Factor Analysis of Personality Theories," Journal. of Individual Psychology: 19, 1963.

Landfield, A., "A Personal Construct Approach to Suicidal Behavior," in Slater, P. (ed.), Dimensions of Intrapersonal Space, Vol. 1, London: Wiley, 1976.

McDermott, J., "R1: An Expert in the Computer Systems Domain," in AAAI 1, 1980a.

McDermott, J., "R1: An Expert Configurer," Rep. no. CMU-CS-80-119, Computer Science Department, Carnegie-Mellon University, Pittsburgh, Pa., 1980b.

Michalski, R. S., "Pattern Recognition as Rule-guided Inductive Inference," IEEE Transactions of Pattern Analysis and Machine Intelligence 2, no. 4, 1980.

Rescher, N., Many-Valued Logic, New York: McGraw-Hill, 1969.

Shaw, M. L. G., and Gaines, B. R., "Externalizing the Personal World: Computer Aids to Epistemology," in Improving the Human Condition: Quality and Stability in Social Systems, Kentucky: Society for General Systems Research, 1979.

Shaw, M. L. G., and Gaines, B. R., "Fuzzy Semantics for Personal Construing," in Systems Science and Science, Kentucky: Society for General Systems Research, 1980.

Shaw, M. L. G., and McKnight, C., "ARGUS: A Program to Explore Intra-Personal Personalities," in M. Shaw (ed.), Recent Advances in Personal Construct Technology, New York: Academic Press, 1981.

Shortliffe, E. H., Computer-Based Medical Consultants: MYCIN, New York: Elsevier, 1976.

Slater, P. (ed.), Dimensions of Intrapersonal Space, Vol. 2, London: Wiley, 1977.

van Melle, W., Shortliffe, E. H., and Buchanan, B. G., "EMYCIN: A Domain-Independent System that Aids in Constructing Knowledge-Based Consultation Programs," Machine Intelligence, Infotech State of the Art Report, Series 9, No. 3, 1981.

Waterman, D. A., and Hayes-Roth, F., An Investigation of Tools for Building Expert Systems, R2818-NSF, Rand Corporation, 1982.

Zadeh, L. A., "Fuzzy Sets," Information and Control, 8, 1965.

Human—Computer Interaction, edited by G. Salvendy
Elsevier Science Publishers B.V., Amsterdam, 1984 — Printed in The Netherlands

An Application of an Expert System to Problem Solving in Process Control
Displays

Author: James P. Jenkins
          U.S. Nuclear Regulatory Commission

ABSTRACT

Results are reported of a human factors experiment of the application of an
expert system, in the form of response tree via a computer simulation of a
nuclear power plant process control problem. Computer simulation allows
implementation and display of plant functions and operator interactions in
the diagnosis of faults in the reactor coolant system and the recovery of
the plant to a safe operating condition. Implications of the findings for
the design and evaluation of similar computer-based-expert systems are presented in the context of human system design criteria. Prior analysis of
operator's acceptance of computerized aids are coupled to these conclusions.
The studies were sponsored by the Nuclear Regulatory Commission as part of a
human factors research program in man-machine interface to provide a technical basis for support to regulatory assessment of advance technology systems
for commercial nuclear power plants.

INTRODUCTION

The need for improved information was dramatically highlighted by the
accident at Three Mile Island. In response to this need and subsequent
requirements by the Nuclear Regulatory Commission, computer applications
in the control room are rapidly being augmented. Control rooms are being
modified to incorporate computer-driven displays and other operator aids
such as the safety parameter display systems required by the NRC. To provide
an independent technical basis for assessing such application, the Nuclear
Regulatory Commission established a human factors research program at Idaho
National Engineering Laboratory's contractor, EG&G, Idaho, in 1981 to perform
experiments and analyses of advanced technology applications to the man-
machine interfaces.   A principal task was analysis of man-computer interaction via expert systems (Bray et al, 1984). Earlier human factors research
at Oak Ridge National Laboratory focused on operator acceptance of computerized aids (Frey & Kisner, 1982).

The capability of modern computer-based systems, coupled with the desire
to help reactor operators avoid errors in diagnosis of system faults and
accident management, has led to the development of artificial intelligence
methods, including expert systems, as candidates to be part of operator
aids. Modelled on human experts, artificial intelligence systems provide a
sophisticated problem-solving technique as well as a vast store of knowledge
to assist the operator in identifying and solving problems, particularly when

the number of alternatives to problem solution is beyond the usual scope of operator capability. Knowledge-based systems, expert-based systems and response trees are all terms used to describe the application of computer-based systems using a natural language interface with the operator to develop a knowledge acquisition subsystem which the operator then uses to assist fault diagnosis and problem solving. In the expert systems experiment performed by EG&G, a response tree method has been used and implemented on a computer-based simulation of a low pressure injection system to cool the reactor core. The response tree consisted of 36 possible solution paths, i.e., cooling system configuration, to affect the cooling function. The operator's task was to identify the best solution within a criterion time and a criterion temperature excursion level of the reactor fuel and align the cooling system to inject water to the core.

DESIGN

The experiment was designed to examine the efficacy of response trees through the effects of two independent variables of interest: Response Tree and Task Difficulty. There were four treatment conditions: a) response tree use was required, b) the response tree was available and its use was optional by the subject, c) subjects were trained on response trees but the aid was inoperable during the scenarios, and d) subjects knew nothing about the response tree and all evidence of the aid was removed from the display situation. Task Difficulty was varied by changing the number (n = 18) and types of failures displayed to the subjects. The experimental design was a 4 x 2 Within Subjects Analysis of Variance with repeated measures on the Within Subjects Variable. Dependent measures were peak core fuel temperature, number of control actions, number of response tree uses, and correctness of the lineup of the low pressure injection system. Twenty-four operators with reactor training were used as subjects in the response tree evaluation. An additional four subjects served in pilot tests to evaluate the procedures, the instructions, and the data reduction methods.

All subjects were trained using response tree training programs depending on the treatment condition which they were in with the exception of subjects in condition d. Each subject learned five operating rules which were heavily emphasized during training. The five operating rules provided to the subjects a frame of reference for evaluating system status as it was changed during the sequence of events in the test scenario. A copy of the operating rules was given each subject as a handout and was available during the test. One of the results of the experiment was that the emphasis on the operating rules was so

successful that almost no violations of them were reported. Individual
training required about 3 hours before testing. A post test questionnaire
was developed to document subjects' opinions about the response tree.

METHODS

   A variety of computer equipment was used for the response tree testing.
Three computer systems were used to run the tests and a fourth computer
system was used for conducting training of the operators prior to the time
of the tests. An experimental display and control system was established in
which the data was presented on a 19" color monitor. Overlaying the color
picture was a transparent touch panel. One computer served for experimental
control and data collection. This computer also provided graphics command to a microprocessor for generating and updating the display. The simulation program was run on a second computer whereby fuel temperature, coolant flow rate, pump and discharge pressure, coolant storage water tank levels,
component status information and accepted component operating commands were
provided. It retained the initial conditions for 18 test scenarios and six
training scenarios. The response tree program was run on a third computer.
It accepted information about component or support system operability and
presented output flow path recommendations on operator request. Subjects
were trained on a PLATO system over a telephone link.

RESULTS

   Three repeated measures analysis of variance were run for the dependent
measures of maximum fuel temperatures reached, number of control activations,
and number of response tree uses. The measures of maximum fuel temperatures
reached yielded two significant effects: the factor of Transient Difficulty
was significant ($p < .01$) and the interaction of Response Tree and Transient
Difficulty was significant ($p < .05$). The significant effect for Transient
Difficulty confirmed that the transients were widely different in their level
of complexity. In general, those conditions, when the response tree was used
or was available for use, took considerable more time than conditions that
did not make the response tree available. It appeared that the use of response tree created a time demand that exceeded the benefit derived based on
the transients and the complexity of the cooling system's problems. The
subjects who had the option of using the response trees apparently did not
exercise the option for the easier transient problems but did use the expert
system on the more difficult problems.

The second analysis of variance was conducted on the number of control actuations made by the subject during each transient problem. The only significant difference was the Transient Difficulty ($p < .05$) which was previously identified as a significant variable.

The third analysis of variance evaluated the subject's style of response tree use. The analysis produced all significant results and effects and interactions ($p < .01$). When the use of the response tree was optional, the subjects tended not to use it. This finding supported the notion that the test scenarios may have been too easy or that the cooling system was not complex enough. A major observation from the experiment is that the response tree did not improve operator performance.

DISCUSSION

Based on an evaluation of the data, the following observations are made:

The subject operators did not use a computer aid for a task they can do for themselves. If an artificial intelligence-based system is to be used, it should aim at a task in which the operators believe they need help and see that help available in the form of an artificial intelligence system. In this experiment, reactor operators felt confident that their background and training gave them sufficient understanding so they could properly align the cooling system in the accident sequences without the help of a response tree. The response tree aid was not significantly employed, despite the favorable opinion expressed by most subjects in a post experiment question-naire.

The level of computer compatibility and the operator's expectation should be made the same through design or training. In this experiment, operators expected that the expert system implemented in the computer "knew" about the failures of the cooling system without being told. The system neither was designed nor functioned as an automatic fault recognition system. Operator training emphasized that failures had to be manually inputted to the response tree aid. However, when under pressure, many subjects acted as though the computer knew about the failures, and they did not have to tell the computer that a valve or pump had failed. This mismatch between computer capability and subject expectation caused confusion and reduced the usefulness of the aid. Operator stereotypes about which tasks a computer should or should not perform must be considered when designing an aid which interacts with the operator's problem solving and heuristics.

The subject operators believed the data provided by the computer and placed high confidence in the data displayed even when the data were incorrect because operator inputs to the computer were incorrect. Care must be taken to ensure that information displayed on such computer-driven displays is correct because the operators believed it.

The role of the rules which was taught to the operators during training was far more effective than was expected from the experimental protocols. A series of priorities were provided to the operator in the rule structure so that if there was apparent conflict between Rule "A" and Rule "X" the priorities allowed the operator to choose one rule over the other rule.

Operator aids are usually developed to help with tasks that are thought to be difficult. The value of the artificial intelligence system may be maximized in two events: a) the implementation by the output of the system which reveals the design basis, and b) the processes by which operators are trained to understand the artificial intelligence system.

Operator acceptance of an expert system also can be influenced by other factors related to design and training. These factors were identified by another human factors project, also part of the man-machine interface program, sponsored and managed by the NRC with Oak Ridge National Laboratory (Frey and Kisner, 1982).

Design factors include: a) user participation with the designer coupled with the objective data, b) appropriate allocation of functions to man, machine, or both, c) minimize magnitude of system response time and minimize its variability, d) characteristics of the dialogue (i.e., the two-way man-computer conversation), e) integration of the system within existing work-stations and places, and f) adequate, correct, and complete documentation for operation and maintenance.

Training factors include: a) content matched to user background, experience and understanding of the system's processes which result in outputs, b) a trainer or training system which is thoroughly pretested, and c) training for subsequent system modifications.

In summary, then, the following guidelines are offered for the application of artificial intelligence-based aids:

The level of computer compatibility within the system and the operator's expectation of the resulting capability should be the same, or nearly the same. This provides the operator with the expected amount of assistance that is intended to be given and which the operator believes he will be given.

Artificial intelligence-based aids may not be used for tasks for which operators feel confident that they can handle without the aid.

Priorities and operating rules developed during the aid's design can be helpful to the operator in performing his tasks as a process control manager whether or not the aid is used.

The degree of integration of controls and displays to allow a holistic presentation to the operator may be equally effective with the operator aid.

Data displayed as a consequence of computer processing in an artificial intelligence system receives either high credance by the operator or very little at all.

REFERENCES

Bray, M.A., Nelson, W.R., Blackman, H.S. and Fowler, R.D. (1983). Response tree evaluation-implications for the use of artificial intelligence in process control rooms. (NUREG/CR-4361), EG&G Idaho, Idaho Falls, Idaho.

Frey, P.R. and Kisner, R.A. (1982). A survey of methods for improving operator acceptance of computerized aids. (NUREG/CR-2586), Oak Ridge National Laboratory, Oak Ridge, Tennessee.

Human—Computer Interaction, edited by G. Salvendy
Elsevier Science Publishers B.V., Amsterdam, 1984 — Printed in The Netherlands

AUGMENTED DISPLAYS FOR PROBLEM SOLVING

Ray E. Eberts

Industrial Eng., Grissom Hall, Purdue Univ., W. Lafayette, IN 47907

INTRODUCTION

Many kinds of problems, to be solved, require the manipulation of images. As examples, Bower (1972) found that groups of subjects told to use imagery are better than a no-imagery control group in solving certain kinds of problems. In a three-term series problem (e.g., Al is taller than Bob, Bob is taller than Carl, who is the tallest?), Huttenlocher (1968) found that, to solve the problem, subjects would often visualize the size of the people and then decide, from that visual image, which one was taller. In other kinds of problems, where subjects are asked to answer relatively simple questions, research has indicated that imagery is used to determine which object (e.g., a mouse or a cat) is larger (Moyer, 1973; Jamieson and Petrusic 1975; and Paivio 1975); imagery is used to determine if objects in different orientations are rotated or reflected from a standard (Cooper, 1975; Cooper & Shepard, 1975); and images can be scanned to solve problems such as the most efficient route to get from one place to another or in trying to recall the people in your high school graduating class by imaging your math class and "looking" around.

In more difficult domains, experts also make use of images to solve problems. Hollan et al. (1980) interviewed expert steam plant operators and found that, instead of storing a series of facts, the experts have what the authors termed a device model, based upon an image of the system, that could be used to diagnose problems. Rasmussen (1981) found that expert troubleshooters use a template of the system to solve problems. Banbridge (1974) found that expert process control operators keep a spatial representation of the current state of the system in mind ready to be used if something unusual occurs.

Although much work has been performed to show how images can be used and how those images can be transformed in various ways, little research has shown how imaging skills are developed. It is assumed, however, in the developmental theories of Piaget (Piaget & Inhelder, 1971) and Bruner (Bruner, Olver, & Greenfield, 1966), that imaging is developed from external actions that a child may perform on an object. Thus, transformations that occur in the real world by manipulating an object can be internalized with enough practice. For example, the human abilities of mental rotation (e.g., Cooper, 1975) and size transformation (e.g., Kosslyn, 1980) are well practiced skills that could have been developed through the years by grasping an object and turning it around in your hand (for rotation) and by looking at an object and walking up closer to it (for size transformations).

In many situations, we do not have the real world external practice which is needed to internalize physical manipulations so that problems can be solved mentally. Interactive computer displays, augmented by graphics, can be used to provide practice for subjects to externally manipulate an image which they may not have had practice with in the real world. After practice, the image can be manipulated internally to solve problems. A set of experiments is summarized below in which subjects were given practice on the external manipulation of a parabola which was subsequently internalized and used to solve problems.

SUMMARY OF EXPERIMENTAL RESULTS

We have little or no practice with the external manipulations of parabolas. Most of us have some idea of what a parabola looks like from our geometry texts but we have little practice seeing how a parabola changes size. A parabola is a very important image because it is a geometric representation of the second order differential equations which describe control characteristics of real world systems such as automobiles, steam plants, and nuclear power plants. Being able to manipulate an image of the control characteristics of these systems may be useful for problem solving.

The experimental method is reported in more detail in Eberts (1983). Briefly, two groups of subjects were trained to track, by manipulating a joystick, a second order system for over six hours. Half the subjects were trained with the parabola augmentation and the other half, the control group, with no augmentation. After practice, subjects were placed in transfer experiments which tested the problem solving skills that were built up and which tested how well the parabola had become internalized (no augmentation was given during the transfer test trials).

For all the transfer experiments, the subjects trained with the parabola augmentation could perform better even with no parabola on the screen. Figure 1 shows the results from an experiment where the subjects were to solve the problem of how to get the system from one state to another state on a static

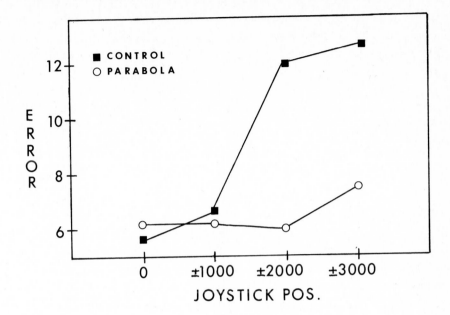

Fig. 1 The error exhibited in getting the system from one state to another state. The acceleration needed corresponds to the joystick position needed to do the task correctly; 0 corresponds to an upright position and ± 3000 corresponds to the two extreme positions.

display by choosing the correct joystick position. The results indicated that subjects were able to mentally manipulate a parabola to find one that would get the system to the required state at the required time and then they matched the correct parabola to a joystick position that would produce it. Figure 2 shows the results from an experiment where the subjects were required to try to solve the problem of controlling the system after the perspective of the system changed from inside-out (e.g., looking outside through the windshield of a car) to outside-in (e.g., looking at the car from above).   Again, being able to internally manipulate a parabola image would be useful for performing this task. Finally, in an experiment where the subjects were required to specify the path of the system, by drawing it in, subjects trained with the parabola were correct 46% of the time and the control group subjects were correct only 25% of the time.   In fact, the mistakes exhibited by the parabola-trained group in this experiment could be attributed to misuse of the parabola image.

Internalization of the parabola is a skill that is built up by externally manipulating the image on the screen. As evidence of this, different groups of subjects were given the same task as that reported in Figure 1 but they were not given prior tracking experience. On half the trials this no experience parabola group had the parabola on the display and, on the other half of the trials, no parabola was given. Figure 3 compares, over two hours of practice, the no experience parabola group to a control group and also to the experienced groups reported in the experiment from Figure 1 (all trials are nonaugmented). Having the parabola on the screen actually hindered performance by the no experience parabola group because they did not have the training or time to develop the imaging skill required for the manipulation of the parabola in problem solving.

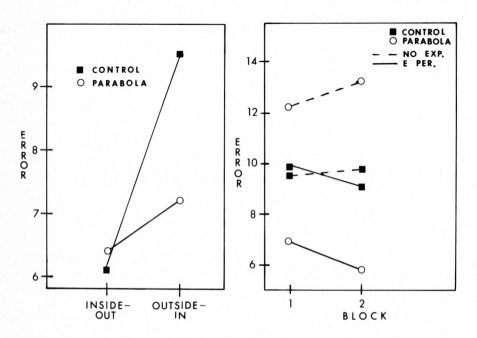

Fig. 2. Root mean square (RMS) error when changing perspective for the two groups.

Fig. 3. RMS tracking error over two blocks of practice for four groups of subjects.

CONCLUSIONS

Imagery can be seen as a perceptual skill that is trained through external practice on physical objects in the real world. Some imagery skills, which can be useful for problem solving but cannot be practiced naturally in the real world, must be developed. Computer augmentation can be used so that subjects can receive practice on these external manipulations. With practice, the external manipulations can be internalized and used for novel problem solving. The set of experiments that were summarized showed how, by geometrically representing equations that describe a simple system, subjects can internalize the system dynamics by internalizing the augmentation. Once internalized, similar mental manipulations can be used to solve system problems.

REFERENCES

Bainbridge, L., 1974. Analysis of verbal protocols from a control task. In: E. Edwards and F. P. Lees (Editors), The Human Operator in process Control. Halsted Press, New York, pp. 146-158.

Bower, G. H., 1972. Mental imagery and associative learning. In: L. Gregg (Editor), Cognition in Learning and Memory. Wiley, New York.

Bruner, J. S., Olver, R. O., and Greenfield, P. M., 1966. Studies in Cognitive Growth. Wiley, New York.

Cooper, L. A., 1975. Mental rotation of random two-dimensional shapes. Cognitive Psychology, 7:20-43.

Cooper, L. A., and Shepard, R. N., 1974. Mental transformation in the identification of left and right hands. Journal of Experimental Psychology: Human Perception and Performance, 1:48-56.

Eberts, R. E., 1983. Internalizing the System Dynamics for a Second Order System. Unpublished Ph.D. Dissertation, University of Illinois at Urbana-Champaign.

Hollan, J., Stevens, A., and Williams, N., 1980. STEAMER: An advanced computer-assisted instruction system for propulsion engineering. Paper presented at the Summer Simulation Conference, Seattle, 1980.

Huttenlocher, J., 1968. Constructing spatial images: A strategy in reasoning. Psychological Review, 75:550-560.

Jamieson, O. G., and Petrusic, W. M., 1975. Relational judgments with remembered stimuli. Perception and Psychophysics, 18:373-379.

Kosslyn, S. M., 1980. Image and Mind. Harvard Press, Cambridge, MA.

Moyer, R. S., 1973. Comparing objects in memory: Evidence suggesting an internal psychophysics. Perception and Psychophysics, 13:180-184.

Paivio, A., 1975. Perceptual comparisons through the mind's eye. Memory and Cognition, 3:635-648.

Piaget, J., and Inhelder, B., 1971. Mental Imagery in the Child. Basic Books, New York.

Rasmussen, J., 1981. Models of mental strategies in process plant diagnosis. In: J. Rasmussen and W. B. Rouse (Editors), Human Detection and Diagnosis of System Failures. Plenum Press, New York.

Shepard, R. M., 1975. Form, formation, and transformation of internal representation. In: R. L. Solso (Editor), Information Processing and Cognition: The Loyola Symposium. Erlbaum, Hillsdale, NJ.

MACHINE INTELLIGENCE IN REAL SYSTEMS: SOME ERGONOMICS ISSUES

S.D. Harris[1] and M.G. Helander[2]

[1]Naval Air Development Center, Warminster, Pennsylvania 18974

[2]Dept. of Industrial and Management Systems Engineering, University of South
Florida, Tampa, Florida 33620

ABSTRACT

Harris, S.D. and Helander, M.G., 1984. Machine intelligence in real systems:
   some ergonomics issues.

   This paper gives an overview of some ergonomics issues in human-machine
symbiosis. Problems of defining performance objectives and quantifying performance are first reviewed and some implications for product liability are
discussed. In order to establish an efficient cooperation between the
machine and the human, it is necessary to incorporate a user model that may
act as an interface. User models may be characterized by their eccentricity,
depth, and vergence, and may comprise both denotational and functional
elements of human personality. An example of a user model in PROLOG is given.

INTRODUCTION

   Classical reference works in the literature of human factors (ergonomics)
have typically included tables comparing human and machine capabilities,
emphasizing the differences between the two. With the recent emergence of
machine intelligence (MI), the distinctions between human and machine components have grown unclear. As Wiener (1948) predicted, machines can today
apparently assume many of the characteristics of their designers. Machines
can analyze problem situations, and plan and execute complicated strategies to
achieve abstract goals. Some machines can speak and understand spoken
messages; others can move with remarkable precision to manipulate objects and
materials in industrial processes. This evolution; increasing similarity
between artifact and artificer, portends an era in which humans and machines
will compete for meaningful work.

   Wiener (1950) warned that there is a need for a new perspective from which
to manage the evolution of computer-based technology. Now more than ever, new
theoretical models, and experimental techniques are needed if human factors
engineers are to function effectively as the user advocate in the systems
engineering process. The objective of this paper is to stimulate the development of new models and methods to meet that challenge.

THE PROBLEM OF PERFORMANCE ASSESSMENT

In spite of the considerable media attentions to applied machine intelligence, it is difficult to assess the real impact of technology. Most high performance systems are used in research, and are often designed to explore
scientific questions within the context of an applied problem. The list of
truly operational MI systems is surprisingly short.

At present, achieving operational status is the only widely recognized index
of performance. The few attempts to develop more nuanced performance measures
have been confined to micro-level analysis, counting the number of rules
invoked to solve a problem, or the amount of computer CPU time consumed. Such
performance measures are useful for addressing engineering questions related to
CPU architecture, or software design but are not especially useful for predicting the performance of an operational system. We allege that the performance
of MI systems would be better represented by also reporting evidence that human
performance is effectively improved by the systems.

DYNAMICS OF HUMAN-MACHINE PERFORMANCE

The behavior of a human-machine dyad is an emergent property of the interaction of the components. If two intelligent agents interact as a system, it
is impossible to ascertain which agent was primarily responsible for the output of the system. It is likewise impossible to assign responsibility for the
behavior of the dyad, because the behavior of each agent is partly a function
of the behavior of the other agent. This should not be especially surprising.
If the human is making decisions based primarily or solely on information provided by the machine, and if the machine is significantly reducing, filtering,
restructuring, analyzing, or otherwise processing information before it gets to
the human, then there is reasonable doubt about which component, human or
machine, actually makes any important decision.

AUTOMATED AUTHORITIES AND PRODUCT LIABILITY

To illustrate the implication of this observation, let us raise the spectre
of a new kind of product liability: Misleading decision aids. There is a
continuing shortage of physicians and well-trained paramedical personnel in the
military. The documented policy that the military has adopted to cope with
this shortage is to replace precious human resources with technical solutions
(LaBerge, 1980). Suppose a MYCIN-like medical diagnostic decision aid (Shortliffe, 1976) were operational at a remote military site and used by "medics"
to diagnose patients. Anecdotal evidence accruing from the experience with
MYCIN indicates that physicians are reluctant to accept the system's recommendations unless then can understand its reasoning (Rich, 1983). Hence, the
critical user would effectively govern the performance of the system. But,

medics are not as well-trained and would therefore be less critical to the system's recommendations. What, then, if the system is wrong, and a casualty results. To whom or what should we ascribe the failure? If the system is designed according to some accepted body of engineering methods and practices, perhaps no one should be blamed; the system developers did the best they could with the resources available. On the other hand, if the system is designed without explicit consideration to the capabilities and limitations of the humans who will use it, perhaps the system's designer should be held account-able (Naval Research Advisory Committee, 1980).

What elements in the system's behavior might mislead a naive user? For one, there is an attempt to personify the MYCIN system by offering recommendations such as "My recommendation is..." rather than using a passive format: "It is recommended that...". The effects of such personification on human decision-making are unknown. Further, the apparent knowledge exhibited by the system due to use of jargon and technical terms has the potential of leading most users into the conclusion that the system is fully competent; maybe even beyond its true expertise.

Consider another, hypothetical example: a weather advisory system for gen-eral aviation aircraft. The weather accounts for most commercial aviation accidents, and for a significant percentage of general aviation accidents. Not much can be done to change the weather, but improvements can be made in fore-casting, analysis of weather information, and presentation of information (Harris, 1982). In fact, analysis of the vast amount of weather-related infor-mation that is available to the cockpit, and presentation of assessments of the implications of weather developments to the aircrew during flight-planning and plan revision, appear to be good candidates for application of artificial intelligence technology. The substrate technologies are already under develop-ment to support implementation of improved weather assessment based on communi-cation and computer-processing aboard aircraft (OTA, 1982).

Consider a weather assessment system that presents itself as an expert on the weather. Several hypotheses can be engendered about the effects of an authoritative "personality" on the decision-making of the aircrew for whom such a system would serve as a consultant. It might be hypothesized, for example, that some people are naturally more deferential than others, and would be likely to accept an authoritative system's recommendations simply because it appears to know what it is talking about. A recent study indicated that 22% of the subjects surveyed (college students) viewed computers as infal-lible (Kerber, 1983). It is likewise quite possible that a relatively ignorant system would lead many pilots astray. Student pilots, or pilots with limited experience might be more apt to go along with the system than "old pros". An authoritative system with incomplete or incorrect knowledge would then mislead a crew into a dangerous situation. The influence of authoritative demeanor on human decision-making is yet unknown.

THE EFFECTS OF STRESS

The amount of information that a human can process per unit time is quite limited. The impact of stress on short-term memory capacity, decision quality, and other aspects of cognitive performance further reduces the processing capability (Broadbent, 1971).

A pilot can therefore probably only consider a few rules and facts about the weather situation during a short interval; particularly under stressful time-critical conditions. The pilot would be aware, however, that the weather advisory system may consider numerous facts and rules during the same time interval. Thus, a pilot might feel safe to delegate important decisions to a computer. Reports of aircraft accidents frequently find that experienced crew-members who recognize a problem will defer action until too late, because they believe another crewmember is aware of and unconcerned about the problem. A system can be considered "expert" because it knows a lot of things about the weather, but will still fail to provide useful advice for some situations because it does not contain rules and facts appropriate to the solution of the problem.

SIMULATED VERSUS SYNTHETIC INTELLIGENCE

Attempts to develop intelligent machines have historically taken two directions, here referred to as "simulated intelligence" and "synthetic intelligence". Simulated intelligence programs are constructed around theories of human cognitive structures. The common research strategy is to develop a model, represent it in a program, present the program with a problem to solve, and compare the result with the performance of human subjects confronted with the same problem. Discrepancies between human and simulation performance suggest changes in the model, and the process is reiterated.

The other approach is to ignore human behavior, and develop completely new principles of intelligence which may be referred to as "synthetic intelligence". The guiding philosophy is that machines are not biological, and thus should not be constrained to behave in the same way as a human. The hope is that there are equally or more efficient approaches to achieving intelligence than those developed through biological evolution. The result of this schism: there are two kinds of machine intelligence (Harris and Owens, 1984).

We propose that human interactions with synthetic intelligence will be markedly different from interaction with simulated intelligence. For example, when synthetic systems gradually fail, the resulting behavior may appear bizarre to the human user. A system that simulates intelligence, however, might be expected to fail in ways that are predictable from the human stand-point. However, it may be that the failure of the synthetic system would be more easily detected and compensated for by a human observer than would fail-ure of a system that simulates intelligence. Which is better as a design philosophy for human-machine systems, simulation or synthesis?

Consider again the example of a weather advisory system. Assessing the weather is a complex problem. The pilot must take into account many objective factors, such as the effects of turbulence on the particular aircraft, and the legal minimum conditions for certain types of operations. Subjective factors are also introduced; for example, whether a pilot is willing to fly into cer-tain types of weather and willing to attempt to land under marginal conditions at the destination airport.

It is clear that a weather advisory system should include a comprehensive model of the objective parameters of the decision problem, but perhaps the recommendations should also be tempered by knowledge of ancillary subjective considerations, as would a human copilot, or, perhaps not! The dynamics of interaction with a machine that is trying to second-guess one's own goals and preferences are simply unknown.

PERFORMANCE ASSESSMENT

Kolcum (1983) indicated that the United States are now building the rudimen-tary components of systems that will place weapons at the disposal of machine intelligence. By failing to comprehend the subtle, complex differences between human and artificial intelligence, we may have already sown the seeds of disaster! It should be patent that performance assessment is not simply a pedantic issue; rather it is a critical issue that should be at the forefront of machine intelligence research.

Performance of the MI component of a system cannot be adequately assessed independently of the other systems components. Licklider (1960) introduced the term "symbiosis" to characterize an intimate, mutually dependent relation-ship between humans and machines. Figure 1 draws upon this concept illustrat-ing that humans and machines have many things in common: (1) they both per-ceive the world, with some subset of that perception shared; (2) both have access to unique and shared knowledge resources; (3) each must communicate that knowledge to the other across limited bandwidth communication channels; and (4) it is not clear who is in charge. Hopson, Zachary and Lane (1981) pointed out that the incorporation of reasoning machines in operational systems, be it military, medical, or transportation systems, has made symbio-sis an important design objective.

The informal definitions of symbiosis proffered by Licklider (1960) and Hopson et al. (1981) capture the general idea of mutual dependence but are not

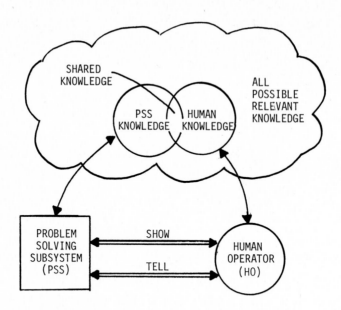

FIGURE 1. An Iconic Model of a Human-Machine Dyad.

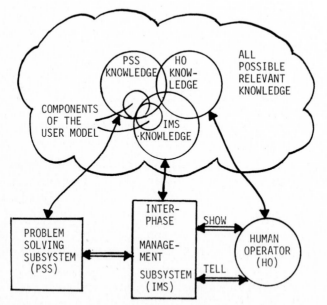

FIGURE 2. Interphase Management Subsystem and Components of the
User Model in the Human-Machine Dyad.

especially useful for engineering purposes. As a more precise alternative
that retains the spirit of Licklider, the following definition is offered:

> Symbiotic intelligence is that state enjoyed by two cooperating
> symbolic computing systems (organic and/or electronic) when, as
> a result of that cooperation, they can successfully and repeatedly
> solve problems that confront them, and when the consequence of
> failure to solve the problems is disintegration of the symbiotic
> system and/or its components.

This definition suggests both a measurable critirion that must be achieved
by a dyad to be considered symbiotic, and implicates certain requisite properties of the system. In sum, what uniquely characterizes a symbiotic system is
the facility with which the human and machine <u>cooperate</u> to solve problems that
bear on the integrity of the individual components (human or machine), or on
the integrity of the dyad. To cooperate, the human and machine must communicate information, and to communicate the information must be sensed by the
receiver, and it must be meaningful to the receiver.

It is therefore necessary to analyze the information processing requirements
imposed by the system upon the human. Predicting what and how much information
to transmit obviously requires a model of the information user's requirements.
The transmitter of the information must contain a user model, in some form
explicit or implicit, else how would it (or its designer) decide what to
transmit.

THE USER MODEL: NUCLEUS OF THE INTERFACE

Every human-machine interface contains a user model, either explicitly
specified and built into the system or implicitly incorporated (by default).
<u>Explicit</u> user models have only recently begun to emerge from research labora-
tories to be incorporated directly into systems as functional components.
<u>Implicit</u> user models reside in the minds of the system designers. More often
than not do they comprise unfounded assumptions about the user population; and
they are usually demonstrably worse than explicit models. Perhaps 99% of all
currently operational human-machine systems employ implicit models. This is
due to the difficulty of finding good engineering documentation that specifies
the user's physical and psychological characteristics. Figure 2 shows a
revised model of human-machine dyad, incorporating an interface management subsystem (IMS). The main purpose of the IMS is to transform information generated in the problem-solving subsystem into a form useful to the human. This
model presumes that the activities within the PSS itself are essentially transparent to the human user, and that the purpose of the interface is to present
the results of the processing in a more palatable form.

User models, such as illustrated in Figure 2, are complex information
structures comprising <u>denotational</u> and <u>functional</u> elements. Denotational

elements record the relatively static attributes or traits that characterize the human(s), for example, age, sex, and job experience. Functional elements of the user model translate the implications of the denotational elements for the behavior of the system.

Models can be characterized in many ways, such as in terms of their eccentricity, depth, and vergency. Eccentricity characterizes the extent to which a user model represents a particular human, or a set of humans (Rich, 1983). Models with maximum eccentricity represent a particular human, and are characterized as individualized, or idiosyncratic models. Models with minimum eccentricity are called normative, or generic models. These models encode general properties of a group of individuals. In reality, most user models lie somewhere between the two extremes.

The depth of the model refers to the type of information encoded in the denotational elements. A model that includes an explicit representation of the human's subjective problem space is referred to as a deep model; whereas one that includes only easily observable properties such as the number of flight hours of a pilot, and the pilot's physical size and weight, is called superficial.

A vergent system incorporates processes that modify the user model, so that it tends (or verges) toward a criterion. In some systems, vergence toward the criterion is automatic whereas in others vergence requires deliberate intervention by the human.

Building a user model

Having confronted the general concept of a user model, one would probably desire to know more about what should go into the make-up of one, for example, the denotational and functional elements. One would hope that something could be learned about what makes a good model by studying what has been tried with success in the past. Unfortunately, previous user models have been quite task-specific. They have little content in common, and can therefore not be used to generate general principles. That state of affairs should not come as a surprise.

The information to be encoded in the user model depends on the nature of the task, part of which could be determined by a task analysis. However, there is idiosyncratic information that should be added in order to increase the eccentricity of the model. Although a clear picture has not emerged, a vast amount of research in such areas as risk taking, cognitive style, and field dependence, strongly suggests that there are higher-order task independent characteristics that significantly influence human problem-solving performance. For example, Anderson (1982) compared his ACT theory with a human subject's performance and found that the subject apparently was more reluctant to abandon a particular problem-solving strategy than was the ACT system.

In a sense, psychological theory is to systems engineering as theoretical physics is to electrical engineering. Psychological variables are the quarks and gluons of information systems engineering. It is apparent that psychological theory must mature to become more useful in systems engineering (Longuet-Higgins, 1981).

AN EXAMPLE OF USER MODEL

An example might serve to clarify some of the ideas discussed above. Consider again a weather advisory system for an aircraft cockpit. The denotational elements of a superficial model record traits such as age, sex, etc., of a pilot, as well as more dynamic features, such as the pilot's recent experience:

```
((pilot name Steve Harris))
((age 36))
((sex male))
((hours in type 400))
((pseudonyms (Commander Hot Dog Steve) ))
((ratings (IFR Commercial) ))
```

The notation used here to represent the hypothetical user model is consistent with the conventions of PROLOG language. Although a user model can assume any of a multitude of forms, a script-like data structure is perhaps the most cogent form (Schank and Riesbeck, 1981). Functional elements of the model prescribe certain behaviors for the interface management subsystem, and for the problem-solving subsystem. For example, the following rules would address the pilot depending upon pilot's sex:

```
((say "sir") ◄———
          (sex male)
          (goal state_recommendation))
((say "ma'am") ◄———
          (sex female)
          (goal state_recommendation))
```

The same user model might be accessible to the problem-solving subsystem (PSS) in order to suggest flight-plan revisions:

```
((recommend "divert_to_bingo") ◄———
          (hours_in_type 100)
          (ceiling_at_destination 50)
          (goal state_recommendation))
```

It may also be useful to represent the pilot's accumulated experience as a function of time, providing an estimate of "currency". The following declarations would represent a pilot with considerable recent experience:

```
((average_flight_hours_per_month 30))
```

This fact would be interpreted by rules that modulate the frequency and type of information to be presented to the pilot.

Finally, consider the possible denotational element:

        ((pilot_personality_type deferential)).

A functional element that references this fact about the pilot's personality might take the form:

        ((assume authoritarian_posture) ⟵——
        (pilot_personality_type deferential))

This could alter the use of certain terms in the system's recommendations in an attempt to increase the probability of acceptance. For example, an authoritarian system might use terms such as "definitely" in place of "possibly," or "take this action" rather than "consider this alternative".

CONCLUSIONS

It is possible to exemplify several factors that should perhaps be included in the user model, and hypothesize their effects on human problem-solving performance. Unfortunately, as with the issues raised above, very little would be substantiated by the research literature. Many aspects of the behavior of human-machine dyads are potentially important but poorly understood.

As we have illustrated in this paper, the consequences of errors in the design of human-machine dyads may have serious consequences. Product liability for example, is a foreseeable problem in machine intelligence systems. We believe it is appropriate to develop engineering methodologies to create explicit user models, and to assess the human-machine dyads. Many of the problems involved in the development of user models must be resolved if machine intelligence technology is to fulfill the promise engendered by media, and sanctioned by the scientific community.

REFERENCES

Anderson, J., 1982. Representational types: A tricode proposal. Tech. Rep. No. ONR-12-1/Dept. of Psychology. Carnegie-Mellon University, Pittsburg, PA.

Broadbent, D., 1971. Decision and Stress. Academic Press, New York, NY.

Harris, S.D., 1982. Holistic Engineering. Proceedings of the Workshop on Standardization for Speech I/O Technology. National Bureau of Standards, Washington, D.C.

Harris, S.D. and Owens, J.M., 1984. Some Critical Issues that Limit the Effectiveness of Artificial Intelligence in Military Systems Applications. Virginia Polytechnic Institute and State University, Blacksburg, VA.

Hopson, J., Zachary, W., and Lane, N., 1981. The Intelligent Use of Intelligent Systems: Problems in Engineering Man-Machine Symbiosis. Proceedings of the 32nd NATO Guidance and Control Panel Symposium on Cockpit Design. NATO, Stuttgart, West Germany.

LaBerge, W., 1981. Keynote Address. In: S. Harris (Ed.), Voice-Interactive Systems: Applications and Payoffs. Naval Air Development Center, Warminster, PA.

Kolcum, E., 1983. U.S. Plans Super Computer for Defence. Aviation Week and Space Technology, April 18.

Licklider, J., 1960. Man-Computer Symbiosis. IRE Transactions of Human Factors in Electronics, 4-11.

Longuet-Higgins, M., 1981. Artificial Intelligence - A New Theoretical Psychology? Cognition, 10:197-200.

Naval Research Advisory Committee, 1980. Man-Machine Technology in the Navy.
   Department of Defense, Washington, D.C.
Office of Technology Assessment, 1982. Review of the FAA 1982 National Air-
   space Systems Plan. U.S. Congress, Washington, D.C.
Rich, E., 1983. Users are Individuals: Individualizing User Models. Inter-
   national Journal of Man-Machine Studies: 18, 199-214.
Schank, R., and Riesbeck, C., 1981. Inside Computer Understanding. American
   Elsevier, New York, N.Y.
Schortliffe, E., 1976. Computer-Based Medical Consultations: MYCIN. American
   Elsevier, New York, N.Y.
Wiener, N., 1948. Cybernetics. Wiley, New York, N.Y.

THE CRAWFORD SLIP METHOD (CSM) AS A TOOL FOR EXTRACTION OF EXPERT KNOWLEDGE

RICHARD A. RUSK[1] and ROBERT M. KRONE[2]

[1]ISSM, Rm. 201, University of Southern California, Los Angeles, CA 90089-0021

[2]ISSM, Rm. 201, University of Southern California, Los Angeles, CA 90089-0021

INTRODUCTION

One of the laments of managers today (Zemke, 1980) is that they do not know how to get the best of the ideas that exist inside their own organizations out where they can be used. They don't seem to believe that individuals will freely provide these ideas nor perhaps that they are worth much if they did. We reject both of these notions. The basic premises of the CSM hold that workers are well informed about many of the issues to which management seeks answers and, given the right circumstances, will provide them. The "right circumstances" would include a positive psychological climate, i.e., one of high trust, openness and respect for the individual and his or her knowledge and skills. This is obviously not simple to attain.

The management literature (see for example Koontz et al. 1984) suggests that one of the best ways to avoid problems in decision making or change im- plementation is to involve those people most impacted in the processes them- selves. Our view would be that organizations do this poorly. Decisions call- ing for major change come as a shock even to those most centrally immeshed in the specific problem areas. The people are rarely asked, either for their opinions or for their ideas. Executives make the argument that they get paid for taking risks and for making decisions and that involving key workers simply takes too long. More astute organizations realize that if people are brought into the decision process, while it initially may take longer, imple- mentation periods are shortened considerably. This frequently results in a shorter overall period for the deliberation and implementation than under conditions of fast executive decision making and the follow on resistance.

It is our contention that this scenario is equally appropriate to human- computer interactions, new system/network implementations, etc.

What then is the best way to bring the most knowledgeable people into the process? Brainstorming, group problem solving Delphi or nominal group tech- niques on suggestion boxes all have their positive aspects. Unfortunately, they also have drawbacks. All of these processes tend to be expensive in terms of the time used to reach consensus. Further, in face-to-face interactions, people tend to protect themselves by not taking controversial postures--they often say "what the boss wants to hear." Also, a position taken in open forum tends to be retained over time, even if found later to be unsound, so as to not be accused of changing one's mind or "looking silly."

Brainstorming, while taking advantage of an "air of creativity" is not known for being a high speed idea generator. In fact looked at literally, it deals only with one idea at a time, its results are difficult to document (if in fact attempted) and discussions easily become jumbles of data that is unretrievable. These same disadvantages can be attributed to the other group techniques in varying degrees.

The Crawford Slip Method (CSM) overcomes many of these prime disadvantages. First, ideas are written. Thus there is an immediate record. Selected individuals are asked to write down their ideas in response to prepared "target" queries. These "targets" are developed by the workshop leaders as those which will best elicit the type of response needed; i.e., pertinent to the critical issues at hand, relevant to the context and designed to stimulate creative thinking. The individuals are selected primarily for their individual station in the organizational hierarchy.

Inputs from individual participants are written on small slips of paper (hence the name) made by cutting a standard sheet of paper in half three times. The resulting 2-3/4" x 4-1/4" inch slips are easy to handle while containing enough space for a single idea. Participants are asked to write the "long way" on the slip and crowd their words near the top edge. This makes later classification efforts simpler. For reasons which will become evermore apparent with use of the technique, they are also asked to write one legible sentence per slip, to use ball points, to spell out acronyms the first time used, to avoid jargon and abbreviations, to use personal pronouns, colorful imagery and imperative verbs freely.

The information which is generated is rapid, safe and independent. Each unique reply is seen only by its author, eliminating the bias of verbalized positions. An average participant can create one slip per minute for about 10 minutes for each target. With 30 people in your group this equates to roughly 1800 ideas in an hour's time! How many ideas did you get in the last hour you spent with a group of this size?

Later categorization of the slip's results in intelligence which is then fed back to management for potential corrective actions.

Examples we have seen lately (Crawford and Demidovich, 1981, 1983; Crawford, 1983; Demidovich and Crawford, 1981, forthcoming; Crawford et al., 1983; Krone, 1982, 1983), demonstrate that the technique works and has been used in a wide variety of environments. New situations, problems or contexts are particularly well suited to the method. Its ability to penetrate deeply into these areas is well documented (Krone and Rusk, 1984a, 1984b; Crawford, Demidovich and Krone, 1984a, 1984b; Zachary and Krone, 1984; Demidovich, Krone and Crawford, being reviewed).

We have described the system, provided sufficient detail for an overview and shown that the use of CSM in the context of this conference--e.g.--Human-Computer Interactions--is appropriate.

In design phases we see potential use of CSM in determining the concerns and expectations of people in the system. Once known, these (and other) concerns can be resolved by management.

In planning and control phases the system could be used to discern policy or procedural issues leading to better strategies of implementation, staffing, or technical resolutions (access issues for example).

In the operational stage, the ideas of the people utilizing the system would be valued as well. Issues such as operational (hardware/software), problems, equipment failures, "bugs" in programs, design of work stations and the interaction of networks all offer opportunity.

In sum, we have contemplated the use of a 60-year old information gathering and diagnostic technique in a modern, technologically complex and turbulent environment, and found it highly relevant and useful. We hope the readers will also.

REFERENCES

Crawford, C.C., Dec. 1983. "How You Can Gather and Organize Ideas Quickly." CHEMICAL ENGINEERING (July 25, 1983), 87-90. Reprinted in IEEE TRANSACTIONS ON PROFESSIONAL COMMUNICATIONS, Vol. PC-26, #4, 187-190.
Crawford, C.C. and Demidovich, John W., "Think Tank Technology for Systems Management," JOURNAL OF SYSTEMS MANAGEMENT, Nov. 1981, 22-25.
Crawford, C.C. and Demidovich, John W., Jan. 1983. CRAWFORD SLIP METHOD: HOW TO MOBILIZE BRAINPOWER BY THINK TANK TECHNOLOGY (Los Angeles, CA: University of Southern California School of Public Administration).
Crawford, C.C. and Demidovich, John W., and Krone, Robert W., 3rd Quarter 1984. "Instructing and Communications: How to Recycle and Improve Expertise by the Crawford Slip Method," EDUCATION AND PROFESSIONAL COMMUNICATION TRANSACTIONS, Joint issues, forthcoming.
Crawford, C.C., Demidovich, John W. and Krone, Robert W., 1984, forthcoming. PRODUCTIVITY IMPROVEMENT BY THE CRAWFORD SLIP METHOD: HOW TO WRITE, PUBLISH, INSTRUCT, SUPERVISE, AND MANAGE FOR BETTER JOB PERFORMANCE (Los Angeles, CA: University of Southern California School of Public Administration).
Crawford, C.C. and Think Tank Team, Winter 1983. "Complexity Crisis: How to Close the Gap between High Complexity and Low Productivity," LOGISTICS SPECTRUM.
Demidovich, John W. and Crawford, C.C., Summer 1981. "Linkages in Logistics: How to Improve Coordination by the Crawford Slip Method," LOGISTICS SPECTRUM, 42-48.
Demidovich, John W. and Crawford, C.C., "Precision in Data Management," DATA MANAGEMENT, forthcoming.

Demidovich, John W., Krone, Robert M and Crawford, C.C., "Computer on Every
    Desk: How To Adjust to the Computer Explosion. Being reviewed.
Koontz, Harold, O'Donnell, Cyril and Weihrich, Heinz, 1984. MANAGEMENT (8th
    Ed.). New York: McGraw-Hill.
Krone, Robert M., "A Systems Improvement Method for Managers," SYSTEMS SCIENCE
    AND SCIENCE. (Proceedings of the 26th Annual Meeting of the Society for
    General Systems Research, Washington, D.C. Jan.5-9, 1982, Len Troncale,
    Ed.), 854-860.
Krone, Robert M., (Fall/Winter 1983). "A Pacific Nuclear Information Group:
    Prospects and Guidelines," JOURNAL OF EAST ASIAN AFFAIRS, Vol. III,
    No. 2, 422-444.
Krone, Robert M. and Rusk, Richard A., "The Crawford Slip Method: How to
    Increase Productivity Through Participation," EXECUTIVE MAGAZINE,
    Orange Co. edition (May 1984), forthcoming.
Krone, Robert M. and Rusk, Richard A., "Applying the Crawford Slip Method in
    Industry or Government," EXECUTIVE MAGAZINE, Orange Co. edition, June
    1984, forthcoming.
Zachary,William B. and Krone, Robert M., Feb. 1984. "Managing Creative In-
    dividuals in High Technology Research Projects," IEEE TRANSACTIONS ON
    ENGINEERING MANAGEMENT, Special Issue on Managing Technical Professionals.
Zemke, Ron, Oct. 1980. "CEO Concerns for the 80's Have HRD Implications,"
    TRAINING/HRD, Vol. 17, No. 10, p. 6.

Human—Computer Interaction, edited by G. Salvendy
Elsevier Science Publishers B.V., Amsterdam, 1984 — Printed in The Netherlands

COGNITION BASED INTELLIGENT TUTORING SYSTEMS[1]

JEFFREY G. BONAR

Learning Research and Development Center, University of Pittsburgh,
Pittsburgh, PA 15260 (USA)

INTRODUCTION

At the Learning Research and Development Center (LRDC) we are developing
intelligent tutoring systems as practical expressions of the principles of
learning and teaching that are emerging from research on novice cognition.
Our approach is to build on past AI experience with intelligent tutoring
systems (Sleeman and Brown, 1982), but using our research to provide explicit
objectives for instruction, important insights about the most difficult aspects
of those objectives, useful diagnostic strategies, and guidance on instructional strategies. Currently, we are beginning development of a decimal
numeration (understanding place value notation in decimal numbers) tutor, an
arithmetic word problem tutor, an algebra tutor, and an elementary programming
tutor.

THREE KINDS OF EXPERTISE

In our cognition based intelligent tutoring systems (CBITS) we use three
kinds of expertise. Domain expertise, characterizes the knowledge and strategies needed for expert performance in a domain. In the domains we are studying -- primary and secondary math and science education -- this expertise is
usually straightforward to understand and implement.

Novice conceptions represent the second kind of expertise used in a CBITS.
These conceptions are the knowledge and strategies typically used by novices.
There is considerable evidence that novices often have detailed, systematic,
and errorful conceptions of how a domain works (Resnick, 1983). Domains where
this has been shown include elementary arithmetic (Brown and VanLehn, 1980),
physics (Chi et al., 1982), and programming (Bonar, 1984). In order to effectively understand novice errors, the CBITS must know about typical alternative

---
[1] This work was supported by the Office of Naval Research under Contract Numbers N00014-83-6-0148 and N00014-83-K-0655. Any options, findings, conclusions, or recommendations expressed in this report are those of the authors,
and do not necessarily reflect the views of the U. S. Government.

novice conceptions.

The third kind of expertise used in a CBITS is <u>teaching expertise</u>. This expertise captures how effective teachers actually instruct students in the domain to be tutored. This knowledge may, for example, be in the form of skill components, ordered in terms of difficulty (see Champagne and Rogalska-Saz (1982)). In this case, the tutor selects more difficult problems by requiring the use of more difficult skill components. A different strategy involves representing the knowledge as concepts to be taught, ordered by conceptual dependence (see Rissland (1978)). With a conceptual approach, the tutor selects more difficult problems by focusing on concepts with more dependencies. In either case, the teaching expertise must be used to assess a student's knowledge and construct the next problem on which a student is to be tutored.

Explicating the second two kinds of expertise have been the focus of much recent work in Cognitive Science (Collins, 1978, Greeno, et al, 1983, Resnick, 1983). The focus of our work is to take what has been learned about the cognitive science of instruction, and apply it to the work of intelligent tutoring.

BUILDING COGNITION BASED INTELLIGENT TUTORS

With the three kinds of expertise discussed above, we are prepared to effectively build on past experience in intelligent tutoring systems (Sleeman and Brown, 1982). In particular we are building on the architecture of the WEST tutor (Burton and Brown, 1982). In that architecture the tutor uses a black-box model to represent domain expertise. For example, an algebra tutor might use a complete search to rank the possible next steps for a student trying to simplify an algebraic expression. It is not likely that an expert would use such a search, so the model gives us little information about how the ideal move was derived, or where a student might go wrong.

The ideal performance, based on our domain expertise, is then compared to the student's actual performance, producing a differential model. In order to diagnose student problems, various issue recognizers detect specific errors and incorrect strategies implicit in the differential model. The particular issues chosen stem from the novice conceptions. Each issue recognizer focuses on specific (mis)conceptions that a novice might have. For example, in the domain of decimal numeration, issues include "correct use of zero as a place holder" and "decimal part of a number specifies the numerator of a fraction" (See Resnick and Nesher (1983) for a complete list of decimal numeration knowledge elements.)

Tutoring is based on the results from these issue recognizers. The knowledge used to make specific decisions about when to intervene and what to tutor next are based on the teaching expertise. For example Champagne and Rogalska-Saz (1982) have developed a detail sequence of subskills to be presented to students learning decimal numeration. Their sequence of skills smoothly moves students from the most basic skills to complete knowledge of the domain.

In many cases, key components of the current generation of intelligent tutors can be improved by using available cognitive science research. The rich cognitive knowledge available to the CBITS we are building can be expected to substantially reduce their complexity compared with present intelligent tutors. For example, the WEST tutor has a major component that works to construct theories relating student performance to possible underlying misconceptions or missing knowledge. In CBITS, much of the knowledge required for this diagnostic process is already understood and can be directly built into the system. As a result, the diagnostic facilities of the tutor may not need to be as powerful, since we have more leverage on what errors the student is likely to make and how those errors relate to the underlying misconceptions.

Building the tutor's representations on the basis of cognitive research not only makes the task easier, it also insures that the tutors' representations will have psychological validity--that is, that they will be matched reasonably closely to human intelligence rather than being purely artificial intelligence constructions. The importance of this is underscored by considering some of the difficulties that have been experienced in attempting to build tutoring systems on the basis of artificial intelligence "expert systems;" systems that were themselves not constructed with human intelligence constraints in mind. Clancy (1982), for example, discovered that the medical knowledge embedded in the MYCIN program, while effective at producing quality medical diagnoses, could not be adapted as an effective tutor. Essentially, MYCIN did not explicitly address how experts used the different kinds of knowledge stored in its production rules. MYCIN's successor, NEOMYCIN (Clancy, 1983), sorts out the purpose and tacit knowledge embedded in its rules. With this knowledge made explicit, a new generation of more effective tutors is being developed. Our intelligent tutoring systems group is fortunate to be able to come at the tutoring task with an understanding of the tacit knowledge used by skilled problem solvers. By understanding the tacit knowledge for a domain, we can design the tutor to teach the exact skills needed and currently missing from standard curriculums.

CONCLUDING REMARKS

We are excited by the opportunity of using intelligent tutoring technology to apply cognitive and educational research directly to the development of more effective educational software. In implementing CBITS, we are generalizing the notion of knowledge and expertise as developed in expert systems, by including novice misconceptions as part of our "expertise." We are encouraged that other expert system applications can similarly benefit from a cognition based approach.

REFERENCES

Bonar, Jeffrey G. Understanding the Bugs of Novice Programmers. PhD thesis, University of Massachusetts, 1984.

Brown, John Seely, and VanLehn, Kurt. Repair Theory: A Generative Theory of Bugs in Procedural Skills. Cognitive Science, 1980, 4: 379-426.

Burton, Richard R., and Brown, John Seely. An Investigation of Computer Coaching for Informal Learning Activities. In Sleeman, Derek and Brown, John Seely (Eds.), Intelligent Tutoring Systems, London: Academic Press, 1982.

Champagne, Audrey B. and Rogalska-Saz, Joan. Cognitive Task Analysis in the Design of Computer-Based Mapping Instruction. American Educational Research Association, New York, March, 1982.

Chi, Michelene T. H., Glaser, Robert and Rees, Ernest. Expertise in Problem Solving. In Sternberg, Robert (Ed.), Advances in the Psychology of Human Intelligence, Hillsdale, New Jersey: Lawrence Erlbaum Associates, 1982.

Clancy, William J. Tutoring Rules for Guiding a Case Method Dialogue. In Sleeman, Derek and Brown, John Seely (Eds.), Intelligent Tutoring Systems, London: Academic Press, 1982.

Clancy, William J. The Epistemology of a Rule-Based Expert System -- A Framework for Explanation. Artificial Intelligence, 1983, 20: 215-251.

Collins, A. Explicating the Tacit Knowledge in Teaching and Learning. Technical Report 3889, BBN, 1978. Presented at the 1978 meeting of the American Education Research Association.

Greeno, J.G., Glaser, R., Newell, A. Research on Cognition on Precollege Education in Mathematics, Science and Technology. In Coleman, W.T. Jr., Selby, C.C. (Eds.), Educating Americans for the 21st Century: Volume 2,: National Science Board Commission on Precollege Education Mathematics, Science and Technology, 1983.

Resnick, Lauren B. A New Conception of Mathematics and Science Learning. Science, April 1983, 220: 477-478.

Resnick, L.B., Nesher, P. Learning Complex Concepts: The Case of Decimal Fractions. Psychonomics Society, 1983.

Rissland, Edwina. Understanding Understanding Mathematics. Cognitive Science, 1978, 2(4).

Sleeman, Derek and Brown, John Seely. Intelligent Tutoring Systems. London: Academic Press 1982.

Human—Computer Interaction, edited by G. Salvendy
Elsevier Science Publishers B.V., Amsterdam, 1984 — Printed in The Netherlands

EXTRACTION OF EXPERT KNOWLEDGE FROM OPERATORS OF DYNAMIC COMPUTER ASSISTED SYSTEMS

WILLIAM D. WEST
Deputy Director of Combat Developments, Fort Knox, Kentucky 40121

INTRODUCTION

The current trend of including microprocessor technology in systems of all types may be attributed to several factors, the most notable being the increasing reliability and capability along with the decreasing size, power requirements and cost of this technology. Perhaps the most significant driving force for the computerization of military equipment, is the need to achieve higher levels of performance from a military force whose size is constrained by national policy to a fixed level. Because of this constraint, each system operator must be able to successfully perform more operations in a shorter period of time. Microprocessor technology offers the capability to provide the system operators with great amounts of assistance in the form of both raw and processed information; however, many questions remain to be answered concerning the most effective techniques to use in its application. These questions have to do with both the quantity and type of data or assistance to be provided at each level of decision making. Some specific questions are:

1) What level of detail should be presented?

2) How much preprocessing of data should be accomplished prior to its presentation?

3) What is the best format for information presentation?

4) What do system operators need to know about the system and its operation to make effective use of the information?

5) Are the skills and abilities of current operators adequate to utilize the system to its capacity?

6) How do expert operators use the information that is available?

7) How can training programs be developed which will assure effective use of the system by the operator?

8) What characteristics of the expert operator's decision process should be incorporated into the system hardware or software parameters?

PROBLEM

Many of these questions are currently being addressed in ongoing research throughout the Army. To answer them, a methodology is being developed which will enable the system developers to understand the decision process of its operators. In many cases, the operators are unable to accurately describe verbally how they use the information or assistance that is provided. Because of the highly dynamic nature of the situation being faced by the operator, they may use a largely intuitive process to arrive at a decision. As the operators advance from beginners to experts, they come to understand the relative impor- tance of the different data items being provided and apply more appropriate weightings to the items in their decision process (Rouse, 81). Our goal is to understand the interrelationships of these variables as used by the decision maker or operator to allow the system developers to incorporate the appropriate level of assistance during the design phase of a project. By understanding the utilization of information by beginners and how it differs from the expert, training plans may be developed to speed the training process.

One area in particular which will be used as a methodology demonstration, involves the determination of the decision process associated with a tank gunners use of the computerized linear predictor fire control system (FCS). The purpose of the FCS is to control the pointing direction of the gun in order to hit the desired target, when either the target or the firing tank, or both, may be stationary or moving. Essentially, the FCS computer must determine the elevation angle and the azimuth, or lead angle required to hit the target, and then implement the solution. Data entry to the FCS computer may be made either automatically, overtly by the gunner, or covertly by sensing the gunner's tracking motions.

TRACKING TASK

The initial impression that one has of the gunner's task, is that it is one of continuous target tracking, but this is not strictly correct. His job is to keep the target centered behind the reticle of the sight, while the computer calculates the indicated dynamic lead solution required to hit the target due to either target motion or firing tank motion. Because the FCS computer is gathering data from the gunner with no independent method of verification, all errors made by the gunner in tracking the target will be reflected in the cal- culated solution of the lead angle at the time of trigger pull, and subsequently at the time of round impact. These errors may be broken down into two main categories, displacement error and tracking rate error. One of the character- istics of tracking performance in a tank which sets it apart from other continuous tracking tasks, is that the tracking error is only important at those times selected by the gunner to pull the trigger. The displacement error at trigger pull has been shown to be much less than the RMS error of a complete

tracking trial as illustrated in Figure 1, unpublished, from research conducted by West (83). The points marked as t01-t06 indicate times selected by
the gunner to pull the trigger. The calculation of the speed of the target is
based on the tracking command signals input covertly to the FCS computer by the
gunner's control movements. Any mismatch between the true angular rate of the
target and the rate indicated by the gunner's control movements will result in
an error in calculating target velocity, resulting in an inaccurate linear
prediction of the future target location.

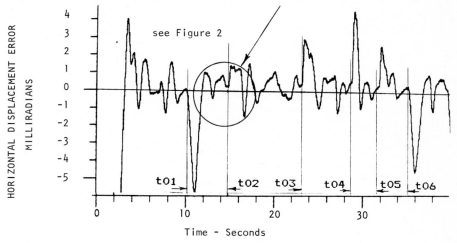

Figure 1. Tracking Error History

The tracking rate error is generally expressed in the angular measure of
milliradians per second, and is indicated by the slope of the displacement
error curve, as illustrated in Figure 2. The importance of the rate error at
round impact time is a linear function of the time of flight to the target,
with miss distance due to this error equal to the rate multiplied by the time-
of-flight. The total error is the vector addition of the displacement error
and the resultant rate error. Typical values of interest for the time-of-
flight range between .5 and 3.0 seconds, based on expected target ranges and
ammunition velocities.

EXPERT DECISION PROCESS

The gunner's decision process can be characterized by the requirement to
make a trade-off between an error source which he can see directly, i.e., the
displacement error, and one which he must estimate, the resultant rate error.
The importance of the rate error in this trade-off process is constantly
changing, as a function of the range to the target, ammunition velocity and
target size. It is clear that while the gunner has been relieved of direct

responsibility for calculating the required lead angle, good performance in the job requires at least some intuitive feel (accurate internal model) for the task which has been allocated to the computer.

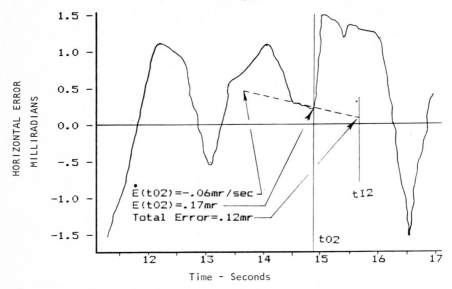

Figure 2. Tracking Error History, Expanded

GUNNER'S INTERNAL MODEL

Preliminary indications from examination of tracking histories, as in Figure 1, are that it may be possible to determine the time duration of acceptable tracking performance required by the gunner before he makes the decision to pull the trigger. For example, Figure 2 indicates a period of relatively smooth tracking for approximately .5 second prior to the decision to shoot. If this duration can be shown to vary with scenario difficulty, it may be related to the gunner's internal model of the importance of the tracking rate error for that scenario. Sheridan, (1974), gives some indication that this time may be linearly related to the rate of information processing required of the operator in this task. Knowing this time would be of importance to hardware designers in matching the machine input requirements to human performance characteristics.

A direct indication of the gunner's internal model is the trade-off between displacement error and rate error which must occur for good performance. Lee (80) has shown, as illustrated by Figure 3, that distributions of these errors at trigger pull show an increasing variance with increasing scenario difficulty. An understanding of how gunners make the trade-off between the displacement error, which they can visualize directly, and the tracking rate error, the importance of which they must estimate, is vital to the development training procedures necessary for optimum system performance.

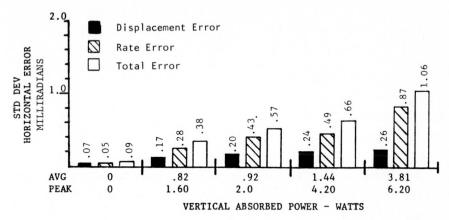

Figure 3. Gunner Performance Variability at Trigger Pull Versus Ride Quality (Measured in Power Absorbed by the Body): After Lee 80.

MODELING THE DECISION PROCESS

Research to model the operator's decision process for this relatively simple two criteria trade-off situation is currently underway at the U.S. Army Armor Center at Fort Knox, Kentucky. The methodology being used involves the determination of the operator's cut-off criteria for each of the decision variables independently. Figures 1 and 2 will be used to explain the procedure. During the entire 45 second trial documented by Figure 1, the gunner determined that there were only six occasions when his tracking performance satisfied simultaneously, his criteria for displacement and tracking rate error. Joint distributions of these errors, similar to those in Figure 3, will be compiled for a variety of scenarios chosen to deliberately vary their relative importance. Once these joint distributions of acceptable performance are determined for an individual gunner, his complete tracking history for all similar scenarios will be analyzed to determine the cut-off criteria for the individual error type. The tracking history will be analyzed for those cases where one of the individual error types was within the limits established for the joint distribution, but the operator chose not to pull the trigger. This will be an indication that the other error type did not meet his standards, and thus establish his decision criteria distribution. For the expert operator, the criteria for each component of error should change as a function of the parameters associated with a scenario.

METHODOLOGY EXPANSION

The technique just explained for the "relatively" simple interaction between the tank gunner and the FCS computer may be expandable to permit examination of more complicated interactions between the operator and the computers in military command and control applications. Large scale net-working of individual computerized simulators, will be used to represent the real time dynamics typical of military operations. Each simulator reproduces with high fidelity, the actions required by individual members of a crew for actual mission performance. Operators of each simulator will be presented with computer generated images depicting the terrain visible through their sighting/sensing systems, and with a CRT display to serve as the two-way interface for data and information transmittal. By monitoring the operator's request for and utilization of the information available and correlating it with his performance and the parameters of the current situation, the value of the information and the best method of presentation may be determined.

REFERENCES

Glumm, M.M., West, W.D., and Lee, R.A., Evaluation of Gunner Station Configura-
    tions for Firing-on-the-Move: Phase II, Technical Memorandum 1-82, US Army
    Human Engineering Laboratory, Tech. Mem. 1-82, 1982.
Lee, R.A., West, W.D., and Glumm, M.M., Evaluation of Gunner Station Configura-
    tions for Firing-on-the-Move, Technical Report No. 12520, US Army Tank-
    Automotive Research and Development Command, Warren, MI., 1980.
Rouse, W.B., Human-Computer Interaction in the Control of Dynamic Systems,
    Computing Surveys, 1981, Vol. 13 No. 1.71-99.
Sheridan, T.B. and Ferrel, W.R., Man-Machine Systems, Information, Control and
    Decision Models of Human Performance, MIT Press, Cambridge, MA., 1974.
West, W.D., Veridical Internal Model Development for an Operator of a
    Predictive Control System, Unpublished, 1983.

Human—Computer Interaction, edited by G. Salvendy
Elsevier Science Publishers B.V., Amsterdam, 1984 — Printed in The Netherlands

INTELLIGENT OBJECT-BASED GRAPHICAL INTERFACES

JAMES D. HOLLAN

Future Technologies, NPRDC, San Diego, California 92152 (USA)

INTRODUCTION

New forms of graphical interaction are being made possible by the current generation of **Display Engines.** These systems, until recently available only in research environments, are rapidly expanding into an increasing variety of exploratory programming applications (Shell, 1983). Their high resolution displays and pointing forms of interaction enable an exciting range of potential applications. The systems range from the new generation of lisp machines from LMI, Symbolics, and Xerox, to a host of 6800-based systems like the Apollo, Iris, and Sun Microsystem machines, to "information appliances" like the Apple Macintosh. With the increased potential for use of graphical interfaces, it seems particularly important to understand how they might effectively be employed and what basis there might be for supporting their use in psychologically principled ways. As one step towards such an understanding, I would like to take the opportunity provided by this conference to reflect on and try to make explicit some of the intuitions that have motivated our work on intelligent graphical interfaces.

For the past several years I have been involved in building an interactive inspectable simulation-based training system. One of the motivations for this research has been an interest in exploring the notion of intelligent object-based graphical interfaces. In the system we have constructed, Steamer (Hollan, Stevens, & Williams 1980; Hollan, Hutchins, & Weitzman, 1984), we provide an interface to allow one to change the state of and monitor a simulation of a complex dynamic physical system via a range of abstract graphically depicted perspectives. Historically our work has been influenced by work on intelligent computer-assisted instruction (Brown, Burton, & de Kleer, 1982; see Sleeman & Brown, 1982 for a survey). It has been inspired by Sutherland's (1963) seminal work on Sketchpad and work on object-based interfaces of the Smalltalk group (now System Concepts Laboratory) at Xerox PARC, especially ThingLab (Borning, 1979).

In the limited space allotted in these proceedings, I would like to highlight three ideas which are at the core of our interface work: **mental models, making visible the invisible,** and **object-based programming techniques.** I will argue that a substantial portion of the usefulness of iconic interfaces is derived from a potentially natural division of communication activities consonant with mental models forms of reasoning, that a quite important type of support is afforded a user by making normally invisible characteristics of a system visible, and that object-based programming techniques provide natural implementation mechanisms.

SUPPORT FOR MENTAL MODELS: MAKING VISIBLE THE INVISIBLE

Understandings of complex dynamic physical systems differ in detail and purpose. For example, the models and knowledge required to operate many pieces of equipment (e.g automated tellers, TVs, automobiles) do not depend on one having deep mechanistic knowledge of the device. In fact, it is a characteristic of a good interface design for such systems that this type of knowledge is neither presupposed nor required for successful operation. In other cases, especially for instructional systems, the whole purpose of an interface is often to support the development of the mental models required to understand mechanism. In instructional applications one is concerned with developing the types of richly structured and robust mental models that are necessary for troubleshooting or that are needed to safely and efficiently operate devices in unusual conditions.

Until we have a better understanding of the models users have about systems and until we more fully appreciate the models we want to encourage users to adopt, the principled design of interfaces is going to be severely constrained. Ideally an interface design should derive from and support the cognitive tasks of the intended users. In the development of Steamer, we have been concerned with the creation of a reactive learning environment in which a student can interact with a simulation of a complex steam propulsion plant in ways that will encourage the development of effective mental models: models which will be useful for reasoning about mechanisms that are required for understanding normal operation of a plant as well as those that are essential for reasoning about and responding to casualty conditions.

Since a major instructional goal for Steamer is to support the development of useful mental models for understanding and reasoning about a complex dynamic system, we have been particularly concerned with making it possible to view and interact with the simulation from perspectives which differ in the level of abstraction at which the system is represented. Graphical interfaces coupled with pointing devices provide an effective way of supporting this form of interaction. With Steamer a student or an instructor can operate the simulation at a level which directly corresponds to interactions with a real plant (opening and closing valves, starting and stopping pumps, etc.) but they can also operate the simulation at more abstract levels (e.g. turning on or off whole subsystems without needing to conceptually decompose those systems) to manipulate global state changes of systems directly. To make such interactions possible we employ highly abstracted views which depict, for example, the whole basic steam cycle involved in powering a ship, views which depict the causal topology of a system by means of animated connections, views which focus on subsystems which might be physically spread out on a ship but which are important to think of as integrated systems, and views which make perceptually available aspects of systems (e.g., rate of change of a signal in an automatic control system) which, although typically not available through standard instrumentation, play quite significant roles in expert reasoning about the operation of the systems.

THE IMPORTANCE OF GRAPHICAL OBJECTS

In order to build useful interfaces, one requires more than bit-mapped displays and pointing devices. If these displays are only used to increase the physical bandwidth of the interface, in terms of the number of bits that can be displayed, then a most important opportunity will be lost: the chance of increasing the **conceptual bandwidth.** A major feature of the Steamer interface is the use of object-based representations which are designed to encourage natural mappings from the interface to the world being simulated and which attempt to provide effective ways for thinking about the simulation. Much of the naturalness of object-based interfaces is based on the tremendous amount of experience and skill people have developed for dealing with physical objects arrayed in space. In other work (Williams, Hollan, & Stevens, 1983) I have argued that there are salient cognitive features of the way people reason about physical systems that involve representations of the world in terms of objects which maintain state information, provide physical and causal topologies, and can be decomposed into more detailed objects. I contend that the naturalness of object-based interfaces, such as employed in Steamer, derives from the common use of abstract objects in reasoning about physical systems. Also interfaces configured from dynamic graphical objects allow a sharing of the work involved in reasoning about the system by maintaining current and past state information, depicting topology, and permitting direct manipulation of state. In addition, hierarchical embedding and decomposition make possible interaction with the system at a level consonant with the requirements of the current task.

The Steamer interface is implemented in Zetalisp using its object-oriented programming facilities, Flavors. This system provides the ability to create multiple instances of objects, to package functionality and share it (even nonhierarchically), to support generic forms of interfaces which permit common forms of interactions with radically different objects, and has facilitated our construction of a powerful graphical editor facility for the rapid prototyping of graphical interfaces.

CONCLUSIONS

The design of human-machine interfaces is still very much an art rather than a science. Design decisions are typically based more on one's experience and informal exploration of design space alternatives than on well understood and empirically validated design principles. Often one has to make tradeoff decisions without being able to fully evaluate the alternatives. In addition, one is rarely able to conduct the types of experiments required to determine which of the myriad potential evaluative dimensions are influenced by a particular design decision. Unfortunately, it is still rare to be able to put forth principled reasons to explain in any deep sense the virtues of even the most successful interfaces. The analysis of the psychological aspects of interface design is still in its infancy and large gaps exist between applications and their scientific underpinnings.

If we are to be successful in building a scientific basis for interface design, it is my view that it will be necessary to appreciate the design of an interface as the construction of a representational system for communication and just as is the case with any other representational system employed by people it is essential to understand the cognitive task the system is attempting to support. Without knowledge of the constraints imposed by the semantics of the task domain and the processing characteristics of both humans and machines, there is little hope of formulating a principled scientific foundation on which to base the design of human computer interfaces. I believe, for example, that it is an egregious error to suppose that one can discuss interface design outside of the cognitive contexts of the task domain in which the interface is embedded and contend that most current investigations, and psychologists seem particularly prone to this, focus too exclusively on a syntactic rather than semantic level of analysis. This often myopic perspective is evidenced in the research literature by the myriad studies concerned with menu structure, formulation of command names, and issues of what type of pointing interface is "best." One potentially more productive perspective is to view human computer interaction as a joint problem solving activity in which there are explicit and implicit obligations and contracts between each member of the interaction. The point I would like to make is that it is very important to keep in mind the whole dialogue structure of the interaction. This includes the important questions of what needs to be "said" and how the communicative functions might be partitioned between the participants as well as the symbology used and the physical mechanisms of interaction. It is from support of this dialogue structure, through effective sharing of the requirements of the task and provision for rapid repair, that successful interfaces evolve.

ACKNOWLEDGMENTS

Work on Steamer has involved the contributions of a number of individuals. I would particularly like to acknowledge the efforts of Ed Hutchins, Louie Weitzman, Bruce Roberts, Larry Stead, and Mike Williams. In addition, discussions with the other members of the Human-Machine Interface project at the University of California at San Diego have influenced my ideas on the principled design of user interfaces. The views expressed in this paper should not be interpreted as representing the official policies of any government agency.

REFERENCES

Brown, J. S., Burton, R. R., & de Kleer, J., 1982. Pedagogical, natural language, and knowledge engineering techniques in SOPHIE I, II, and III. In Sleeman, D., & Brown, J. S. (Eds.) *Intelligent Tutoring Systems*. New York: Academic Press, 227-282.

Borning, A., 1979. ThingLab - A Constraint-Oriented Simulation Laboratory, Xerox SSI-79-3 and Stanford STAN-CS-79-746.

Hollan, J. D., Hutchins, E., & Weitzman, L. STEAMER: An Interactive Inspectable Simulation-Based Training System, *AI Magazine*, in press.

Hollan, J. D., Stevens, A., & Williams, M. D., 1980. STEAMER: An advanced computer-assisted instruction system for propulsion engineering, *Proceedings of Summer Computer Simulation Conference*, published by the Society for Computer Simulation, 400-404.

Sheil, B., 1983. Power tools for programmers, *Datamation*, 29, 131-144.

Sutherland, Ivan E. 1963. Sketchpad: A Man-Machine Graphical Communication System, Ph.D. thesis, MIT, Cambridge, Mass.

Williams, M. D., Hollan, J. D., & Stevens, A. 1983. Human reasoning about a simple physical system. In Gentner, D., & Stevens, A. (Eds.) *Mental Models*. Hillsdale, New Jersey: Erlbaum, 131-153.

Human—Computer Interaction, edited by G. Salvendy
Elsevier Science Publishers B.V., Amsterdam, 1984 — Printed in The Netherlands

AN ISOMORPHISM BETWEEN FAULT TREE ANALYSIS AND LISP DATA STRUCTURES

M.R. Lehto, D.R. Clark, and J.M. Miller
Dept. of Industrial and Operations Engineering, University of Michigan,
P.O. Box 7995, Ann Arbor, MI, 48107.

INTRODUCTION

In this paper, it is assumed that two things are isomorphic when they are identical in respect to properties of interest to us. The following discussion will define some of the commonalities between fault tree analysis and LISP data structures. The implications of this isomorphism will then be explored.

WHAT IS FAULT TREE ANALYSIS?

Fault tree analysis (FTA) is a general technique used in systems safety to analyze potentially hazardous events. In FTA, a logic structure is developed which models the flow of undesirable events within a system. This logic structure is called a fault tree and is composed of connected nodes. The fault tree is a directed graph in which nodes further down in the tree trigger higher level nodes. The nodes are either logic gates or events, while the connections describe the logical relationships of the nodes. Development of the fault tree (Malasky, 1974) involves data collection and preliminary hazard analysis to determine the relevant events and their logical relationships. The resulting fault tree is then simplified and used to evaluate hazards.

Figure 1 illustrates a simple fault tree. At the top of the tree, A is the final undesired event. Event A occurs when either the set of events [B,D,E] or [C,D,E] occur. The set of events [B,C,D,E] contains low-level events, while [A] contains the top-level event. The logical-causal flow of events is modeled by connected logic gates. Only AND and OR gates are shown here, but many other types of gates are commonly used in fault tree analysis (Malasky, 1974).

WHAT IS A LISP DATA STRUCTURE?

LISP is a high-level computer language, used extensively in artificial intelligence, which is especially suited for symbol manipulation. LISP data structures are symbolic (S-) expressions, and can be numbers, atoms, strings, or lists (Charniak, et al., 1980). Each S-expression is a syntactically-legal program which is evaluated by the LISP function EVAL; such expressions use or are defined by other S-expressions. In LISP programming, functions (a special type of S-expression) are defined and used to manipulate S-expressions.

Figure 2 illustrates a LISP data structure equivalent to the fault tree shown in Fig. 1. The data structure defines the conditions under which [A]

298

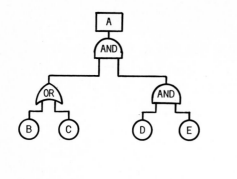

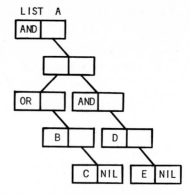

FIGURE 1. A SIMPLE FAULT TREE   FIGURE 2. A SIMPLE LISP DATA STRUCTURE

evaluates to True. As should be apparent from Fig. 2, LISP data structures are binary trees. Each cell within the tree has two pointers which point to symbolic expressions further down in the tree. Another way to represent this data structure is given by the LISP list notation. In list notation, the fault tree shown in Fig. 1 is the following list:

(COND ((AND (OR B C) (AND D E)) 'A))

or equivalently,

(COND (A 'A))

For either list, the LISP interpreter returns A if the logical conditions defined by the fault tree are satisfied.

THE ISOMORPHISM

    A casual examination of Figures 1 and 2 immediately reveals basic similarities between the two data structures. Table 1 lists basic properties of each structure and maps these properties from one structure to the other. The first mapping shown in the table indicates that the directed tree structure of a fault tree is equivalent to the directed binary tree used in LISP. The logical equivalence of binary and general trees is well established (Martin, 1977). The only difference is that the binary representation may require additional nodes to represent an arbitrary tree (e.g., Fig. 2 requires one more node than Fig. 1). This discrepancy, of course, has no influence upon logical

TABLE 1. A MAPPING BETWEEN FAULT TREE ANALYSIS AND LISP DATA STRUCTURES

Fault Tree Analysis . . . . . . maps to . . . . . . LISP Data Structure

Fault Tree Analysis	LISP Data Structure
Directed Tree	Directed Binary Tree
Top Undesired Event	An Atom Set to a LISP List
Primary or Low Level Events	Atoms
AND or OR Gates	AND or OR Reserved Words
Other Logic Gates	User Defined Functions
Links	Pointers
Probabilistic Links	User Defined Functions

equivalence. The logical equivalence becomes more intuitive when the logic structure of a fault tree is carefully considered. In other words, a fault tree is actually a hierarchical collection of IF-THEN rules. The IF portion of a rule is the state of the lower level events entering the logic gate, while the THEN portion is the output of the logic gate. The COND statement used earlier to define the LISP list is, of course, an example of an IF-THEN rule.

The next four mappings shown in Table 1 define the equivalence of nodes used in the two basic structures. First, the events shown in Fig. 1 directly correspond to LISP atoms in Fig. 2. For a high-level event, the atom's value can be set to a LISP list (for example, event A is defined by a list). The LISP list defines the logical relation of the high-level atom to low-level atoms. Another straight-forward approach which can be used to represent more complicated events in LISP is to attach property lists to the atoms. Logic gates used in FTA can also be defined by equivalent LISP data structures. AND and OR are already defined as reserved words in most versions of LISP. More sophisticated gates can easily be defined by writing LISP functions which simulate these gates. The links used between nodes in Fig. 1 are equivalent to the pointers used in Fig. 2. More sophisticated links, such as probablistic links are often used in FTA. LISP pointers do not adequately represent such relations; user defined LISP functions, however, could model these probablistic relations.

IMPLICATIONS

"The complex and arduous process of building an expert system can require years of effort. Much of the work is knowledge acquisition, extracting knowledge from human experts and representing it in machine-usable form." (Waterman and Hayes-Roth, 1983)

The isomorphism between FTA and LISP data structures becomes especially important when the difficulty in obtaining expert knowledge in machine readable form is considered. Existing knowledge encoded within fault trees is in a form usable by an expert system or other computer program. This point is illustrated by the existence of computerized FTA programs. But more importantly, the heuristic nature of existing expert systems directly corresponds to the knowledge structure of a fault tree. (As noted earlier, a fault tree can be decomposed into a collection of rules or relations.) Consequently, knowledge from fault trees can be directly transferred into an expert system. For example, the REACTOR expert system uses fault tree-type data (Nelson, 1982).

A second major implication is that the general approach used in FTA may be useful for extracting expert knowledge. As noted by Buchanen, et al. (1983), it may be difficult to obtain expert knowledge consistent with the knowledge representation used within the computer program. This problem could be alleviated if the knowledge of the expert was directly mapped to a program compatible representation. In other words, eliminating the step wherein the expert's knowledge is transformed into a formal representation by the computer expert might be helpful. Extracting knowledge in the format of fault trees directly results in a _formal_ representation of the expert's knowledge. Also, a large population of human experts is familiar with the general fault tree approach.

The final point is that there is a large data bank of knowledge stored within fault trees. Table 2 summarizes several application areas of fault tree analysis. Classically, this data has been collected for large systems such as nuclear power plants, space projects, or missile systems. However, fault trees or other similar tree structures are useful in a wide variety of alternative settings. For example, Lehto and Miller, (1983) apply this approach when evaluating the effectiveness of warnings. Similar examples include MORT (Johnson, 1973), or generic cause trees for common consumer accidents (Hendrickson, et al., 1976). Subsequently, it must be concluded that recognition of this general isomorphism has the potential to greatly increase the application and development of expert systems.

TABLE 2.   REPRESENTATIVE APPLICATIONS OF FAULT TREE ANALYSIS

Application Area	Amount of Data Present	Reference
Nuclear Power	Large	WASH-1400
Consumer Products	Small	NBSIR 76-1097
Aero-Space Projects	Moderate	Mearns (1965)
Industry	Moderate	MORT
Aviation	Moderate	Connor & Hamilton (1980)

REFERENCES

Charniak, E., Riesbeck, C.K., and McDermott, D.V., 1980. Artificial Intelligence Programming. Erlbaum, Hillsdale, N.J., 323 pp.
Buchanen, B.G., et al., 1983. Constructing an Expert System. Chapter 5 in Building Expert Systems, edited by Hayes-Roth, F., Waterman, D.A., and Lenat, D.B. Addison-Wesley, Reading Mass., 444 pp.
Connor, T.M. and Hamilton, C.W., 1980. Evaluation of Safety Programs with Respect to the Causes of General Aviation Accidents. DOT/FA78WA-4159, ASP-80-2, 216 pp.
Hendrickson, R.G., Robertson, E.M., and Kelley, R.V., 1976. Illustrative Generic Standard for the Control of Thermal Burn Hazards in Household Appliances. National Bureau of Standards, NBSIR 76-1097, 49 pp.
Johnson, W.G., 1973. MORT: The Management Oversight and Risk Tree. Journal of Safety Research, 7(1), 4-15.
Lehto, M.R. and Miller, J.M., 1984. Warnings and Instructions: A Review, Evaluation, and Recommendations. Working Document.
Malasky, S.W., 1974. System Safety: planning/engineering/management. Hayden Book Company, Rochelle Park, N.J., 339 pp.
Martin, J., 1977. Computer Data-Base Organization. Prentice-Hall, Englewood Cliffs, N.J., 713pp.
Mearns, A.B., 1965. Fault Tree Analysis: The Study of Un-likely Events in Complex Missile Systems, Systems Safety Symp., Seattle, WA., June 8-10.
Nelson, W.R., 1982. REACTOR: An Expert System for Diagnosis and Treatment of Nuclear Reactor Accidents. CONF-820874-1, 7pp.
U.S. Atomic Energy Commission, 1974. Reactor Safety Study - Appendix II (Vol 2) PWR Fault Trees, WASH-1400, 618 pp.
Waterman, D.A. and Hayes-Roth, F., 1983. An Investigation of Tools for Building Expert Systems. Chap. 6 in Building Expert Systems, edited by Hayes-Roth, F., Waterman, D.A., and Lenat, D.B. Addison-Wesley, Reading Mass., 444 pp.

Human—Computer Interaction, edited by G. Salvendy
Elsevier Science Publishers B.V., Amsterdam, 1984 — Printed in The Netherlands

THE EFFECT OF FORCED VISUAL WORK ON THE VISUAL NERVOUS SYSTEM

M. SAITO

Dept. of Health Administration, Faculty of Medicine, University of Tokyo,

7-3-1 Hongo, Bunkyo-ku, Tokyo 113

INTRODUCTION

   Much concern about psycho-physiological effect of machine-paced and computer-paced work on industrial workers has been aroused and led to investigation. In the computerized production lines, workers are hardly any chance to control the lines by themselves for confirming their works. Vitality level of workers under paced work conditions has been disclosed by interpreting brain activity during working time (Hashimoto, 1960, Oshima, 1979, 1981). Oshima suggested that an appearance of antagonistic relation between two functions is a manifestation of man-adapting to environment. In this paper, interaction between brain activity and oculo-motor activity as well as the amplitude of inhibition and excitation of each function during working time are discussed to assess occupational stress of workers engaging to the environment rapidly revolutionized by new technology.

METHOD

Subjects in the field

   Two groups of visual workers, young female workers (N=37, aged 18 to 22) and young male workers (N=48, aged 18 to 23), were tested on the actual production lines.

Working conditions

   Workers are not allowed to carry out their work with their own pace and are forced to work with a given pace with 2 times of 15-min. recess and a 45-min. lunch time in a day.

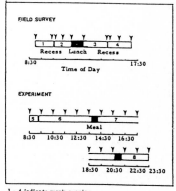

1 - 4 indicate work session
5 - 8 indicate free time (non-work) session
Y indicates measurement was carried out

Fig. 1 : Data collection protocol in the field survey and in the experiment

They are subjected to visual inspection (search of defect on glass bottles) in four working sessions as shown in Fig. 1.

Testing conditions

Testing was carried out 5 times in the morning session and also 5 times in the afternoon session.· Each test was made immediately after a continuous work of forced visual work. Subjects were requested to take adequate sleep at night before testing day. Pre-test was provided in the day before.

Measuring items

1) Ocular accommodation: Oculo-motor activity in the eyes is tested by assessing the amplitude of accommodation. The H-S-9B autographic astheno-meter was used as a tester (Suzumura, 1974). 2) Brain activity: Activity level of cerebral neocortex in the visual nervous system was evaluated by measuring frequency of critical flicker fusion (CFF). The CFF tester developed by Shibata Chemical Engineering Co., Ltd. was applied.

Subjects in the experiment

Five male students (aged 22 to 27) including one with ametropic eyes part-icipated for the experiment of 15-hr. testing. This experiment was planned to study originally a different purpose in the past. Parts of the results were used for comparing with those of forced visual workers in the field. Test in the experiment was carried out every one hour as shown in Fig. 1.

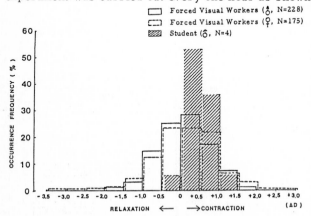

Fig. 2 : Frequency distribution of changes in ocular accommodation (Dptr) between the initial value and the value after work in 8-hr working day

RESULTS

Oculo-motor activity

Occurrence of the changes in ocular accommodation after visual work appeared 53.9% for male and 47.2 % for female in the range of -0.5 dptr～+0.5 dptr, and 86.3% for male and 81.6% for female in the range of -1.0 dptr～+1.0 dptr. Strong contraction

of accommodation which exceeds +1.5 dptr occurred only 4.4% for female and

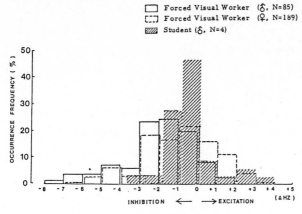

Forced Visual Worker (♂, N=85)
Forced Visual Worker (♀, N=189)
Student (♂, N=4)

Fig. 3 : Frequency distribution of changes in the CFF
value between the initial value and the value
after work in 8-hr working day

1.4% for make workers. Occurrence in the contraction side (indicating as plus) was 54.9% for male and 56.8% for female. Thus, distribution appeared similarily between male and female workers, whereas in student group 88.9% of the changes in accommodation distributed in the range of 0 dptr ～+1.5 dptr.

Activity in the central nervous system

Activity in the brain of male workers during working time trends to the direction of inhibition. Occurrence of the changes in CFF value after work appeared 89.5% for male and 68.3% for female workers towards the side of inhibition. Strong inhibition such as -8.0 Hz ～-4.0 Hz was observed 15.3% for male and 8.9% for female. There are 31.7% for female and only 10.5% for male workers of which changes appeared toward the side of excitation. In student group, 75% of occurrence appeared in the range of inhibition, 0 Hz ～ -2.0 Hz, while 19.4% was toward the side of excitation.

Interaction of two functions

As shown in Fig. 4, mean CFF value of five students slightly increased right after starting at 8:30 am and increasing phase continued for about 3 hours. Then it gradually decreased till around meal time which seemed to provide a slight recovery. On the other hand, hourly variation of mean ocular accommodation except for one student with ametropic eyes trends to increasing with a decrement in the final phase. Hourly variation direction of each function was compared during 15 hours. A periodic

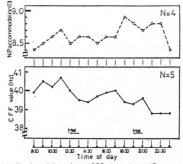

FIG4 Hourly variations of mean CFF value and mean NP accommodation

306

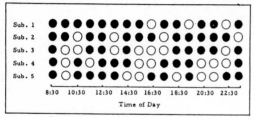

Sub. 1
Sub. 2
Sub. 3
Sub. 4
Sub. 5

8:30 10:30 12:30 14:30 16:30 18:30 20:30 22:30

Time of Day

O indicates antagonistic reaction and ● indicates non-
antagonistic reaction between CFF value and n.p.
accommodation

Fig. 5 : Interactive variation pattern in autonomic
nervous system and in central nervous
system of male students for 8:30 to 23:30

appearance of antagonistic reaction between oculo-motor activity and brain activity was observed as shown in Fig. 5. There are not a specific rhythm, but antagonistic phase continues 1 to 3 hours followed by non-antagonistic phase (unchanged or changing to the same direction) for 1 to 4 hours, except for one student (sub. 1) who had worked during night before testing day.

DISCUSSION

A hypothesis raised at the beginning of the survey was that the changes in ocular accommodation before and after work might be larger amplitude than a physiological variation, -0.5 dptr ~ +05 dptr, as shown by Yamagi (1968) and Otsuka (1969). It was found that most of the changes occurred in the range of -1.0 dptr ~ +1.0 dptr, and occurrence of strong contraction was very low even though workers were required to concentrate during work. As previously reported about visual workers by Saito (1981), changes for contraction occurred in the morning session and seldom appeared in the afternoon session. Activities in oculo-motor function in the afternoon session appeared decreasing or relaxing in comparison with initial value. This trend of variation is apparently discriminating with the case of student whose changes in accommodation were activated in the same period with working time, 830-1730 (Saito, 1982). A periodic appearance of antagonism in which activation of oculo-motor function is accompanied by inactivation in the central nervous system as observed in students was disordered for forced visual workers with short antagonistic reaction only in the morning session. Workers seemed to adapt to working condition for only a few hours in the morning. Their concentration seemed not to continue from 830 to 1730.

REFERENCE

Hashimoto, K. (1960) Fatigue, Corona Publ. Co., Ltd., Tokyo
Oshima, M. (1979) A study on fatigue, Dobun Shoin, Tokyo, pp 24-26
Oshima, M. (1982) Human-approach to unknown, Dobun Shoin, Tokyo pp 114-140, 206-214
Otsuka, H. & Shikano, S. (1969) Clinical ophthalmology, Kanehara Publisher, Japan, pp 273-294
Saito, M., Tanaka, T. & Oshima, M. (1981) Eyestrain in inspection and clerical workers, J. Ergonomics, Vol. 24, No. 3, pp 161-173
Saito, M., Kishida, K. & Hasegawa, T. (1982) Ocular accommodation variability of visual inspection workers in shift work system, Shift work: its practice and improvement. Center for academic publications Japan, pp 47-55
Suzumura, A. (1973) Measuring method of accommodation by accommodo-polyrecorder (H-S-9B), Report 24, Institute for Environmental Medicine, Nagoya Univ.
Yamagi, R. (1968) Study on pseudomyopia, Japanese J. of ophthal., Vol. 72, 10, pp 135-200

Human—Computer Interaction, edited by G. Salvendy
Elsevier Science Publishers B.V., Amsterdam, 1984 — Printed in The Netherlands

307

BINOCULAR AND TWO-DIMENSIONAL EYE MOVEMENTS ANALYSER FOR PHYSIOLOGICAL
EVALUATION OF VDT OPERATIONS

SUSUMU SAITO

Dept. of Industrial Physiology, National Institute of Industrial Health,

Nagao 6, Tama-ku, Kawasaki, 214 (Japan)

ABSTRACT

Saito, S., 1984. Binocular and two-dimensional eye movements analyser for
    physiological evaluation of VDT operations. Proc. First USA-Japan Conf.
    on Human-Computer Interaction, Honolulu, Hawaii

    In order to physiological consideration of VDT (visual display terminal)
operations, constructed was the system for measuring horizontal and vertical
ocular motilities of both eyes with accuracy. Versional eye tracking
experiment with covered unilateral eye gave binocular horizontal dissociation
(exophoria of covered eye) in both the saccadic and fixation phases. Binocular fixation point computed from the value of eyeball deviation (divergence)
in the fusion-free condition was further than several recommended viewing
distances from VDT operator to CRT screen.

INTRODUCTION

    As current rapid rate of VDT usage increases, many problems concerned with

health and safety of occupational video viewing workers have been argued and

discussed in various fields (Cakir et al., 1980, Grandjean et al., 1980, NRC,

1983). The majority of questionnaire surveys elucidate that VDT operators

complain of eye strain and visual fatigue. These eye impairments were more

frequent in VDT operators than traditional office employees (Laubli et al.,

1981). The present experiment deals with the oculomotor function as one of

the most important physiological sides of VDT operations. A system for pre-

cise measuring and computing of two-dimensional eye movements of both eyes

was constructed and investigated was the system evaluation and binocular

interaction in eye tracking.

DETECTION OF EYE POSITION

    For measuring eye movements, a number of techniques have been developed

through physiological and other researches (Robinson, 1968, Leigh et al.,

1983). Utilized method in this study for detecting eye position is corneal

reflection technique. The virtual image of each eye created by projection

of an infra-red emitting diode onto the eye is focused on a two-dimensional

MOS (metal oxide semiconductor) image sensor which has 320 (H) x 244 (V)

pixels and then converted into NTSC video signal. Fixation point of each eye

can be displayed on a monitor TV as so-called eye mark superimposed on a
visual sight of a subject. Simultaneously, the video signal is fed to
electronic decoder in order to convert the fixation position into corresponding analog voltage. The eye movements can be measured even when a subject

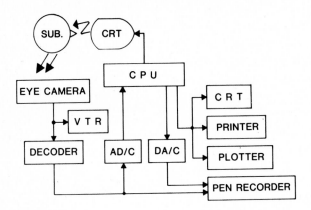

Fig. 1. The system for analysis of binocular and two-dimensional eye
movements.

puts on his spectacles. There was not significant difference in calibrated
linearity and accuracy between myope with glasses on and emmetrope without
glasses. The equipment is incorporated into the NAC eye mark recorder V.

SUBJECTS AND EXPERIMENTAL PROCEDURES

Studies were made on 14 healthy adult persons aged 30.8 ± 6.1 (mean and
standard deviation) years old and they had no known visual defects except for
some myopes. A subject was seated on a chair and his or her head was placed
on a chin holder with metal fittings providing additional support to reduce
the head movements.

A character "+" was exposed as a target to a subject on a CRT located 45 cm
apart from the eyes. The position of a target was randomly changed on a
two-dimensional CRT screen with statistically descriptive range of variance
of its randomness at intervals of 2 sec. A subject was instructed to fix his
eyes to a target as quickly as possible. After repeating the sequence 48
times, a trial finished and then data processing set in. An amount of a
target displacement was set at 9.2 degrees on an average as to horizontal and
vertical directions regardless of different degrees of position randomness.

DATA PROCESSING

At the beginning of an experimental trial, calibration of measuring system was automatically accomplished. Four channel data of eye positions corresponding to horizontal and vertical co-ordinates of fixation point of each eye were sampled by A/D converter with 33 msec period and with 12 bit resolution. Then the data were fed to 16 bit micro-computer system for signal processing and graphic display of measured fixation points loci. The corneal reflex method employed here has a limited spatial resolution about 0.5 degrees and utilized image sensor for detecting an eye mark also has a similar limitation. To overcome these drawbacks the accuracy or resolution of measured eye movements was advanced by averaging a number of sampled data.

The data taken in were divided into two phases and analysed; first the saccadic phase subsequent to onset of a target presentation, secondly the fixation phase to a stationary target. The initial 363 msec were decided as saccadic phase after consideration of saccadic reaction time (Saito et al., 1974), the following duration was categorized as fixation phase. All the data were evaluated in each phase as mean and standard deviation of algebraic differences between target and eye positions every sampling period. Binocular differences between a target and eye positions in both horizontal and vertical directions were also appreciated as the indices of heterophoria or latent strabismus of a subject. Several examples of measured results are shown as follows.

ACCURACY OF SACCADE AND FIXATION

Saccadic accuracy in the study was represented by saccadic error which meant

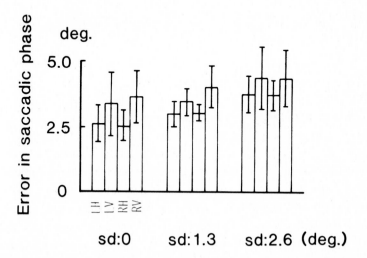

Fig. 2. Saccadic accuracy. Degree of randomness of target movement was noted by sd. LH, LV, RH and RV in the figure stand for Left or Right eye and Horizontal or Vertical direction of movement, respectively.

integrated positional difference between a target and eye data during saccadic phase as described above. Mean and standard deviation of 14 subjects to three different levels of randomness were demonstrated in Fig. 2. As already noted total amount of saccadic travel among the three conditions was almost the same. The saccadic accuracy increased with decrease the randomness of target movements. When a target was stationary, absolute value of subtractive eye

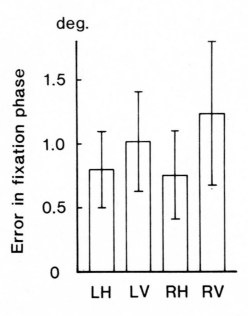

Fig. 3. Fixation error to a stationary target.

data from a target position was computed as an index of fixation error (Fig. 3). Averaged fixation error of 14 subjects in this study was 0.95 degrees with standard deviation of 0.40 degrees.

DIFFERENCE BETWEEN BOTH EYES IN BINOCULAR OR MONOCULAR VISION

   Binocular conjugate eye movements in the same direction are called versions. Similarly to the measurements of fixation, absolute value of subtractive left eye position from right was computed every sampling period in each horizontal and vertical direction, respectively. The value represents binocular differences of ocular motility as index of heterophoria or latent strabismus.

   In Fig. 4, the averaged value of binocular differences in usual binocular vision is illustrated by dotted horizontal lines. The grand mean and standard deviation in the condition were 0.84 and 0.28 degrees. In the same figure, dissociated eye position during eye tracking with monocular vision is represented by histogram. This study was done as follows. Initially, with both

eyes viewing, the measuring system was calibrated and a series of eye tracking
trial was executed. Then the same sequence was attempted when the cover was
placed before a unilateral eye, and finally, tried with covered another eye.
Six healthy subjects participated in the test. All the subjects examined
showed exophoria that is divergent visual axes in the fusion-free condition.
The phenomenon corresponds to hetrophoria or latent strabismus (Lehigh et al.,
1983, Moses, 1970). This is not pathological but normal physiological

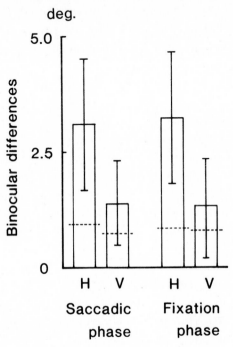

Fig. 4. Dissociated eye position in fusion-free condition. Dotted lines
are the levels of binocular fusion condition.

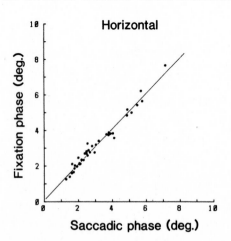

Fig. 5. Size of heterophoria in two phases.

oculomotor function. The amount of deviations between both eyes when unilateral eye was covered was almost the same in saccadic and fixation phases as shown in Fig. 4. It is demonstrated from another side that the magnitude of binocular deviations shown in saccadic phase closely coincided with those in fixation phase. Fig. 5 shows a close relationship of binocular deviation sizes between saccadic and fixation phases. The relation agreed well as described by the following linear regression equation:

$$Y = 0.997X + 0.119 \qquad (r = 0.986) \tag{1}$$

where Y = deviation angle in fixation phase; X = those in saccadic phase; r = correlation coefficient.

In other words, dissociated position or heterophoria was maintained an almostly constant deviation during the sequence of saccade and fixation. This means that even an covered unilateral eye is placed without fusion mechanisms under the normal condition of eye movement control system. Under-lying physiological mechanisms seem to be similar to precise saccadic eye movements in completely dark room (Saito, 1975). Grand mean and standard deviation of exophoria measured in the present study were 3.16 and 1.43 degrees, respectively. From the value, the distance of an imaginary or hypo-thetical binocular fixation point with fusion-free condition can be obtained theoretically as 73.0 cm on an average. The range of the distance, consider-ing a standard deviation, is within 57.0 cm and 101.2 cm apart from eyes. Though the values may change with the physiological attributes of persons to be examined, these distances obtained here are relatively long in comparison with the already recommended viewing distances from VDT operator to CRT screen by several authorized organizations. The guideline recommended by NIOSH, as a typical example, has proposed that the viewing distance should be within 400 mm and 700 mm (Bergman, 1980).

REFERENCES

Bergman, T., 1980. Health Effects of Video Display Terminals. Occupational Health and Safety, 49, 6:24-28, 53-55.
Cakir, A., Hart, D.J. and Stewart, T.F.M., 1980. Visual Display Terminals, John Wiley & Sons, Chichester.
Grandjean, E. and Vigliani, E. (Editors), 1980. Ergonomic Aspects of Visual Display Terminals, Taylor & Francis, London.
Laubli, T., Hunting, W. and Grandjean, E., 1981. Postural and Visual Loads at VDT Workplaces II. Lighting Conditions and Visual Impairments. Ergonomics, 24:933-944.
Leigh, R.J. and Zee, D.S., 1983. The Neurology of Eye Movement, F.A. Davis, Philadelphia.
Moses, R.A., 1970. Adler's Physiology of the eye, The C.V. Mosby, St. Louis.
National Research Council, 1983. Video Displays, Work, and Vision, National Academy press, Washington, D.C.
Robinson, D.A., 1968. The Oculomotor Control System: A Review. Proc. IEEE., 56:1032-1049.

Saito, S., Tsukahara, S., Fukuda, T. and Yoshida, T., 1974. Some character-
    istics of EEG alpha activity during tracking eye movements. Fukushima J.
    Med. Sci., 20:97-106.
Saito, S., 1975. Association of eyelids with the control system of eye
    movements. Fukushima J. Med. Sci., 21:113-124.

Human—Computer Interaction, edited by G. Salvendy
Elsevier Science Publishers B.V., Amsterdam, 1984 — Printed in The Netherlands

EFFECTS OF REST BREAKS IN CONTINUOUS VDT WORK ON VISUAL AND MUSCULOSKELETAL COMFORT/DISCOMFORT AND ON PERFORMANCE

Helmut T. Zwahlen, Andrea L. Hartmann, and Sudhakar L. Rangarajulu
Department of Industrial and Systems Engineering, Ohio University,
Athens, Ohio 45701

Based on the concerns about potential chronic effects on the visual and musculoskeletal system and prolonged psychological distress, the National Institute for Occupational Safety and Health (1981) has recommended that

1. A 15-minute work-rest break should be taken after two hours of continuous VDT work for operators under moderate visual demands and/or moderate workload.

2. A 15-minute work-rest break should be taken after one hour of continuous VDT work for operators under high visual demands, high workload and/or those engaged in repetitive work tasks.

It was noted (National Academy of Science, 1983), however, that "moderate" and "high" visual demands and workloads are not defined by NIOSH, and that no comparison is made between VDT jobs and comparable non-VDT jobs on these parameters. In a preliminary study (Zwahlen, 1983) with three VDT operators we found that the average screen viewing time was only 14% for a data entry task and 34% for a file maintenance task, and therefore questioned whether the many reported complaints about eye troubles are really caused by the screen itself. To further investigate this question and others the following experiment was conducted.

METHODS

Six subjects, all female and experienced typists, wearing no glasses or contacts, three of them 18, one 26, one 30 and one 53 years old, were tested during two full working days in a VDT workstation. A 15 minute rest break was given in the middle of the morning and of the afternoon session in addition to a 45 minute lunch break. At the beginning and end of each workperiod a questionnaire on discomfort (see legend in figure 2) was displayed on the screen; the subjects could respond to the eighteen questions by pressing the minus - key from column 00 to 72, according to the level of their discomfort. The scale went from column 05 "no, not at all", over 20 "only very little", to 36 "somewhat", 49 "quite a bit" and 64 "yes, very much so".

A task mixture was used: in the data entry task the information had to be keyed in according to an original, in the file maintenance task the subjects had to find errors on the screen (every line had at least on) and correct according to an original file. The files consisted of names for chemical compounds, stock numbers with 10 characters (e.g. G7J18G2Y7), addresses, phone and bin numbers, prices and eight digit location codes.

In two of the four sessions the original file was a hard copy, while in the other two sessions the same information was displayed on the right half of the screen. The experimental design for these two data presentations was completely balanced.

The subjects were working under an incentive pay scheme. Their performance (keystrokes per minute and errors per file) was continuously monitored by an Apple II computer system which was also driving the IBM 3101 VDT (fitted with a glare filter) used by the subjects to enter and to display the information. An Armstrong Tascon Lighting fixture illuminated the work area. An IBM char was used; the keyboard height was adjustable. A gulf & Western, Applied Science Laboratories 1998 computer controlled eye monitoring system collected eye scanning and pupil diameter data in a nonobtrusive way.

RESULTS AND DISCUSSION

Figure shows that the rest breaks are highly beneficial in reducing musculoskeletal discomfort. The scores for these questions (see also fig. 2) were consistently higher, especially for the neck and back, than the scores for the visual discomfort questions which also did not decrease as much and as consistent over the rest and the lunch breaks. For both visual and musculoskeletal discomfort there still is, despite the breaks, a considerable cumulative effect over the working day. In numerous field studies (see NIOSH, 1981 and NAS, 1983) the reported incidence and intensity of visual complaints were usually similar or even higher than the musculoskeletal problems. In this laboratory study a modern display unit was placed in an environment with appropriate non-glare lighting; on the other hand the focusing requirements of the eye monitor system were such that the subjects had to be asked to move their head as little as possible, which could be a major cause for high musculoskeletal discomfort levels in neck and back.

Discomfort scores for the first and second day as well as for the two data presentation modes were quite consistent. Looking for more than 80% of the time at the screen when working with a split screen as compared to less than 40% when working with a hard copy caused - as shown in figure 2 - only a minimal or no additional increase in both visual and musculoskeletal discomfort scores.

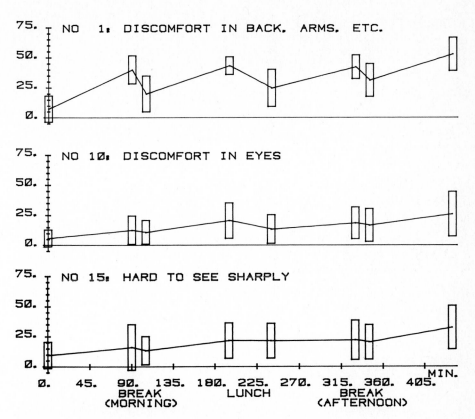

FIG. 1 Group averages and standard deviations of the successive discomfort scores for one musculoskeletal and two visual questions for 6 VDT operators and both working days (N = 12).

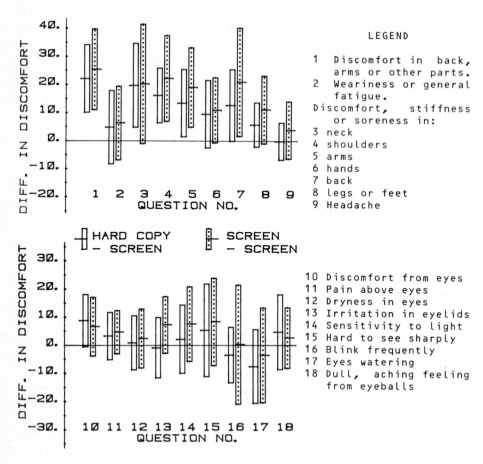

FIG. 2. Group averages and standard deviations of the differences in discomfort scores over each 90 minutes of continuous VDT work for 6 VDT operators, 2 full working days and two different data presentations (N = 24 for each condition).

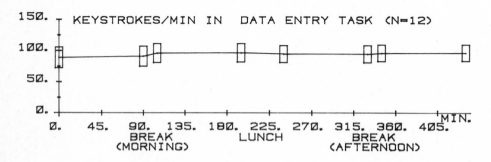

FIG. 3. Group averages and standard deviations of the keystrokes per minute that the 6 VDT operators made in the data entry task over both working days (N = 12).

The subjects maintained their performance fairly well over both working days (Figure 3). Keystrokes per minute were in general slightly higher after the breaks, but they also increased during the sessions due to the learning effect. For the errors there was no consistent trend.

CONCLUSIONS

Based on these results we may conclude that 1) the amount of time looking at the screen has no major influence on both visual and musculoskeletal discomfort, that 2) rest breaks should be scheduled primarily to relieve musculoskeletal stress, that 3) two rest breaks in addition to the lunch break appear not to be sufficient to adequately reduce musculoskeletal and visual stress in continuous VDT work characterized by high data acquisition and processing demands, and that 4) there are no obvious reasons why clerical work using well-designed VDTs under appropriate non-glare lighting conditions in easily adjustable workstations should produce any effects which are fundamentally different from any other sedentary non-VDT work.

ACKNOWLEDGEMENTS

This study was partially supported by the National Institute for Occupational Safety and Health. The authors wish to especially acknowledge the contributions of Dr. Olov Ostberg, Visiting Scientist at NIOSH, and Dr. Michael J. Smith, Chief of the Motivational and Stress Research Section, DBBS/NIOSH.

REFERENCES

National Institute for Occupational Safety and Health, 1981. Potential Health Hazards of Video Display Terminals. DHHS (NIOSH) Publication No.81-129, Cincinnati, 75 pp.

National Academy of Science, 1983. Video Displays, Work and Vision. National Academy Press, Washington, D.C., 273 pp.

Zwahlen, H.T., 1983. Measurement of VDT operator performance, eye scanning behavior and pupil diameter changes. In: Proceedings of the Human Factors Society 27th Annual Meeting, Norfolk, Virginia, Volume 2, pp. 723-727.

Human—Computer Interaction, edited by G. Salvendy
Elsevier Science Publishers B.V., Amsterdam, 1984 — Printed in The Netherlands

Toward a (truly) Intelligent Terminal:
A NEW PROCESS OF VDT SCREEN LAYOUT DESIGN

Dennis J. Streveler
University of California - San Francisco
Section on Medical Information Science
San Francisco, CA 94103 U S A

- - - - - - - - - - - - - -
A human decides <u>what</u> and <u>why</u> data
appears on the screen, a machine
decides <u>where</u> and <u>how</u>.

INTRODUCTION

As much of computer science advances, an important aspect of the science is allowed
to languish, devoid of software tools, without objective measures, and with no synergistic relationship to hardware design. Although more and more process decisions are
deferred until execution time, screen design is still hard-coded and bound at
compilation time. While nearly everyone agrees that VDT design is among the most
important aspects of the man-computer interface [Bailey82], little energy has been
expended to modernize and automate this design activity.

THE MODERNIZATION PROCESS

Until now, the term "intelligent terminal" has been used to describe visual terminal
devices which exhibit little, if any, intelligence. Although video terminals contain
sophisticated processors, which are fast computers in their own right, their inherent
power has been devoted largely to such mundane tasks as screen refreshing, screen
editing, function key servicing and the like.

The ultimate goal of this research is to define a (truly) intelligent terminal: one
which actively participates in the creation of an appropriate external interface -- a
terminal which <u>designs its own screen layouts</u>, and one which does this in real-time,
<u>on-the-fly</u>. The following machines are described in an attempt to prescribe a
reasonable path to that goal.

1. The <u>Evaluator</u> (implemented)

The Evaluator is a machine which objectively analyzes an existing screen design and
provides feedback to the designer regarding the design's spatial structure. It provides

322

information concerning:

Loading and density (both global and local)

Complexity

Association

Alignment (and other visual cues)

Aesthetics (balance and symmetry)

It does not analyze semantics, only form. Even this basic information is useful to the screen designer, especially in cases where one alternative design must be chosen over another.

We present below some sample output from The Evaluator. First, the original screen design is shown. The screen instance is an actual example from a popular, if somewhat dated, system used for entering and retrieving information concerning medical encounters.

```
                         *CLINIC HEALTH REPORT*
  BARLETTA,TONY  #666884444                    PROBLEM:  2 HEADACHE
  MALE AGE: 41 DOB: JAN 26,  36                VISIT: 3
     AUG 30, 77
       WT: 186    TEMP: 98.8    BP: 140/60

  SUBJECTIVE
     PAT CONTINUES TO HAVE PERIODIC SPELLS

  OBJECTIVE
     MONITOR

  PLAN
  TESTS
     COMPLETE BLOOD COUNT
        HEMATOCRIT (42-50 ): 45
        WHITE BLOOD COUNT (4500-11000 MM3): 12000*
        RED BLOOD COUNT (4.6-6.2 MILLION/MM3): 5
     POTASSIUM (3.5-5.0 MEQL): 6*
     SODIUM: 123

  MEDICATIONS
     ACETOPHENAZINE: 2 TABS FOR 3 DAYS
```

Next is the graphic output of the 'boxing analyzer'. This process provides feedback concerning the likely visual association of fields. It indicates which sets of fields can be inscribed by a rectangular box drawn completely in white-space. Our example points out some possible problems: Box #3 and #4 indicate a possible improper association. Box #6 contains data which is orphaned from other vital signs appearing in Box #2. Box #10 is large and ungainly, showing little internal organization. Box #2 contains the patient's name, a vital piece of information, which is included with several other unrelated items.

BOXING ANALYSIS

```
.........................+1--------------------+.............................
:                        |*CLINIC HEALTH REPORT*|                           :
+2-----------------------+ +--------------------+3+-------++4---------+      :
|BARLETTA,TONY  #666884444|+5-+                  | PROBLEM:||2 HEADACHE|     :
|MALE AGE: 41 DOB: JAN 26,||36|                  |VISIT: 3 |+----------+     :
|  AUG 30, 77             |+6-+-------+          +---------+                 :
|  WT: 186    TEMP: 98.8  ||BP: 140/60|                                     :
+7-----------------------+ +----------++---------+                          :
|SUBJECTIVE      +8---------------------+                                   :
| PAT CONTINUES |TO HAVE PERIODIC SPELLS|                                   :
+9---------+-----+---------------------+                                    :
|OBJECTIVE |                                                                :
|  MONITOR |                                                                :
+10--------+-------------------------------------+                          :
|PLAN                                            |                          :
|TESTS                                           |                          :
|   COMPLETE BLOOD COUNT                         |                          :
|      HEMATOCRIT (42-50 ): 45                   |                          :
|      WHITE BLOOD COUNT (4500-11000 MM3): 12000*|                          :
|      RED BLOOD COUNT (4.6-6.2 MILLION/MM3): 5  |                          :
|   POTASSIUM (3.5-5.0 MEQL): 6*                 |                          :
|   SODIUM: 123                                  |                          :
+11---------------+------------------------------+                          :
|MEDICATIONS      +12---------------+                                       :
| ACETOPHENAZINE: |2 TABS FOR 3 DAYS|                                       :
+-----------------+-----------------+.......................................:
```

The next figure, output from the 'hot-spot analyzer', provides information regarding relative data densities across the display. One can discern from this plot where the areas of high data content exist, and how many separately distinguishable areas exist in the topography. In our example, we find only one significant 'hot spot', the area around the laboratory test results. The rest of the display is somewhat uninteresting. Note that from this representation, we can clearly see that the display is significantly off-center (out of balance).

HOT SPOT ANALYSIS
[Character set used to show increasing "heat" is: .`-:=\X@#]

The last figure, results of the 'alignment analyzer', provides information regarding the extent and nature of the use of columnar alignment in the display layout. Notice that, in this example, there are relatively few instances of alignment, especially in the important area containing the laboratory test results. We expect that an improvement in alignment in this area might enhance the readability of the data.

```
ALIGNMENT ANALYSIS
                              ⌐CLINIⅭ ⱨEALTⱨ ⱤEPORT⌐
⌐ARLETTA,TON⌐  ⌐66688444⌐                            ⌐ROBLEM⌐  ⌐ ⱨEADACHⱤ
MALⱤ ⱯGE⌐ ⌐⌐ ⱣOB⌐ JAN 26⌐  ⌐⌐                        ⱴISIT⌐ ⌐
    ⱯUG 30⌐ 7⌐
       ⱲT⌐ ⌐8⌐   ⱮEMP⌐ Ᵽ8.⌐     ⱣP⌐ ⌐40/6⌐

⌐UBJECTIVⱤ
    ⱣAⱮ ⱵONTINUEⱵ ⱮⱰ ⱨAVⱤ ⱤERIODIⱵ ⱵPELLⱵ

ⱰBJECTIVⱤ
    ⱮONITOⱤ

ⱣLAⱨ
ⱮESTⱵ
    ⱵOMPLETⱤ ⱣLOOⱰ ⱵOUNⱮ
        ⱨEMATOCRIⱮ ⌐42-5⌐ ⌐⌐ ⌐⌐
        ⱲHITⱤ ⱣLOOⱰ ⱵOUNⱮ ⌐4500-1100⌐ MM3)⌐ ⌐2000⌐
        ⱤEⱰ ⱣLOOⱰ ⱵOUNⱮ ⌐4.6-6.⌐ MILLION/MM3)⌐ ⌐
    ⱣOTASSIUⱮ ⌐3.5-5.⌐ ⱮEQL)⌐ ⌐⌐
    ⱵODIUM⌐ ⌐2⌐

ⱮEDICATIONⱵ
    ⱯCETOPHENAZINE⌐ ⌐ ⱮABⱵ ⱤOR ⌐ ⱣAYⱵ

STRENGTH OF ALIGNMENTS (number of alignment "runs" in each column)
2..2..2...1..1..1....1.1..1........................................... LEFT
........11.1....1...1.2.1.....1....................................... RIGHT

ALIGNMENT STATISTICS
    Total LEFT  Strengths      12
    Total RIGHT Strengths       9
```

2. The Suggestor (being implemented)

The Evaluator is a passive machine; The Suggestor attempts a more active role in screen design. Like The Evaluator, it operates on the canonical form of a screen design. It seeks to remedy any discrepancies in the measures it discovers by presenting alternatives to the designer. If a screen is poorly balanced, it rearranges the 'boxes' to improve the overall balance. If information is grouped improperly, the machine proposes other configurations by using other predefined templates. The screen design task is accomplished through an interactive dialog between machine and designer. The human's role is to thwart any suggested change which would adversely affect the intended semantics of the design.

3. The Experimentor (implemented)

To drive The Suggestor, rules must be formulated concerning "good" screen design. Unfortunately, few empirical data now exist.[Galitz81] One measure of human performance, visual search speed, is of particular interest. If factors which enhance that measure, and antagonists which detract from it, can be isolated, described and validated with empirical data, then the rules needed to fuel an active design machine can be stated.

The Experimentor is a self-running experiment. It presents questions via a voice synthesizer and alternative screen designs via a visual terminal. It times and logs the subject's response. The subject indicates he has successfully completed the visual search task (i.e. found the datum requested verbally by the voice synthesizer) by typing the first character of the target field. Data from the log becomes input to later statistical analysis. From experiments proctored by this machine, a set of guidelines, aimed at improving human performance in visual search tasks, can be extracted.

4. The Layout Machine (being described)

While The Evaluator and The Suggestor operate on canonical forms, The Layout Machine operates on a representational form. It can design its own alternative screen formats from scratch, given only a high-level, hierarchical representation of the desired screen layout.

An example of a representational form for a "credit screen" in an Accounts Payable system is provided. An informal grammar follows. Note that the grammar is reminiscent of other familiar forms, like the hierarchical data structure representation of the languages COBOL and PL/I. Additional clauses which direct and constrain the machine have been added.

```
declare 1 credit_information,
        2 name_and_address FIRST,
            3 name                      picture x(20),
            3 address   occurs 2        picture x(20),
            3 city                      picture x(13),
            3 state                     picture xx,
            3 zip                       picture 9(5),
        2 credit_status TITLE "Credit Summary" UNORDERED,
            3 last_payment,
                4 last_payment_date     picture xx/xx/xx,
                4 last_payment_amount picture $,$$9.99,
            3 current_balance           picture $,$$9.99,
            3 aged_balance   occurs 5   picture $,$$9.99;


    <level>  <object-id>  [TITLE <string> | NOTITLE ]
         [OCCURS <integer> ]
         [PICTURE <picture-spec>  [FILL <loading%> ] ]
         [IMPORTANCE <importance> | BOX]
         [BEFORE <before-field-list>]
         [AFTER   <after-field-list>]
         [FIRST | LAST]
         [ORDERED | UNORDERED]
         [TEMPLATE       <positive-template-list>]
         [NOT TEMPLATE <negative-template-list>]
```

5. The Intelligent Terminal (the ultimate goal)

The description of a machine which creates screen layout designs on-the-fly is now possible. The Layout Machine can be fitted with a set of heuristics which assure adequate response time. A response time of 0.3 seconds for this task might be rea-

326

sonable for many applications. The time required to choose an appropriate design is, of course, a function of how exhaustive a search of alternative designs is warranted. And this machine can be imbedded in the terminal itself.

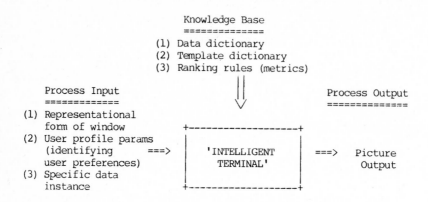

```
                            Knowledge Base
                            ==============
                        (1) Data dictionary
                        (2) Template dictionary
                        (3) Ranking rules (metrics)

      Process Input                    ||                Process Output
      =============                    \/                ==============
  (1) Representational
      form of window          +--------------------+
  (2) User profile params     |                    |
      (identifying    ===>     |    'INTELLIGENT     |   ===>     Picture
      user preferences)       |     TERMINAL'       |            Output
  (3) Specific data           |                    |
      instance                +--------------------+
```

As a result of the screen layout process being deferred until execution time, the machine has the opportunity to design an optimal layout, which is sensitive to the particular user at the controls, and to the particular data instance being displayed.

REFERENCES

Bailey, Robert W., Human Performance Engineering: A Guide to System Designers, Prentice-Hall, 1982.

Card, Stuart K. et al, The Psychology of Human-Computer Interaction, Erlbaum, 1983.

Engel, Stephen E. and Richard E. Granda, Guidelines of Man/Display Interfaces, IBM Technical Report TR 00.2720, December 1975.

Galitz, Wilbert O., Handbook of Screen Format Design, Q.E.D. Information Sciences, Inc., Wellesley, Mass., 1981.

Ramsey, H. Rudy and Michael E. Atwood, Human Factors in Computer Systems: A Review of the Literature, Science Applications, Englewood CO, Technical Report SAI-79-111-DEN, September 1979.

Shneiderman, Ben, Software Psychology: Human Factors in Computer and Information Systems, Winthrop, 1980.

Streveler, Dennis J. and P.B. Harrison MD, "Measuring the 'Goodness' of Screen Designs: An Example from Clinical Medicine", Proceedings of the Seventeenth Annual Hawaii International Conference on System Sciences, January 1984, vol. 1., pp.423-430.

Streveler, Dennis J. and Anthony I. Wasserman, "Quantitative Measures of the Spatial Properties of Screen Designs", Proceedings of INTERACT'84, London, September 1984 (in press).

Tullis, Thomas S., "The Formatting of Alphanumeric Displays: A Review and Analysis", Human Factors, vol.25, no.6, December 1983, p. 657.

NOTE

Details concerning the machines described in this paper are available from the author at the address shown above.

Human—Computer Interaction, edited by G. Salvendy
Elsevier Science Publishers B.V., Amsterdam, 1984 — Printed in The Netherlands

TWO-HAND NUMERIC KEYBOARD DESIGN FOR FINANCIAL DATA PROCESSING: A MATHEMATICAL
SIMULATION OF OPERATOR KEYING BEHAVIOUR

S.W.T. CHEUNG AND G.F. RABIDEAU

Systems Design Engineering, University of Waterloo, Waterloo, Ontario, Canada
N2L 3G1

INTRODUCTION

Prior work (Rabideau et al, 1982) used fast touch-keying female operators to
measure mean inter-key times of one-handed finger movement patterns on a 10-key
numeric KB. Such operators use only three fingers and thumb for most keystrokes. Some Asiatic operators have complained of hand and wrist pain after
one-handed keying. Use of both hands would reduce the keying load/finger.
It might also effect mean inter-key time savings. Paucity of research funds
however, limited this phase's objective to mathematical simulation of two-
handed keying to preliminarily compare potential two-handed keying speed with
the NCR Inc. empirically-derived data on one-handed inter-key times obtained as
noted above.

METHOD

This study design required definition and analysis of those finger movement
patterns required for two-handed keying. Several numeric key configurations
also were defined. Inter-key time estimates were derived from the prior study's
results by comparing movement pattern geometries of one- vs. two-handed keying.
Next a simulation model and algorithm were selected and applied to both sets of
keyboard layouts to determine movements and inter-key times for a batch of 1000
"dollar amounts", e.g., $129.50.

Finger movement patterns and mean inter-key times

A total of 17 finger movement patterns had been identified in the prior
empirical study. Mean inter-key times ranged from 136 to 179 ms, the most rapid
being lateral rollover and lateral hurdle. "Lateral" (as opposed to "medial")
and "up" (vs. "down") patterns tended to be faster than their opposites. In the
present study, the authors shredded some one-handed patterns (hurdles) further,
consequently identifying nine more (or 26) one-handed 10-key KB movement
patterns.

The authors also defined 13 types of two-handed finger movement patterns. Each is identified in Table 1 which also lists estimated mean inter-key times obtained by extrapolation from the one-handed results. The two <u>alternate hand</u> times are 70 ms and the remaining times range from 136 to 179 ms. Two-handed keying movement patterns are fewer and simpler because the KB provides at least eight home-key positions and it lacks the "up" and "down" movements required for one-handed, three-finger keying of 10-key matrices.

TABLE 1

Calculated two-handed KB inter-key times for 13 types of movements.

Pattern	ms	Pattern	ms
Alternate Hand L-R[*]	70	Medial Single Hurdle	155
Alternate Hand R-L[**]	70	Repeated Keying	155
Lateral Rollover	136	Medial Shift Keying	159
Lateral Single Hurdle	137	Medial Double Hurdle	167
Lateral Shift Keying	145	Lateral Triple Hurdle	169
Medial Rollover	147	Medial Triple Hurdle	179
Lateral Double Hurdle	153		

[*] L-R: left to right hand   [**] R-L: right to left hand

Numeric key configurations

Eight two-handed numeric KB layouts were defined as shown in Table 2. Simple and mirror-image progression with and without even-odd digit split were used in the layouts. Effects of response stereotypes, e.g., expected left-to-right digit value increase, weren't considered in making the layouts, hence some are possibly non-optimal. Key locations of any successively-keyed pair of digits serve to define that keying's finger movement pattern.

TABLE 2

Two-handed KB layouts used in the keying simulation.

Layout designation	Direction(s)	Key Amount Layout	
1. simple L-R order	L → R →	1 2 3 4 5	6 7 8 9 0
2. reverse R-L order	L ← R ←	0 9 8 7 6	5 4 3 2 1
3. converging mirror-image	L → R ←	1 2 3 4 5	0 9 8 7 6
4. diverging mirror-image	L ← R →	5 4 3 2 1	6 7 8 9 0
5. even-odd L-R split	L → R →	1 3 5 7 9	2 4 6 8 0
6. even-odd R-L split	L ← R ←	9 7 5 3 1	0 8 6 4 2
7. converging mirror/split	L → R ←	1 3 5 7 9	0 8 6 4 2
8. diverging mirror/split	L ← R →	9 7 5 3 1	2 4 6 8 0

The financial data

A standard set of 1000 "documents", actually dollars/cents amounts was used in the simulation. Digits per amount ranged from three to six, the four frequencies being 3 = 215, 4 = 687, 5 = 92, and 6 = 6. Mean digits/amount was 3.9

and median, 2.5. Some of the 10 digits are more popular than others. Frequencies by digit value are (in descending order): zero = 1284, one = 503, two = 420, five = 403, three = 275, four = 226, six = 220, seven = 206, eight = 183 and nine = 167.

Simulation models and algorithm

Two mathematical models were required for the one- and two-handed KB operational simulations, respectively. A pseudo-code algorithm (Dyck et al, 1979) was utilized with Fortran IV and structured WATFIV dialect. These and their flow charts are omitted herein because of their length (see Cheung, 1984). The simulation calculated: (1) key-pair frequencies per batch; (2) inter-key times for each KB type and layout; and (3) total keystrokes/finger for each configuration.

RESULTS

Inter-key time comparisons

Table 3 compares total inter-key times (to nearest ś) across both one- and two-handed KB configurations. One-handed inter-key time/batch is 448 s, while mean time/batch for two-handed KB layouts is 340 s. Hence two-handed keying could cut inter-key time ~ 24 percent.

TABLE 3

Inter-key times (in s) per KB and layout for entry of 1000 amounts.

One-handed	Two-handed layout number							
	1	2	3	4	5	6	7	8
448	339	339	340	337	340	342	343	339

Two-keying movements - alternate hand and repeat digit - may restrain variability across the KBs. Alternate hand comprises 43 percent of finger movements/ batch and 26 percent of total inter-key time; for repeat-digit it comprises 28 percent of movements and 37 percent of inter-key time. Although the repeat-digit time (155 ms) was extrapolated from the one-handed results, alternate hand time (70 ms) was set at one-half of the one-handed rollover time. It could actually be greater; if it were doubled, i.e., 140 ms, it would add 88 s or less to the two-handed batch times for a total of ~ 400 s.

DISCUSSION AND CONCLUSIONS

This study's design and its simulation suggest that use of two-handed KBs to key financial data could increase productivity. Also, it has shown that KB development should seek to balance finger and hand workload. Table 4 presents percentages of keystrokes by finger for current one-handed vs. potential two-handed operation.

TABLE 4

Percentage of all keystrokes made by each digit for two KB layouts.

One-handed KB					Two-handed KB	(left)				(right)			
digit: T	1	2	3	4	digit: 4	3	2	1	1	2	3	4
%	33	24	26	17	0	13	7	8	16	23	5	6	22

The foregoing table shows imbalance of finger loading in "%" of total keystrokes". Perhaps the several digits should differ in terms of workload, e.g., weaker digits being assigned key numbers which have relatively low frequencies. However, such design measures cannot be capriciously made. Configuration is a "system" problem. Research must resolve effects of key location expectancy stereotypes on relative ease of learning and eventual error rates, given certain numeric key configurations. In other words biomechanical, cognitive and perceptual-motor variables must be included in experimental designs.

A logical next step should involve experiments to resolve KB design issues - both biomechanical and perceptual motor - to choose those two-handed parameters which best attenuate strain, facilitate learning and permit optimal keying speed and accuracy. The authors note that this task has but demonstrated probable practicality and efficiency of two-handed financial data keying.

REFERENCES

Cheung, T.S.W., 1984. Two-handed numeric keyboard design in financial data processing machines. MASc thesis, Department of Systems Design Engineering, University of Waterloo, Waterloo, Ontario, Canada, 150 pp.
Dyck, V.A., Lawson, J.D., and Smith, J.A., 1979. Introduction to computing. Reston Publishing Company, Inc., Reston, VA.
Rabideau, G.F., Lee, R.P.J. and Meguire, P.G., 1982. Inter-key times and digit keying sequences of 10-key numeric touch-keying operators. Proceedings of Eighth Congress of the International Ergnomics Association, Tokyo, August 23-31, pp. 178-179.

Human—Computer Interaction, edited by G. Salvendy
Elsevier Science Publishers B.V., Amsterdam, 1984 — Printed in The Netherlands

VDT AND HUMAN PERFORMANCE

M. AOKI, T. OHKUBO, Y. HORIE and S. SAITO

College of Industrial Technology, Nihon University, 1-2-1, Izumi, Narashino,
Chiba (JAPAN)

ABSTRACT

AOKI, M., OHKUBO, T., HORIE, Y. and SAITO, S., 1984. VDT and human performance

The purpose of this research is to clear the correlation between the lowering
of the arousal level during VDT work and task performance. In this experimentation, therefore, two types of VDT works of which difficulty was different from
each other were performed for 120 minutes and EEG, CFF, near point of eyes
accommodation, etc. were measured. As a result, significance of α wave (8 Hz)
was recognized 30 minutes after the experimentation was strated, indicating
that there was an apparent correlation between the increase of the α wave and
the error generation ratio. The results were more apparent in easier VDT work
items.

INTRODUCTION

Due to the rapid development of electronics technology, computers have now
become common tools for industries to promote the automation of production lines.
With those computers, the productivity has successfully increased, as well as
the quality of products has been improved. The industries then have made
further efforts to reduce as many workers as possible, while expecting energy-
saving and safety to be more enhanced.

This automation, however, is resulting in compelling workers to involve in
supplementary jobs not yet automatized or monotoring jobs (stand-by work type).
That is, workers are forced to work under the condition of excessive reduction
of work load. (E.L. Wiener & R.E. Curry, 1980)

Such jobs will not only reduce the workers' arousal level, that is, leading
them to the status of considerably high level of error potentially, and at the
same time bring stress to them. (A.D. Swain & H.E. Guttman, 1980). Thus those
jobs will badly affect workers both physiologically and psycologically.

This experimentation, thus, aims at examination of the relationship between
the arousal level during work and task performance by giving a simple visual
work (CRT monitoring job) which will bring monotonous phenomenon to workers.

METHODS

Work contents

To make the subject feel monotony, each of the subject was isolated in a room and given two different types of tasks done by using a CRT display and a keyboard.

One of the tasks was continuous addition of single digit numbers (Kraepelin Task); one-digit random numbers except 0, 1, and 2 (40 characters x 10 lines) were displayed on the CRT display and a pair of numbers to be added were indicated by the cursor. When an answer was given, the cursor moved to indicate the next one pair of numbers. The response was made by using the ten key (0 to 9).

Another work task was character-erasing. Japanese Katakana characters (47 characters) were displayed on the CRT display in a format of 40 characters x 10 lines just in the same way as the Kraepelin Task. 4 characters to be erased were specified beforehand and when the cursor came to the characters, the key 1 was pressed. When the cursor came to non-specified characters, the key 2 was to be pressed.

Working hours and measured items

The experimentation was performed continuously for 120 minutes. The experimentation was suspended every 30 minutes to measure the CFF and near point of eyes accommodation (N.P).

The EEG and task performance were measured continuously. In the experimentation, the monopolar lead method was used for EEG, in which a reference electrode was set on vertex (Cz) and an indifferent electrode was set on ear.

The EEG original waveform was recorded on recording paper, and the integrated value of instantaneous element which were analyzed for each crossover frequency band via a power spectrum analyzer was measured every 10 seconds. The instantaneous frequency bands used were 7 in total; 5 to 7 Hz as θ wave element, 7 to 9 Hz, 9 to 11 Hz, and 11 to 13 Hz as α wave element, and 13 to 16 Hz, 16 to 20 Hz, 20 to 30 Hz as β wave element.

Subjects and test conditions

As the subjects, 5 healthy man university students, aged 21 to 23, were selected. The brightness of the CRT display was 124 cd/m^2 (green characters display) and 34 cd/m^2 (black backgroung) constant. The lighting in the test room was 650Lx and was completely artificial.

RESULTS and DISCUSSION

The two types of experimentation were expected to bring monotonous feeling to the subject. They were repetitive works requiring recognition, judgement, and response and were to be done within short time of period respectively. When the character-erasing Task was compared with the Kraepelin Task, the character-erasing task was easier than the Kraepelin Task in any item of recognition, judgement, and response actions.

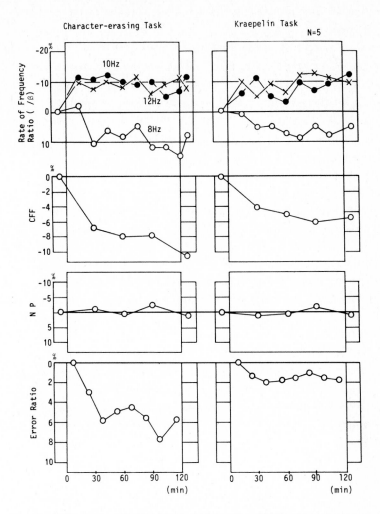

Fig. 1 Difference of stress caused by the difficulty of work tasks

Figure 1 shows an average value of the measured results in EEG. CFF, NP and task performance (error rate) for each work performed for the five subjects.

   The each variation of CFF, which was shown as the increase/decrease ratio to the prework values, lowered 30 minutes after both the experimental works were started. The lowering was particulary remarkable in the character-erasing Task, and some subjects dozed off during the work. The measured results of EEG shown in the top step of the Figure 1 are the variation checked every 15 minutes in comparison with prework values after processing was made as each percentage for β wave (13 Hz to 30 Hz) of the center frequencies 8 Hz, 10Hz and 12Hz. The proportioning of both 10 Hz and 12 Hz was reduced for both the works, while that of 8 Hz increased.

The proportioning increased by about 10% 30 minutes after the character-erasing Task was started, and by 15% just before the work was finished. Also in the Kraepelin Task, it increased by 4% 30 minutes after the work was started, and 8% in 75 minutes, indicating significant lowering of the arousal level.

When the variation of EEG was compared with the variation rate of measure values of CFF (five points in time) sequentially which were obtained every 30 minutes, it was found that the variation of the 8 Hz element was high, corresponding to the lowering of CFF.

The error rate (ratio between errors and all responses) throughout the Kraepelin Task was within 2%, but the error rate in the character-erasing was 6% in 30 minutes, and it increased by 7.9% in 90 minutes. As for the number of responses, the average number of responses per one minutes in the first 15 minutes of the work was 48.3 ± 1.82 ($X \pm SD$) in the Kraepelin Task, while it was 65.5 ± 4.6 in the character-erasing task. In the time band in which the highest error rate was shown, the number of responses was 47.8 ± 2.3 (30 minutes) and 53.8 ± 6.8 (90 minutes) respectively. Reduction of the number of responses and the delay of the response time were recognized in the character-erasing task.

The third step in Figure 1 shows NP variation, but no significant extension tendency due to both the experimentations and working time elaspe was recognized. No correlation with other measured items was also observed.

As can be seen from the measurement results, the arousal level of the brain was not activated by repetitive operations within a minimum unit time, and a monotonous vigilance effect (30 minutes effect; so called by A.D. Swain et al.) was confirmed. The mechanism of its generation is that the effect was caused not by the abuse of one's brain or fatigue of one's body, but because the brain was not activated. Therefore, the effect cannot be expected to be improved simply by inserting a rest between two working periods, and it becomes necessary to take up a countermeasure of changing the organization into an operation having different contents.

REFERENCES

A.D. Swain & H.E. Guttman; Handbook of Human Reliability Analysis with Emphasis on Nuclear Power Plant Applications, NUREG/CR- 1278 (DRAFT) (1980)
E.L. Wiener & R.E. Curry; Flight-deck Automation: Promises and Problems, Ergonomics, 23-10, p.995 (1980)

Human—Computer Interaction, edited by G. Salvendy
Elsevier Science Publishers B.V., Amsterdam, 1984 — Printed in The Netherlands

ERGONOMIC AND STRESS ASPECTS OF COMPUTERIZED OFFICE TECHNOLOGY

Michael J. Smith, Ph.D.

Applied Psychology and Ergonomics Branch, Division of Biomedical and Behavioral Science, National Institute for Occupational Safety and Health, Centers for Disease Control, Public Health Service, U.S. Department of Health and Human Services

ABSTRACT

Office computerization is growing at an astronomical pace with estimates that industrial firms in the private sector will spend $1 trillion between 1982 and 1986 on computers and related supplies and personnel (OTA, 1983). Currently, over 50 percent of the U.S. workforce is in offices with one in five office workers using a computer terminal. By the end of the next decade one in two office workers will be using a computer terminal (OTA, 1983). This proliferation of computer automation can pose significant problems for managers and workers alike. This paper will explore the major problem areas keying in on the VDT as the central human/computer interface. Some suggested solutions to the problems are offered.

INTRODUCTION

It should be obvious to even the casual observer that the level of technological achievement in the last twenty years has been faster than the previous 2,000 years, and that this rate of development is occurring at an ever increasing pace. Even more impressive, this technology is being translated into use almost immediately. Indeed, there is little lag between the development and its application.

This quickened rate of development and instant application of technology has not occurred without problems as well as benefits; economic, social and health. The economic benefits accrue because work can be done more efficiently. However, there are problems concerning the high cost of implementing the new technology at the workplace. Many times the new technology requires that the current technology be scrapped and an entirely new work process be installed. This obsolescence can be so significant that the current technology has little economic value. To add to this loss, the new technology is often very expensive, and therefore, the economic investment in new technology is often high. However, if an industry fails to use the new technology, it may lose the ability to produce competitive products (e.g., the automobile industry), and the economic losses due to uncompetitive products can be fatal. There is little choice economically; new technology has to be utilized to its fullest availability and capability.

The social benefits are the new jobs and the associated improvement in living conditions that can occur. The problems are complex and are related to the economic problems. Mankind has evolved from a pre-agricultural society to fixed agricultural communities, mercantile city/states, industrialized cities/countries, and finally to the automated/computerized society of today because of technological improvements. Each of these levels of mans' evolution in work has had its own unique social systems, norms and modes of behavior which focused on the work technology. Thus, the hours of work activity, the times and content of meals, the sleeping patterns, the type and style of educating children, the roles for men and women and many other aspects of society have been affected by the work processes of that technological time. Today's technology has brought about significant changes in social structure and social roles. It has reduced the physical demands of jobs so that women are participating in all types of work in greater numbers. Thus, the raising of children is not the only primary facet of their lives, and thus, the way in which children are raised has changed. Additionally, women are gaining opportunities for the more prestigious, better paying high technology jobs that have previously been the sole domain of men.

Education has been changing to deal with new technology, although in many cases, it has not been changing fast enough, so that there is a lack of qualified scientists, technicians and machine operators to apply the new technology in the workplace. Even so, education is evolving with technology, so that today six year old children are learning how to use personal computers at school, and many colleges and universities are requiring that those who wish to graduate be literate in computer languages. In essence, the new technology impacts the work process and has far reaching implications for the economy, and social structure.

The relationship between new technology and health can best be examined in an occupational stress framework (see Levi, 1972). In this model, features of the work environment and job content (stressors) can have an influence on emotions and biological processes (stress) which can lead to ill health given chronic exposure with no intervention to mitigate the stress influence. A feeling for the types of potential problem areas can be envisioned by determining the stressors that are associated with new technology. These can be grouped into environmental conditions, job task demands and management related psychosocial influences. One way to examine these factors would be by using the example of the video display terminal - the ubiquitous computer component symbolizing the advent of new technology in the modern day office. For a more complete examination of this issue see "Health Issues in VDT Work" by M.J. Smith (1984).

Environmental Features and Ergonomics

Typically, new technology is introduced into an existing work environment which requires modifications to ensure compatibility. Usually such changes are not recognized until after the new technology is put into use. In the case of VDTs, traditional offices have had to be retrofitted to adapt to the needs of the new technology, and often such renovation cannot be easily accomplished. For example, VDTs generate heat which can produce discomfort for employees and malfunctioning of the VDTs. To counteract this problem, airconditioning is added to current ventilation systems which sometimes are not designed to handle the additional load. It is then difficult to regulate the temperature and humidity evenly throughout the entire building because of uneven airflow. Resultant hot and cold spots, and the drying of the air by the airconditioning give rise to skin irritation and general feelings of discomfort from VDT users.

The visual environment is another critical aspect which is often problematic when new technology is introduced. The environmental requirements for VDTs for proper visual functioning and comfort is much different than for work using hard copy (books, computer printouts). When retrofitting is done, typically the optimal visual environment cannot be achieved for both hard copy and VDT use, and compromises have to be made. It is quite clear, for instance, that work in which the user looks only at the VDT screen, and not at any hard copy, requires less illumination than work that requires the operator to read hard copy. Some experts feel that general illumination levels should be kept low, and if additional illumination is necessary for a particular job task, then task lighting (illuminating just the material to be read at a higher level) should be utilized.

Glare is the single most detrimental environmental factor for VDT operators because it reduces contrast and increases the amount of visual effort. Glare is best controlled by eliminating its sources, or modifying the source to limit the extent of glare. Proper placement of the video display screen, to eliminate reflections from glare sources, is the most effective means of glare control. VDT screens should be positioned parallel to windows, as well as parallel and between luminaries. Some modern offices are made with full length glass exterior walls, which make it almost impossible to place a VDT parallel to windows. When positioning is not feasible, then modifications must be made to the glare source. In the case of windows, curtains, or blinds, or shades can be used to block out the incoming light. For luminaries, it is possible to install fixtures that focus the light downward, such as parabolic wedge reflectors, which act to reduce the amount of light dispersion, and hence the amount of reflected glare. If glare persists, some modification must be made to the VDT. The most effective method is to use a filter over the screen, which provides for the absorption of incoming light rays and reduces the amount of reflections from the screen surface.

Job Task Demands and Ergonomics

Job task demands can be grouped into the physical requirements of the activity and the "thinking" or cognitive aspects. In terms of job task demands, new technology has a tendency to reduce the amount of physical energy expenditure, to make certain tasks more repetitive, and to reduce the amount of "thinking". Moreover, the need for greater attentiveness to the ongoing process tends to limit the amount of socialization and interaction possible with other workers. This impact does not discriminate between professionals, technicians or clerical workers. For many jobs, the technology can reduce the number of tasks that are perceived as tedious or boring, (such as the checking of grammar or spelling in newspaper writing and editing). This is a positive feature, enabling more time to be spent in creative work. There are instances, too, where the technology robs jobs of their creative interest, reducing users' involvement to recurring, simplistic responses. The latter are more typically reported by VDT operators.

The physical task demands are related to loads imposed by workstation design, and to the workload and workpace requirements. In terms of workstation design, it has been demonstrated that VDT technology imposes increased loads on operator vision and musculature which have to be counteracted by proper environmental and workstation design (see Dainoff, 1982; Smith, 1984). Those environmental factors that influence vision have already been discussed. The workstation design issues center around the concept of making the workstation flexible enough so that it can be adjusted to accommodate different users and different work task requirements.

As is the case in retrofitting the office environment, office furniture often needs to be replaced to better meet the change in physical work requirements posed by the new technology. With the VDT, provisions should be made for a work table that allows for separate adjustment of the keyboard and the screen in terms of height and distance away from the body. The table surfaces should be tiltable to allow for the most appropriate angle of viewing and keying. The work table should also have sufficient work area so that the operator does not have to stretch too far, or twist and turn in awkward positions. Copy holders should be supplied to reduce the wrist angle between the keyboard and work table. In addition, each workstation should have a chair that allows for adjustment of seat pan height and lumbar support height and depth. These furniture requirements are needed to deal with the increased postural demands imposed by the VDT technology.

In addition to workstation design, aspects of workload and workpace also have to be addressed when dealing with the physical task demands. Workpace and workload requirements for VDT operators are often set primarily by the capacity or limits of the computer system to which the VDT is connected, and typically the capacity of the operator to meet these demands is overlooked. This occurs for two reasons. First, the companies that market the technology sell the system to the purchaser based on claims of increased efficiency and reduced manpower needs. If manpower is reduced, then those who are left have to do more work more quickly. If the amount and rate of work are set by the capacity of the machine and not based on "human factors", then the human component of the system usually breaks down. Secondly, the persons who install and bring the technology "on-line" are engineers and computer scientists who understand computers quite well, but typically do not know a great deal about human capabilities or capacities. It is imperative that when new technology is installed that workload and workpace be established using "human factors" principles.

Job Task Demands and Stress

Once the physical demands have been controlled and adjusted, it is necessary to look at the psychological demands that are imposed by new technology. These concern job content, control over the work process, performance monitoring, and social isolation. Automation has the greatest negative influence on those jobs that inherently had little content to begin with. If automation causes further fragmentation and simplification of work and repetition of tasks, it can produce boredom. It is important that new technology reduce the repetitive, meaningless tasks, leaving the human operator those tasks that require "thinking" and promote the meaningfulness of work. Given the adaptive capabilities of computers, this should not be hard to achieve, but research has shown the opposite can occur (Smith et al, 1981).

Control of the work process is a significant factor in the development of job stress. This has been demonstrated by several researchers (Karasek et al, 1979; Cooper and Marshall, 1976; Smith, 1981) and appears to be one of the primary stressors imposed by computerized technology. The computer system usually has control over operator access to the system. In addition, it controls the programs that can be accessed and the rate at which work can be processed. Every-now-and-then it "crashes", or produces an unexplained delay in processing that demonstrates to the user his complete lack of control over the system. This reinforces the perception of the user that the computer system is in control and that very little user control can be exercised over the job task aside from turning the computer off.

While it is impossible to completely avoid computer breakdowns, it is possible to minimize their occurrence through scheduled maintenance (programmed downtime) and prudent adherence to the limitations of the technology. Thus, to overload a computer system with more users than it was designed to handle is to ask for these types of "crashes" and "delays in response" and their resultant stress.

While it is quite difficult to deal with the breakdowns, it is somewhat easier to have "user-friendly" software that provides the user with control over the work task and access to diagnostic messages to help when problems occur. This is a relatively new area of computer technology, but it holds the key to increased human efficiency in using computers, and hence, increased system efficiency. It is also possible to increase user control by allowing greater decision making on how work gets done (the methods used, scheduling), and allowing alternative work procedures if they can be carried-out efficiently and effectively while not disrupting other users.

Another aspect of control that has a psychological identity of its own is the use of performance feedback. When the computer is used to "tattle" to a supervisor about user performance, then the user feels a loss of control over the work process, as well as feelings of alienation and hostility toward the computer and supervisor. Performance feedback can be used to enhance the user's control by feeding the information directly back to the user to let him know how he is doing. This should be done at least every hour or sooner to get the maximum benefit (Smith & Smith, 1966). This increases the feeling of control over the work process and reduces the ill feeling produced by constant negative supervisor interaction about performance.

Computerized systems, involving individual users at fixed workstations, greatly reduce social interaction, which has traditionally been one of the more pleasant aspects of clerical office work. It is well established that social support of coworkers is an important buffer in controlling the health consequences of job stress (LaRocco et al, 1980). However, with the use of VDTs, it is often not possible to have social interaction during the work task activity. Therefore, social interaction during non-task periods must be enhanced and encouraged. This can be accomplished by providing special work break facilities in close proximity to the work areas, and by allowing groups of workers to go on break together.

Management Related Psychosocial Influences

A major factor, which produces worker resistance to automation, is that automation often appears at the workplace "out-of-the-blue" without worker knowledge of the impending change in the work process. It is very important for the successful implementation of computer automation, and subsequent enhancement of worker health and performance, that organizations have a transition policy that includes worker participation in all stages of the automation process. Thus, affected workers should be involved in the planning phase of automation. This will aid in worker acceptance of the changes in work processes, and ensure that worker concerns are aired. It will provide them with a fuller understanding of the computer system, its capabilities, and their role in the work process.

Training of the users in their new job requirements is a neglected aspect of computer automation. Most training offered to users is of limited scope and is not sufficient to develop skills, nor to build the user's confidence in his ability to use the system properly. Thus, users often are forced to experiment with the system to determine how it works, sometimes with disastrous results. Training should start with an explanation of why the new technology is needed, and its benefits to the company and to the user. The equipment and computer system should be thoroughly explained, indicating the strengths and weaknesses of the system. Then, there should be intensive training from the vendor's instruction manual that explains how the system works, and the system's specific functions. Training should be followed-up by practice in the functions learned with a skilled user available to coach the trainees as needed.

Fear for job security is one of the greatest concerns brought about by new technology. This is natural, since automation sometimes displaces workers. A company that invests time and energy in developing the skills of workers, through training, demonstrates a desire to keep its valuable resources, and often reduces worker fears of job loss. However, there are other job security problems related to computerization. One is the possibility of being downgraded because the computer system takes over some of the worker's functions, making the job less complex. The main purpose of computerization is to do work more efficiently and productively, not just to simplify work. Thus, companies should develop a cautious policy regarding workers' downgrading when new technology is introduced, since worker productivity will depend not only on the technology, but also on workers' desire to apply the technology effectively. In addition, companies must develop career paths for VDT users, so that advancement can be attained for those who are good performers. Being locked into a highly repetitive job, which has very little content or meaning, with no chance for advancement is a major source of job stress, and a disincentive for a large category of computer system users.

Finally, employee monitoring by computers creates a dehumanizing work environment in which the employee feels controlled by the machine. When performance monitoring is then used by supervision to control performance, employee perception of work pressure and workload is very high, thus producing stress responses. In many cases, keystroke-by-keystroke information is kept on employees, and then used by first-line supervisors to pressure them into increasing their performance. For the most effective employee performance and to enhance stress reduction, supervisors should use positive motivational and employee support approaches. Secondly, supervisors should be skilled operators, who can assist those operators having technical difficulties. Thirdly, supervisors should receive training in employee support approaches, thus helping to buffer the effects of other stressful job demands.

CONCLUSIONS

Computerized technology has the capability to greatly enhance the jobs of office workers by reducing undesirable, repetitive work tasks that require little thought, and increasing the content of jobs by providing greater task variety and meaning. However, this technology also has the opposite capability; that is, to reduce office jobs to assembly-line systems in which job meaning is lost. The overall impact of the decision to enhance or degrade jobs through computerization will influence the economic benefits of computerization, the social and cultural development of segments of society, and the health of the affected workers. In order to protect the health of those office workers affected by computerized technology, a management philosophy has to be adopted that will encompass considerations for: (1) adequate environmental and workstation design, (2) elimination of stress-producing job demands, and (3) provisions for more meaningful and positive work experience with needed worker training and career development.

REFERENCES

Cooper, C.L. and Marshall, J. "Occupational sources of stress: A review of the literature relating to coronary heart disease and mental ill health." Journal of Occupational Psychology, 1976, 49, 11-28.

Dainoff, M.J. "Occupational stress factors in visual display terminal (VDT) operation: A review of empirical research." Behaviour and Information Technology, 1982, 1, 141-176.

Karasek, R. "Job demands, job decision latitude, and mental strain: Implications for job redesign." Administrative Science Quarterly, 1979, 24, 285-308.

LaRocco, J.M., House, J.S. and French, J.R.P. "Social support, occupational stress and health." Journal of Health and Social Behavior, 1980, 21, 202-218.

Levi, L. Stress and Distress in Response to Psychosocial Stimuli. New York: Pergamon Press, Inc., 1972.

OTA. Project proposal on information and communication technologies and the office. Washington, D.C.: Office of Technology Assessment, United States Congress, 1983.

Smith, K.U. and Smith, M.F. Cybernetic Principles of Learning and Educational Design. New York: Holt, Rinehart and Winston, Inc., 1966.

Smith, M.J. Occupational Stress: An Overview of Psychosocial Factors. In G. Salvendy and M. J. Smith (Eds.) Machine Pacing and Occupational Stress. London: Taylor and Francis, Ltd., 1981, 13-19.

346

Smith, M.J., Cohen, B.G.F., Stammerjohn, L.W., and Happ, A. An investigation of health complaints and job stress in video display operations. Human Factors, 1981, 23, 387-400.

Smith, M.J. Health Issues in VDT Work. In J. Sandelin, J. Bennett, M.J. Smith and D. Case (Eds.) Visual Display Terminals, New York: Prentice Hall, 1984.

Human—Computer Interaction, edited by G. Salvendy
Elsevier Science Publishers B.V., Amsterdam, 1984 — Printed in The Netherlands

COMPUTER TECHNOLOGY:STRESS AND HEALTH RELEVANT TRANSFORMATIONS OF
PSYCHOSOCIAL WORK ENVIRONMENTS

G. JOHANSSON

Department of Psychology, University of Stockholm, S-106 91 Stockholm (Sweden)

ABSTRACT

JOHANSSON, G., 1984. Computer technology: Stress and health relevant transformations of psychosocial work environments.

The chapter reviews research attempting to identify psychosocial factors in
the environment which may lead to harmful stress, as well as psychosocial conditions which may serve as buffers against such harmful effects. Computerized
administrative work and supervisory control tasks in process industries serve
as examples. They indicate that, in order to avoid the introduction of new
stressors as well as stressors familiar from mechanized mass production, the
application of computer technology must be accompanied by careful analysis and
deliberate adjustment of the work organization.

BACKGROUND

The research that will be reviewed in this chapter forms part of a long-term
project concerning stress, coping and health as relted to the psychosocial work
environment (e.g., Frankenhaeuser & Gardell, 1976). The aim of the various
studies has been to identify psychological and social factors in the work environment associated with perceived strain and ill-health. We also want to identify possible protective factors, i.e., psychosocial conditions which may serve
as buffers protecting the person from harmful stress effects. This line of research ultimately aims at contributing to intervention and prevention, not only
at the individual level, but at the systems level as well.

Our research strategy includes methods and concepts from social psychology and psychobiology. Interviews, questionnaires and observations are used
to describe significant aspects of the psychosocialwork environment. For the
assessment of the individual's reaction to the environment we also monitor physiological functions during work. One of the notions underlying the use of physiological and biochemical techniques in human stress and coping research is
that the load which a particular environment places on a person can be determined by measuring the activity of the body's organ systems, which are controlled by the brain and reflect the level of arousal. In our case, the physiological functions include blood pressure and heart rate in addition to the uri-
nary excretion of adrenaline, noradrenaline and cortisol. These hormones can be

reliably assessed in urine samples which can be obtained in field settings without interference with the daily routines of the individual. For the interpretation of these physiological parameters it is also necessary to get indications of the individuals experience of the situation. For this purpose the participants in our studies give quantitative self-ratings of mood and arousal.

Adrenaline and noradrenaline usually facilitate both mental and physical adjustment to acute environmental demands. However, a growing body of research findings (e.g., Elliott & Eisdorfer, 1982) indicate that frequent or longlasting mobilization of such adaptive reactions may contribute to the development of psychosomatic disturbances, among them cardiovascular disease. Recent stress research in the laboratory and in the field has drawn attention to two types of psychosocial conditions at work which tend to be of particular importance for the generation and modulation of stress reactions. Conditions characterized by stimulus overload and underload are both stressful in the sense that they put high demands on the organisms capacity to adapt to environmental conditions. Empirical evidence shows that well-being and performance reach a maximum when the environment offeres a moderately intense and moderately varied inflow of stimulation (Frankenhaeuser & Johansson, 1981). Another important aspect of stressful conditions reactions concerns the individual's possibility to exert control over the situation. A lack of control in almost invariably associated with feelings of distress, whereas being in control may prevent a person from experiencing distress. Thus, personal control may act as a buffer which serves to modulate the intensity of the stress reaction and may also decrease the risk of individuals developing disease (e.g., Frankenhaeuser, 1979).

COMPUTERIZED ADMINISTRATIVE WORK

All large information systems which require continuous updating involve the constant feeding of new data into the system. Computer-based systems have the advantage of making such updating very rapid and making the most recent information instantly available to large groups of users, even those at a considerable geographical distance. The initial establishment of such systems usually requires the entering of large amounts of data which have been accumulated in paper files over many years. Office automation has, unfortunately, meant that data-entry work has been concentrated within special personnel categories who have had few, if any, other tasks.

This development illustrates how an increase of technology intensity in white-collar jobs may introduce negative elements which were previously seen only in industrial production. A number of investigations have shown that boredom, coercion, mental strain, and social isolation are more widespread and intense among workers whose jobs are severely circumscribed as to autonomy, variety, skill, and social interaction (for a recent review, see e.g., Gardell, 1982). Recent research also indicates that such work conditions may increase the level of biological stress reactions and damage health (Johansson, Aronsson & Lindström, 1978; House, McMichael, Wells, Kaplan & Landerman, 1979).

In the blue-collar sector attempts have been made to avoid such unwanted negative consequences and costs by means of alternative ways of organizing production (e.g., Gardell, 1981). Unless counter- measures are taken also in the white-collar sector there is a risk that the new technology will create highly repetitive tasks which will require little skill, allow little social interaction, and generate the type of negative consequences associated with mechanized mass production. Data-entry work is a case in point.

Data-entry work

We studied these problems in an insurance company which used visual display units (VDU) connected by telecommunication to a central computer (Johansson & Aronsson, in press). The study was conducted in two stages. In the first part a questionnaire was used to obtain an overall picture of positive and negative aspects of computerization for different types of work.

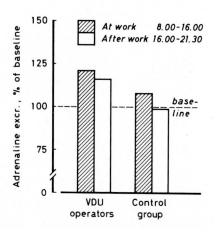

Fig. 1. Mean excretion of adrenaline during and after work for VDU operators and a control group. All values are given as a percentage of control values measured at home on a day off. (Johansson & Aronsson, 1984.)

On the basis of the questionnaire data two subgroups were selected for the second part of the study. One group, a data-entry unit, spent more than 50 % (sometimes as much as 90 %) of their working hours at the computer terminal; their work was of a routine kind, intellectually undemanding and performed at high speed. The other group used the computer no more than 10 % of their time. These were typists and secretaries with fairly flexible and variable tasks including social interaction.

The results indicated that the group which spent the major part of their work day at the VDU had slightly higher catecholamine levels than the control group during work. This difference between groups increased in the evenings, which were spent, by both groups, quietly at home. In other words, the workers took longer to unwind, if they had spent many hours doing attention- demanding routine work at the computer terminal. This "slow unwinding" was reflected also in responses to the questionnaire. The data-entry group reported significantly more mental fatigue after work (Fig. 2). These results give a clear example of how attention-demanding, repetitive and physically constricted work results in effort and tension, which may encroach into leisure time (cf. Johansson et al., 1978; Gardell, 1982).

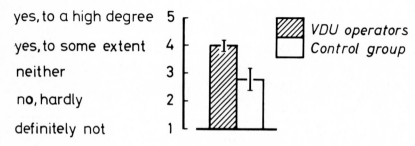

Fig. 2. Mental fatigue after the end of work for a VDU group and a control group (Johansson & Aronsson, 1984).

Dependence on equipment

The tendency to concentrate routine VDU tasks within certain groups of workers also make these groups dependent on the technical equipment and eliminate most of their personal control on occasions when the computer systems go down.

Our study of white-collar work in an insurance company (Johansson & Aronsson, in press) provided a possibility to study the psychobiological reactions of workers during an interruption of the normal operation of the computer system. The VDU group, which was described above, was subjected to a breakdown lasting four hours (although the duration of the breakdown was unknown until the end of those four hours).

For the VDU group, the majority of which did data-entry work, an interruption meant that they could carry out no work. Their own work, therefore, piled up, which increased the next days work load. During the breakdown we investigated self-ratings of mood and alertness as well as indicators of physiological arousal such as heart rate, blood pressure, and excretion of adrenaline and noradrenaline. These data were then compared to corresponding results from a day of normal operations. The results showed that - although no work could be carried out - feelings of fatigue and being rushed were more pronounced than during normal operation. All physiological measures were elevated during the breakdown period. For adrenaline excretion and diastolic blood pressure the differences were statistically significant.

Again, the cause of these potentially harmful reactions is found in an unsatisfactory organization of work. The feelings of fatigue and being rushed reported by the VDU group while waiting for the system to start operating are very understandable. They reflect the anticipation of the next days higher work load and the lack of perceived personal control in this situation.

To get rid of this source of stress is partly a question of eliminating technical deficits and increasing the availability of computer systems. However, it is equally important to eliminate the routine, repetitive data-entry tasks at the VDU. Spreading this necessary but monotonous task over larger groups, e.g., by entering data where they are generated, will considerably decrease the impact of computer breakdowns on employees strain and health.

SUPERVISION OF COMPLEX TECHNICAL SYSTEMS

In production industries, the introduction of new technology has had quite different consequences for the psychological job content than it has had in the office. One interesting example is provided by supervisory tasks in process industries such as chemical plants, refineries, power stations, the paper and pulp industry, etc. Although centralized remote control of such processes has been possible for a long time, the introduction of computers has accentuated certain elements in the operators task which may increase the mental work load. There is, for instance, a tendency to make the computer take over as much as possible of the process control, leaving the operator in an increasingly passive work situation while demands for attention and high performance remain the same or even increase.

The psychological job content of process-control tasks is determined to a great extent by the percentage of work hours spent in each of the following major task categories: (1) Supervisory control during normal operations, (2) supervisory control and interventions when faults arise, (3) start-up/shutdown procedures, (4) work outside the control room and (5) interruptions of operation. During periods of passive and routine supervision there are few demands on the operator except that of keeping attentive and ready for action.

Tasks in which passive supervisory control is the dominating element offer unsatisfactory conditions for performance and well-being. However, jobs which involve a mixture of various elements will enhance the maintenance of an optimal level of stimulation which in turn will promote performance as well as

general well-being (Frankenhaeuser & Johansson, 1981). The situation of passive supervision, infrequently and unpredictably interrupted by temporary work
overload is also detrimental for several other reasons.

The switch from passive supervision to active information processing and
decision making under time pressure may become extremely demanding and is associated with intense psychobiological stress reactions. Furthermore, highly
automated systems which assume the human to be passive, do not allow the operator to exercise his/her skill and process understanding. This will most
probably lead to an erosion of operator qualifications and, thus, to worse
performance. Such de-skilling will also decrease the level of personal control
perceived by the operator. In this way a diminished role of the human in man-
machine systems becomes stressful, not only at times of process disturbances
but continuously during monotonous supervision of the process.

These conditions were investigated by Johansson and Sandén (1982) in a
study of two groups of control-room operators. One of these groups performed
process-control work dominated by passive supervisory control. They supervised
stable, continuous processes such as oxygen production and power generation.
In a monotonous work situation their task was to remain passive but alert until disturbances in the production process called for their attention and action. They had only limited possibilities to predict the character of the next
disturbance and the time of its occurrence. It was a situation which offered
little external stimulation and a low level of personal control.

The second group was involved in production planning and control. They used
telephone, radio and computer communication to coordinate the activity in several parts of a steel mill. These operators worked under time pressure and at
a high level of stimulus input, but according to questionnaire and interview
data they felt well qualified for their jobs and their work produced feelings
of high motivation and job satisfaction. This situation involved elements of
stimulus overload but also good opportunities for personal control in the work
situation. Both groups carried a large responsibility for efficient and safe
production flow.

Both groups showed a marked increase in levels of adrenaline output during
daytime work. Although the two types of tasks were very different there was,
however, no statistically significant difference between their average levels
of adrenaline excretion. They differed significantly, however, in their experience of the work situation. Active production control was associated with
feelings of being rushed and under stress, but also with intense job involvement and job satisfaction. Passive supervisory control, on the other hand, was
associated with feelings of monotony and a vague feeling of uneasiness, especially during night shifts. Only half of this group felt that the job provided
them with personal satisfaction.

Both groups were satisfied with the possibilities of learning new things in work and with the fact that they managed to perform a difficult and complex job. At the same time, feelings of monotony and anxiety when facing process failures were much more pronounced in the process-control group.

Our interpretation of these results is that a situation of passive supervisory control with continuous demands for attention and action readiness can give rise to effort and strain which are comparable to those of a job containing complex information processing and decision making under time pressure. The difference lies in the emotional quality of the experience. While the effort of an active planning and coordination task tends to be associated with positive feelings, the effort experienced in a passive, uneventful situation is associated with feelings of monotony, uneasiness and insecurity.

CONCLUSIONS

Empirical evidence shows that under certain circumstances the introduction of computer tecnology may add to the stressfulness of work routines. Conditions such as those described above - the introduction of repetitive, fragmented tasks in office work and an increase of passive, supervision of complex production processes - should be modified so that future work condition become better adjusted to basic human needs and potentials.

Provided that we define the direction in which we wish to change the psychosocial content of work, the flexibility of computer technology ought to enhance efforts to combine efficient production with safe and healthy work environments.

The research reported in this paper has been supported by the Swedish Work Environment Fund.

REFERENCES

Elliott, G.R. and Eisdorfer, C., 1982, (Editors), Stress and Human Health. Analysis and Implications of Research. A study by the Institute of Medicine/National Academy of Sciences. New York: Springer Publishing Company.

Frankenhaeuser, M., 1979. Psychoneuroendocrine approaches to the study of emotion as related to stress and coping. In: H.E. Howe and R.A. Dienstbier (Editors), Nebraska Symposium on Motivation 1978. University of Nebraska Press, Lincoln, pp. 123-161.

Frankenhaeuser, M. and Gardell, B., 1976. Underload and overload in working life: outline of a multidisciplinary approach. J. Hum. Stress, 2: 35-46.

Frankenhaeuser, M. and Johansson, G., 1981. On the psychophysiological consequences of understimulation and overstimulation. In: L. Levi (Editor), Society, Stress and Disease, Vol. IV: Working Life. Oxford University Press, London, pp. 82-89.

Gardell, B., 1981. Strategies for work reform programmes on work organization and work environment. In: B. Gardell and G. Johansson (Editors), Working Life: A Social Science Contribution to Work Reform. John Wiley & Sons, Chichester, pp. 3-13.

Gardell, B., 1982. Scandinavian research on stress in working life. Int. J. Health Services, 12: 31-41.

House, J.S., McMichael, A.J., Wells, J.A., Kaplan, B.H. and Landerman, L.R., 1979. Occupational stress and health among factory workers. J. Health Soc. Behav., 20: 139-160.

Johansson, G. and Aronsson, G., 1984. Stress reactions in computerized administrative work. J. Occup. Behav. (In press.)

Johansson, G. and Sandén, P.-O., 1982. Mental belastning och arbetstillfredsställelse i kontrollrumsarbete (Mental load and job satisfaction of control room operators). Rapporter (Department of Psychology, University of Stockholm), No. 40. (English summary.)

Human—Computer Interaction, edited by G. Salvendy
Elsevier Science Publishers B.V., Amsterdam, 1984 — Printed in The Netherlands   355

A MODEL FOR HUMAN EFFICIENCY: RELATING HEALTH, COMFORT AND PERFORMANCE IN
THE AUTOMATED OFFICE WORKSTATION

M. DAINOFF

Department of Psychology, Miami University, Oxford, Ohio 45056 USA

ABSTRACT

A general approach to human work efficiency is presented which integrates
the dynamic fatigue model of Grandjean with resource allocation concepts
from cognitive psychology. Within this framework, experimental evidence is
presented which demonstrate performance and health complaint changes as a
result of ergonomic optimization of video display terminal workstations.

INTRODUCTION

The worker of the future is likely to be an information worker, linked to
a system of computerized procedures via a Visual Display Terminal (VDT).
Guiliano (1982) has predicted that for the U.S., 40-50% of the total
workforce will be utilizing such equipment by the end of the decade, and
there is no reason to expect that the situation will be any different in
other industrialized countries. Unfortunately, this process of automation
does not seem to have occurred without its cost. Concerns regarding health
problems associated with VDT work have been circulating since the mid-1970s.
However, evidence for such concerns (regarding their existence as well as
putative cause) has been controversial (see Dainoff, 1982; National Research
Council, 1983 for reviews).

With respect to a major source of health complaints--visual and
musculoskeletal fatigue--the traditional illness approach which looks for
impacts of specific disease vectors on specific target organs has not been
particularly useful. Effects which may be present are more likely to be
result of multiple clusters of causal agents which have cumulative and
diffuse effects on multiple body systems (Amick and Celentano, in press).
Accordingly, the purpose of this paper is to present an alternative
perspective in which the focus is on efficiency of resource utilization
rather than illness.

FATIGUE AND RESOURCE ALLOCATION

We take, as a point of departure, the dynamic fatigue model of Grandjean
(1969). In this approach, the individual is seen as generating a kind of

generalized fatigue as a result of coping with a variety of demands, both physical and psychological. The rate of fatigue buildup is proportional to the cumulative intensity of the demand. Thus, the discomfort experienced by working at a keyboard which is too high is added to the discomfort experienced from performing a repetitive data entry task under high productivity pressure. Normally, fatigue recovery occurs by means of work-rest breaks during the day, and through rest and relaxation after work. If, however, the cumulative buildup of fatigue across the typical workday is sufficiently and consistently large enough, normal recovery mechanisms are not sufficient, fatigue begins to accumulate from previous workdays, and the individual enters a state of chronic fatigue or stress. presumably, this generalized state of debilitation is manifested in a variety of physical symptoms which are superimposed on any specific localized symptoms of strain or chronic trauma (e.g., wrist disorders, back disorders--see, for example, Arndt, 1983).

Within this perspective, let us consider the following possibility. Following the Grandjean (1969) model discussed above, discomfort which arises from improper working conditions may, if intense enough, lead to chronic health problems (physical and/or psychological). Such health problems will, in the long term, generate significant costs to the parent organization. However, it is also plausible that, in the short term, such discomfort will interfere with daily work performance, thereby making the employee less productive.

This proposition can be made more explicit by combining the Grandjean approach with the so-called resource allocation model taken from cognitive psychology (Kahneman, 1973; Norman and Bobrow, 1976; Navon and Gopher, 1979). By freely adopting the basic concepts of this model, we argue that the human operator possesses, at any moment, a finite amount of information processing capacity. These resources can then be allocated among a variety of information processing mechanisms or functions. The linkage with the Grandjean model is that we assume that fatigue accumulation accompanies the expenditure of productive work accomplished relative to the resources expended.

Therefore, on this model, to the degree that an individual experiences discomfort attributed to poor workplace design, he/she devotes performance resources to coping with the sources of that discomfort, and, consequently, has fewer resources to devote to the primary task. We can also distinguish between fatigue accumulated in productive work (accomplishing the task) and non-productive fatigue (coping with avoidable discomfort). The likely result is: (a) performance deficit, (b) post-work accumulation of fatigue,

(c) a combination of each of the above. (A similar suggestion was made by Branton, 1976, regarding seating.)

Within this framework, a systems perspective (Meister, 1978) is required in order to take into account the complex of interactive and interdependent elements which characterize the modern automated office workplace. A research strategy utilizing this perspective is described. This strategy involves creation of an optimal (state-of-the-art) system, which is then systematically degraded. If the same task is required under both conditions, estimates of relative efficiency can be obtained. Figure 1 describes potential outcomes from such experiments.

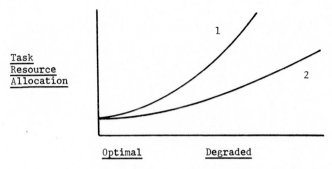

Fig. 1. Predicted levels of resource allocation in two VDT tasks as the workstation is systematically degraded.

As the workstation is degraded, the resource allocation function increases. This reflects the argument that the need to cope with suboptimal working conditions requires allocation of additional resources in order to maintain a constant level of performance. Simultaneously, expenditure of such resources should generate levels of fatigue (in Grandjean's use of the term) at greater rates than would be the case in the optimal workstation. On the other hand, should such additional resources not be forthcoming, performance will drop off.

Different task demands will generate different resource allocation functions. Figure 1 depicts functions for two hypothetical tasks. (For simplicity, these functions are assumed to be normalized to the same optimal level, thereby indicating relative increases in resource allocation.) The task demands in Task 1 would be such as to require greater amounts of resource allocation as the system became degraded, as compared with Task 2. These differential allocation functions would presumably be reflected in some combination of system output measurement plus operator fatigue symptom rate.

The practical benefit of such an approach is in the suggestion that, for any given task-workstation combination, some departure from optimality may be tolerated with only modest costs in additional resource allocation. this formulation would seem to provide a useful alternative to the ergonomic checklist approach seen in many sources (e.g., Cakir, Hart, and Stewart, 1980). Such checklists are useful for determining initial conditions of optimality, but give no hint as to priority of recommendations. In practice, funds available are likely to be insufficient to provide optimality in all cases, and decisions must be made as to which ergonomic recommendations, if any, should be given top priority. The system degradation approach should provide an experimental procedure to determine ranges of tolerance and relative effectiveness of different systems components, enabling such decisions to be made more effectively.

EXPERIMENTAL EVIDENCE

The author and colleagues have conducted a series of such experiments while at the National Institute for Occupational Safety and Health. The investigations involved a comparison of optimal vs. degraded working conditions at a video display terminal (VDT) task. Groups of entry-level typists, after a day of training, performed data entry work for 3 hours per day for four days, alternating between optimal and degraded conditions on different days. Performance measures and subjective complaints were assessed.

Experiment 1 involved a global comparison of optimal and degraded ergonomic workplace conditions, incorporating differences in lighting and glare, as well as postural differences determined by the adjustability of chairs and working surfaces. In the optimal condition, the chair was push-button and adjustable with a support pad in the lower lumbar region of the back. The terminal workstand allowed independent adjustment of keyboard and display screen. A copy holder and wrist rest were provided. These ergonomic design features allowed each operator to individually assume an optimal posture such that the feet were flat on the floor, the lower back was supported, leg-trunk and thigh-trunk angles were approximately 90 degrees, elbows were at or slightly below, the level of the home row of the keyboard, wrists were supported, the angle of view to screen center was approximately 20 degrees, and the copy was held upright at the same distance from the eyes as the screen. Lighting and glare control were controlled by the use of a specialized VDT overhead lighting fixture utilizing a parabolic lens, and by the placing of a contrast-enhancing anti-reflection filter over the terminal face.

In the degraded condition, an ordinary office chair with no lumbar support was set at a standard height. An adjustable terminal-stand was employed as above, in this case, maladjusted . so as to simulate those suboptimal postures which had been observed in field investigations. This resulted in the keyboard being too high, the screen too low, the wrists unsupported, and the copy lying flat on the desk. In addition, high levels of glare were present on the screen face.

The second experiment consisted of a replication of the first, but, in this case the only postural factors were compared. Lighting conditions were equated.

The results of both studies were that operator <u>efficiency</u> was greater under optimal working conditions than under degraded conditions. Efficiency, in this series of studies, is assessed in terms of increased performance and decreased levels of physical complaints. Performance was measured by work output in keystrokes per minute, with a penalty for errors; an incentive pay system was set up based on this performance formula.

Nearly all workers performed better under optimal conditions than under degraded conditions; the average improvement (as assessed by differences in earned incentive pay) was 24.6% in Experiment 1, and 17.5% in Experiment 2.

Physical complaints were assessed by means of a discomfort checklist administered before and after each experimental session. As expected, most subjects showed increases in reported musculoskeletal complaints at the end of the session; however, these levels were 39.86% higher under degraded conditions in Experiment 1, and 33.71% higher under degraded conditions in Experiment 2.

The combination of lower performance and higher complaints under the degraded conditions support the system degradation model described above. In addition, it may be noted that Experiment 2, which represented a less severe level of system degradation, also resulted in somewhat lower effects of such degradation, as reflected in performance as well as complaint levels. Thus each experiment may be regarded as an individual point on one of the allocation functions depicted in Figure 1.

REFERENCES

Arndt, R. Working posture and musculoskeletal problems of VDT operators--review and reappraisal. <u>American Industrial Hygiene Association</u>, 1983, <u>44</u>, 437-446.

Amick, B.C. and Celentano, D.D. Human factors epidemiology: an integrated approach to the study of health issues in office work. In B.G.F. Cohen (Ed.), <u>Human Aspects in Office Automation</u>. Amsterdam: Elsevier, 1984.

Branton, P. Behavior, body mechanics, and discomfort. In E. Grandjean (Ed.), Sitting Posture. London: Taylor & Francis, 1976.

Cakir, A., Hart, D.J., and Stewart, T. Video Display Terminals. New York: Wiley, 1980.

Dainoff, M.J. Occupation stress factors in VDT operation: a review of emperical literature. Behaviour and Information Technology, 1982, 1, 141-176.

Dainoff, M.J. Video display terminals: the relationship between ergonomic design, health complaints, and operator performance. Journal of Occupational Health Nursing, 1983, December, 29-33.

Dainoff, M.J., Fraser, L., and Taylor, B.J. Visual, musculoskeletal, and performance differences between good and poor VDT workstations. Proceedings of the Human Factors Society 26th Annual Meeting, Seattle: 1982.

Grandjean, E. Fitting the Task to the Man: An Ergonomic Approach. London: Taylor & Francis, 1969.

Giuliano, V. The mechanization of office work. Scientific American, 1982, 247, 148-164.

Kahneman, D. Attention and Effort. Englewood Cliffs, N.J.: Prentice-Hall, 1973.

Meister, D. A Systematic Approach to Human Factors Measurement. San Diego, Cal.: Navy Personnel Research and Development Center, 1978.

National Research Council (NRC). Video Displays, Work, and Vision. Washington, D.C.: National Academy Press, 1983.

Navon, D., and Gopher, D. On the economy of the human-processing system. Psychological Review, 1979, 86, 214-255.

Norman, D. and Bobrow, D.J. On the analysis of performance operating characteristics. Psychological Review, 1976, 83, 508-510.

WORK LOAD OF PROGRAMMERS AND OPERATORS WITH VDU

T. HASEGAWA[1], M. KUMASHIRO[1], K. MIKAMI[2] AND T. OKUBO[3]
[1]University of Occupational and Environmental Health, Japan
[2]Hokkaido Institute of Technology
[3]Nihon University

INTRODUCTION

Visual display units (VDUs) are used in various fields and as a result, the effect of VDU work on VDU operators is now highlighted. A study was made of VDU operators at a workplace where VDUs were used at low frequency and the self-paced work system and of VDU operators at another workplace where VDUs were used at higher frequency but with frequent breaks. How the differences in the frequency of VDU use would affect the variations in the psychophysiological functions of the VDU operators was investigated.

METHOD

A total of 15 subjects were employed in two groups. The first group comprised nine male programmers (23 to 33 years old) in a system development company. They prepare, input and debug programs with VDUs, all at their free pace. They work from 9:00 to 17:00 with an hour's recess for lunch. Work with VDUs accounts for 40% of the working hours (Case 1). The other group was six female operators (25 to 31 years old) in a telephone directory assistance firm. When they receive an inquiry for a telephone number, they retrieve the telephone number through their VDU and answer the inquiry. The time taken to answer one inquiry is 15 to 180 sec. The waiting time until the next inquiry is received is between 5 and 15 sec. The operators work from 9:20 to 16:50 on the morning shift and from 14:20 to 19:30 on the afternoon shift. They continuously work for 40 to 70 min before they have a 20-min break. They rest for 40 min from 12:00 on the morning shift and from 16:20 on the afternoon shift. Work with VDUs accounts for about 80% of the working hours (Case 2).

The critical fusion frequency (CFF), near-point accommodation and subjective feelings of fatigue were investigated. The programmers were measured for these items before and after work in a one week. The telephone directory assistance operators were examined for the CFF before and after each continuous work and were investigated for the other items four times per day. The period of survey was two weeks for the morning shift operators and one week for the afternoon shift operators.

RESULTS

Case 1

Figure 1 shows the changes in the CFF of the subjects. The CFF after work was 0.2 Hz lower than before work. No significant differences were observed between the CFF of the subjects before and after work.

Figure 2 shows the changes in the near-point accommodation of the subjects. The near-point accommodation after work was 0.2 diopter better than before work. No significant differences were recognized between the values of near-point accommodation before and after work.

Figure 3 presents the changes in the rate of complaint of subjective feelings of fatigue. The rate of complaint of fatigue after work decreased 3.5% for the first category of subjective feelings of fatigue (dullness and drowsiness), increased 8.7% for the second category (difficulty of concentration) and rose 4.8% for the third category (physical discomfort), as compared with the rate of complaint before work. "Feel fatigued in the eyes" was the only item for which the rate of complaint after work was higher than 25% (actually 52.2%).

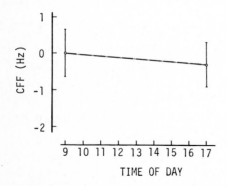

Fig. 1. Variations of critical fusion frequency (CFF) values for male programmers.

Fig. 2. Variations of near-point accommodation for male programmers.

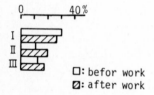

□: befor work
▨: after work

Fig. 3. Mean self-rated of subjective feelings of fatigue for male programmers. I;first category(dullness and drowsiness), II ;second category(difficulty of consentration), III;third category(physical discomfort)

Case 2

Figure 4 provides the changes in the CFF of the subjects when they worked without VDUs. When the morning shift operators worked with VDUs, the CFF exhibited a significant drop at four times, or 11:00, 11:20, 14:50 and 15:10, as compared with the CFF before work. When the afternoon shift operators worked with VDUs, the CFF showed a significant drop at 16:20 and 18:30, as compared with the CFF before work. When the CFF after work with VDUs was compared with the CFF after work without VDUs, no significant differences were observed between the morning and afternoon shift operators. The rate of decline in the CFF at each point of time was calculated to be lower than 5%, a criterion proposed for mental work. The patterns of CFF variation in work with and without VDUs were similar to the pattern of CFF variation reported for a monotonous-shaped work.

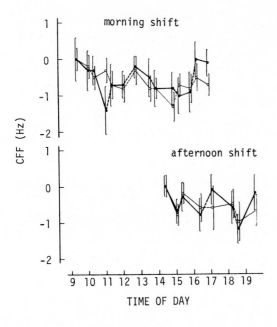

Fig. 4. Variations of critical fusion frequency (CFF)values for female operators.
—●— ;with VDU,
—○— ;without VDU

Figure 5 shows the patterns of variation in the near-point accommodation of the operators. When the morning shift operators worked with VDUs, the near-point accommodation decreased 0.3 diopter at 12:00 and exhibited a significant difference from that before work. When the afternoon shift operators worked with VDUs, the near-point accommodation significantly improved at 17:00 and 19:30, as compared with that before work. When both the morning and afternoon shift operators worked without VDUs, the near-point accommodation did not significantly changed from that before work.

Figure 6 gives the rate of complaint of subjective feelings of fatigue of the operators. The rate of complaint of the morning shift operators after work with and without VDUs decreased for the first, second and third categories in that order. When the afternoon shift operators worked with VDUs, their rate of complaint was the largest for the first category, followed by the third category. The rate of complaint for the second category was lower than before work.

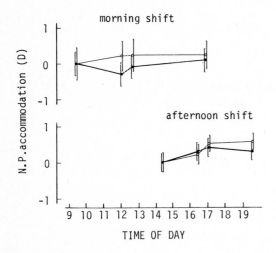

Fig. 5. Variations of near-point accommodation.
●—;with VDU,
—○—;without VDU

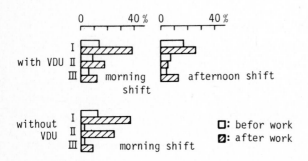

Fig. 6. Mean self-rated of subjective feelings of fatigue for female operators. I;first category(dullness and drowsiness),II ;second category(difficulty of consentration),III;third category(physical discomfort)

CONCLUSION

The results of this project suggest that when programmers use VDUs at low frequency and at their own pace, and when operators use VDUs at higher frequency but with frequent breaks, they do not experience appreciable drops in their psychophysiological functions. On the contrary, they felt an increase in irritation, boredom and depression depend on a computer-paced work system.

Human—Computer Interaction, edited by G. Salvendy
Elsevier Science Publishers B.V., Amsterdam, 1984 — Printed in The Netherlands

STRESS AND FACTORS OF PRODUCTIVITY AMONG SOFTWARE DEVELOPMENT WORKERS

A. ZAVALA[1]

[1]SRI International, 333 Ravenswood Avenue, Menlo Park, California 94025

INTRODUCTION

SRI International is conducting a study to examine the human factors that affect the productivity of software development workers. Two goals of this study are to identify (1) key issues and factors of productivity and (2) testable hypotheses about factors, such as stress, correlated with productivity. This paper describes some initial results of correlational analysis between stress and other work-related factors.

Stress

Factors affecting software developer productivity that have been addressed in the literature include costs (Moralee, 1981), cost estimation, time estimation, and increasing computer program size (Boehm, 1981). Although some studies have examined the relationship between stress, aggressive lifestyles, and behavior in the work environment of non-software developers (e.g., Chesney and Rosenman, 1980a,b; Salvendy and Sharit, 1982), few have examined stress among software development workers. Chesney and Rosenman (1980a) reviewed the relationship between coronary heart disease, stress, work behavior, and a behavior pattern called Type A, a hard-driving, aggressive lifestyle in which devotion to work is often a central element. The incidence of coronary heart disease as a risk factor appears to be high in Type A individuals, who describe themselves as eager and challenged and who rise to meet competition (Cohen, 1978:243).

The A-Scale

At SRI International, Chesney and her colleagues continue to refine a measurement for the Type A behavior pattern: the Chesney A-Scale. The A-Scale (Chesney, et al., 1979) consists of twenty statements that people use to describe themselves (e.g., "I am an outgoing person"; "I usually make up my mind quickly"). A responder rates the degree of truth or falseness of each item. The A-Scale provides an indication of stress-related behavior patterns.

STRESS AND PROGRAMMER PRODUCTIVITY

Approach

Data for SRI's productivity study are being gathered by administering a
survey to individuals in nine participating companies, which vary in size,
product, and location. Survey items were developed based on findings from
literature reviews and on interviews of two or three people at each host
company (Zavala, 1984). A-Scale items were incorporated into the survey.

SRI has sent a total of 400 surveys to host companies. The results presented
below are based on analysis of the 200 surveys returned to date. The reliability
index of the productivity survey, as measured by Chronbach's Alpha (Nie, et al.,
1977), is 0.94.

Analysis

Initial analysis has focused on determining the relationships between the
A-Scale and productivity survey subscales identified previously (Zavala, et al.,
1979) and listed in Table 1. Because of the relationship found by Chesney (1980a)
between scores on the A-Scale and stress, the A-Scale is used here as an indicator of stress.

Pearson product-moment correlation coefficients were calculated between the
A-Scale and survey subscales. The correlation between scores on the A-Scale
and software developers' self-reports of productivity was 0.163 ($p^* < 0.02$;
$N^\dagger$ = 199), i.e., the higher the stress, the lower the productivity. Also
significant was the correlation of 0.453 ($p < 0.003$; N = 42) between the self-
report of the worker's productivity and the supervisor's rating of that worker's
productivity.

Table 2 presents the correlations, significance, and sample size between
stress and survey subscales. Only correlations significant at better than the
0.1 level are included. All except one of the correlations are negative.
Negative correlations indicate that a low value on a given factor is associated
with a high value on the stress score.

Table 2 shows that software developers feel less stress when they can work
autonomously, are respected by their supervisors, and see opportunities to
advance; have the skills, knowledge, experience, education, and ability needed
to do their jobs; are satisfied, have good attitudes and high morale; feel
their jobs meet their expectations; assume responsibility on their own and
have a concern for the quality of their work; have the resources (tools, job

---

*Probability that correlation would occur by chance.
†Sample size.

TABLE 1

Subscales of the Productivity Survey

LEADER BEHAVIORS--Supervisor solves management problems, checks equipment, is pleasant, treats workers as equals.

WORKER BEHAVIORS--Workers are autonomous, sense the respect they get from their supervisor, see opportunities to advance.

DELEGATION OF AUTHORITY--Supervisor encourages workers to make their own decisions and passes authority on to them.

CAPABILITIES OF THE WORKER--Skills, knowledge, experience, education, ability, and training that the worker brings to the job.

STRICTNESS--Company management and policy are strict and strictly enforced; supervisors criticize readily.

EQUIPMENT DESIGN--Equipment is difficult to use because of inadequate dials, controls, switches, pedals, and layout.

SATTITUDE--Satisfaction and attitude of worker is good, morale is high, stress is low, job meets expectations.

EXTERNAL INFLUENCES--Government regulations, social and political situation in the country.

SAFETY--Company strives toward safety; worker feels positively about OSHA, and adopts an attitude of working safely.

SELF-RESPONSIBILITY--Worker takes responsibility on his own; has concern about his work quality.

RESOURCES--Worker feels he has tools, job aids, manuals, parts, and materials in sufficient quantity and of sufficient quality to do the job.

THE COUNTRY'S SITUATION--Worker feels the country's social and political changes will not affect the company or his job.

SOCIAL AND WORK BEHAVIORS--Worker has positive relationships with others in the work setting; feels good about work setting.

PAY AND CONDITIONS OF WORK--Worker feels good about pay, reviews, raises, and physical conditions (e.g., noise, temperature).

WORK CONDITIONS--There is adequate lighting, ventilation, and job stability.

OVERTIME AND PERSONAL PROBLEMS--Worker gets and enjoys getting overtime; has few personal problems.

RESPECT FOR THE WORKER--Worker receives respect from peers and supervisors; has self-respect; feels his work quality is high.

JOB PROBLEMS--Worker does not get to stand up and move around much; job is driving him to drink; gets eyestrain, etc.

THE COMPANY--Company has clear goals, good leadership, good workflow and technology, low turnover, and little confusion.

ECONOMIC NEEDS--Worker has a sense of economic well-being; job meets basic needs for food, clothing, shelter.

RESPONSIBILITIES AND AMOUNT OF WORK ACCEPTED--Worker gets enough work to do; worker wants and gets sufficient responsibilities.

SPECIFIC COMPANY POLICIES--Workers feel length and number of rest periods are adequate; training, size of department, and layout are good.

CRISES--Worker did not get expected raises or promotions, lost loved ones, or had a serious health problem.

PRODUCTIVITY--Worker's estimate of his or her own productivity.

PROGRAMMING--A composite of all survey items relating to software development.

TABLE 2

Correlations between Stress (A-Scale) and Productivity Factor Subscales

Item	Correlation[*]	p[†*]	Sample Size
Worker behaviors	-144	048	189
Worker capabilities	-146	053	177
Sattitude	-170	018	192
Self-responsibility	-274	0001	198
Resources	-133	086	198
Social behavior	-244	0006	196
Respect for the worker	-258	0003	193
Job problems	-168	02	192
Personal crises	+152	034	194
Productivity	-163	02	197
Programming	-165	019	200

[*]Leading decimals omitted.

[†]p = probability that correlation would occur by chance.

aids, manuals) needed to do their jobs; have positive relationships with their colleagues and feel good about the work setting; are respected by their peers; have few physical stresses (e.g., eyestrain); have few personal crises related to pay raises, promotions, health, or loved ones.

CONCLUSIONS

This analysis shows software developers as a group of individuals whose work and productivity are influenced by stress. Stress and lowered productivity appear to go together. The workers apparently are concerned about the quality of their work and seem to enjoy responsibility. Finally, the Chesney A-Scale seems to be a useful device for diagnosing stress among software developers.

Of interest are the findings that high stress scores correlate with a lack of fit between the worker's capabilities and job demands. These findings are consistent with the suggestion by Chesney et al. (1981) that successful programs to reduce risk of coronary heart disease resulting from stress will be designed to remedy the lack of fit between employees and their work situations.

The results of the present study are useful because they identify specific areas in the software developer's work situation where a lack of fit is likely to have the greatest detrimental effect. These areas would be good candidate areas where productivity improvement programs can be expected to have a high probability for success.

In an insightful review of occupational stress, Sharit and Salvendy (1982) point out that the area of stress is multi-factorial. The findings of the present study support that assertion as it applies to software developer productivity. Thus, further work is necessary to understand more clearly the interrelationships of stress among software developers and other factors that affect their productivity.

It must be recognized that the results presented here are preliminary; it is necessary to conduct these analyses on a larger sample to verify the stability of these results. More data continue to arrive for this project, and current project plans are to conduct that verification.

ACKNOWLEDGMENT

This paper is based in part on work supported by the National Science Foundation under Grant No. MEA-820040. Any opinions, findings, conclusions, or recommendations expressed in this paper are those of the author and do not necessarily reflect the views of the National Science Foundation.

REFERENCES

Boehm, B. W., 1981. Improving Software Productivity. Proceedings, Twenty-Third IEEE Computer Society International Conference, Washington, D.C., pp. 2-16.

Chesney, M. A., Ward, M. M., Black, G. W., Swan, G. E., Rosenman, R. H., 1979. Type A/B and Environmental Control: Too Much or Too Little. American Psychological Association, 1979, New York.

Chesney, M. A., Rosenman, R. H., 1980a. Type A Behavior in the Work Setting. In: P. Cooper, Current Concerns in Occupational Stress. Wiley, London.

Chesney, M. A. and Rosenman, R. H., 1980b. Type A Behavior Patterns: Recommendations for Modification, Consultant, 20:216-222.

Chesney, M. A., Sevelius, G., Black, G. W., Ward, M. M., Swan, G. E., and Rosenman, R. H., 1981. Work Environment, Type A Behavior, and Coronary Heart Disease Risk Factors. Journal of Occupational Medicine, pp. 551-555.

Cohen, J. B., 1978. The Influence of Culture on Coronary-Prone Behavior. In: T. M. Deabroski, S. M. Weiss, J. L. Shields (Editors), Coronary-Prone Behavior, Springer-Verlag, New York. pp. 243-252.

Moralee, D., 1981. ADA: Software Engineering Language of the Future?, Electronics and Power, July/August, pp. 556-562.

Nie, N. H., Hull, H. C., Jenkins, J. G., Steinbrenner, K., and Brent, D. H., 1977. Statistical Package for the Social Sciences (SPSS), 2nd ed., McGraw-Hill, New York.

Salvendy, G., and Sharit, J., 1982. Occupational Stress. In: Salvendy (Editor), Handbook of Industrial Engineering, Wiley, New York.

Salvendy, G. (Editor) 1982. Handbook of Industrial Engineering, Wiley, New York.

Sharit, J. and Salvendy, G., 1982. Occupational Stress: Review and Appraisal. Human Factors, pp. 129-162.

Zavala, A., Kaplan, R., Fitz-Enx, J. A., Hards, K. E., Sherman, N. R., and Kyllonen, P., 1979. Measurement of Factors Affecting Productivity at Four-Phase Systems, Inc., Inpsych, Cupertino.

Zavala, A., 1984. Some Correlates of Stress Among Software Development Workers. Paper presented at the Eleventh Conference on Production Research and Technology, Carnegie-Mellon University, Pittsburgh, PA.

Human—Computer Interaction, edited by G. Salvendy
Elsevier Science Publishers B.V., Amsterdam, 1984 — Printed in The Netherlands

MEASURES FOR IMPROVING OCCUPATIONAL HEALTH OF PEOPLE WORKING WITH VDTs AND ROBOTS IN JAPAN

H. TOGAMI and K. NORO
University of Occupational and Environmental Health, Japan, 1-1 Iseigaoka, Yahata Nishi Ku, Kitakyushu 807 (Japan)

ERGONOMIC MEASURES FOR VISUAL DISPLAY TERMINALS (VDTs) IN JAPAN

The problem that has drawn the largest attention lately to this gap is the health of visual display terminal (VDT) workers. The problem was first discussed in papers and reports in the United States and Europe from the last half of the 1960s to 1970. Given the estimated VDT dissemination rate of about 10% then, this fact credits these authors with excellent foresight and approach. Japanese researchers belatedly showed their first interest in the problem in 1980 when a few Japanese attended a workshop in Milan, Italy (Noro et al., 1980). The problem aroused the interest of the Japanese society in the last half of 1982 and attracted widespread attention in the first half of 1983 when a survey report of Microwave Inc. (1983) of the United States was introduced in Japan's major newspapers. J. O'Hare (1982) pointed out in the IEA Newsletter that only a few Japanese researchers presented papers on the problem at the IEA' 82 Tokyo congress.

Table 1 lists main ergonomic studies and activities on the health of VDT workers in Japan.

TABLE 1

Main ergonomic studies and activities on health of VDT workers in Japan.

---

o Study commissioned by Toyota Foundation (1981)
o Study on adaptability of old workers to VDT as part of activities of Old Worker Adaptability Research Committee (1981)
o VDT Work Research Committee (1982)
o Industrial Hygiene Research Committee (1983)
o OA Safety and Health Assurance Research Committee (1983)
o Study commissioned by Ministry of Labor (1983)
o The Committee on Occupational Health Measures in response to office automation and its various implications (the Ministry of Labor) (1984)

The changes in dissemination rates of VDT units from 1981 to 1986 (forecast) are shown in Table 2.

TABLE 2

Proportions of business machines from 1981 to 1986.

Type of machine	1981	1986 (Forecast)
General-purpose computers	87.1	88.2
On-line terminals	70.2	76.6
Facsimile terminals	60.2	65.1
Office computers	36.1	47.2
Word processors	34.0	42.1

These high dissemination rates of VDT displays highlight delays in research and remedy for the problem.

VDT Work and Occupational Health - A Provisional Guideline - (Japan Industrial Safety and Health Association, 1984), published on February 28, 1984 concerning industrial hygiene control in VDT work and listed in Table 1 will be explained next. The guideline was prepared by a research committee composed of specialists and established to study the industrial hygiene measures necessitated by office automation. One of the authors, Noro, is a member of the committee. The Labor Ministry directed the labor standards bureaus of the prefectures to furnish companies and other organizations where VDTs are used with instruction by referring to the guideline. The guideline is tentative, however. It covers the principles of industrial hygiene control, how to carry out industrial hygiene control and concrete items. The concrete items are concerned with environmental control, work control, health control and industrial hygiene education. Compared with the standard DIN 66234 of West Germany, report* of the NIOSH of the United States and booklet** of the Health and Safety Executive of the United Kingdom, the Japanese guideline is characterized by the emphasis placed on the overall occupational health management system.

OCCUPATIONAL HEALTH MEASURES FOR INDUSTRIAL ROBOTS IN JAPAN

How about the situation with industrial robots?

Fig. 1 shows the number of industrial robots installed in each of the world's main countries.

The diagram indicates that the number of industrial robots installed in

---

* NIOSH, Potential Health Hazards of Video Display Terminals, June 1981.
** Health and Safety Executive, Visual Display Units, 1983.

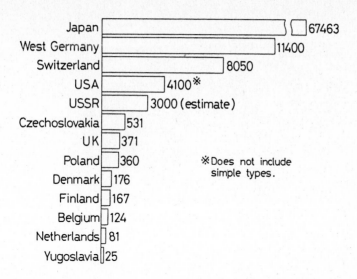

Fig. 1. Number of industrial robots installed in major countries in
        1981.

Japan is far larger than in any other country. This sudden spread of robots has
been giving rise to many problems (Noro et al., 1983). Occupational health
measures in a broad sense are urgently required in this respect. Two principal
measures are already taken to this end in Japan.

Personnel administration by companies (proposal by economic council)

After deliberation of an outlook for the Japanese economy by the year 2000,
the Long-Term Outlook Committee (chaired by Saburo Ohkita) of the Economic
Council, an advisory body to the Prime Minister, compiled a report on three
fields of industrial society, employment and national life.

The report thinks it necessary to develop opportunities for people 65 years
old and older to work according to their individual willingness and capability.
It also calls on the companies to modify their personnel administration policies
based on liftime employment, such as by transferring workers displaced by robots
to new jobs and reducing working hours commensurate with productivity improvement.

Safety regulation of industrial robots

The Japanese Ministry of Labor had been studying for some time amendments
to the Occupational Safety and Health Regulations as part of safety assurance
for workers engaged in work with industrial robots. The results of the study
were promulgated as "Ordinance concerning Amendments to Occupational Safety and
Health" on June 20, 1983.

374

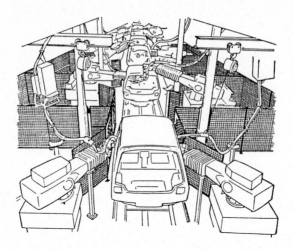

Fig. 2. Safety fence and interlock switch for press forming
robot.

CONCLUSION

The two problems mentioned above suggest the following. Safety regulations
were promptly established for industrial robots, because the problems involved
are technically clear; that is, the mechanical motions of the robot and the
injuries the operator may suffer are in clearcut relations. The effect on the
worker of the workplace environment where the robot is placed, as pointed out by
Noro, is not yet fully investigated and thus calls for immediate study.

The delay in taking occupational health measures for work with VDTs is due
to the fact that the problems involved are medical ones, mainly concerned with
eye-related complaints. If the complaint is eye fatigue, it is difficult to
essentially distinguish the eye fatigue from the eye fatigue pointed out by
Ramazzini in 1700. This ambiguity of the problems and the Japanese tendency of
limiting workers' health control by workplace doctors within factory-attached
dispensaries combined to cause the delay in taking appropriate measures.

REFERENCES

Japan Industrial Safety and Health Association, 1984. VDT Work and Occupational
    Health - A Provisional Guideline -. Tokyo, February.
Microwave Inc., 1983. Microwave news video display terminals: Health and safety.
Noro, K. and Tsuchiya, K., 1980. Method of caluculating inspection time of sam-
    ple on visual display by measurement of eye movement. In: E. Grandjean and
    E. Vigliani (Editors), Ergonomic Aspects of Visual Display Terminals. Milan,
    Italy, pp. 147-152.
Noro, K. and Okada, Y., 1983. Robotization and human factors. Ergonomics,
    26(10), pp. 985-1000.
O'Hare, J., 1982. Ergonomics international. November.

Human—Computer Interaction, edited by G. Salvendy
Elsevier Science Publishers B.V., Amsterdam, 1984 — Printed in The Netherlands

Attitude Changes Accompanying a Large Scale Automation Effort

Fred Fallik, Ph.D.
Internal Revenue Service
Washington, D.C.

I. BACKGROUND

Over the past few years, an intensive effort has been made by the Internal Revenue Service to improve its efficiency and effectiveness by automating many of its office functions. To date, the most extensive effort in automation has been the "Automated Collection System" (ACS).

ACS is designed to improve the office procedures by which delinquent taxes are collected. Compared with the previous methods of collecting such taxes, the ACS involved several dramatic changes in record keeping, taxpayer contact, workflow, office environment, and administrative procedures. So far as possible, delinquent account information was computerized and taxpayer contact was improved by installing an automated telephone dialing system.

The Human Resources Technology (HRT) Group became involved in the ACS project from the standpoint of assuring that psychological, social, and physiological factors were considered in the design of the new work environment. A major aspect of our efforts in this regard was to measure the effects of the ACS automation effort on employee attitudes. More specifically, we proposed to conduct a study which would:

a. Measure the changes in work attitude over time as a result of the ACS experience.
b. Identify, so far as possible, those factors which result in different work attitudes.

II. METHODOLOGY

To provide a test period for the new ACS equipment and procedures, four "pilot" sites were designated to begin on-line operation in May, 1983. After a period of five months of learning and testing, the remaining 16 ACS sites were to begin a planned phase-in of ACS operations. Two of the original ACS pilot sites were, unfortunately, not able to begin immediate operation due to a vendor default. These two sites did, however, begin operating in September, 1983.

To measure the attitudinal effects of this change from a relatively unautomated to an automated environment, the HRT Group designed an attitude survey which was administered to all ACS employees in the four pilot sites and to a control group of employees in two districts matched to the ACS sites. The control group employees performed the same functions as the ACS employees but under the older non-automated procedures and with manual record keeping and telephone equipment.

The attitude survey itself was composed of 109 items of which six items
required a narrative response. The remaining 103 items required the respondent
to select the most appropriate answer from a number of alternatives. Space was
provided for respondent comments in each section. The questionnaire was
comprised of five sections: 1. employee background, 2. work process, 3. work
environment, 4. work equipment, 5. general satisfaction issues. The section of
questions on work equipment was omitted from the control group's questionnaire
since the equipment was not available at those sites.

The questionnaire was administered three times during the pilot period.
The first administration took place in May, 1983, just prior to the beginning
of the pilot period, that is, before any of the respondents had had any
experience in the ACS environment. The purpose of this administration was to
establish a base-line of data against which later attitude change could be
measured. The second administration of the questionnaire was in late June and
was used to measure initial reaction to the ACS. The third and last
administration of the qeustionnaire was in early October and was used to
measure relatively stable work attitudes. In all, over 300 employees took part
in the study. For the purpose of analysis, the results from all four pilot
sites were combined as were the results from the two control sites.

III. RESULTS

A full presentation of the study's results would, of course, be impossible
given the space limitations. The number of possible comparisons among and
within questionnaire administrations is almost limitless. We have specifically
excluded all results which might be site specific. That is, differences due to
variations in managerial style or culture are ignored here. The analyses that
are presented below are what, for us, represented the most significant general
findings that have potential applicability beyond the IRS as a unique agency.
The results presented below are divided into two major sets of comparisons.
First, the trends in job satisfaction from the first to the third
administration will be discussed. Second, some significant findings related to
employee tenure will be discussed.

A. Longitudinal Changes

From the first to the third administration of the questionnaire a period of
approximately five months had elapsed. During this period of time several
significant changes in attitude had occurred both within the pilot sites and in
the control sites. The tables below serve to summarize the attitudinal changes
that occurred from the first to the second to the third administration,
comparing pilot sites with control sites.

	Table 1: Work Process Administration			Table 2: Work Environ. Administration			Table 3: Work Satisfaction Administration		
	1	2	3	1	2	3	1	2	3
Pilot	2.81	2.78	2.80	2.62	2.73	2.68	2.97	2.84	2.86
Control	2.49	2.40	2.40	2.20	2.15	1.97	2.51	2.49	2.48

The three tables above display the average satisfaction level of employees on a 1 to 4 scale (1=very dissatisfied, 2=dissatisfied, 3=satisfied, 4=very satisfied). Table 1 incorporates items which relate to the procedures, work flow, challenge, etc. of the job. In each of the three administrations of the questionnaire, the pilot sites are more satisfied than the control sites. A slight drop in satisfaction among the pilot sites occurred in the second administration, but satisfaction levels appear to have stabilized by the third administration.

Table 2 above summarizes the responses to items centered around the attractiveness and comfort of the physical work environment using the same satisfaction scale. Again, the control group demonstrates significantly lower satisfaction levels on all three administrations. Satisfaction levels within the pilot sites increased from the first to the second administration and then dropped on the third. Notice that employees tend to be less satisfied, in general, with their work environment than they are with the work process.

Table 3 again indicates that the control sites are significantly lower in satisfaction levels than the pilot sites in terms of satisfactions with the people and work itself. Within the pilot sites the initial high levels of satisfaction dropped somewhat on the second administration and had more or less stabilized by the third administration. Note also that, of the three areas, work process, work environment, and work satisfaction, employees indicate the highest levels of satisfaction with the work itself and the people they work with.

B. Tenure Differences

While the data summaries provide an overview of the differences among pilot and control sites on the three administrations, they tend to obscure differences among pilot sites and between employee groups across sites. One of the most consistent of such trends within the pilot sites can be attributed to the amount of experience employees had had with the IRS. All respondents were divided into two groups, those with more than 18 months experience and those with 18 or less months as an employee of the IRS. These two groups differed dramatically from each other in many areas.

The social and demographic characteristics of the two groups showed several differences. Newer employees tended to be better educated than older employees. Almost 53% of the newer employees had a college or graduate degree compared to 24% of the long term employees. Newer employees tended to have a higher percentage of males (46%) than long term employees (16%). As you might expect, they were also younger and had fewer people dependent on them.

Future job expectations of the two groups differed. Only 3% of the newer employees indicated that they plan to be working at their current job within the next few years compared to 14% of the long-term employees. Asked why they might leave, newer employees cited salary/benefits, advancement opportunities, and hours of work as reasons more frequently than long-term employees.

The level of satisfaction between newer and long term employees also differed. Both groups were equally satisfied with the work process but long-term employees were significantly more satisfied with the work environment than the short-term employees. Similarly, long-term employees were more satisfied with the work itself and the people with whom they worked.

IV. Summary and Conclusions

The results presented here merely touch on some of the major trends in the project. From these analyses, the following inferences might be drawn.

* Employees expectations prior to the implementation of new work technology are high. Satisfaction with the work process remained about the same over the course of time, satisfaction with the work environment increased slightly, but general job satisfaction decreased from the first administration.

* Generally, employees tend to be less satisfied with the environment in which they work than with the procedures used to accomplish their job. They tend to be most satisfied with the people they work with and the job itself.

* Employees who are not involved in the implementation of the new technologies tend to become more and more dissatisfied with their current work equipment and procedures. This appears to be almost a "negative Hawthorne effect."

* Employees who had experience using the non-automated work procedures tend to appreciate the effects of the change more than those who are relatively new to the job. Long term employees may be more realistic and have greater job stability than those who have had only a short term of employment.

Human—Computer Interaction, edited by G. Salvendy
Elsevier Science Publishers B.V., Amsterdam, 1984 — Printed in The Netherlands

PSYCHOSOCIAL ENVIRONMENTS CREATED BY COMPUTER USE FOR MANAGERS & SYSTEMS ANALYSTS

Barbara G.F. Cohen

Applied Psychology and Ergonomics Branch, Division of Biomedical and Behavioral Science, National Institute for Occupational Safety and Health, Centers for Disease Control, Public Health Service, U.S. Department of Health and Human Services

ABSTRACT

Twenty-three (23) personal interviews were conducted with supervisors and computer systems analysts as part of a health evaluation of 300 office workers using VDTs in their work. This sample of professionals utilizing VDTs revealed a host of job stressors that can affect worker health and well-being. Middle management personnel and computer specialists' perceptions of their working conditions indicate a need for improvement in human relations and in human factors that can be generalized to many workplaces.

INTRODUCTION

As a result of various health complaints reported at a federal government office facility, the National Institute for Occupational Safety and Health (NIOSH) responded to the agency's request to investigate the matter. The floor plan utilized an open office concept, having private offices around the perimeter and a maze of free standing partitions subdividing the rest of the building. The office area was renovated and the ventilation, air-conditioning, and heating systems had not been altered with this renovation. Consequently, temperatures and air flow were found to be uneven, producing hot and cold spots that were unsatisfactory from the workers' perspective.

Since this federal agency's operations primarily involve data services, more than 80% of the 300 employees located in the facility utilized VDTs in their work. Previous studies of VDT users (Smith et al, 1981; Stammerjohn et al, 1981; Cohen et al, 1981; Dainoff, 1982) have indicated excessive visual and musculoskeletal discomfort as well as general stress reactions arising from ergonomic, job design and organizational factors connected with such operations. Thus, the NIOSH evaluation focused on these concerns. Data collection included: (1) worksite observations and measurements of illumination, glare and workstation design, (2) visual examinations, (3) a stress and health symptoms questionnaire, and (4) individual semi-structured interviews of a sample of computer systems analysts and managers. This paper will focus on the interview data which elicited computer systems analysts' and supervisors' perceptions of stressors at their work sites. The purpose of interviewing this group was to ascertain a more complete understanding of the presence of any job stressors potentially affecting employee health than may have been revealed through the standardized health questionnaire and ergonomic observations. These perceptions will be discussed in the context of the ergonomic, visual, and health related findings obtained in the study.

METHOD

Subjects:

Twenty-three workers were randomly selected from the rosters of supervisors and computer systems analysts to participate in the interviews. As most of the supervisory positions and analysts in this agency were male, the interviewed sample was comprised of 21 males and two females. Their ages ranged from 30 to 50 years of age with a mean of 41 years. Their length of service in this agency ranged from 1 to 24 years with a mean of 12.6 years. Length of service in their present position ranged from 6 months to 10 years with a mean of 7 years.

Supervisors as well as analysts used computers in their work. However, none of the interview group spent more than one hour continuous on the VDT as the access to terminals was limited due to the many employees needing the equipment. Thus, these workers took turns in sharing use of the VDT terminal and averaged about 4 total hours per day on the terminal. If the computer system crashed during any one of their one hour periods at the terminal, they lost their turn and the information on the system. This delayed the work and obviously frustrated the workers.

Interview Method:

A semi-structured interview lasting about 20 minutes, was designed to discern positive and negative aspects of each participant's job. All participants were asked a series of open-ended questions about their job, their feelings, and their health. Positive and negative factors were obtained by asking respondents the things they liked best and least about their jobs. Examples of questions asked and responses are given below.

RESULTS

Job Factors:

To the question what do you like best about your job, the most frequent
reply (48% of responses) was enjoyment of the work itself. It was evident
that the agency's mission was important to the study participants, and this
seemed to enhance their interest. Moreover, to many of the interviewees,
the computers appeared to be more than just tools to complete assignments.
They were fun to use. Irritation arose over not being able to use them
often enough or long enough as well as having to deal with overloaded
systems (83%). The next most frequent response describing desirable job
attributes dealt with task flexibility (26%), working at one's own pace
(20%), and, particularly for supervisors, interacting with people (26%).
Being called upon to use special effort or talent to perform particular
tasks was perceived as a positive factor so that those who experienced such
a challenge liked that aspect of their job. By the same token, those who
did not feel challenged mentioned its absence as a problem. Likewise, the
employees who perceived that they had flexibility over their work schedules
and manner of accomplishing assigned tasks saw this as a positive factor.
Those with heavy workloads and unrealistic deadlines for completion
complained of the lack of control and flexibility. Several supervisors
indicated interest in their staff as they discussed efforts to secure better
equipment, improved work conditions, and more promotions for them.
Supervisors expressed their frustration when unable to achieve these goals.
Other replies of positive factors included the variety of tasks, peer group,
importance of the job, intellectual stimulation, being busy, having
responsibility, completing one's own work, and simply enjoying the
computers. On the other hand, dissatisfaction with equipment was the most
frequent complaint and 83% acknowledged a number of specific shortcomings.
(For example, there was an insufficient number of terminals for the amount
of users, too much down-time because the system was insufficient to handle
the amount of data, and delayed response time. Overall, it was felt that
the existing equipment was outdated and failed to do the job required).

Ergonomic Issues:

Prominent problems related to ergonomic issues concerned the lighting
(39%), the lack of space for working and for storage (22%), and the poorly
designed chairs (17%). Requests for desk lamps to improve illumination were
refused by upper management. Some employees brought in their own lamps and
their own humidifiers in spite of being told they were prohibited.

Ergonomic observations confirmed the impressions gathered in the interviews. Worksite illumination levels in most areas were found to be inappropriate for the work activity and the visual demands. The ergonomic analysis also showed glare problems on all the terminals. Glare on the screen washed out characters, thus intensifying workers' visual efforts. Workstations (chairs, desks, VDT consoles, etc.) all lacked adjustability to adapt them to comfortable user heights and positions. Many terminals had fuzzy characters that could produce readability problems.

Management Issues:

The supervisors and computer systems analysts interviewed voiced significant complaints about upper management (52%). Dominant were feelings that upper management was unconcerned about employee health, more concerned over paper forms than with employees, and unaware of the work itself or work problems. Moreover, it was perceived that management wasted time by causing duplication of effort as well as putting up barriers to progress. Among negative descriptors alluding to leadership were terms such as "ambiguous", "disorganized" and "unreasonable". Since top management often changes with new political appointees, several employees were disturbed by the lack of continuity.

Environmental Issues:

Environmental conditions causing discomfort to this group centered mainly on ventilation problems such as not enough air, air not circulating and smoke-filled air (96%). Some offices were reported to be stifling and hot, others as cold. NIOSH's investigation determined that the uneven climatic conditions in the building required further evaluation by a ventilation engineering specialist. Several environmental issues were related to the open office design. There were complaints about partitions blocking the air from circulating yet not high enough to block out smoke. Many workers indicated that they experienced difficulty in concentrating because of noise from conversations either behind the partitions or in the aisles (22%). Having a quiet place was felt to be necessary for debugging programs and noise was a great annoyance. Lack of privacy was a concern issues for others (35%). Finally, supervisors regretted the loss of feeling and working as a unit after their staff members had been dispersed to various areas in the open office.

Health Issues:

When asked how they felt at work and at the end of the day, the majority of interviewees complained of dryness of eyes, nose, throat, and/or skin (57%). The second most common types of complaint involved sinus infections, allergies, frequent colds or flu (52%). The third most common type of complaint alluded to burning, itching eyes and headaches (49%). Other symptoms reported in frequency of occurrence were fatigue (35%), bronchial infections (9%), depression (4%), hypertension (4%), weight gain (14%), and nose bleeds (4%). These interview data corresponded with the findings from the visual examinations, ergonomic analyses, and health responses from the survey questionnaire.

The questionnaire findings on the frequency rankings of employees' health complaints for the previous year were: (1) respiratory problems, (2) visual disorders, (3) musculoskeletal disorders, (4) psychological problems such as irritability, depression periods, high tension, severe fatigue, and (5) stomach disorders. The interview group differed only in that the frequency of dryness of eyes, nose, throat and/or skin was the most common category of complaints.

DISCUSSION

The purpose of the interviews was to ascertain a more complete understanding of the presence of any job stressors potentially affecting employee health than may have been revealed by the stress and health questionnaire or the ergonomic worksite observations. The findings indicate that the interviews do offer such additional insights.

A profile of the interview participants suggests that the workers seek responsibility and challenge, feel strongly about the importance of their work, and take much pride in a job well done. Because of the amount of personal investment involved in their work, roadblocks to completing the job or to the quality of the output can be a significant source of aggravation. The sample of managers and computer analysts interviewed expressed a great deal of frustration with the upper management and with the procedures that govern the outcome of their work as well as with the inability to secure good equipment to perform the job. Furthermore, concern for their subordinate's health and well-being as well as their productivity appears to intensify the irritation middle management and the first-line supervisors experience. On the other hand, this concern for subordinates may also account for the relatively low levels of employee job stress that were noted in the written survey.

Survey questionnaire analyses revealed that except for a high level of physical discomfort, scores on job stressors as indicated on questionnaire scales such as heavy workload, role ambiguity, and conflict, boredom, lack of staff or peer support did not indicate that this group of VDT operators perceived unusually stressful working conditions. In fact, the employees perceived even more staff support, less feelings of being controlled by their supervisors, and more autonomy than established normative data (Insel & Moos, 1974) and than other VDT operators from previous research (Smith et al, 1981).

In summary, the interviews indicated that the prominence of psychological problems such as irritability, depression, tension, severe fatigue and of psychosomatic disorders like stomach ailments as reported in the survey instrument was due not only to inadequate climatic and ergonomic conditions but to organizational factors that impeded the progress of their work, factors that were not measured by the questionnaire.

REFERENCES

Cohen, B.G.F., Smith, M.J., Stammerjohn, L.W. Psychosocial factors contributing to job stress of clerical VDT operators. In Machine Pacing and Occupational Stress, Salvendy, G. & Smith, M.J. (Eds.) London: Taylor and Francis, 1981, 337-345.

Dainoff, M.J. Ergonomics - the physical pain. Computerworld: Office Automation, March 31, 1982.

Insel, P. & Moos, R. Work Environment Scale - Form S. Palo Alto, California:
Consulting Psychologist Press, 1974.

Smith, M.J., Cohen, B.G.F., Stammerjohn, L.W., Happ, A. An investigation of health complaints and job stress in video display operations. Human Factors, 23(4), 1981, 387-400.

Stammerjohn, L.W., Smith, M.J., Cohen, B.G.F. Evaluation of work station design factors in VDT operations, Human Factors, 23(4), 1981, 401-412.

VII. APPLICATIONS OF HUMAN-COMPUTER INTERACTIONS

Human—Computer Interaction, edited by G. Salvendy   387
Elsevier Science Publishers B.V., Amsterdam, 1984 — Printed in The Netherlands

HUMAN INTERACTION WITH ONLINE RETRIEVAL SYSTEMS

MYER P. KUTZ

Electronic Publishing Division, John Wiley & Sons, Inc. New York, New York

ABSTRACT

   The purpose of this paper is to discuss challenges faced by primary
publishers when they elect to distribute their publications (which are original
works) through online retrieval services. Until recently the bulk of the
materials distributed through the online services were secondary publications,
which consist of abstracts and indexes to the primary literature. Librarians
comprise nearly all of the online market for secondary services. The primary
publishers are attempting to reach beyond the library community to end users,
i.e., the professionals who read primary publications. This paper describes
the accommodations that the online services, in concert with the primary
publishers, have had to make in order to serve a broad-based group of users who
do not wish to become information specialists, but demand that the online
services be so user-friendly that virtually no training is required to use them.

   To make a long story short, the private companies (called vendors),

government agencies and university centers that developed online retrieval

services (also called search services) did so in order to make available

secondary publications to libraries and information centers. Major online

retrieval services used by libraries and other information centers are:

   1. DIALOG (Lockheed Information Systems)

   2. ORBIT (System Development Corporation - SDC)

   3. BRS (Bibliographic Retrieval Services, Inc.)

   4. MEDLINE (National Library of Medicine)

   5. THE NEW YORK TIMES INFORMATION BANK (The New York Times)

These search services made available databases consisting mainly of secondary

or bibliographic information. Many of them were traditional library

reference media such as Chemical Abstracts and Engineering Index. With the

advent of the online services additional abstracting and indexing services

have appeared. Two examples of organizations producing guides to business

literature are ABI/INFORM, which is produced by a subsidiary of the Louisville

Courier Journal, and Management Contents. The range of databases is now

staggering, as can be seen by perusing the leading guide. The Directory of

Online Databases[1], published by Cuadra Associates in Santa Monica, now lists

2,225 databases. Examination of a sub-set of online databases - those dealing

with business - illustrates the range of information now available, which goes

far beyond such typical business and management bibliographic databases as

ABI/INFORM adds about 2,500 records a month to its database. But a recent list

of online business databases compiled from the Cuadra directory starts with a

textual-numerical database on U.S. economics called the A. Gary Shilling

Economic Forecast. This database contains more than 200 time series of historical and forecast data for the U.S. economy including national product and income accounts, consumer price indexes and other macroeconomic indicators. The list of online business databases concludes with the Zip Code Demographic database, which contains demographic statistics for over 35,000 U.S. postal zip codes. These statistics include population, income and housing. Access to the data can be by individual zip code, state, county, postal region, postal section and zip code range.

As recently as 1981 Charles T. Meadow and Pauline (Atherton) Cochrane in their book Basic of Online Searching[2] write "The major buyers of search services today are libraries – academic, special, public and even school libraries. They may resell the service to their clients free or share the cost. Some, but not all, libraries encourage their users to learn to search for themselves. Most, however, employ highly trained specialists who may be called by such titles as Search Specialists or Data Systems Librarians. These intermediaries assist the user or perform the search for the user." But LEXIS, and online retrieval service operated by Mead Data Central, a subsidiary of the Mead Corporation (whose main business is paper and forest products), had been selling an online information directory to end users. Mead had positioned LEXIS, (which is a family of files (called libraries) that contain the full text of court decisions, statutes, regulations and other primary and secondary materials) in law schools. People training to become lawyers learn to use this search service to rapidly research court decisions. These people continue the practice when they go to work in law firms and have become one of the first groups of end users who do their own searching. Mead originally distributed its libraries through dedicated phone lines and, more importantly, dedicated terminals specially designed to be particularly user-friendly. The service became profitable partially because, as conventional wisdom had it, lawyers were able to pass along the costs of online searching to their clients, but also because of the user friendliness. But this is getting ahead of our story.

From the outset, the major search services tended to cultivate intermediaries as customers with special status. By and large, online searching, which could be done using non-dedicated terminals coupled through telephone lines to the search services' computers, was not user-friendly. Most professionals, particularly business people, who had tried online searching found it something they did not wish to try again. It even seemed that some intermediaries would seize upon this difficulty as a guarantee of job security. One encountered situations in which intermediaries told end users that online searching was too difficult for them and they were well advised not to even bother to learn how to do it.

A case could be made that the search services conspired with the intermediaries to perpetuate this situation. To be sure, the rapid proliferation of databases required continuing education for intermediaries. They had to learn the contents of each new database and the methods for retrieving the new pieces of information. The search services set up training sessions and user meetings. At certain major conventions, such as the annual Online conventions in London in December and in New York in April, database publishers and producers gave product reviews in which they described the features of new databases. It required a great deal of study to keep up with the field.

The pricing algorithms used by the search services made it even more unlikely that end users would become involved in online searching. Most algorithms involved charges based on the amount of access time plus, in some cases, the amount of material retrieved. Such algorithms, which involved stiff prices, on the order of $1.00 or more per minute of access time for commercial databases, made it extremely expensive for untutored searchers to thrash around for minutes at a time. There was a penalty for learning on the job. A branch of the online literature was devoted to search strategies that minimized the cost of searching. If the end user paid for the cost he was well advised to let an expert do it.

To further limit online access time and make searching more efficient many searchers became dependent on thesauri, which were published collections of terms used by indexers and abstractors working on a particular bibliographic database. Such thesauri contain terms such as descriptors assigned by indexers or names of authors, titles, or individual words occuring in titles or abstracts. Having a list of interrelated terms helped define searches more precisely.

The search services that provide access to bibliographic information trained searchers to use set theory. Searchers employed three operators: the AND operator, to find elements in a new third set which are in a first set and also in a second set; the OR operator, to find elements in a third set which are either in a first set or second set or both; the NOT operator, to find elements of a third set which consist of those parts of a first set which are not also part of a second set. Meadows and Cochrane justified the teaching of the use of such operators as follows: "The kinds of commands most familiar to beginning searchers are the set combination commands, probably because to those unfamiliar with computers, this type of command is almost intuitive." The operators were necessary because, as Meadows and Cochrane put it "The reason for having set combination is that it is rarely enough to define a set in terms of a single term, even if the term is a descriptor assigned by an indexer. Usually you will find that there are several terms with similar meanings, all of which you would like to use in a search, and there may be correlated terms that you want to find together in selected records."

But the services also developed proximity operators, which seem to this untutored searcher to be not only easier to understand, but also far more powerful. Examples of proximity operators are ADJ (for adjacency), WITH and SAME. On BRS, for example, the proximity operators permit natural language searching. With the ADJ operator one looks for words next to one another; with the WITH operator, for words appearing in the same sentence; with the SAME operator, for words appearing in the same paragraph. The concept can be extended profitably in databases with tabular information. The ADJ operator functions the same, i.e., it permits searching for words next to one another. But, table titles can be treated as sentences, and the tables themselves can be treated as paragraphs. More importantly, the proximity operators are extremely useful when searching the full text of articles, rather than citations, or in addition to them. With more and more full text databases going online, proximity operators are becoming more and more useful.

To illustrate I will use an example from the Kirk-Othmer Encyclopedia of Chemical Technology database, which can be searched on BRS. Suppose we are looking for tables which contain the tensile strength of aluminum. It is possible to type in a search statement which says that we are looking for tables where the word aluminum appears in the same table as the word tensile adjacent to the word strength. The first answer to the search, incidentally, is a table in the chapter on adhesives, which gives tensile strength values for low, medium and high strength aluminum.

Worse yet, from the point of view of making online searching user-friendly, have been the commands for displaying answers or printing them (if your terminal is a printer or is attached to one). On BRS, which is a powerful, and, in many ways attractive system, the print command is particularly user-unfriendly. To illustrate, let us go back to the tensile-strength-of-aluminum example, and let us suppose that we are already signed onto the Kirk-Othmer database on BRS, which itself is so torturous a procedure that inexperienced searchers often find it intimidating. The screen would read as follows:
BRS - search mode - enter query
   1_:

To find tables which contain information about the tensile strength of aluminum one would type in this search statement:

aluminum same tensile adj strength.ta.

The spacing must be as precise as shown. The search system is most unforgiving in this way and an error message will appear if any rule has been violated, even in the slightest way.

Once the searcher has typed in the above search statement, the system provides the following answer:

RESULT   10

What this means is, there are ten articles in the Kirk–Othmer database which contain tables that satisfy the search statement. These tables may provide the tensile strength of aluminum or they may provide the tensile strength of some aluminum alloy or they may simply have the words aluminum, tensile and strength in such combination that although the search statement is satisfied, the searcher's question is not answered.

In order to look at the first table which satisfied the search statement, the searcher must type in the following print statement:

..p 1 hits/doc=1

Again, the spacing must be exact. If any mistakes in spacing are made, or too many dots are typed in front of the letter p, or if some other mistake is made an error message will appear. This message will not identify the error. By typing in ..p the searcher has informed the search service to deliver answers to the questions. By typing in the numeral 1 the searcher has referred the system to questions that are in set 1. Typing in the word hits informs the system to print the tables that satisfy the search statement. Typing in doc=1 informs the system that the searcher wishes to look at answers only in the first article where the system has found them. Here is the first table that satisfies the searcher's question. As mentioned earlier, it is from the Adhesives article. Note that it gives a range of answers and so might be particularly useful.

Table 1. Approximate Tensile Strength of Materials (Kirk-Othmer Encyclopedia
of Chemical Technology, Third Edition, Volume 1, Martin Grayson,
Editor, 1978, John Wiley & Sons, Inc., New York, New York)

Material	Tensile Strength, MPa[a]
glass fibers	4000
alloy steels	2000
titanium	1400
nylon fibers	800
carbon steels	700
high strength aluminum	650
magnesium	380
medium strength aluminum	280
alumina ceramics	200
glass-filled nylon	170
low strength aluminum	100
EPOXIES	90
nylon	70
acrylics	70
hard rubber	55
phenolics	55
wood composition board	35
black rubber	30
gum rubber	10
foam plastics	2
concrete	1
foam rubber	0.4

a 1 MPa = 145 psi.

It has occurred to the database publishing community - and to database
vendors as well - that menu-driven protocols would be far less intimidating to
untrained end users. Recently, with the encouragement of publishers, vendors
began to offer menu-driven protocols that were far more tedious to use than
the standard protocols, but allowed for database access by end users with a
minimum amount of training. At first the vendors made these protocols
available at off-peak hours, i.e., after 6:00PM local time - and at lower than
standard access usage rates. The idea was to encourage end users who were in
their offices late or wished to search on home computers to begin to use online
services. These services were called Knowledge Index (on Dialog) and BRS
After Dark. Shortly thereafter several publishers pursuaded BRS to make the
menu-driven software available at peak hours and at usage rates that might
encourage end users to begin doing their own searching rather than relying
on intermediaries. This group of publishers includes ABI INFORM, Grolier
(which included Academic American Encyclopedia in this new service), John
Wiley & Sons (which included the Harvard Business Review), and Management

Contents.

The menu-driven software does indeed make searching easier. Trained
searchers find it repetitious and tedious, and it is expected that novice
searchers will in time reach similar conclusions. But it is expected that the
menu-driven protocols will make novice users comfortable enough with searching
so that they will convert to using standard protocols, which are far more
efficient. Because it is taking so long for knowledge of online searching to
filter through to end users I expect that it will be at least a year or two
before the menu-driven systems draw substantial numbers of users into online
searching.

What will speed the process is the development of so called gateway systems,
which combine menu-driven software with simplified access to the online
services and then to the databases. It is early days for these gateway
systems, but they have already begun to proliferate, much as one would expect
given the statistic that last year there were more modems sold in the United
States than personal computers. A great number of people are interested in
going online and searching the world's significant technical and medical
literature. They'll do so once they learn about the nature of online systems,
and then learn about an easy way to access the information they need.

REFERENCES

Cuadra, Ruth N., Abels, David M., Wanger, Judith, Directory of Online
    Databases, Cuadra Associates, Inc., Santa Monica, California, 1984

Meadow, Charles T., Cochrane, Pauline A., Basics of Online Searching,
    John Wiley & Sons, Inc., New York, New York, 1981

Grayson, Martin (Editor), Kirk-Othmer Online, John Wiley & Sons, Inc.,
    New York, New York, 1983

Human—Computer Interaction, edited by G. Salvendy
Elsevier Science Publishers B.V., Amsterdam, 1984 — Printed in The Netherlands

SOME FUNDAMENTAL PROBLEMS OF APPLICATION OF INDUSTRIAL ROBOTS IN PRODUCTION
LINE

T. OHKUBO, M. AOKI, Y. HORIE, S. SAITO and Y. UENO

College of Industrial Technology, Nihon University, 1-2-1, Izumi, Narashino
    Chiba (JAPAN)

ABSTRACT

OHKUBO, T., AOKI, M., HORIE, Y., SAITO, S. and UENO, Y., 1984. Some funda-
    mental problems of application of industrial robots in production line.

The progress of industrial robots development technology in recent years in
Japan is remarkable, but it is very difficult to obtain instruction manuals on
concrete description of how to introduce robots into industrial job sites. If
obtained, the contents except for part of them are very poor. This, it seems,
might have been prevented the introduction or use of robots from being made
properly. And as a result, those robots could not be used effectively. The
worst case was that even labor accidents were caused by robots. In some other
cases, robots were not harmonized with men.
    This research therefore aimed at pointing out various causes of the above
problems to be generated when industrial robots are to be introduced, considering them from the ergonomics point of view. The research was made through case
study examples.

INTROUDUCTION

Industrial robots developed in the United States in the first half of 1960s
have kept on increasing in practical use and introduced in many corporations in
the world. This tendency is getting all the more strengthened now. Especially
in Japan, the retention rate of industrial robots, centering on major corporations at the beginning, has been kept increasing rapidly since 1980. We have
almost 42% of all industrial robots now in use in the world. As robots have
spreaded so widely, the cost of robots has also lowered. This has further spur-
red on the introduction of robots not only in major corporations but also in
medium and small corporations.

The use of such industrial robots will bring various merits such as enhanced
productivity, stableness of quality, energy-saving etc. Various useful functions which substitute human labors have also been developed for those industrial
robots along with the progress of science. However, due to lack of proper
instruction manuals describing concrete procedures and notes on introducing
those robots, robots have not always been used effectively; workers have had
to involve in monotonous jobs making up for functions of robots or suffer from
excessive work load because their working pace was set in accordance with the

functions of robots. Thus, at worst, labor accidents were caused by robots, generating problems which have never seen before in relation to man-robot-environmetal system.

This research, therefore, aimed at considering problems and requirements to occur when robots are to be introduced through practical cases and intended to facilitate workers to be harmonized with robots in comfortable and safety work conditions, where no men are sacrified by robots.

(1) Work suitable for robotization viewed from human work characters

The common ideas to be thought of at first when industrial robots are introduced will be improvement of productivity, stableness of quality, and energy-saving. If they are considered from a view points of man's working characteristics, the following three potential factors should be examined first checking if the three points are contained in the work for which robots are introduced.

(i) Existance of works in limited conditions

Works in limited conditions are works unfavorable to workers, such as heavy physical labor and works under injurious conditions. These works, when carried out by men, are often too hard and their procedures are too complicated for workers. Thus, industrial robots, if used in such works, will be very useful. And in those limited conditions, robots would play their roles most effectively. However, there may be some cases in which the work may be beyond the functional capacity of robots. In this case, workers must help part of the work processes performed by robots.

(ii) Exsistance of monotonous work and its rate

This case may be a case in which industrial robots are used effectively. These days, labor itself has been freed from conventional heavy muscle labor and turned into lighter and easier one, by which workability and quality are more enhanced. On the contrary, there have appeared a new type of physiological and psycological problem -- stress -- which have less seen before; workers have come to feel jobs uninteresting and dull, or receive strengthened physical fatigue on their bodies partially.

The fatigue generated under such work status, even if the work is light and easy physically, will be great psycologically or mentally. As a result, the work may be dehumanized. In Japan, middle aged part-time woman workers apt to involve in such jobs; the rate has now reached over 66%. Their work load, when combined with house-keeping labor, is often led directly or indirectly to diseases.

(iii) When sophisticated skills are required:

Any job, more or less, requires skills. Skilled jobs can be roughly classified into complecated job and simple job. However, it is very hard to determine
those jobs quantitatively. Because, even if an attempt is made to evaluate a
skillful job objectively according to the degree, only vague expression like
"about this much" can be made actually. Also because workers master jobs which
require skillfulness through their body in a long time of period, that is,
intuitions, it is very difficult to give an objective index to them.

Problems in skilled jobs are that jobs to be done.only by skilled workers
have been placed out of factory automation, and therefore no harmony could not
have been kept between skilled workers and automatic machines. This further
resulted in forming a vicious circle of shortage of skilled workers.

Besides the three points mentioned above, robots should substitute for all
works of which productivity is lowered directly or indirectly and works which
will cause occupational diseases.

(2) Notes on introduction of robots

To promote robot systems with which productivity is enhanced and workers can
work in a comfortable environment, detailed investigation and analysis of works
on the spot should be made first, then difficulties and problems to occur when
robots are introduced must also be solved before designing optimum work systems,
However, in practical, medium and small corporations in Japan are not equipped
with optimum conditions yet under which robots can operate effectively. It is
of course very hard to introduce robots as are to work sites which were only
reformed mechanically. Before introducing robots to those medium and small
corporations, at least the following conditions must be satisfied.

(i) Work condition

In almost cases, work conditions are not optimum for workers. Thus, if robots
are introduced in such job sites with much noise, vibration, and dust, robots
may malfunction. In addition, when an abnormality occurs in robots, no workers
may be noticed, thus the abnormality may be developed to labor accidents. It is
very important therefore to check if the work environment is satisfied with
required conditions mentioned above for introducing robots. If not, the necessary improvement must be made beforehand.

(ii) Reserving a proper working space

Robots must be installed in a place with enough space to perform inspection
and maintenance for robots and workers can move smoothly and in safe around the
robots during operation. In addition, the structure and quality of the floor

on which robots are installed must stand for the weight of robots.

(iii) Work load influences on workers

There may be various types of work load influenced on workers. Problems are that workers are forced to do a work beyond his capability or to do a work in which he cannot give fully play to his ability.

One of the purpose to introduce robots is to free workers from such the circumstances. However, at present, industrial robots cannot substitute for workers load completely yet. Therefore, if robots are used for works with high work load, workers are often forced to do supplemental and monotonous works which cannot be done by robots for a long time of period. In such the case, the quality of the workers' work load may be completely different from conventional one.

(iv) Work items

To understand what kind of work workers are doing instead of robots, both qualitative and quantitative analysis will be needed for workers' working status and processes of parts.

To grasp works objectively will provide this research with very important materials required for determining the optimum operation of robots as well as pointing out and inprovement of problems in work contents. Especially, it is indispensable for knowing procedures when robotizing skilled works.

(v) Robot operator

To operate industrial robots effectively, experts who educated on computer programming, system monitoring, and inspection and maintenance for robots should be reserved beforehand.

When introducing industrial robots, especially for medium and small corporations, general-purpose robot systems would be better. And the robots operators should be qualified for not only operating robots, but also qualified hopefully as robot system designers capable of corresponding to change of designs of products or model changes effectively and speedily.

(3) A case study on applicability of robots in production line

A case study was carried out at a factory based on items mentioned in (2), to know the necessity and applicability of the afore-mentioned considerations;

(i) Outline of subject factory and purpose of robots introduction

As the subject factory in the case study, a valve maker (capital:$700,000, employees:350) was selected. The factory is planning to introduce assembly robots in near future. The valve maker is a medium-sized corporation, manufacturing more than 1000 types of valves and joints. The maker has already used N.C. machine tools for processing materials, and the assembly lines are subject to robotization this time.

The purpose of introducing robots were for the three points such as stableness of quality, energy-saving of productionlines, learning techniques of industrial robots.

(ii) Research methods

Ther research-subject assembly line used conveyor system. Survey and evaluation were thus made for evaluating the man-machine-environmental conditions from a view of three points as mentioned below;

(a) Layout of the work site

At first, an layout diagram of the work site was made, then flow of parts, products, and workers are checked and analized.

(b) Work contents

A video analysis was made for each worker's action and posture in processes in which parts are changed into products. Particularly, checks were made carefully whether there were any works causing labor accidents or labor diseases in the assembly line.

(c) Work load

Subjective symotoms of fatigue by the I.F.R.C. (Industrial Fatigue Research Commitee)were also checked, as well as conceptional or experienced feelings of workers for ordinary works were investigated and analized through a questionnaire survey made in advance.

The assembly line to be robotized were participated by 10 workers in total (8 woman and 2 man part-time workers). The number of production processes were 14 in total. Thus, one worker had to be in charge of two or more processes. Numbers of workers for the research were, therefore ten.

(iii) Research results and discussions;

(a) Layout of the work site;

Figure 1 shows the layout diagram of the work site. Viewing the work site from objective data obtained by measuring it, the site was also used as a temporary stock place of products and parts during operation. Therefore, it was concluded that the flow of workers, parts, or products were not always done smoothly. Considering the work area of robots to be introduced, the present floor space was insufficient.

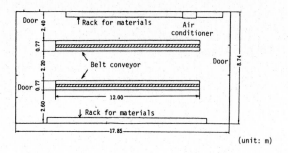

Fig. 1 The layout diagram of the work site

(b) Work contents;

  The work on the spot was compared with that in the standard work manual. As a result, it was turned out that the work was not standardized yet. Even the same work, when done by others, was done in different ways and there were also many useless actions in workers. For example, workers were often busy in looking for parts around the factory. In other words, there was much room for improving the present work system and it seemed to be possible to reform the system and must be improved before robots are to be introduced.

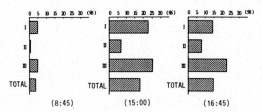

Fig. 2 Symptoms of feeling fatigue for totally 21 subjects.

(c) Work load;

  Figure 2 shows the results of the subjective symptoms of fatigue. "Eye strain" and "stiff shoulders" were the main symptoms. They were followed by appeals of "pain in the lower back" and "weary feet". It was remarkable that monotony seemed to be more serious for workers than the above fatigue problems. The work on the assembly line looked that monotonous.

  Thus, introduction of robots to the pertinent work site would be considerably effective, but problem is that the present technical level of robots will not be able to cope with the pertinent work completely. Even if robots are introduced, there are still some supplemental work left to workers (e.g. visual inspection, exchange of tools, etc.). And it is also considered that another monotonous works will be generated with the replacement of the system.

(4) Conclusion

There are a lot of corporations which have already introduced industrial robots and have added up much profits actually. However, conventional way of introducing such industrial robots to improve the productivity and make the quality stable may not cope with problems occurring between robots and workers. Another type of problems will be generated in relation to the man-machine-interface. Such introducing way would not be preferable for man.

When viewing such the problems from results obtained from the research this time, the primary will be that no standard work method has been established in those works. It is natural that there will be generated much unncecessary actions of workers since even the same process is never be done in the same way. Such the work system would never bring high productivity.

Another renewed recognition through the case study was that most assembly works, even if they are light and easy to do, make workers feel monotonous.

Considering these research results, it is found that introducing of industrial robots does not always result in the improvement of the productivity and obtaining of immediate effect on freeing worker from monotonous works. Actually, however, it is more important to fulfill the required conditions to introduce (mentioned in (2)). It was convined again that this cannot be neglected to provide an effective work system.

Corporation managers with for introducing those industrial robots eagerly now that factory automation has been rapidly advanced, but they also should consider some effective measures mentioned earlier part so that a harmonious relations between workers and robots can be kept well in a macro-viewed work environment without sticking to short-run profits.

REFFERENCES

1) Research Institute of the Japan Small Business Corporation. 1984.
    Research on the development of production systems by use of micro computers
    (I)
2) Research Institute of the Japan Small Business Corporation. 1984.
    Research on the development of production systems by use of micro computers
    (II)
3) Yokomizo, Y. 1983, Industrial Robots, J. Ergonomics, Vol. 19, No. 5.
4) Nagamachi, M and Anayama, Y. 1983. An Ergonomic study of Industrial Robot
    (1) - The experiments of unsafe behavior on robot manipulation -,
    J. Ergonomics, Vol. 19, NO. 5.

Human—Computer Interaction, edited by G. Salvendy
Elsevier Science Publishers B.V., Amsterdam, 1984 — Printed in The Netherlands

A Quasi-Natural Language Interface for UNIX

Purna Mishra, Barbara Trojan, Robert Burke, and Sarah A. Douglas
Departments of Computer Science and Psychology, University of Oregon, Eugene, OR

INTRODUCTION

One of the primary goals for human factors research in computer science is to develop systems which are more adaptive to differing user categories. This paper presents one solution to building adaptive systems—a quasi-natural language interface directed to optimize the performance of casual users of UNIX.[*] The major contribution we make to the development of natural language interfaces is to empirically assess and define the background knowledge and goals of casual users that form the context for their queries.

What is a casual user and how could a quasi-natural language interface be appropriate? Casual users have learned the initial concepts of using a computer system, in this case UNIX, but only infrequently make use of it. In addition, casual users are individuals who have expertise with some other computer system, in our study a DEC10 running TOPS-10. This prior knowledge will influence how they conceptualize a new system (Douglas & Moran, 1983). We also assume that casual users know basic classes of computer tasks but may lack knowledge of how to translate these tasks into the appropriate commands in UNIX; or they may know the command lexicon and syntax but may be uncertain of the effects of the commands (the semantics). These elements of a casual user's knowledge should be recognized by interface designers in order to facilitate efficient user operation and to provide appropriate feedback that allows the casual user to develop an accurate model of the new system. The interface should provide a transition to the typically terse command language preferred by experts.

LIMITATIONS OF EXISTING ON-LINE HELP SYSTEMS

A brief review of the existing on-line help for the UNIX command language reveals some of its limitations and the reasons for a more extensive quasi-natural language interface. UNIX has three forms of help available: prompting, the *help* command, and the *man* command which can match keywords and invoke pages from an on-line manual. These three existing on-line help facilities are fairly limited. While *help* lists some useful commands and their functions, such as *cat* for *concatenate files*, it fails to list information on other useful tasks such as copying, deleting, etc. Thus, it is woefully incomplete. The on-line manual appears to be a useful feature, but it, too, has limitations. The depth of information is invariant: users must wade through much detail to find relevant information. Secondly, the amount of information presented usually fills the screen causing users to lose their work context. Dunsmore (1980) found on-line documentation took valuable time away from problem-solving. Prompting, while preserving the work context,

---

[*] We use the word *quasi* to denote that we wish to specialize the natural language interface to the types of questions, problems and knowledge consistent with our empirical studies, rather than providing a generalized natural language processor with potential overhead in real-time response. Quasi-natural language systems are interpreters that translate natural language questions into formalized command/query languages. Other examples include the natural language interfaces to database query systems.

suffers from terseness, and casual users require additional documentation on the parameters. This causes them to use the on-line manual which in turn proves inadequate.

Experiment One: User interaction with existing UNIX on-line help

We were particularly interested in how casual users perform in the UNIX environment with currently available help systems. We devised a core set of fifteen file manipulation tasks, representing tasks that had practical utility during a typical UNIX session. Each task was represented by a schematic picture showing the before and after state of its objects (e.g. a file, a display, etc.). To verify that the pictures communicated the tasks well, ten expert UNIX users were shown thirty file manipulation tasks and asked to match the task with the correct UNIX command displayed in an accompanying list of 25. Half of the task items were pictorial representations of 15 file tasks and half were verbal representations of the same task goals, designed to be equivalent. The verbal items were of the nature, "You want to see your directory on the screen." Times were kept for each task and spontaneous comments were recorded. The study basically confirmed that pictures were acceptable testing materials.

Two of the items that required multiple commands were too difficult (only 30% correct responses) and were eliminated from further testing materials. For the remaining tasks the 5.6% error rate was judged to be acceptable. An analysis of task times favored the use of verbal tasks (sentences, 19.04 secs.; pictures, 26.3 secs.) but the overall F test in the ANOVA was not quite significant ($F=5.06$; $df=1,8$; $p<.06$). There was a significant interaction effect in the study ($F=5.34$; $df=1,8$; $p<.05$). Experts were significantly faster on verbal items only when they had completed the pictorial items first. The reverse presentation sequence showed no difference in task time when sentences and pictures were used to represent the task.

To evaluate the casual user's experience with the on-line help system in UNIX, we tested five users, all with some previous, but infrequent UNIX experience. Significantly, one became so frustrated with the *man* command that he quit the session on the third task. The remaining four users completed all tasks with a mean session length of 10.6 minutes and required an average of 21.6 seconds to complete each task that they knew. On tasks for which they requested information, the mean task time jumped to 108.2 seconds, 44.1 seconds of which was spent accessing information. Overall, the 13 tasks (representing 25% of the total tasks) on which the *man* command was used consumed a disproportionately large 67.7% of the session time. Even more striking is the fact that users issued 37 separate command requests in order to find the information they needed for the 13 tasks. Clearly there are striking costs in time and errors for casual users when they use available help systems for UNIX.

Another approach to the data is to analyse the typescript protocols as a way of assessing the effectiveness of system prompting. Not only is the on-line prompting time consuming, it is apparently not helpful to the users in correcting their errors. For example, one user repeated the same syntactic error three times during the session. The correct UNIX command name was typed (in this case *cp*), but the TOPS-10 new = old file syntax was used. In each case the system responded "cp: cannot open filea.1", but the user didn't modify the initial command syntax, even though the *man* command for *cp* had been used at the beginning of the session.

COLLECTION OF USER BACKGROUND KNOWLEDGE

We have noted that our casual users have had previous TOPS-10 experience, and have some evidence which supports our claim that prior experience influences their interaction with the acquisition of the UNIX system. We thus attempted to collect data about how users translate internal representations of tasks into a command language format and how they formulate queries for information to do so.

Experiment Two: Query representation

For this we used the revised set of thirteen file manipulation tasks described previously in experiment one. Twenty users, experienced with a DEC10 running the TOPS-10 operating system, viewed the pictures and wrote queries about how to do the task on a new system. From this pool of 260 responses, we analysed the words chosen to represent the tasks as well as the structure of the queries. As might be expected, this free-form task produced a large variety of responses. However, we expected and found evidence of the influence of their prior DEC10 system knowledge. In each of the fifteen tasks, the most frequent word used to describe the task was the TOPS-10 command. Further, the new = old syntax of TOPS-10 file transfer commands were evident. One subject framed all queries in the TOPS-10 syntax. Some tasks such as "delete" showed good agreement across respondents, while others such as "display file contents" showed much variation. Queries contained from 3 to 9 command synonyms and showed from 3 to 6 syntactic constructions. Evidently there is marked variance in the ease with which a task can be conceptualized. This points out the creative productivity of natural language with which any natural language processor must cope.

FUNDAMENTAL DESIGN: UFO (UNIX FILE ORIENTER)

These experimental studies suggest that a quasi-natural language interface might be an improvement for casual users since free-form questions could provide more detailed lexical, syntactic, and semantic variations. Consequently, our new interface, UFO (UNIX File Orienter), handles the following types of user inputs:

(1) UFO accepts natural language requests for information on how to perform a task, e.g. "How do I delete a file?" or "How can I copy one file into another?".

(2) UFO accepts natural language requests for information on the effects of a command, e.g. "What would happen if I type rm file.1?" or "Does rm delete a file?".

(3) UFO accepts and executes natural language commands based on a data base of user lexical, syntactic and semantic variances, e.g. "Delete file.1". The user is always given the format of the UNIX command, an explanation of the effects, and queried whether it should be executed. If the command cannot execute, the reasons are given.

(4) UFO is transparent to UNIX and users can type standard UNIX commands. If the command cannot execute, the reasons are given.

Two versions of UFO have been built. Both programs have approached the problem of natural language understanding by parsing with a semantic grammar. After the input is decoded into the type of query, the system either translates it into the correct UNIX command or produces an explanation from a stock of replies. Since real-time response is of critical concern, the first version was discarded in favor of what we consider a more powerful approach.

UFO Version One

Version One took inspiration from UC, a UNIX natural language interface under development for several years (Wilensky, 1984). The parsing process used approximately 100 semantic patterns for sentence recognition focused on verb semantics. Unlike the UC system, our semantics were not defined by Conceptual Dependency theory but by details of user knowledge in attempting to perform file management tasks: goals of the query and knowledge of both UNIX and TOPS-10 command semantics including pre- and postconditions (effects) of commands. This semantics was integrated with syntactic and lexical knowledge. After 100 fundamental patterns were added, extensive testing with a few users indicated that though the system was able to handle many queries, important distinctions would only cause many more patterns and a final result of degraded response time. This is in fact what has happened with UC which now contains 675 patterns and a response time of one minute. UFO runs on a VAX/750 and UC on a VAX/780.

UFO Version Two

Version Two of UFO is based on the Word Expert Parser of Small (1982). The parsing is based on semantics stored in a lexicon of 450 words and a set of situation-action rules for each semantic type. The parsing uses the important distinctions that occur between words found in a sentence to finally build up a representation of the semantics of the type of query in terms of UNIX knowledge. This parser is considerably improved in its ability to parse varying sentence configurations and includes mechanisms for interpreting references through context. It has proven capable of handling misspelled, semantically ambiguous, and grammatically incorrect sentences by interacting with the user for further clarification. Its performance is quite adequate and within real-time constraints.

FUTURE EXTENSIONS AND CONCLUSIONS

We plan a highly controlled study of casual users who have UFO available by evaluating measures of task time, UFO use time, and user ratings of confidence and satisfaction. Additional data will be gathered from a keystroke analysis of the session terminal log. Repeated UFO use should produce increased user efficiency and some evidence for the claim that appropriate feedback increases the likelihood of improving a casual user's performance. The authors suggest that a system designed to be adaptive and to account for prior knowledge is best suited for casual users, even within a fairly limited natural language interface.

Our key research focus for the next phase of the project requires that we understand more about how different kinds of knowledge change the type of explanation delivered by the system. The current version of UFO does not have a sophisticated user model, other than to assume prior knowledge of the TOPS-10 system. The messages it delivers to the user do not vary based on any contextual model of a particular user's knowledge. Asking a specific question always delivers the same explanation. It seems obvious that a natural language system that begins to help different types of users from computer-naive novices to experts will have to maintain an internal representation of that particular user's knowledge. Further empirical study will focus on precisely this issue: what kinds of explanation are expected in different levels of expertise and what kinds of inferences can the system make about the knowledge of the user from the question asking behavior of the user.

REFERENCES

Douglas, S. & Moran, T.P. Learning operator semantics by analogy. In *Proceedings of the American Association for Artificial Intelligence* (Washington, D.C., August 22-26). AAAI, Menlo Park, CA, 1983, pp. 100-103.

Dunsmore, H. Designing an interactive facility for non-programmers. In *Proceedings of ACM 80* (Nashville, Tenn., Oct. 27-29). ACM, New York, 1980, pp. 475-483.

Small, S. Viewing word expert parsing as linguistic theory. In *Proceedings of the Seventh International Joint Conference on Artificial Intelligence* (University of British Columbia, August 24-28, 1981). AAAI, Menlo Park, CA, 1982, pp. 70-76.

Wilensky, R. Talking to UNIX in English: An overview of an on-line UNIX consultant. *AI Magazine*, Spring 1984, pp. 29-39.

Human—Computer Interaction, edited by G. Salvendy
Elsevier Science Publishers B.V., Amsterdam, 1984 — Printed in The Netherlands

Clyde: A Unix* Tutor

Adam E. Irgon**, Bell Communications Research, Piscataway, New Jersey 08854
John C. Martin**, ITT Advanced Technology Center, Shelton, Connecticut 06484

Introduction

Clyde is a knowledge-based assistant that teaches new users of the Unix operating system. The program is not a tutorial or sophisticated user-invoked help mechanism in the vein of Wilensky's UC (Unix Consultant)   Rather, it is a program which simulates the command level of the operating system, monitoring the session and interrupting the user to offer advice and warnings only when warranted.

The literature on Unix abounds with superlatives describing its elegance and power. But as Norman   points out, Unix often seems cryptic and unnatural to a beginner. Clyde uses teaching by example to help the frustrated beginner overcome the inevitable problems of learning the finer points of Unix. Clyde avoids undue repetition by deactivating its teaching of a concept when that concept is learned, just as a human tutor would teach a topic only as long as necessary.

The System

One of the primary goals of the Clyde program is to maintain absolute transparency. Until Clyde has advice to give, using Unix through Clyde is equivalent to using normal Unix. When this happens, the user receives a suggestion from Clyde, and the user's command is passed to Unix for normal processing as Clyde once again disappears. The program keeps a permanent profile of each user's progress, and uses this profile to ensure that a user is taught about a certain command only once in a single session, and a predetermined number of times over multiple sessions.

What Clyde can teach

Clyde teaches a variety of topics: some particular to Unix, and others applicable to many operating systems. In this section, we show some of the topics that Clyde can teach about, showing user input preceded by %, and Clyde's output preceded by >.

History

The Berkeley Unix Cshell *history* facility is one of the more powerful general purpose Unix facilities available to the user. Surely though, few users would infer the existence of such a facility. Clyde provides the necessary information at an opportune time. There are actually three ways to reexecute commands using the history facility. For example typing **!-3** would reexecute the command that was executed three commands ago, **!23** would reexecute the 23rd command from the current session, and **!c** would reexecute the last command that began with a **c**. Clyde teaches about all three methods when a full command is unnecessarily typed.

---

* *UNIX is a trademark of AT&T Bell Laboratories*
** *This work was done at Brown University, Department of Computer Science, Providence, RI*

Directory Hierarchy

A valuable feature in Unix is the ability to create subdirectories. This allows easy organization of files by topic, and is actually more efficient in terms of disk access. A user with an overgrown home directory and no subdirectories is taught about the Unix directory hierarchy, and how to take advantage of it. In addition, the **cd** (change directory) command is fertile ground for user inefficiency. Clyde is prepared to teach about many aspects of **cd** including using **cd** with no parameters to return to the home directory, and using **cd c** instead of **cd /a/b/c** when in directory **/a/b**. Clyde also teaches about **cd ..** for ascending the directory hierarchy, and **cd ∼/foo** and **cd ∼foo** for abbreviating pathnames.

Wildcards

Although this facility is not unique to Unix, it is certainly very powerful and warrants teaching. Clyde recognizes several common situations for wildcard usage, and offers advice accordingly, as in the following sequence which removes files.

```
% rm fah
% rm fah1
% rm fah2
> Instead of typing:    rm fah
>                       rm fah1
>                       rm fah2
> you may prefer to use a feature known as wildcards. By typing
> 'rm fa*', all of the above files would have been deleted without
> deleting any other files from your current directory.  The '*'
> matches zero or more characters when specifying filenames.  Your
> current directory is displayed in response to the command 'ls -a'.
```

Improvements on inefficient multiple command sequences.

Clyde recognizes a variety of correct but inefficient command sequences, and informs the user of a better command in much the same way as Shrager's *Wizard* program. Among these sequences are the use of redirection of input and output (Unix commands < and >) where pipes (Unix |) would be more appropriate, and the redundant typing of a filename to a text editor when using the default filename would be more advantageous. The following section of a user session illustrates these situations.

```
% vi process-date.c
% cc process-date.c
% date >today
% process-date.o <today
> If you were trying to redirect the output of date to become the
> input of process-date.o, you could have used the Unix "pipe"
> facility as follows:
>            date | process-date.o
> Note that this method avoided the creation of the file today.
% vi process-date.c
> The Unix text editors often may be invoked by simply typing the
> appropriate editor name, since they assume the last file edited
> by you. In this case, typing 'vi' will invoke editing of the file
> process-date.c, and restore your latest cursor position within
> that file.
```

Forking Processes

Clyde recognizes several appropriate situations for creating background tasks using forks (Unix command **&**), such as formatting documents and queueing prints, and explains the benefits of invoking additional processes.

Command analogs

Users moving from another operating system to Unix may inadvertently type a command particular to the familiar system. Clyde has a fairly extensive vocabulary of these commands and is able to suggest the appropriate Unix analog. Clyde also takes the opportunity to show how to use the Unix **alias** facility, which allows users to choose an alternate name for a Unix command.

Dangerous commands

This category includes commands such as **rm** * (remove all files) and **wall** (write to all users). Should the user input one of these commands, Clyde explains the consequences of the command and asks for user confirmation before passing the command to Unix for execution.

Implementation

Clyde takes a number of steps to process a command. First, a preprocessor breaks the command line into tokens. Since Unix treats upper and lower case letters differently, Clyde checks to ensure that the case is correct. Then, it examines the input to see if an analogous command from another operating system was mistakenly typed. With an error of this type, it tries to guess what Unix command the user desires, asks for confirmation, and attempts to process the correct command. The input is then passed to an Augmented Transition Network (ATN) parser which has arcs of the form:

```
(topic    actions    currently-active    times-taught    maximum-times-taught)
```

Topic is the name of the Unix command. If there is a need to explain this topic, then this symbol is passed to a routine called *teach-about* which then displays the text. *Actions* are a group of Lisp expressions, primarily Frail assertions and retrievals. *Currently-active* is a flag that is set false if the topic has been taught during this session. *Times-taught* is a counter incremented over sessions, until it equals *maximum-times-taught*, at which point the whole arc is deleted.

If no active ATN arc matches the user input, the typed command defaults to a catchall arc which does nothing and the command is handed off to Unix as it is in the other cases. If a matching active arc is found, the action associated with that arc is performed. This may be an assertion to the Frail database, or a lookup in the Frail database followed by a tutorial message to the user. When a user is taught about a concept, the arc is not removed, but is instead made inactive for the current session, so that the user is not taught any given topic more than once in a session. There is also a counter associated with each arc that a knowledge base editor can set, so that a user is taught a particular concept only a fixed maximum number of times over all sessions before an arc is permanently removed from the ATN. When a user demonstrates successful grasp of a Unix concept by using it, the program removes the appropriate arc from the ATN permanently with the assumption that it need not be taught about. Each user's updated personal ATN is written to a file at the end of every session, so that Clyde keeps a record of a user's knowledge. As the number of arcs in the ATN approaches one, the processing time decreases.

410

Clyde is implemented in Franz Lisp, and runs under Berkeley 4.1a Unix. The database is represented in the Frail knowledge representation system. Frail is a frame based deductive retriever, with other extensions such as a problem solver and marker passing. The ability to extend the knowledge base in Clyde is highly desirable, and it is fairly easy to do. The Unix expert must define a new frame with slots for the needed properties, add a new arc to the ATN, write a short action routine which either asserts or retrieves frame instances, and possibly write text to explain the new concept to the user.

Clyde's performance is reasonable but there is a noticeable overhead for every command. The Franz Lisp call that passes Unix commands through to the operating system adds approximately two seconds to every command execution. The problem is that a new shell is started for every command passed through, which is time consuming. This would be unacceptable if Clyde was to be widely used. An alternate scheme of executing the Unix commands was tried: setting up a separate process that continuously communicates with Clyde. This solved the speed problem, but introduced some output problems.

Clyde is a research project that could be made quite practical to use. In a timesharing environment, the overhead of a Lisp job per person is somewhat of a problem, but we believe that Clyde would work very well on a Unix based workstation where there is more computational power available for each user. However, there are some important lessons for anyone contemplating a project such as this. First, it is important to use a programming language that interacts well with the operating system. Franz was good in this respect compared to some Lisps, but there are a few Unix features that we had to simulate in our program because they would not work otherwise (e.g. history). Second, while the techniques we used would be useful for building knowledge based tutors for other operating systems and user interfaces, the effort might be better spent in making new user interfaces that are easier to learn and use.

Acknowledgments

We thank Jeff Shrager, whose Wizard project inspired us to do this system. Thanks also to Mike Gavin, Dave Johnson, and Matt Kaplan for amazing wizardry with Frail, Unix, and Franz Lisp. Thanks to our advisor Eugene Charniak for his help, and to various people on Usenet who told us about their Unix pet peeves. This paper has benefited from the comments of Ruven Brooks, Adele Howe, Simon Kao, Dan Neiman and Rudy Ramsey.

References

Charniak, E., Gavin, M., and Hendler, J. *The Frail/Nasl Reference Manual.* Technical Report CS-83-06, Brown University, Department of Computer Science, 1983.

Norman, D. A. The Trouble with UNIX. *Datamation:* 139-150, November, 1981.

Invoking a Beginner's Aid Processor by Recognizing JCL Goals. Technical Report MS-CIS-81-7, University of Pennsylvania, 1981.

Talking to UNIX in English: An Overview of UC. In *Proceedings of American Association for Artificial Intelligence.* Pittsburgh, PA, 1982.

Human—Computer Interaction, edited by G. Salvendy
Elsevier Science Publishers B.V., Amsterdam, 1984 — Printed in The Netherlands

ERGONOMICS IN THE AUTOMATED OFFICE: GAPS IN KNOWLEDGE AND PRACTICE

S.L. SAUTER AND R. ARNDT

Preventive Medicine Department, University of Wisconsin, 504 N. Walnut
Street, Madison, WI 53705 (USA)

Informational limitations impede the application of ergonomics in video
display terminal (VDT) workplaces. One limitation is the inconsistency among
manufacturers' product designs, sets of published recommendations, and user
practices. Limited empirical data on the effects of various designs and
recommendations complicate the issue further. The following VDT chair design
and use data provide a sampling of this problem.

Nineteen U.S. and European office chairs suitable for VDT work were
assessed with respect to about a dozen features commonly cited as important
from an ergonomic perspective. One was minimum seat height. The mean value
for this parameter (pan at top-front) was 44.7 cm ($\underline{SD}$=2.1 cm). For five of
the chairs, manufacturers' brochures reported minimum pan heights to be 5 cm
or more lower than our measure. A recommendation of 40 cm is found in the
National Research Council (NRC) report (Video Displays, Work, and Vision,
1983), and Bell Laboratories (Video Display Terminals: Preliminary Guidelines
for Selection, Installation and Use, 1983) recommends 15 inches (38.1 cm).
None of the chairs we assessed met either recommendation. After we statistically adjusted the pan height by subtracting distances for seat compression
($\underline{M}$=1.6 cm, $\underline{SD}$=0.6 cm; with 0.15 kg/cm^2) and maximum cylinder compression (9
chairs, $\underline{M}$=1.2 cm, $\underline{SD}$=0.8), only one chair met the 40 cm recommendation and
none the 38.1 cm recommendation.

Popliteal height is frequently given as the upper limit for pan height
(Floyd and Roberts, 1958). The rationale is to avoid thigh compression.
None of the chairs could be adjusted low enough to match the popliteal height
of the 5th percentile woman, even with seat and cylinder compression distances subtracted.* Adjusting the popliteal height upwards 3.3 cm for heels
did not affect the outcome (3.3 cm = mean increment in popliteal height with
heels from our own assessment of female operators). Seven chairs were too

---

*Popliteal height anthropometric data from the NRC report were used.

high for the adjusted popliteal height of the 50th percentile female, and 11 too high for the 30th percentile.

It has been suggested that thigh compression is of concern mainly in tasks requiring a forward lean (Burandt and Grandjean, 1963). In a field study by Grandjean et al. (1983), VDT operators were seen to lean back. The data show seat heights in excess of expectations from popliteal height alone (only 10% < 45 cm). We surveyed 35 dialogue (no paper) VDT operators using modern "ergonomic" chairs for evidence of leg discomfort. Observations showed that 23 of the 35 operators had their seat heights adjusted above their popliteal heights (including shoes). The mean discrepancy was 3.0 cm (SD=1.6 cm). Of these 23 operators, 22 reported no leg discomfort. Other than a report by Pottier et al. (1969), there seems to be little empirical data on the relationship between leg nervous or circulatory dysfunction and chair seat design/height adjustment.

Discrepancies also exist for the back rest/lumbar support. After the work of Akerblom (1948), Grandjean (1981) has recommended lumbar support 10-18 cm above the pan. The NRC recommendation is for adjustability in a similar range (10-20 cm above the pan). This value is at variance with the Bell recommendation for a lumbar height of 9-10 inches (22.9-25.4 cm). The Bell recommendation does not mention vertical adjustment. Both recommendations differ from the products we evaluated. Of the 19 chairs, only two adjusted the full range of 10-20 cm, and only five to 25.4 cm, although over half adjusted to 22.9 cm. None of the chairs had a back rest size of 50 cm high (M=38.1, SD=6.0), which seems recommended in the NRC report. A variant of one of the 19 chairs had a back rest of 56 cm, and the backs of seven chairs could be adjusted upwards to 50 cm. Fitting trials with a lumbar support ("Posture Curve," New York, N.Y.) for 35 "file update" VDT users resulted in a mean preferred lumbar apex height (above compressed seat) at the upper limit of the Bell recommendation (M=27.0 cm, SD=3.4 cm). The height was uncorrelated with stature (r= -.08) and the pan-to-C7 distance (r= -.02).

Similar conflicts also exist for arm rests. The Bell manual indicates that a 10 inch high (25.4 cm) arm rest is preferred. None of the chairs with arm rests (13/19) had an arm rest height of 25.4 cm (seat uncompressed), and only one (by 0.6 cm) with the seat compressed. On the basis of anthropometric data by Diffrient et al. (1981), the 25.4 cm preference exceeds the elbow height of the 99th percentile male. However, a nontrivial discrepancy (about 4 cm) exists between the upper limit of elbow height presented by Diffrient et al. (about 25.4 cm) and by the NRC (29.4 cm), and the NASA Anthropometric Source Book (Webb Associates, 1978). Arm rest heights (compressed seat) of the chairs we evaluated compared favorably with the

Diffrient et al. (1981) recommendation of 21.6 cm ($\underline{M}$=22.2 cm, $\underline{SD}$=1.7 cm).

Another limitation is difficulty in application and interpretation of existing specifications by office personnel. For example, in ergonomic workshops we have conducted for purchasing agents and interior designers, it has become evident that the current form of specifications for seat and back rest angles are of little utility in chair selection or evaluation. Tangent lines cannot be fit to the contours of many chairs, and thus accurate assessment of these parameters is nearly impossible. The same is true for lumbar support. In a recent workshop, participants provided lumbar support height measures ranging over 13 cm for the same chair using the documents mentioned above as guides. Even the assessment of pan height resulted in a measurement range of several centimeters.

A third related concern is simply the limited availability of tutorial literature or training in the area of VDT ergonomics. For example, we surveyed heads of two dozen major U.S. contract furnishing firms and found that 50% rely exclusively on product manufacturers for information and assistance on ergonomic questions. Eighty percent indicated there was insufficient ergonomic information available to meet their firm's needs. During a VDT ergonomics workshop in the spring of 1984, we surveyed representatives of over 100 different midwest firms which utilized VDTs. Approximately two-thirds of the attendees had direct responsibility for furniture purchase. Of these individuals, over 50 percent reported they depended primarily upon magazines, trade publications, or vendors and manufacturers for ergonomic information. About two-thirds reported they had difficulty in obtaining needed information.

All of the limitations described here represent important obstacles to the implementation of ergonomics in the VDT workplace. While improved availability and presentation of information is needed, more critical and central to the correction of all of these problems is improvement of the VDT ergonomics knowledge base. Controlled studies of VDT users are needed to empirically examine the performance, comfort, and health implications of various recommendations, product designs, and worker preferences. The importance of data of this type is underscored by the recent work of Grandjean et al. (1983). While the focus of the present discussion is restricted mainly to the chair, uncertainty regarding the significance of recommended design solutions extends to numerous other features of the VDT workplace (see Rupp, 1981).

414

ACKNOWLEDGEMENT

We thank Sheri Knutson for her assistance in this work.

REFERENCES

Akerblom, B., 1948. Standing and sitting posture. Nordiska Bokhandeln, Stockholm.

Burandt, U. and Grandjean, E., 1963. Sitting habits of office employees. Ergonomics, 6:217-228.

Diffrient, N., Tilley, A.R., and Harman, D., 1981. Humanscale. MIT Press, Cambridge, MA.

Floyd, W.F. and Roberts, D.F., 1958. Anatomical and physiological principles in chair and table design. Ergonomics, 2:1-16.

Grandjean, E., 1981. Fitting the task to the man. Taylor and Francis, London.

Grandjean, E., Hunting, W., and Pidermann, M., 1983. VDT workstation design: Preferred settings and their effects. Human Factors, 25:161-176.

National Research Council, 1983. Video displays, work and vision. National Academy Press, Washington, DC.

Pottier, M., Dubreuie, A., and Monod, H., 1969. The effects of sitting posture on the volume of the foot. Ergonomics, 12:753-758.

Rupp, B.A., 1981. Visual display standards: a review of issues. Society for Information Display Digest, April.

Video Display Terminals: Preliminary Guidelines for Selection, Installation and Use, 1983. Bell Telephone Laboratories, Short Hills, NJ.

Webb Associates (Editors), 1978. Anthropometric Source Book, Volume I: Anthropometry for Designers. U.S. National Aeronautics and Space Administration, Scientific and Technical Information Office.

Human—Computer Interaction, edited by G. Salvendy
Elsevier Science Publishers B.V., Amsterdam, 1984 — Printed in The Netherlands

A CASE STUDY ON THE VDT TASKS AND HUMAN CHARACTERISTICS

Y. HORIE, T. OKUBO, M. AOKI and S. SAITO

College of Industrial Technology, Nihon University, 1-2-1, Izumi, Narashino, Chiba (JAPAN)

ABSTRSCT

HORIE, Y., OKUBO, T., AOKI, M. and SAITO, S., 1984. A case study on the VDT tasks and human characteristics.

.Investigation was made on burdens on VDT workers from a view point of Ergonomics, the burdens also having actively been investigated in Europe and the United States so far. Also in Japan, many corporations of various kinds of industries, universities, and gevernmental research institutes have carried on basic and application researches related to thr problems. In this research made through a questionnaire survey, the present circumstances of VDT workers in Japan are investigated to find out what is the key point in those problems from a view point of Ergonomics.
The questionnaire survey method is used in this investigation, asking workers; age, sex, height, eye sight, experience, working hours, content of physical fatigue, desk and chair status during work concerning working postures. The office room temperature, humidity, noise, and lighting were also checked as enviromental conditions.
As a result, some correlations are found in particular between sex difference and work items, as well as between working hours and rest intervals. In general, almost workers used ordinary clerical working desks and chairs and complained that they did'nt have enough or any space for placing materials on their desks.

INTRODUCTION

Office work in Japan had been centered on writing and calculation using Japanese abacuses until five years or so. Recently, however, the work has been rapidly changed from such desk work to VDT work called "OA (Office Automation) revolution" due to development of electronics technology. This change of work is estimated to further be accelerated in future. In such the circumstances, the burdens of workers must have been considerably changed both in quality and quantity.

Workers health troubles caused by VDT work has now become serious social problems. Eliminating such troubles and protective management for those problems are thus intensely watched, although in Japan efforts for solving such the problems were just started.

There may be various fatcors causing those problems, but one of the major causes will be the fact that emphasis of the development for computer equipment has been put mainly on the development of hardware inside systems and the coordination among men, machines, and envitonment systems has been throught little of or neglected. However, the guide line for such VDT work is now being gradually established on the basis of materials obtained through basic and application researches having made by the government, universities, and corporations.

In this investigation report, such the present circumstances of VDT workers were focused on using the questionnaire survey method, trying to find out the key point for solving mental or physical problems of the VDT workers in Japan.

METHODS

The questionnaire was performed for 9 corporations (103 men and 50 women VDT workers). The items of the questionnaire were: age, sex, height, eye sight, experience, working hours, working items, content of physical fatigue, desk and chair status during work. The temperature, humidity, noise, and lighting in the office are also measured along with the performance of the questionnaire.

RESULTS

Simple total

The results of the questionnire were as follows: Workers of 24.8% involved in VDT work for "2 to 3 hours" per day, 17.6% for "1 to 2 hours", and 11.8% for "0 to 1 hour". It was also found that the workers of 36.0% involved in VDT work continuously for "1 to 2 hours", 18.3% for "2 to 3 hours", and 17.0% for "0 to 1 hour".

Job items were as follows: 63.4% of them were on "development" while 36.3% were on "data input". "When a rest is taken" was answered as follows: workers of 76.5% was "when I feel it necessary", while 23.5% was "periodically". For the part of fatigue, the answer of 41.8% of workers was "eyes", 21.5% "shoulders", 10.1% "arms", 13.8% "loin", and 3.4% "the back, etc."

69.9% of workers were satisfied with the height of their desks, but 86.3% of them wished for more working space for their desks. Many workers complained that there were no space for placing materials on their desks.

Cross total

The correlation between the height of workers and "working pose", "satisfaction with chair", or "height of desks" was recognized. The taller they were, the higher their desks became, thus their satisfaction with chairs became less and their posture becames poor.

Considering VDT working hours on a day, the correlation is found between working hours and taking rests; if their working hours are less, they take a rest as required, but if the working hours exceed 6 hours, they tend to take a rest periodically.

The correlation between sex difference and difference of working items was also found; almost all woman workers involved in "data input job". Man workers who involved in such data input job were less experienced, while woman workers who involved in development job were much experienced in VDT work.

As for working posture, woman workers were good, sitting deeply on their chairs, while man workers had poor posture sitting forward and resting their weight on the back of chairs.

TABLE 1
VDT workers feeling of satisfaction

Item	Age(year)	Sex	Height
Satisfied	22 - 24	Woman	160 - 165 cm
Unsatisfied	28		170 - 175 cm
Undecided	- 24, 24 - 28, 30 -	Man	- 160 cm, 165 - 170, 175 -
Item	Eye sight	Experience	Working hours/day
Satisfied	0.5 - 1.0	Less than one year	More than 7 hours
Unsatisfied	1.5 -	3 to 4 years. more than 5 years	
Undecided	- 0.5. 1.0 - 1.5	1 to 3 years 4 - 5 years	Less than 7 hours
Item	Continuous working hours	Working item	Taking a rest
Satisfied	5 to 7 hours	Data input	Periodically
Unsatisfied	3 to 5 hours, more than 7 hours	Development	
Undecided	Less than 3 hours		As required
Item	Fatigue portion	Working posture	Footwear
Satisfied	Eyes, back	Sitting backward, sitting intermediate	Leather shoes
Unsatisfied	loin, arm	Sitting forward	Sandals
Undecided	Shoulders, face, none		Sneakers

Analysis by quantative theory class III

As a result of the Hayashi's quantative theory class III, the problem
causes of VDT work were classified into three types; workers are satisfied
with jobs, unsatisfied with jobs, or undecided.(Reffer to Table)

DISCUSSION

From the above results, the conclusion will be as follows: Woman workers
were satisfied with their jobs more than man workers, and younger and shorter
workers were satisfied more than older and taller ones. As for experience,
workers with experience of "less than one year" were satisfied, but they were
getting more unsatisfied as thy were more experienced. In other words, they
seem to be ubsatisfied when they grow accustomed to their jobs.

Shorter time of period was spent in "data input job", while rather longer
time of period was spent on "development job". In most cases, their jobs were
finished or suspended within 5 hours, but jobs, if it takes more time to finish
them, were done continuously until tyey were completed.

"Development jobs" were mainly done by man workers, and rests were also
taken as required, while "data input jobs" were done by woman workers, and
rests were taken periodically.

Workers looked satisfied more with "data input jobs" because the working
hours were comparatively short and rests could be taken periodically. As for
desks, there were many complaints heard about the small working area, although
they were satisfied with the height of their desks.

In the investigation of working posture, it was found that "taller workers",
"workers with shorter working hours", and "older workers" were apt to sit
forward and rest on the back of their chairs, and less satisfied with their
jobs. In many cases, woman workers were sitting backward on their chairs. It
was remarkable that there were many workers appealing fatigue of "eyes" in the
questionnaire.

REFFERENCES
Cakir. A, Hart. D.J. & Stewart. T.F.M: The VDT Manual (Darmstadt: Inca-Fiej
    Research Association) 1979
Hayashi.C: Plan and Practice of Marketing Research (The Nikkan Kogyo Shimbun
    Ltd.,) 1964
Läubli. T, Hünting. W, & Grandjean. E: Visual impairments related to environ-
    ment in VDT operators, p.85 - 94, Ergonomic aspects of VDTs, (Taylar &
    Francis) 1980
Nakasako. M, Hünting. W, Läubli. T, Grandjean. E: Constrained posture and some
    Ergonomic Problems of VDT operators. J. Science of Labour Vol. 58,No.4
    p.203 - 212, 1982

Human—Computer Interaction, edited by G. Salvendy
Elsevier Science Publishers B.V., Amsterdam, 1984 — Printed in The Netherlands

MEDICAL DECISION MAKING BY MEANS OF MAN-MACHINE DIALOGUE

Tomio SEKIYA[1], Akira WATANABE[2] and Makoto KIKUCHI[1]

[1]Medical Engineering Dep., National Defence Medical College,Tokorozawa,Saitama
359 (Japan)

[2]Institute of Medical Electronics, University of Tokyo, Hongo, Bunkyo-ku, Tokyo
113 (Japan)

ABSTRACT

The objective of this study is to develop an algorithm for helping physicians
in diagnosis, based on the statistical patient data.   An attempt was made to
represent the complicated multi-dimensional disease space (i.e., symptom space)
in a simple graphic form.   The disease space of congenital heart disease is
reduced to two-dimensional disease regions using trigonometrical polynomials
without loss of information.   The advantage of this method is that a diagnosis can be made simply by examining the relationship between each two-
dimensional disease region and a curve representing   patient's symptoms.

INTRODUCTION

One of the major objectives of the computer-aided diagnosis is to construct
an algorithm for medical diagnosis which is hopefully help physicians in accuracy as well as insight.   The theoretical approaches to this aim have been
made since Ledly and Lusted [1959] used Bayes' theorem or Boolean algebra.

The disease space is multi-dimensional and composed of symptom points.   The
region of a disease covers points corresponding to the patients with the particular disease.   When the disease region has a complicated structure, it will
more efficiently be analyzed by representing the situation in a graphic form.
This happens frequently in medical diagnosis.

Watanabe [1965] proposed an algorithm for congenital heart disease, where
the each disease region is represented as a sum of sub-region with the contour
and distances presented in a graphic form.   However, any efficient interactive method of representing the multi-dimensional disease space has not been
developed.

In this study, we represent the disease space by a method of trigonometrical
polynomials representation (Andrews, 1972).   Each set of symptoms of a patient is expressed in the form of curves in the 2-D plane.   This method has
two advantages.   First, we are accustomed to examining intuitively plots of
functions (2-D curve).   Secondly, they may be infinite-dimensional.

This means imbedding high dimensional data in an easily visualized form of the function.   The physician can see, in an interactive way, the local structure around the patient point in the multi-dimensional disease space.

INPUT DATA

A set of symptoms of each case is represented by a 51-dimensional vector in a multi-dimensional disease space. Every component of 51-dimensional vector assumes three value [-1, 1, 0] corresponding to normal, abnormal and unsettled or missing situations, respectively. 190 cases four congenital heart diseases without any complication, who had been operated on at the University of Tokyo Hospital were used for analysis—47 cases of auricular septal defect (ASD), 36 cases of ventricular septal defect (VSD), 47 cases of patent ductus arteriosus (PDA) and 60 cases of tetralogy of Fallot (TF). The 51 symptoms chosen for analysis were 10 subjective (No.1 - 10), 6 physical (No.11 - 16), 29 phonocardiographic (No.17 - 45) and 6 electrocardiographic (No.46 - 51) findings.

ROCEDURE   AND RESULTS

An analysis of a 51-dimensional symptom space was attempted by a HP-9845B desk-top computer with $1/6\mu s$ clock time, 56 KB core.   In the trigonometrical polynomials representation, if the data is k-dimensional, each data point X^T = (x_1, x_2, ..., x_k) is mapped into a function

$$f_X(t) = x_1/\sqrt{2} + x_2\sin t + x_3\cos t + x_4\sin 2t + \text{.......}$$ (1)

This function is then plotted over the range $-\pi < t < \pi$.   Then we can map k-dimensional data into 2-D space without loss of data information.   This method has a feature that the multivariate data is expressed in a pattern like time series.

Fig.1 is an example of trigonometrical polynomials representation, in which each center of gravity of four kinds of disease are plotted.   Maximum amplitude is normalized in such a way that the maximum value = $\pm$1.

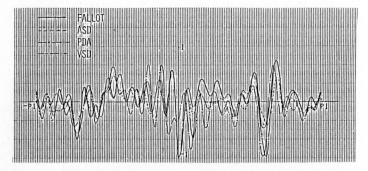

Fig.1 Plots for the center of gravity of every category

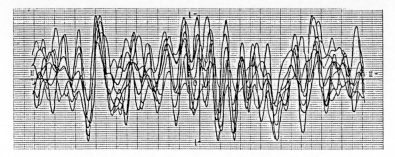

Fig.2 Trigonometrical polynomials representations for PDA

In Fig.2 all of the data belonging to PDA category are shown.   By drawing the
envelope of these curves, four templates are obtained corresponding to each disease (Fig.3).

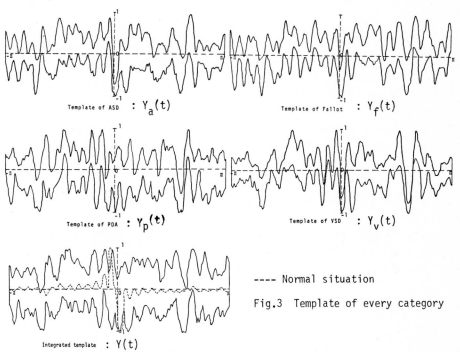

Template of ASD : $Y_a(t)$

Template of Fallot : $Y_f(t)$

Template of PDA : $Y_p(t)$

Template of VSD : $Y_v(t)$

Integrated template : $Y(t)$

---- Normal situation

Fig.3 Template of every category

   If one curve (a patient point), is contained in the template region completely, we can determine that belongs to one category (disease).   Comparing
the   templates of four category, there is at least one points where overlap
does not occur.   These points are tabulated in Table 1 which are used for the
classifying the diseases.   Fig.4 is the flow chart for the classification,
where $Y_p(t)$ and $Y_a(t)$ denote the templates of PDA and ASD, respectively, and $f(t)$
is a given set of data.   The integrated template $Y(t)$ is an envelope formed
by absorbing all the four templates.   By using this method we can classify all
of the 190 cases of congenital heart disease completely.

TABLE 1

Classifying points of templates

	PDA	VSD	ASD	Fallot
PDA		$-\pi/81$	$-\pi/81$ $-38\pi/81$	$15\pi/81$
VSD			$-13\pi/81$	$-13\pi/81$
ASD				$29\pi/81$
Fallot				

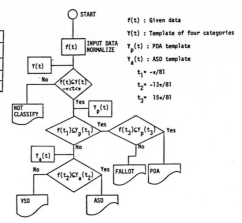

$f(t)$: Given data
$Y(t)$: Template of four categories
$Y_p(t)$: PDA template
$Y_a(t)$: ASD template
$t_1 = -\pi/81$
$t_2 = -13\pi/81$
$t_3 = 15\pi/81$

Fig.4 Flow chart for the classification

DISCUSSION

The advantages of this method are as follows:

(1) The data compression is achieved using all the measured data without loss information.

(2) The diagnosis is little affected by missing data if their number is less than five to eight.

(3) In the process of diagnosis physicians can see the relationship between ε disease region and the curve representing patient's symptoms on a CRT display in an interactive way.

REFERENCES

Andrews, D.F., 1972. Plots of high-dimensional data. Biometrics, 28 : 125-13ε
Watanabe, A. et al., 1965. Analysis of the symptom space. Dig. of 6th Int. Cc on Medical Electron. & Biol. Eng., 136-137

ACKNOWLEDGMENT

The authors wish to thank Professor M. Saito and Dr. K. Ikeda, Institute of Medical Electronics, University of Tokyo for valuable discussions and Profes K. Hiramatsu for cooperating them with the data processing.

Human—Computer Interaction, edited by G. Salvendy
Elsevier Science Publishers B.V., Amsterdam, 1984 — Printed in The Netherlands

AN EXPERIMENTAL PLAN FOR ASSESSING THE ADVANTAGES OF USING INTERACTIVE
COMPUTER GRAPHICS IN TRAINING INDIVIDUALS IN BASIC ORBITAL MECHANICS

J.P. YORCHAK, J.E. ALLISON, and V.S. DODD
Martin Marietta Denver Aerospace, P.O.Box 179, Denver, Colorado 80201

INTRODUCTION

Recent advances in computer graphics technology make it possible to depict complex two- and three-dimensional concepts realistically. Since orbital analysts (individuals that monitor satellites in space) must understand very complicated three-dimensional concepts and interrelationships, the use of computer graphics could significantly enhance their training by depicting satellite orbits in a "3-D" fashion. Therefore, we predict that with graphics-based training, these individuals will learn orbital mechanics concepts faster, and their attitude toward their training will be more positive than individuals trained using conventional methods (manual-based training relying on text and diagrams).

Research supporting this hypothesis is described below. Booher (1975) found that mixtures of pictorial information and verbal instructions were superior to verbal instructions alone in facilitating performance on three types of perceptual motor tasks. In addition, Arnold and Dwyer (1975) found that when pictorial information was added to verbal information concerning the physiology of the heart, high school students showed better performance on knowledge and comprehension tests. Rigney and Lutz (1976) extended these results to an interactive computer graphics training environment. They found that students trained with interactive graphics representations of electrochemical processes performed better on posttests than students trained with written materials alone.

We hope to replicate these findings, and in addition, we hope to demonstrate that individuals trained with interactive graphics are able to apply their training to new situations more effectively than individuals trained with conventional methods. To test our hypothesis, two versions of a lesson on basic orbital mechanics will be experimentally compared.

METHOD

Thirty Martin Marietta employees with no prior training in orbital mechanics will be randomly assigned to one of two training groups--an interactive graphics group or a conventional training group. A 10-15 page training manual (Manual A) which defines basic orbital mechanics concepts will be given to all subjects. The training apparatus for the graphics group consists of an Evans & Sutherland (E&S) Multi Picture System graphics workstation, function buttons, and a pad of analog dials (the function of the dials will be explained in the next section). The E&S system is hosted on a VAX 11/780 minicomputer. Subjects in the conventional training group will receive a second manual (Manual B) providing further elaboration of the orbital mechanics concepts in both text and pictorial form.

Both groups will begin their training by reading brief descriptions of the six orbital parameters from Manual A. The six parameters necessary to completely specify a satellite orbit are; inclination, semi-major axis, eccentricity, longitude of the ascending node, argument of periapsis, and time of periapsis passage. The descriptions in Manual A emphasize the relationships between the values of the orbital parameters and the size and shape of the satellite's orbit and ground trace. In the interactive graphics group, the definition of each concept will be followed by a graphics elaboration. This elaboration is designed to permit direct interaction with the six parameters through the analog dials. In this way, these subjects may change the values of any of the six parameters and immediately see the effect of those changes on the satellite's orbit as well as its ground trace. The format of the dynamic graphics display is shown in Figure 1. In the conventional training group, Manual B will be substituted for the interactive graphics elaboration given to the other group. Since each group receives identical information from Manual A, training groups differ only in terms of the type of elaboration they receive.

Following the training session, both groups will complete identical posttests consisting of recall, recognition, and concept application problems. The concept application problems are included in the posttest to assess how well each subject is able to apply what he/she has learned to new situations. Learning will be measured by performance on the posttests. Ten semantic differential scales (Osgood, Suci, and Tannenbaum, 1957) will also be included to assess the subject's attitude toward his/her training.

A MANOVA will be performed on the performance and attitude scores. Additionally, correlations between attitude scores and performance scores will be examined to see if attitudes toward training are related to actual performance.

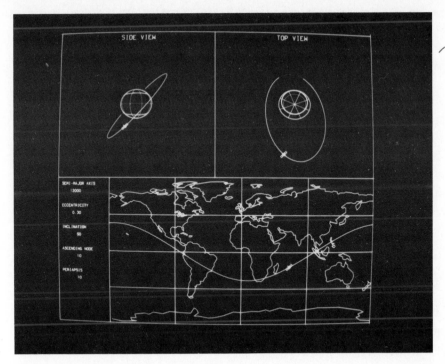

Fig. 1. Photograph showing the format of the display used by the dynamic graphics training group.

SUMMARY

When learning new material, the learner's task is to internalize a model that characterizes the relevant domain of knowledge (Norman, 1983). We anticipate that dynamic computer graphics will aid this internalization process by depicting the external world in a realistic and understandable fashion. Rigney and Lutz (1976) found that students trained with an interactive, animated computer graphics representation of electrochemical processes performed better on a posttest than students trained using text material; they also had more positive attitudes toward the training session. We anticipate similar results for this experiment. Additionally, we are interested in the effect that method of training has on a subject's ability to deal with novel information. Mayer (1981) suggests that when transfer of training to novel situations is the goal, it is important to use methods of training which foster deeper understanding: one method that seems to aid training in this way is the use of conceptual models during training. Since the computer graphics displays used in our training system are designed to aid the development of conceptual models, individuals trained with interactive 3-D computer graphics should perform better on new problems than subjects trained with conventional material.

ACKNOWLEDGEMENTS

   This research was supported by Martin Marietta Denver Aerospace through Independent Research and Development project D-47R, "Computer Generated Display and Control Technology". (This paper is released under the Export Administration Regulation GTDA 379.3)

REFERENCES

Arnold, T.C. & Dwyer, F.M., 1975. Realism in visualized instruction. Perceptual and Motor Skills, 40:369-370.

Booher, R.H., 1975. Relative comprehensibility of pictorial information and printed words in proceduralized instructions. Human Factors, 17:266-277.

Mayer, R.E., 1981. The psychology of how novices learn computer programming Computing Surveys, 13: 25-35.

Norman, D.A., 1983. Some observations on menta. models. In D. Gentner & A.L. Stevens (Editors), Mental models, Hillsdale, NJ: Lawrence Erlbaum.

Osgood, C.E., Suci, G.J., & Tannenbaum, P.H., 1957. The measurement of meaning. Urbana: University of Illinois Press.

Rigney, J.W. & Lutz, K.A., 1976. Effect of graphic analogies of concepts in chemistry on learning and attitude. Journal of Educational Psychology, 68: 305-311.

COMPUTER-ENHANCED TELECOMMUNICATIONS   /

GEORGE J. BOGGS
Telecommunications Research Lab., GTE Laboratories Inc., 40 Sylvan Rd., Waltham
MA 02154

ABSTRACT

Boggs, G.J., 1983. Computer-enhanced telecommunications. Proc. of the First
USA/Japan Conf. on Human-Computer Interaction, 1:

The evolution of telecommunications networks to digital technology is creating a
new form of human/computer interaction. In the context of digital telecommunications networks, the computer serves as a mediator for human/human communication.
Human factors attention is necessary to insure that computer-mediated communications actually enhances telecommunications services. An example of the role of
human factors in the development of a computer-enhanced voice teleconferencing
service is described. The enhanced voice teleconferencing service is based on
binaural hearing, and employs computer technology to resolve many of the human
factors problems found in extant voice teleconferencing systems.

INTRODUCTION

The human/computer interface has been targeted as an area in need of major
research activity for the future (Chapanis, Anderson and Licklider, 1983). Conventionally, user interactions with computers have been for the purpose of directing a computer to perform some task for the user. However, the evolution of
analog telecommunications networks to digital technology is creating a new form
of human/computer interaction, and will require a broader concept of the human/
computer interface.

The emergence of the digital telecommunications network has the potential to
affect profoundly the ways that people communicate. Digital telephone networks,
for example, frequently employ microprocessors to digitize and process speech
signals for transmission. In this context, the computer serves as a mediator for
human/human communication. As computer-mediated communications become more common, human factors attention to this form of the human/computer interface will
become more important.

One · of the major advantages of computer-mediated communications is the
flexibility offered by digital technology. In telephony, microprocessors can be
programmed to compress the bandwidth of voice signals (Richards, 1973). Voice
compression results in more efficient use of existing network service capacity,
thus reducing end user costs. Beyond the obvious advantage of using digital
technology to reduce the cost of network services, digital technology can also
be used to enhance telecommunications services. The task of human factors in
this context is to insure that enhanced services actually result in increased
utility for the user.

This paper describes the development of a computer-enhanced voice teleconferencing service. The development process was carried out in two stages. The first

stage, conceptual development, included a human factors analysis of existing voice teleconferencing systems and the identification of human factors strategies to compensate for interface deficiencies. The second stage involved the actual design of an enhanced digital voice teleconferencing system based on the human factors design strategies identified during the first stage.

CONCEPTUAL DEVELOPMENT

Human Factors Analysis

Voice teleconferencing does not require new and sophisticated network resources, since voice conferences are usually conducted using the extant telephone network. However, voice teleconferencing systems have not gained the wide acceptance that one might expect from a cost and convenience viewpoint (Olgren and Parker, 1983). As Olgren and Parker cogently point out, the major reasons for user avoidance of voice teleconferencing are human interface deficiencies.

The monaural nature of current voice teleconferencing restricts the quality of the interaction. Simultaneous talking by two or more participants results in unintelligible speech signals. The decrement in intelligibility is particularly evident when the simultaneous voices are acoustically similar (i.e., all male or female), or when the channel is noisy (Kantowitz and Sorkin, 1983). The usual human factors solution to this problem is voice switching. Voice switching, however, restricts participation because only one person is allowed to speak at a given time. Other participants cannot interrupt the speaker or interject comments as often happens during face-to-face conferences.

Another human factors problem is speaker identifiability. Unless participants are well-acquainted with each other's voices, it is often difficult to identify participants on the basis of voice characteristics alone. In fact, Olgren and Parker (1983) suggest that voice conference participants should be well-acquainted to avoid this problem. Unfortunately, this is not often feasible.

Human Factors Strategy

Given the major problems described above, a human factors strategy was sought to eliminate these problems. Fortunately, a simple strategy was available that capitalizes on a natural ability of human auditory processing. Binaural hearing processes can be exploited to enhance intelligibility during simultaneous talking and to improve speaker identification.

Binaural hearing is listening with both ears. Binaural hearing allows the auditory system to localize sounds in the azimuthal plane. When a sound source propagates from a location to the right or left of a listener, the sound signal reaches the two ears at different times. This is referred to as interaural time delay. The auditory system simply estimates the magnitude of the time disparity, and the apparent location of the sound source is largely a function of the magnitude of the interaural time delay (Mills, 1952).

Binaural hearing provides other advantages in addition to the obvious advantage of sound localization. For example, binaural hearing is responsible for the well-documented "cocktail party effect." The cocktail party effect was so named because it allows one to selectively listen to one speaker in the presence of several other, potentially interfering, ongoing conversations. If a binaural voice teleconferencing interface could be developed, the potential exists for permitting simultaneous talking with no appreciable degradation in intelligibility for a given speaker.

Binaural hearing can also be exploited to improve the identifiability of conference participants. In the context of a psychological experiment, Geiselman and Crawley (1983) report that knowledge of a speaker's spatial location significantly enhanced the listener's ability to identify the speaker. One would expect this result theoretically, since stimuli that differ along two or more dimensions are more readily identified than stimuli that differ along only one dimension (Pollack and Ficks, 1954). Therefore, binaural teleconferencing may be an appropriate strategy for remediation of the speaker identifiability problem.

SYSTEM DESIGN

A new voice teleconferencing system design should meet two major criteria. First, the new system must be compatible with the extant telephone network. Second, any new design for user equipment must be convenient to use and low in cost. This section describes a novel voice teleconferencing system based on binaural principles that meets both of these criteria. The new design will affect two aspects of a voice teleconferencing system: the user instrument and the teleconference bridge. Space limitations preclude a discussion of the user instrument. It should be noted, however, that the use of binaural voice signals forces the use of stereophonic headphones as a part of the user instrument.

Teleconferencing Bridge

The teleconference bridge is the heart of the binaural teleconferencing system. Consistent with the major theme of the paper, the bridge design is based entirely on digital technology. A teleconferencing bridge is basically an electronic device that receives and mixes the voice signals for transmission via the telephone network.

A binaural teleconferencing bridge must perform two tasks. First, the monaural speech signal must be split into two separate channels, and one channel must be delayed relative to the other (to simulate the interaural delay). Second, the bridge must compress the speech to transmit two channels of speech along a telephone network designed for single-channel voice transmission. These two tasks are easily handled by a digital bridge.

Dividing a single channel of speech into two separate channels is a simple task for a microprocessor. As each speech interval is sampled and digitized, the resulting sample is written into two separate buffers for storage. One of the buffers is immediately output, and the other is stored for a brief period before output. This delays one channel relative to the other, creating the binaural ef-

430

fect. The magnitude of the delay, and therefore the apparent spatial location of the speaker, is software-controlled. Each speaker can be assigned a unique spatial location. This design requires a separate microprocessor for each participant in the conference, with a master microprocessor to control the delay (apparent location) for each participant. The output channels for each participant are then digitally mixed and prepared for transmission.

The use of digital technology also permits the bridge to transmit the two-channel signals over the telephone network. The standard telephone network has a bandwidth of 64 kilobits per second. Sophisticated digital coding schemes, however, permit speech to be digitized and transmitted at less than 64 kb/sec with very little loss in speech quality. In fact, adaptive delta modulation is a coding technique capable of encoding and transmitting high quality voice signals at a rate of 32 kb/sec. If adaptive delta modulation is used, digital samples from the two channels can be interleaved and transmitted over low-cost 64 kb/sec voice-grade telephony channels.

CONCLUSIONS

The above description of a binaural teleconferencing system exemplifies the potential contribution to be gained from a synergistic relationship between human factors and digital telecommunications engineering. The design, using standard components and the extant network, represents a potential enhancement for voice teleconferencing systems.

Aside from enhancing the voice teleconference interface, the teleconferencing example explicitly shows the utility of expanding the concept of human/computer interaction to encompass computer-mediated communications. There are many potential application areas for human factors involvement. Applications that immediately come to mind are signal compression (for both voice and video), signal enhancement and videoconferencing. The potential benefit of computer-enhanced telecommunications is enormous. For this potential to be realized, however, the human factors community must broaden its scope to include this important new area of human/computer interaction.

REFERENCES

Chapanis, A., Anderson, N.S., and Licklider, J.C.R., 1983. User-computer interaction. In: Research Needs for Human Factors, National Academy Press: Washington, D.C.
Geiselman, R.E. and Crawley, J.M., 1983. Incidental processing of speaker characteristics: Voice as connotative information. Journal of Verbal Learning and Verbal Behavior, 22: 15-23.
Kantowitz, B.H. and Sorkin, R.D., 1983. Human Factors: Understanding People-System Relationships. Wiley: New York.
Mills, A.W., 1958. On the minimum audible angle. Journal of the Acoustical Society of America, 30: 237-246.
Olgren, C.H. and Parker, L.A., 1983. Teleconferencing Technology and Applications. Artech House: Dedham, MA.
Pollack, I. and Ficks, L., 1954. Information of elementary multidimensional displays. Journal of the Acoustical Society of America, 26: 155-158.
Richards, D.L., 1973. Telecommunication by Speech, Wiley: New York.

Human—Computer Interaction, edited by G. Salvendy
Elsevier Science Publishers B.V., Amsterdam, 1984 — Printed in The Netherlands

FROM PROTOTYPE TO PRODUCTION: THE MATURING OF OCEAN'S USER INTERFACE

NELSON HAZELTINE

Research and Development, NCR Corporation, Dayton, Ohio U.S.A.

INTRODUCTION

OCEAN is the Order Configuration and Entry Advisor for NCR Corporation.
It is an expert system that applies principles of artificial intelligence to
the task of converting a sales order for an NCR computer into a specification of a computer that can be manufactured. The OCEAN knowledge base
contains information about the components of NCR computer systems, interrelationships among components, and constraints.

OCEAN has several benefits for NCR. First, it reduces the time spent on
configuring an order when compared to the previous manual method. Second,
configuration errors, regardless of the complexity of the order, are virtually eliminated; thus avoiding costly modifications in the field. Third, by
incorporating expert order entry and configuration knowledge into OCEAN, the
training time of new order entry personnel is substantially reduced.

The OCEAN development proceeded in two stages: the prototype stage and
the deliverable stage. The goal of the OCEAN prototype was to provide a
convincing demonstration of the applicability of artificial intelligence to
the tasks of order configuration and entry. To succeed in proving the
feasibility and utility of the basic concepts, the OCEAN prototype had to be
usable by order entry and configuration personnel so that its correct
operation could be verified. As a practical matter it was necessary to
concentrate most of the development resources on the fundamental artificial
intelligence issues, rather than on developing a full-blown, final version
of the user interface. The goal of the delivered system was to achieve the
benefits as outlined previously.

This paper will describe the requirements for the user interface and
indicate the features of the end user interface that evolved over time.
From this one experience a set of suggestions is developed that may be used
in subsequent expert system interface design.

DEFINITION OF INTERFACE REQUIREMENTS

There are generally three classes of individuals associated with a system like OCEAN, each with separate interface requirements. First there are the knowledge engineers who are experts in applying artificial intelligence techniques and who are able to handle all types of interfaces into the system including the LISP programming language used to develop the system. Their interface requirements center on a development environment and will be documented elsewhere. Second, there are the knowledge base maintenance personnel who must have some rudimentary knowledge of knowledge engineering principles and of the LISP programming language. The third class, the primary focus of this paper, are the actual end users, which in the case of OCEAN are order entry personnel.

PROTOTYPE INTERFACE DEVELOPMENT

For the prototype, the designers of the system did not attempt to develop the deliverable or final interface since end users did not know the interface features they preferred. The designers selected an environment sufficiently robust that it was not necessary to expend much effort on the initial user interface, thus allowing the developers to concentrate most of the development resources on the fundamental AI issues. Through interviews with the expert order entry personnel knowledge engineers formulated a conceptual idea of the user interface. The conceptual idea was used as a guide in selecting key interface features for the prototype that would be sufficient to demonstrate the feasibility of OCEAN.

The resulting prototype interface was intelligible to the expert user and could be taught to lesser-trained users, although it was expressed in awkward English which included some system development terminology that was difficult for the average person to understand. This was acceptable as a temporary measure during the validation of the prototype.

A key interface feature missing from the prototype was an explanation facility to explain why OCEAN made a particular decision on a part or what parts resulted from a given package. Instead, the prototype version of OCEAN had a trace facility that showed the steps being performed in the configuration of an order. While a trace facility is acceptable for a prototype, it was found to be inadequate for a production system which needs to explain its actions to the end user.

DELIVERABLE INTERFACE DEVELOPMENT

After the prototype was demonstrated successfully, work on the deliverable interface began. The prototype interface was modified to accommodate an English dialogue that was more natural and understandable. The system development terminology was replaced with NCR order entry terminology that could be understood by the end user. In addition, tools were provided to ease the work of order entry personnel in typing in an order, such as prompting the user for specific information. Abbreviation of OCEAN commands also saved keying time.

During the prototype stage, the user had few options available for control of OCEAN. OCEAN now gives the user many options, all expressed in an English-like language that provides a powerful control over the flow of OCEAN processing. To manage the wide choice of options, the end user has an OCEAN help facility that lists the options available at each step of processing.

One of the present options is an explanation facility, which adds an important capability for assessing the accuracy of OCEAN as well as for training new order entry personnel. With this facility, the user can now ask OCEAN to explain why it made a certain decision on an order. The explanation function is selective, allowing the user to concentrate on specific features of the order, rather than the entire explanation of the order. The specifications for the explanation facility were derived by asking the order entry personnel what kinds of questions they would ask of a human expert. The designers responded by providing an explanation facility that answered questions the way a human expert would have answered the questions. The explanation facility may be used during the processing of an order as well as after an order is processed to explain decisions made by the expert system.

A significant improvement in the present version of OCEAN compared to the prototype is the provision of knowledge base maintenance tools. Now, rather than having to be a very skilled knowledge engineer, with in-depth knowledge of LISP programming, a good management information system programmer can maintain the knowledge base through the use of OCEAN commands for adding, deleting, or modifying knowledge base information, though as of now some knowledge of LISP is still necessary.

Another key feature of the present interface is the use of modular print routines for modifying the format of output. This allows easy change in the presentation of printed output.

FUTURE PLANS FOR INTERFACE ENHANCEMENT

Tables, charts and graphs will be added to graphically portray component relationships and provide guidance to alternate selections where there are choices. Techniques such as pointer selected options ("mouse" control and menu selections) will be added to the English-like language interface presently provided. An important enhancement will be the addition of electronic file transfer from OCEAN to the factory's automated manufacturing control system without the need for manual operations. Improvements will include further reduction of the need for LISP programming knowledge by the knowledge base maintenance personnel through the use of additional OCEAN commands for knowledge base maintenance.

SUGGESTIONS FOR EXPERT SYSTEM INTERFACE DESIGN

The OCEAN experience indicates the following key suggestions for expert system interface design:

- Involve the end user early in the design of interfaces but don't expect the end users to have strong preferences.
- Develop the interface concepts before the prototype interface design.
- Use the interface concepts to guide the selection of the prototype interface techniques.
- Use early demonstrations of the prototype interface to design the delivered system interface.
- An explanation facility is an absolute requirement for the delivered system; the explanation should be in the style of a human expert.
- For the delivered system, the user interface should utilize the natural and understandable language of the user; the prototype can live with something less.
- Relieve the end user of having to remember arcane computer commands and procedures.
- Give the end user control over the expert system so the end user can achieve his/her goals more quickly.
- Minimize the amount of keying required by the user.

Human—Computer Interaction, edited by G. Salvendy
Elsevier Science Publishers B.V., Amsterdam, 1984 — Printed in The Netherlands

A COMPUTERIZED DATA BASE FOR IDENTIFYING INDUSTRIAL ACCIDENT SCENARIOS

Kenneth R. Laughery[1]

[1]Psychology Department, Rice University, Houston, Texas 77251, U.S.A.

INTRODUCTION

This paper presents the results of an ongoing project to develop a computerized data base for industrial accidents. The effort includes a coding scheme for representing accident data as well as analytic procedures that can be used by managers and others responsible for safety. In most large manufacturing operations a considerable number of accidents involving injuries occur each year. Most of these injuries are minor, although some are serious. A typical ratio of minor to serious injuries is about 25 to 1. In the past much of the work done in analyzing industrial accidents has focussed on incidents involving serious injuries such as those defined as OSHA recordables. Yet, an enormous amount of important safety information is contained in the less serious injury events.

While using computers to store data about industrial accidents may be a convenience, the more significant issues concern the types of information coded about each accident and the procedures for analyzing the data. In this project two categories of data are coded for each accident, demographics and the accident scenario. The analytic procedures include straightforward tabulations of demographic data as well as techniques for exploring the dynamic aspects of the accident events.

The accidents coded and analyzed in this project occurred at Shell Oil Company's Deer Park Manufacturing Complex in Deer Park, Texas. This complex i the Company's largest manufacturing facility in the United States, employing approximately 3300 people. Shell has a standard reporting procedure and form for recording information about accidents. The form is completed for any incident which results in an employee reporting to the first aid station. Details of the accident reporting procedures at Shell have been presented by Laughery, Petree, Schmidt, Schwartz, Walsh and Imig (1983). To date, 3526 accidents have been coded and partially analyzed.

THE CODING SCHEME

The data coded for each accident included demographics and the accident scenario. Twenty-one variables make up the code.

Demographic Code

Twelve variables were used to represent information about the employee and the time and place of the accident.

Badge Number	Time of Day
Sex	Day of Week
Age	Month
Job Classification	Day of Month
Date of Employment at Shell	Year
Date Starting Current Job	Location

Accident Scenario Code

The concept of an accident scenario was introduced by Drury (1983). The purpose of the scenario code is to represent the dynamic elements of the accident event. To put it more simply, the code is intended to describe "what happened." The strategy in developing the scenario was to breakdown the accident into a series of time sequenced elements. The scenario has four "dynamic" (event) codes and four "descriptor" codes. The dynamic elements are:

Prior Activity. The task in which the employee was engaged when the accident occurred. Fourteen different activity codes were used. Examples would be handling materials and assembling equipment.

Accident Event. The event that initiated the accident sequence. Sixteen different event codes were used. Examples would be tool slipped and employee tripped.

Resulting Event. An intermediate event that followed the accident event and that occurred because of the accident event. There were ten event codes. Examples are the employee fell (perhaps after tripping) and material was released from containment (perhaps a toxic chemical). Not all accidents have a resulting event; some accident events lead directly to the injury.

Injury Event. The event that produces the injury. There were twelve codes. Examples would be hit a stationary object and contact by a stationary fluid. A simple example of the above code would be an employee was in transit (prior activity), tripped (accident event), fell (resulting event) and hit his head (injury event) on a piece of machinery. The four descriptor elements of the code are:

Agent of Accident. The tool, equipment, substance, etc. involved in the accident event (43 codes).

Source of Injury. The tool, equipment, substance, etc. involved in the injury. (43 codes).

Type of Injury. Contusion, fracture, burn, etc. (18 codes).

Part of Body Injured. Eye, back, arm, etc. (17 codes).

In the above example, the agent of accident would be the object over which the employee tripped. The source of injury would be the machinery against which the head struck. The type of injury might be a laceration, the body part would be the head.

ANALYTIC PROCEDURES

The purpose of the analyses is to help managers identify safety problems and to suggest priorities for safety improvement efforts. A secondary purpose (although important to some users) is to compile a variety of safety and accident reports that are common to most organizations. This latter purpose can usually be satisfied by straightforward frequency analyses of the demographic variables. The identification of problems and the development of intervention strategies can be especially helped by analysis of the scenario code. In other words, understanding how accidents are happening is crucial to the development of effective safety programs. A scenario analysis program has been developed to examine patterns in the accident events. The four event variables described above are used for generating the patterns. The program is structured to enable an individual, e.g., a manager, to sit at a terminal and request scenario frequencies for any subset of the data base (3526 accidents at present) that can be defined by any combination of values of any of the variables. Examples of the situations for which scenarios can be obtained are:

All accidents under a particular manager's responsibility.

All thermal burns, back injuries, eye injuries, etc.

All accidents involving machinists (high accident rate group).

All accidents while assembling/disassembling equipment.

RESULTS AND CONCLUSIONS

Although the computerized data base has only recently been implemented at Shell's facilities, the results of some scenario analyses have already identified possible interventions for improving safety. One example concerns back injuries (a serious problem in manufacturing industry). Scenarios of back injury accidents indicate two common patterns. The first is the expected materials handling tasks where an employee was lifting some object. The second, however, had not been so obvious, at least not the frequency with which it occurred; namely, situations where the back was injured while turning a valve. This result was of particular interest to the plant engineers since the data showed a basic problem was the awkward location of many valves. The second example concerns eye injuries. The scenarios for these injuries showed the major problem to be inadequate goggles and safety glasses, a finding of interest to the industrial hygienists.

On the basis of the work completed in this project to date, a few conclusions seem warranted. First, the large volume of data concerning accidents in manufacturing industry is extremely useful for improving safety. The computer is a most appropriate tool for storing and analyzing such data. Second, scenario data and analyses are especially helpful in the development of intervention strategies. The key here is understanding how accidents happen, the dynamics of the events. Finally, such information systems must be designed with a variety of users in mind. Managers, safety engineers, industrial hygienists and design engineers are examples of the different types of people who will find such accident data helpful. The system must, of course, be "friendly" to them all.

REFERENCES

Drury, C. G. and Brill, M., 1983. Human factors in consumer product accident investigation. Human Factors, 25: 329-342.

Laughery, K. R.; Petree, B.L.; Schmidt, J.D.; Schwartz, D.R.; Walsh, M.T. and Imig, R. C., 1983. Scenario analyses of industrial accidents. Proceedings of the Sixth International System Safety Conference, Houston, 8-2.1 - 8.2.21.

Human—Computer Interaction, edited by G. Salvendy
Elsevier Science Publishers B.V., Amsterdam, 1984 — Printed in The Netherlands

CONSIDERATIONS IN DEFINING OFFICE AUTOMATION: A CASE STUDY OF THE
WORLD BANK - EASTERN AFRICA REGION, WASHINGTON, D.C.

Benjamin C. AMICK, III [1] and Janet DAMRON [2]

[1] Department of Behavioral Sciences, The Johns Hopkins University, School of
Hygiene and Public Health, 615 N. Wolfe St., Baltimore, MD 21205

[2] Office Technology Officer, Eastern Africa Region, The World Bank,
1818 H St., NW, Washington, D.C. 20433

INTRODUCTION

Office automation is not a single event either having positive or negative
effects on the worker, but a process of change in the office environment.
Office automation is the utilization of resources (i.e. financial, human and
technological) to improve the effectiveness of the process of work. The computer is only one of many technologies and must be studied within the context
of the larger office system. The purpose of this paper is to examine and
describe the process of change resulting from the introduction of automation
into the office environments of the Eastern Africa Region of the World Bank.

OFFICE SYSTEMS

Examination of the variability in the tasks a worker performs and how this
variability changes after automation is one way to begin to understand the
consequences of office automation from a systems perspective. A task is any
activity the worker performs during the course of the day in the work process
using the available technologies in the work environment. Task variability
is the patterned set of daily or weekly tasks a person performs in his/her
job.

The office environment is a system where work is carried out by a definite
number of workers. The introduction of computers into the office environment
to replace other technologies not only changes specific tasks but their variability. For example, changes in the amount of time spent at one task may
necessitate changes in the amount of time spent at other tasks, especially
since office automation does not immediately remove older technologies such
as the typewriter. Considering the office as a system, the amount of time a
secretary spends working on a VDT must be seen as part of the daily task variability, along with time spent at the typewriter and doing other tasks
needed to complete her job. Therefore, to understand the implications of the

introduction of automation technologies into the office environment, changes in task variability must be examined.

OFFICE AUTOMATION AT THE WORLD BANK

The Eastern Africa Region of the World Bank is divided into 3 main units; a Projects department with 9 divisions, and two Programs departments (Programs I and Programs II) with a total of 5 divisions. Their main task objective is to identify, process and supervise loans made by the Bank to underdeveloped nations in Eastern Africa, and provide technical assistance to its borrowers as required.

Prior to the introduction of computerized word processing into the Region a central word processing unit (CWPU) for the entire Bank was used to produce final reports. Initial drafts would be prepared on the typewriter then sent to the CWPU for further processing. A regional task force in 1980 proposed gradual introduction in the Region of word processing in a decentralized mode and discontinuation of the use of the central facility. A principal reason for the introduction of the automation technology was to improve the efficiency of both word and information processing capabilities within the units of the Region. The objectives for office automation were defined by the regional task force as: (1) reduce typing workload and improve the quality of printed output; (2) increase efficiency in report production and administrative work; (3) increase effective use of time and talents of staff at all levels; and (4) improve effective working relationships and teamwork.

The automation of offices in the Eastern Africa Region involved not only technological changes, but organizational ones as each organizational unit took full control of the word processing task. Philips/Micom 2001 units with dual disk drives and printers, were introduced into all divisions, using a bilingual word processing software package to meet the French language requirements. Workstations were placed in special rooms with appropriate workstation furniture, lighting and sufficient ventilation. Acoustical covers were placed over the printers. Along with the introduction of the above technologies, the Region organized a series of in-house training courses in word processing, system administration and special seminars on health and environmental issues. Each organizational unit had overall control or their workstation(s).

METHODS

The data to be used in this paper were compiled from task evaluations carried out by the second author at the World Bank in 1981 and 1982. Figure 1 shows the time sequence of these evaluations with respect to the introduction of office automation technologies. A secretarial workload inventory was conducted prior to the introduction of the automation technologies (Time 1-T1) and another after their introduction (Time 2-T2). The inventory is a one week diary·of tasks (plus leave) carried out by secretaries and filled out on a day-to-day basis. Information from each inventory is not linked, so pre-test and post-test comparisons are based on group data and not individual data. The workload inventory was carried out over two weeks to estimate task variability, as these patterns cannot be reliably estimated over a day or two. Even one week may be inadequate because of the time of year the data are being gathered. Therefore, a two-week period, with each week separated in the same fiscal quarter, is likely to be the most effective way to esti-mate patterned task variability. Over 90% of the secretaries completed and returned the diary for two week periods at both times. After the post-test, a semi-structured interview (Time 3-T3) was given to 80% of the secretarial, 50% of the research/administrative assistants, and 49% of the higher level staff in the Region. Regional staff at T3 was 119 secretaries, 35 assistant level and 220 higher level. These interviews were designed to describe the effect of office automation on the overall work process, rather than focusing only on the secretarial staff as the workload inventory did.

Figure 1: Time Sequence of Evaluations at the World Bank

Time 1 (T1)	Time 2 (T2) /a	Time 3 (T3)
(Jan–Feb 1981)	(Nov–Dec 1981/Jan–Feb 1982)	(June–July 1982)
Workload Inventory	Workload Inventory	Follow-up
Pre-test	Post-test	Interviews

/a Major introduction of equipment in April, May, June of 1981.

To determine whether differences in task variability were statistically significant a nonparametric test, Wilcoxon matched-pairs signed-ranks test, was used (Siegel, 1956). This statistic not only tests the direction of the differences within pairs, but the magnitude of the difference. It gives more weight to a pair which shows a large difference than one that shows a small difference. The unit of analysis was the percentage of time during a week period an individual spends at a task. It was hypothesized that the intro-duction of automation technologies changes the task variability - people will spend more time at some tasks and less time at others. Since the direction of change is unknown for all tasks, a two-tailed test of significance was used.

RESULTS

Analysis of the task variability showed there were significant differences
(0.02 < p < 0.05) in the amount of time spent at various tasks after the
technological change. A breakdown of the data by the three departments
reveals that the significance is primarily due to the Projects department
having the largest number of secretaries. Both the Programs I & II units did
not show statistically significant differences, but they did show interesting
changes, demonstrating how changes in the amount of time spent at one task
affects others. The remainder of this paper discusses only differences in
task variability for the Eastern Africa Region and not the separate units to
point out the advantages of looking at task variability rather than a single
task.

The direct effect of the new technologies was to change the amount of time
spent typing on typewriters and on the computer. At T1, 33% of a secretary's
time was spent at the typewriter and 2% on the computer. Although there were
no computers in the Region, some secretaries were able to spend time on them
at the CWPU. This changed drastically after the automation system was
installed. At T2, 26% of a secretary's time was spent working at the computer and 26% at the typewriter. Assuming a person works 80 hours in two
weeks, this means a secretary spent 1.5 hours at the computer prior to the
installation and 21 hours after. This represents greater than a 1000%
increase in the amount of time spent at a terminal. Concommitant with this
increase was a 21% decrease in the time spent at the typewriter (27 hours at
T1 and 21 hours at T2). Overall, there was a 50% increase in the number of
hours spent typing during a two week period (28.22 hours at T1 compared to 42
hours at T2). This increase was mainly caused by discontinuing the use of
the CWPU.

To examine the effect it had on other tasks, we examined 10 tasks with the
largest magnitude of change. These, in ascending order, are: typing on a
word processor, typing on a typewriter, errands, xeroxing, recording leave
and attendance, filing, telephoning, routing materials and making arrangements. These tasks reflect a broad spectrum of what a secretary's job encom-
passes. At T1 they represent 81% (64.7 hours) of all time spent on the job,
while at T2 they represent 91% (72.6 hours). Obviously, other tasks not mentioned or reported were not carried out as frequently at T2. Overtime
increased 170% from T1 to T2. There was a 17% decrease in the time spent
doing tasks other than typing (36.5 hours at T1 compared to 30.3 hours at
T2). The two largest changes were in errands and xeroxing. There was a 34%
decrease in the amount of time spent doing errands (5.4 at T1 and 3.6 at T2),
and a 22% decrease in time spent xeroxing materials (7.7 at T1 compared to
6.0 at T2). These data show increased time spent typing has been offset by a

decrease in the time doing other tasks the job requires. Since the time spent at most other tasks also decreased, this must have had an effect on the work group, which includes higher level staff along with secretaries.

To ascertain what consequences the changes had for the work group as part of the office system the semi-structured interviews (T3) were carried out after the second task inventory. When asked whether there were problems with the new technology, 71% of the secretaries (S) and 79% of the higher level (HL) staff felt the number of drafts had increased. Also, secretaries felt that other workers did not realize how much time was involved in making changes. HL staff did not seem to realize that making corrections required reprinting, and at times repagination of text. In effect office automation and the decision to discontinue the use of the CWPU had increased the typing workload and time pressure on secretaries to complete drafts. In the work-load inventory this was reflected in the increase in the amount of time spent typing.

In general, secretaries (71%) were satisfied with the location of the terminals, however, 71% of their supervisors would prefer to see the machines close to the secretary's desk. The major problems identified by the HL staff were: telephones not being answered, lack of secretarial support to type urgent messages, delays in filing, and a general decrease in secretarial support. These were confirmed by the decreased amounts of time spent doing these tasks reported at T2. It is not clear whether this was due to the location of the word processing equipment or the increases in the typing workload. Two findings support the latter view. First, the feeling that the typing load had not decreased by both secretaries (43%) and HL staff (71%). Second, 43% of the secretaries report they frequently worked more than 4 hours continuously on a CRT. Probably both of these factors have contributed to reduce the amount of time a secretary had to spend on general tasks.

Advantages to the decentralized word processing system reported by secre-taries in the interviews were that the technology had given them the oppor-tunity to learn a new skill which increased their mobility and marketabil-ity. Along with HL staff, they felt there was a better quality to the reports (79% for HL and 65% for S). There were discrepancies between the higher and secretarial level staff among other advantages cited. Higher level staff reported with greater frequency that office automation had given divisions more control (43% HL compared to 14% for S), that it saved time (65% HL compared to 36% for S) and that they liked the ability to make fast corrections (57% HL compared to 21% for S). These differences point to the need to examine the office as a system, as it appears that automation has had more positive affects on some people's jobs than others. Therefore, the organization of the work process is an important component to examine when

trying to understand the impact of office automation. It is also important
to understand that the change process is a gradual one as it requires changes
in work habits and methodologies.

DISCUSSION AND IMPLICATIONS

The process of change in the office system brought about by office automation, has been shown to affect a broad range of tasks the secretary does in
her job in the Region. One characteristic of the office system, task variability, was significantly different after automation. The interviews
revealed that although there was a recognition of improvement in the quality
of work, the decrease in time availability for other tasks had a somewhat
negative impact on the overall office system. These findings are similar to
those by Huuhtanen (1984), who found that there was more work to be done. He
also found that computerization made work interesting, a finding supported by
this evaluation. At this stage of the change process the typing workload has
increased, but the quality of output was judged to be better by all members
of the work group.

Higher level staff in the Bank expressed a greater degree of satisfaction
with the new decentralized word processing system compared to secretaries.
This shows how office automation differently impacts on people depending on
their job in the organization. Smith (1981) has shown that professionals and
clerical workers differ on a wide variety of job dimensions, job attitudes
and health outcomes. Further evaluation at the World Bank will try to clarify the reasons for the differences.

The implications of this research in defining the impact of office automation, are that the human-computer interaction is only one part of an automated office system. To understand the change process that office automation
brings to the work environment, this must be viewed as a system with a set of
working relationship and tasks that people devote time to, on a patterned
basis. Office automation is a technological, structural and organizational
process of change carried out within the organization to improve the effectiveness of the work process. In the Eastern Africa Region these were arti-
culated in the four objectives of a decentralized word and information processing system. It is too soon to know whether objectives will be achieved.
What is known is that there are both positive and negative effects, and that
only by viewing the office as a system can the relationships between these
effects be understood.

REFERENCES

Huuhtanen, P., 1984. "Office Automation. A study of the Impacts of
    Computerization on the Job Content, Workload and Work Organization of
    Payroll Clerks", Mimeograph.
Siegel, S., 1956. Nonparametric Statistics for the Behavioral Sciences.
    McGraw-Hill: New York, NY.
Smith, M.J., et al, 1981. "Investigation of Health Complaints and Job Stress
    in Video Display Operations". Human Factors, 23(4): 387-400.

Human—Computer Interaction, edited by G. Salvendy
Elsevier Science Publishers B.V., Amsterdam, 1984 — Printed in The Netherlands

449

Problems in Vocal Man-Machine Communication

Michael G. Joost

Dept. of Industrial Engineering, North Carolina State University, Box 7906,
    Raleigh, NC   27695-7906 (USA)

ABSTRACT

   Automatic speech recognition and synthesis (voice I/O) presents a
situation not often encountered in the study of man-machine communication.
While research has been carefully conducted exploring and guiding the
evolution of visual displays and keyboard entry, the potential revolution of
verbal communication has been largely ignored.   As a result, a new
technology exists for which we are poorly prepared; where an attempted
application often fails because there are insufficient implementation
guidelines.

   Although a substantial amount of research has been directed toward voice
I/O, most of it has dealt with the development of better processing hardware
or recognition/synthesis algorithms. Too often, voice I/O is perceived as
little more than a vocalization of the visual/keying processes of more
traditional technology without an appreciation of the different cognitive
requirements of a verbal transaction.

   Before voice I/O can become a mature, viable communication medium, a
number of answers must be generated. Topics of particular relevance include
training, motivation, selection, sensory and cognitive loading, as well as
performance aiding and error detection and correction. This paper raises a
number of questions requiring further study.

INTRODUCTION

   Given the convenience and flexibility in vocal human communication, it
has long been a dream of mankind to have machines that could communicate
vocally. While pioneering work was pursued in the 1930's and 1940's, this
research resulted in equipment capable of speech to image translation
(Potter et al., 1947). It was not until 1952 that machine recognition of
speech was achieved. While development progressed at an increasingly rapid
pace, it was not until 1972 that the first commercial word recognizer was
available.   Since that time, the recognition frontier has moved from
isolated word-speaker dependent systems through isolated   word-speaker

independent systems to connected word-speaker dependent and is approaching
connected word-speaker independent capabilities (Lea, 1980).

Just as human communication requires more than hearing, machines require
more than automatic speech recognition. Developments in automatic speech
production progressed in parallel with those in recognition with a perceived
inversion in the speed with which capabilities progressed. Given the
phonetic research of the 30's and 40's there was a much firmer starting
point. The sounds that had to be produced were known so it was a "simple"
matter to produce these sounds and string them together in the necessary
temporal sequence to create speech. Unfortunately, specifying the
necessary, correct phonetic strings was/in an art with few adepts and, thus,
recent progress appears slow. Consequently, most recent research has
centered around two points, more effective text-to-speech algorithms and
alternatives to phonetic generation of speech. Proponents of the former
emphasize the potential of an unlimited speech vocabulary while those
pursuing the latter exploit the fact that seldom is a situation so
unstructured that an unlimited vocabulary is necessary.

From these modest beginnings, an industry has evolved with the potential
of revolutionizing the way in which humans communicate with machines. In
thirty years, the technology has gone from the laboratory to the field and
in twelve years the number of suppliers of voice I/O products has gone from
one to in excess of 170 vendors.

In spite of this, it has been only recently that major advances in
automatic speech recognition and synthesis have made limited voice
communication feasible. As in most technological advances, the human user
has been, to some degree, ignored as available resources are used to
overcome technical problems. It is often assumed that the use of these
systems is so straightforward that there should be no difficulty in use;
almost everyone communicates verbally every day. This is somewhat ironic
since these voice systems are often being promoted as the ultimate man-
machine interface.

VOICE INPUT/OUTPUT RESEARCH AREAS

Users, potential users, consultants, and vendors of voice I/O equipment
were interviewed regarding their perception of research needed to enhance
the usefulness of automatic speech systems. Out of this interchange, a
number of ideas emerged including product development and improved

understanding of the vocal transaction process. Table 1 presents the major man-machine communication categories. As can be seen, the first six categories deal with automatic speech recognition, the seventh with speech production, and the final three deal with both speech input and output.

TABLE 1

Relevant research needs

---

1. Error detection/correction in automatic speech recognition
2. Partial speaker independence and template sharing
3. Training and retraining of both user and hardware
4. Effects of frustration
5. Vocabulary size and selection
6. Language independence
7. How to design effective verbal displays
8. Design of vocal transactions to optimize throughput and errors
9. Effects of noise
10. Identification of factors affecting the acceptance of voice I/O

Description of needed research

Error detection and correction are concepts that take on several forms depending on perspective. In its simplest form, this is the process by which a user examines the current entry (by whatever display mechanism is available) and is allowed to correct errors. most existing systems allow only the very crudest of correction techniques, i.e. erase everything including the error and correct entries and reenter the necessary information. Obviously, this is a time-consuming, cumbersome, and inefficient process. More advanced systems are applying syntactic, grammatical, and logical rules to automatically correct entry errors. These, however, are not out of the laboratory environment, require substantial computing power above the needs of the recognizer, and assume intimate knowledge of the transaction structure; a knowledge that is often lacking. Interim solutions which take little additional computing resources and place fewer constraints on transactions are needed. These imply the mechanisms by which humans detect and correct mistakes need to be better understood as well as a "free-form" contextual editing capability needs to be developed.

When a potential user examines the feasibility of an application of voice I/O, a large investment of time is involved. This time is not only that of the system integrator, but also the production personnel who are ultimately to use the system. Speaker-dependent systems, which comprise the majority of today's hardware, require that each user register his voice. When the vocabulary is small, this is only a minor inconvenience, but when the necessary vocabulary is large, the time requirements may be on the order of 50 to 100 hours. Few organizations can afford this loss of production. For this reason, if there exists a "generic" speaker or pool of speakers, it may be possible for the user to be productive from the start with a somewhat greater error rate. Determining the existence of such a "generic" speaker and procedures for selecting such speakers would be a major task, but the potential gains could spell the difference between a successful implementation of voice and an application where implementation would be too costly.

Very little quality data are available to evaluate the long-term stability of voice systems. This raises questions about the need for repeated training or retraining of users and reregistering the users with the hardware. These data would permit the more realistic assessment of the ultimate cost of systems and provide reasonable evaluation of the need of systems that adapt automatically to changes in voicing patterns or inflection.

Inevitably, when speech input is used, recognition errors occur. When these errors occur, the user's level of frustration is often increased. Some individuals react to this frustration better than others. To date, four modes of reaction have been observed including "giving up," anger, "random" attempts to find the accepted vocalization, and a very systematic attempt to replicate the user's perception of the target utterance. If coping strategies can be identified, then these may be useful for selection of user candidates or developing training methodologies to reduce the accompanying frustration.

In many cases, this frustration may be reduced through the judicious choice of the vocabulary to be used in an application. By careful selection of words, it is possible to reduce the level of confusion and, thus, reduce the number of misrecognitions experienced by the user. Currently, if this process is attempted at all, it is accomplished by guesswork. Consequently, its effectiveness is dependent on the skill of the analyst.

The recognition systems currently available have been designed with English or Japanese as the use language. It remains to be seen whether they work as well with other languages which may have as great or greater need of the technology. As an example, consider Chinese which is a tonal language (English and Japanese are not) with an unmanageably large symbol set (more than 4000 characters). If voice input will not work for Chinese, the alternative is translation or anglicization (or its equivalent) if computers are to be substantial long-term value.

When considering voice output or synthesis, even after assuming the vocalization is reliably understandable, many questions remain about the optimal design of verbal displays. Many have attempted to merely vocalize the information as it would appear on a visual display. Given the differences in modality, however, this is adequate in only the simplest of situations. Humans speaking to other humans use many cues not available to the computer. To be effective, voice I/O systems may have to anticipate the need for additional cues and provide some approximation of these cues. Included in this set of needs may be high-speed scanning capabilities and control of information rescanning and presentation speed. Without these capabilities, effective speech output for more than rote, short messages is unlikely to be feasible.

All systems today have a limited vocabulary size. Typically, at any point in time, the limit ranges from 50 to 350 words. This limit is not, however, too stringent since the vocabulary can be paged to include only the current set of alternatives. In spite of this, a user may feel constrained if, even rarely, he is told his entry is not known to the system. The effects of this perceived constraint could be minimized if it were possible to design a dialogue which guides the user to use only the available vocabulary. While preliminary work has been done in this area, most of it is still in the laboratory and is of minimal practical use.

Finally, even after all of the above techniques have been developed and refined, there is still a potential problem of user acceptance. Several organizations with wide current user bases have reported that while initial response to speech I/O were good, productivity fell off rapidly for a variety of apparently psychological factors that very few have yet attempted to evaluate.

As can be seen from the above discussion, a number of questions remain to be answered before speech I/O becomes a commonplace man-machine

454

communication modality. Many of the research areas can borrow from allied research from other related fields, but there are a number of unique opportunities available to investigate relatively virgin territory.

REFERENCES

Lea, W. (Editor), 1980. Trends in Speech Recognition. Prentice-Hall, Englewood Cliffs, New Jersey.
Potter, R.K., Kopp, G.A., and Green, H.C., 1947. Visible Speech. D. van Nostrand Company, New York.

Human—Computer Interaction, edited by G. Salvendy
Elsevier Science Publishers B.V., Amsterdam, 1984 — Printed in The Netherlands

DESIGNING SPEECH RECOGNITION INTERFACES FOR TALKERS AND TASKS

David Isenberg [1], Douwe Yntena [1&2] and Ray Wiesen [1]

[1] Verbex, 2 Oak Park, Bedford, MA
[2] Harvard University, Cambridge, MA

To a human factors engineer, the design of a talk-and-hear interface is not like the design of conventional type-and-see interfaces. We feel that there are four main reasons:

(a) The structural properties of the speech medium,

(b) The shortcomings of today's speech technology,

(c) The human as speech producer and perciever, and

(d) The tasks that speech is asked to do.

We shall discuss the causes and implications of these sources of difference, but then we will consider a few points common to all design.

Structural properties of the speech medium. In the usual type-and-see interface, an input to the machine stays on the screen until the user takes some action to dismiss it. The user deals with outputs similarly. Speech, on the other hand, is evanescent; once uttered, it is gone. If the user needs another exposure to the output (perhaps because it was not understood, or the user's attention was distracted) then some way of displaying it again must be provided. And if the user may need to "see" the input just uttered (perhaps to verify that she said the right thing) then some way to display the input should be provided. It is this property of the speech medium that most clearly differentiates a talk-and-hear interface from the usual type-and-see system.

The designers have to decide, input by input and output by output, what must be done about redisplaying the message. Should the display be auditory or visual or both? In a package sorting task, our colleagues recently found that verification feedback slowed down throughput so significantly that it was better to let an occasional recognition error slide through.

Shortcomings of today's speech technology. Today's speech technology is error-prone, both on input to the recognizer and on output when the speech is synthesized. These errors can be due to the machine, or to speech errors of the user. On output, synthesized voice is not as intelligible as human speech. Errors of timing and intonation can often confuse a listener despite recent advances in this art.

For the designer, this suggests the classic solution; keep alternative messages few in number and acoustically distinct. Often this requirement trades off with the naturalness, the stimulus-response compatibility as it were, of a chosen vocabulary item. This implies that the designer choose a vocabulary guided by principle, but then try out the items decided upon and solicit feedback about how natural they feel in actual use. If the recognizer has the capacity for activating context dependent subsets of the vocabulary, this can keep the number of active alternatives down. In an automobile inspection task with a 20 word vocabulary, only "left", "right" and "rear" could appear before "door"; once "door" was recognized, 85% of the candidates for the preceding word were eliminated.

Certain speech recognition capabilities remain elusive. People can ofter understand speech in negative signal-to-noise ratios; machines cannot. People can separate meaningful speech from time-varying noises; machines cannot. Pronunciation varies as a function of talker, dialect, rate of speech, and other factors; we need algorithms that know how to throw away this variation. A machine that could do phonetic analysis as people do it would make problems of talker differences, dialect and accent, and restrictions on vocabulary size tractible.

The human as speech producer and perciever. For the most part, the designer addresses problems of voluntary changes in pronunciation with pragmatism and common sense. Because the speech production mechanism is not a dedicated system, the user needs to know (and it never hurts to state such things explicitly) that chewing gum, smoking and drinking coffee are not activities that are consistent with high recognition performance, that spoken inputs need to be clear and consistent, and so forth. We once had a case of a worker who trained one of our speaker-dependent machines using formal dialect. After some weeks, we were called back to the plant to investigate a decline in recognition performance to find that this worker had used the machine enough so it felt familiar to him and was now speaking to it in a friendly colloquial dialect. Except for rare cases like this, there is a practice effect for users of speech recognition systems; successful recognition rate increases over the first few weeks of use as if the machine were training the user. On the output side of the talk-and-hear interface, the main human factor to consider is the limit of short-term memory. This, in effect, is our display size.

The kinds of tasks that speech is asked to do. Tasks that talk-and-hear interfaces do well today are ones that involve simple data input, usually with hands and eyes busy. Sorting mail, luggage and packages, inspection tasks involving cars and electronic components, and shipping and recieving applications have all been implemented efficiently using today's speech

technology. These are much simpler than text editors, message systems and
other interfaces that more commonly concern the human engineer these days.
We do not have to worry so much about presenting large menus or complex data
structures in ways that people can easily understand. We worry little about
efficient forms of command abbreviations. We get a lot of mileage from those
three little words, " keep it simple".

   A talk-and-hear system at work. Our colleagues recently designed a
baggage sorting interface for the main hub of a major airline. Some a
priori design decisions were made. To keep the information rate down, we
divided the vocabulary into two subsets that the user could select by saying
"East Coast" or "West Coast". The destinations were city names because they
felt natural to the users, rather than flight numbers, which upper management
preferred. As expected, some problems arose when the system went on line.
In the East Coast sub-vocabulary, "Austin"-"Boston" and "Dallas"-"Dulles"
were frequent confusions; the solution was to route confusible destinations
to adjacent piers so it was easy for workers loading the carts to correct the
confusions. A squealing clutch on a conveyor belt also caused some errors;
to fix it we had to adjust a reject parameter and get the users to train the
system right next to the offending clutch. Speech recognition increased
throughput from 15 to 35 bags per person/minute, with about 2 bags per 1000
missing their plane.

   Design principles. Can we use our experience with speech interfaces to
test the generality of design principles proposed from experiences with type-
and-see interfaces? Surely such principles should be independent of interface medium. We find ourselves agreeing with some of the 5 principles proposed by Norman (1983) (e.g. "Low level protocols are critical."),while we
take strong issue that others apply to speech tasks (e.g. "Data retrieval
dominates activity.") We find that our designs are successful to the extent
that we really understand the users and the task that they do, then build a
prototype, and test and modify it iteratively until we converge upon a learn-
able, workable and pleasant system. This formula for success is simply a re-
statement of the four principles of Gould and Lewis (1983); though we should
point out that they are not principles OF design, but more properly
principles FOR designers. Iterative test and redesign of our principles will
yield a set of generic design principles that work.

458

REFERENCES

Gould, J.D. and Lewis, C. (1983) Designing for Usability - - Key Principles
    and What Designers Think. Presented at CHI83. Boston, MA
Norman, D.A. (1983) Design Principles for Human-Computer Interfaces.
    Presented at CHI83, Boston, MA

ADDENDUM

Human—Computer Interaction, edited by G. Salvendy
Elsevier Science Publishers B.V., Amsterdam, 1984 — Printed in The Netherlands

RELATIONS BETWEEN MAN AND COMPUTERRIZED SYSTEM

M. OSHIMA

Medical Information System Development Center

ABSTRACT

Oshima, M., 1984. Relations between man and computerrized system

This paper is described about perspective concepts of medical information system by 56 men of learning and experiences, which are divided in basic items, characteristics of system, human factors of medical information system, suggestion for introduction of medical information system, and subject of R & D of new systems. These results suggest the future concept of man—computer system interaction.

The questionaire was held for 56 men of learning and experience about medical information system. The results was brought to some coclusions. These results are considered to be very important for relationship between man and medical information system.

Table 1 shows the basic items. These are the basic conditions to establish the principle of medical information system.

TABLE 1. Basic Items of Medical Information System

1. Understand of medical information
2. Establishment of science of medical informatics
3. Establishment of methodology for systematization
4. Standardization of medical information system
5. Synthesizing many medical information system
6. Establishment of curriculum of medical informatics
7. Completion of education for medical informatics

The many items were commented about characterristics of systems. The contents of these items are sometimes not so concrete, but are able to be established. These items means the necessity for adaptation and matching of characteristics of systems to human characteristics. Therefore, the study of human characteristics is very important for establishment of medical information system.

TABLE 2. Characteristics of System (I)

1. Non-uniformity	6. Community oriented system
2. Non-fixing	7. Flexibility of system
3. Compacting system	8. Intelligency of system
4. Totalization of system	9. Ducom oriented system
5. Medical care oriented system	

462

TABLE 3. Characteristics of System (II)

---

10. Japanese styled system
11. Principle of one-patient-one-medical history
12. Plinciple of one-patient-one-medical record
13. Information exchange between communities
14. Common and generalized terminal
15. Harmony between centralized and distributed processing
16. Balancing of systems
17. Speedup of coversion
18. Input of information at occurent place
19. Connection to large computer
20. Optimal layout
21. Service oriented system

Next is the items of human factors of medical information system.
Of course these items are based upon the man oriented principles. The problems
of VDT is included in these items. As other items the flexibility and
availability, simple operation and prevention of operation mistakes et al.

TABLE 4. Human Factors of Medical Information System

---

1. Usability and availability
2. Simple operation
3. Practice of human factors of CRT-display
4. Prevention of operation mistake
5. Speedup of convention
6. Protection of privacy
7. Quality control and reliability
8. Efficiency
9. Economics
10. Safety
11. Matching of man-machine system and man-computer system
12. Intelligibility of system
13. Social acceptability and acceptability
14. Rationalization of man-computer interaction
15. Matching for thinking sequence
16. Humanized system

Next is the suggestions for introduction of medical information system.
In these items 13 items are commented as Table 6. Some items are called
from 13 items: that is to say, precision of target and object, step by step
introduction of system, and sufficient preparing time et al.

Next is the problem of research and development of new systems as shown in
Table 7.

TABLE 6. Suggestions for Introduction of Medical Information System

1. Precision of target and object
2. Step by step introduction of system
3. Sufficient preparing time
4. Adjustment of situation in advance
5. Common understand for medical information
6. Financial insure
7. Decision making of priority and importance
8. Attendance of end user
9. Leadership of top manager
10. Adjust to needs
11. Appropriate selection of maker
12. To hold the phase of improvement
13. Importance for leadership of top manager and accummulation by subordinates

TABLE 7. The Subjects of Research and Development new systems

1. System to be able to estimate the future
2. Health care system
3. System to cooprate with many organization
4. Image information system
5. Patient data base system
6. System to product medical record
7. Primary health care system
8. Medical record management system
9. Data base of medical information
10. Data maintenance system
11. Health risk evaluation system
12. Data returning system
13. Medical thesaurus
14. Data transmittance system
15. Systematization of middle wided hospitals
16. Popularizing system
17. Cooperation
18. Aimming at 10 years after

In conclusion, human being has to match with the surrounding conditions, and the surrounding conditions has to adjust to human being. This is very important principle at the period of science and technology.

Human—Computer Interaction, edited by G. Salvendy
Elsevier Science Publishers B.V., Amsterdam, 1984 — Printed in The Netherlands

A STUDY ON THE CHANGE OF VISUAL FUNCTION IN CRT DISPLAY TASK

K. AOKI[1], N. YAMANOI[2], M. AOKI[3] and Y. HORIE[3]

[1]Dept. of Health Administration, Faculty of Medicine, Univ. of
Tokyo, 3-1, Hongo 7-chome, Bunkyoku, 113 Tokyo (Japan)

[2]Institute of Medical Electronics, Faculty of Medicine, Univ. of
Tokyo, 3-1, Hongo 7-chome, Bunkyoku, 113 Tokyo (Japan)

[3]College of Industrial Technology, Nihon University, 1-211 Izumi-
cho, Narashino 275 (Japan)

INTRODUCTION

Computerization of clerical work have increased the use of
CRT display terminals, and a greater number of the workers
are complaining the eyesight fail and eye strain and pains
(Ohashi and Aoki, 1982). Therefore it is important to measure
the visual load of 'CRT display work. The perpose of this
study is to assume the visual load through measurement of the
change of visual function of the workers during CRT display
task.

METHODS

Task

Four hundreds of one figure random numbers (3 to 9) were
displayed on CRT display of the micro computer. The subject
calcurates the sum of a pair of one figure numbers which were
indicated randomly by the cursol on the CRT display. The subject
must input the answer through the key board.

One continuous work time was 15 minutes and each subject
was requested to perform 6 series of this task, so the total
CRT display work time was 90 minutes.

CRT display

14 inches CRT display was used in this study. The luminance
of character was 124 cd/m^2 and of background was 34 cd/m^2.
The contrast between character and background was 3.6:1.
The color of character was green in this case.

The illuminance on the CRT display was 350 lux and that on
the key board was 650 lux.

Measurement

The measurement of visual function and fatigue of subjects
was carried before the experiment and between the continuous
works (each 15 minutes). As visual function, visual acuity,
near point and accomodation time(contraction time and relaxation
time) was measured. CFF was tested as mental fatigue and subjects
reported fatigue symptoms. The task performance of each subject
(number of answers and number of errors) was recorded automaticaly
in the computer memories.

Subjects

Nine male students aged 21 to 23 performed the CRT display
task. Three of them used spectacles for myopia.

```
8 5 9 9 6 4 5 3 4 8 6 5 4 7 3 9 9 9 7 7 6 6 7 4 6 9 5 9 8 5 3 9 9 3 9 8 7 8 3 9
7 6 7 8 6 3 9 5 4 4 3 6 3 6 7 7 6 3 4 5 3 5 9 8 4 8 5 8 4 8 3 5 7 7 5 4 9 7 7 8
5 5 6 6 7 6 4 3 9 5 8 4 5 8 8 4 5 3 9 7 8 8 7 8 3 6 3 7 4 7 6 4 7 7 9 5 7 9 5 3
9 3 3 7 4 5 3 7 3 4 8 6 9 4 8 7 3 7 5 7 6 3 5 7 8 8 6 8 8 5 5 9 9 4 8 3 7 8 5 3
8 6 8 6 9 4 8 7 9 9 9 9 5 6 7 3 6 6 9 7 5 5 6 5 8 9 6 5 9 4 8 6 6 7 8 8 3 7 9 9
9 6 4 9 4 6 6 9 7 4 8 3 5 5 3 4 4 4 7 5 7 7 3 8 4 8 3 4 6 6 6 9 8 8 5 4 9 9 8 4
5 5 8 9 9 4 7 3 7 5 8 7 6 7 5 7 8 6 6 7 3 6 9 8 8 6 3 3 8 5 7 7 6 3 3 4 9 7 3 9
7 6 6 6 8 6 3 6 9 7 9 6 7 9 3 7 4 3 4 9 3 8 5 9 7 4 6 3 6 3 4 8 9 4 7 9 6 9 5 9
7 9 9 5 7 5 6 6 3 8 8 8 5 7 4 9 8 9 9 6 3 6 7 7 9 8 8 8 5 9 7 8 4 6 8 4 7 8 6 5
6 6 9 7 3 7 5 7 6 7 8 8 6 9 4 6 8 3 9 3 3 5 9 3 9 4 7 3 7 4 7 4 9 7 3 3 5 9 4 3
```

Fig. 1. An example of random numbers displayed on the CRT.

RESULTS AND DISCUSSIONS

The visual acuity was measureed before and after CRT display
task, but there appeared only small change in this experiment.
Fig. 2. shows the change rate of eye accomodation time. The
relaxation time was prolonged as the work time passed but the
contraction time prolonged at 15 minutes and left at constant
level from 15 to 90 minutes. There appeared only small change
on the distance of near point.

Fig. 3. shows the relation between the performance of CRT
display work and work time. The number of answers in each 15
minutes was increased gradually but the error number was increased
too, especially after 75 minutes CRT display work.

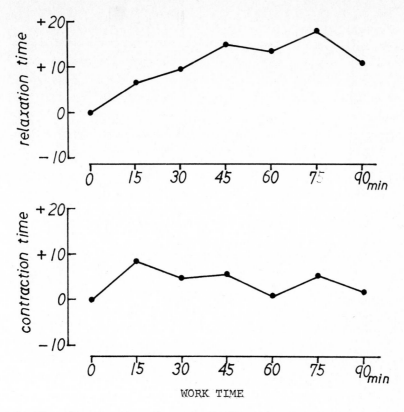

Fig. 2. The change rate of accomodation time. (mean rate of 9
subjects)

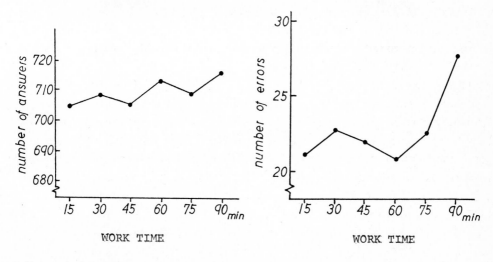

Fig. 3. The performance of CRT display task. (mean number of 9
subjects)

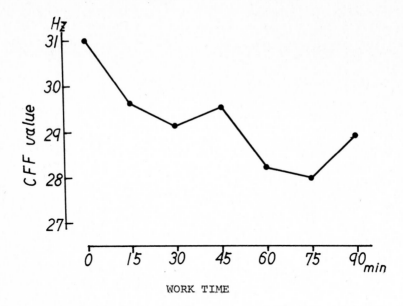

Fig. 4. The change of CFF value. (mean value of 9 subjects)

The relation between the work time and CFF value was shown in Fig. 4. The CFF value was 31 Hz before the work then went down to 28 Hz after 60 or 75 minutes work. The change rate was about -10%. The fatigue symptoms reported by the subjects was increased in number after the CRT work especially in the eye strain.

From the result mentioned above, CRT display task affected on the visual function of the subjects, especially on the relaxation time in the accomodative functions. The mechamism of the delay of reluxation time was not clear but it was assumed that the ciliary muscle was related in this fact.

REFERENCES

Grandjean, E. and Vigliani, E.(Editors), 1980. Ergonomics Aspects of Visual Display Terminals. Taylor & Francis, London.
Ohashi, M. and Aoki, K., 1982. A Study on Visual Function of VDU Operators. Proceedings of the 8th Congress of the International Ergonomics Association. Tokyo, pp. 560-561.

AUTHOR INDEX